BIKING USA's
RAIL-TRAILS

Where to Go ■ What to Expect ■ How to Get There

BY SHAWN E. RICHARDSON

Adventure Publications, Inc.
Cambridge, MN

Other Books by Shawn E. Richardson
Biking Missouri's Rail-Trails
Biking Ohio's Rail-Trails
Biking Wisconsin's Rail-Trails

BIKING USA's
RAIL-TRAILS

Where to Go ■ What to Expect ■ How to Get There

Text, research, & cartography by Shawn E. Richardson (OH), Dr. Jack McDonald (MD), Nick Decker (Missouri DNR), Robyn Blanpied (HI), the City of Albuquerque (NM), Floyd Hickok (ND) and David Owens (TX).

Photography by Shawn E. Richardson, Dr. Jack McDonald, Nick Decker (Missouri Dept. of Natural Resources), Robyn Blanpied, Floyd Hickok and the City of Albuquerque

Cover and Interior design by Jonathan Norberg

Due to the changing trail conditions, Adventure Publications and the author are not held responsible for any injury or damage caused by either direct or indirect information in this book.

First Printing 2002
Second Printing 2004

ISBN 1-885061-41-2

Published by
Adventure Publications, Inc.
820 Cleveland Street South
Cambridge, MN 55008
1-800-678-7006

Printed in the U.S.A.

This book is for Betsy Boone-Abraham (KY), Mark J. Ballenger (OH), Tom Edwards and Mary Gleason Boone (KY), Tom Edwards Boone Jr. (KY), Tina Davy (KY), Dean Focke (OH), Daniel L. Hasch (KY), Henry Christain Herrmann III (OH), Steve Hubner (WI), Terri Kay (IL), Kevin Keach (MO), Robert G. Koenig (OH), Jill C. Richardson Lang (KY), Diane Lin (IL), Tammy Lin (IL), Michael Longest (OH), Robert Longest (OH), Kathaleen McFeeley (OH), Ryan McFeeley (OH), Tom and Susan McFeeley (OH), Seneca Murley (IL), Dr. Delton Richardson (GA), Dr. Harold Edward and Antonia Calvert Richardson (KY), Jim and Jill Schwartz (OH), Steven M. Slucher (KY), Felice Tacktill (NY), Terry Whaley (MO), and my wife Joyce A. Richardson (OH) for joining me in trail blazing across U.S.A.'s rail-trails.

A special thanks goes to all of the trail groups and trail builders across the United States of American for making our nation a wonderful place to be proud of and for helping me complete my research. A special thanks also goes to my wife Joyce A. Richardson who took her time to "sag drive" the trails for me and for helping me out with the final touches of the maps for this book. A special thanks goes to Dr. Jack McDonald (MD), Nick Decker (MO), Robyn Blanpied (HI), David Owens (TX), Floyd Hickok (ND) and the City of Albuquerque (NM) for providing me with additional photography for the trails in this book. Finally, a special thanks goes to all the recreationalists who will be enjoying these trails.

This book is in memory of the American families whose lives were affected by the September 11, 2001 New York City and Washington, D.C. bombings.

This book is also in memory of Delton B. Richardson.

Contents

Introduction

I researched and created Biking U.S.A.'s Rail-Trails as a guide to U.S.A.'s major off-road multipurpose trails and rail-trails. It provides tourists, weekend travelers, outdoor lovers, and recreationalists with a resource list to allow them to easily find each trail.

Most of the trails described herein have a smooth surface to allow users to bicycle, mountain bicycle, walk, hike or travel by wheelchair. Many are opened to cross-country skiers during the winter months and some even allow horseback riding. Best of all, these trails prohibit motorized vehicles from using the them at any time, providing a safe alternative to users throughout the year. Check each individual trail to make sure it allows for your intended use.

While the book does not include any detailed maps for these trails, a locator map and description of each trail can be found under each state's listing of trails (see "Contents" to locate your state of interest). Addresses are provided for each trail under "U.S.A.'s Bicycle Information Contact by State" so readers can obtain more information concerning their trails of interest. Also, many trail maps are found in books written for several states under "U.S.A.'s Rails-to-Trails Guide Books" on page 312.

The maps and information in Biking U.S.A.'s Rail-Trails are current as of 2002. Future editions will include trails currently under development. If you find that any of the maps need corrections, or if you have discovered trails not listed, write to me in care of Biking U.S.A.'s Rail-Trails, P.O. Box 612, Worthington, OH 43085. I hope this book makes trailblazing across the United States of America more convenient and enjoyable for you, and whenever you use these trails, always keep in mind the safety tips listed in the back of this book.

Happy Trails!

Shawn E. Richardson, 2002

Boats, Trains & Automobiles

This book is primarily a rails-to-trails guide book for smooth surfaced trails for bicycling. However, it is important to expand this book to include towpaths-to-bike paths and highways-to-bikeways.

Rails to Trails

A bike trail converted from a former railroad right-of-way; this is the Mountain-Bay State Park Trail (Delly Trail) in Wisconsin.

Towpaths to Bike Paths

A bike path converted from a towpath along a canal right-of-way; this is the Towpath Trail (Ohio & Erie Canal) in Ohio.

Highways to Bikeways

A bikeway converted from an abandoned highway no longer used by motor vehicles; this was the former U.S. Route-66 over the Mississippi River between Missouri & Illinois.

The Rails-to-Trails Conservancy

Founded in 1985 with the mission of enhancing America's communities and countryside, the Rails-to-Trails Conservancy is a national nonprofit organization dedicated to converting abandoned rail corridors into a nationwide network of multi-purpose trails. By linking parks, schools, neighborhoods, communities, towns, cities, states and national parks, this system will connect important landmarks and create both a haven for wildlife and a safe place for everyone to bicycle, walk, in-line skate and travel by wheelchair. Rail-trails meet demands for local recreational opportunities and connect with long-distance trails to make it possible to ride continuously across a state and eventually from coast to coast without encountering a motorized vehicle. For more information, contact the Rails-to-Trails Conservancy, 1100 17th St. NW, 10th Floor, Washington, D.C. 20036 or call 202-331-9696.

Biking USA's Rail-Trails (Book and Website)

www.bikingusarailtrails.com

Biking USA's Rail-Trails, by Shawn E. Richardson. This guide provides tourists, weekend travelers, outdoor enthusiasts and recreationalists with information about the USA's major multi-purpose trails and rail-trails. State locator maps show where the major trails are, and information such as surface type, trail length, trail use and more is provided for each trail.

The Biking USA's Rail-Trails website is a companion to the book, and was designed to promote and provide information about the most prominent and scenic rail-trails across the country. The website gives examples of rail-to-trail, highway-to-bikeway and towpath-to-bikepath conversions. Under "trails and photos," mileage charts, a locator map USA's top rail-trails, and pictures from nearly every state are shown. Fun and games with questions and puzzles relating to rail-trails can be enjoyed under "rail-trail trivia." Of course, all of the answers can be found in **Biking USA's Rail-Trails**.

Help Keep Us Updated

Are there any new bike trails in your area? Did we not list a major bike trail which should have been included in this book? Have any trails listed in this book gone through any changes? Whether the trail has changed in length, surface, types of trail use, address, phone number, web page address or even the trail name itself, we would like to know so you can help us keep this publication accurate and up to date.

Please copy this page, answer the questions, and send it to Biking U.S.A.'s Rail-Trails, P.O. Box 612, Worthington, OH 43085. This will help us give our trailblazers the best and most accurate information for biking U.S.A.'s rail-trails.

Exact Trail name

Which State(s)?

Was any part of this trail formerly a railroad?

Vicinity? City (Street or spot) to City (Street or spot)

Trail Length (miles)?

Trail Surface?(concrete, asphalt, smooth crushed gravel)

Trail Use? (Yes or No)
Bicycle_____   Cross Country Skiing_____   Mountain Bicycle_____
Snowmobile_____   Walking-Hiking_____   Wheelchair Use_____   Roller Skating or
Roller Blades_____   ATV Use_____   Golf Cart Use_____   Horseback riding_____
Trail Users Fee_____   Horse & Buggy or Horse & Wagon_____

Address for Trail Information?

Phone Number for Trail Information?

Web Page for Trail?

Is the trail smooth enough for a touring bicycle?

When (Year) was the trail (First Section) built/open?

To make our research easier, could you provide us a map of the trail showing mile posts and parking spots?

Are there any other adjacent bike trails near by?

Are there any local bicycle route guide maps of your area? If so, where could we find them?

Any other comments?

Please answer these questions completely and send this page to the address above. Thanks for you input.

Trail User's Fee for Certain Trails

Certain trail organizations as well as certain state DNRs invest dollars to acquire rail corridors and then transform them into smooth-surfaced bicycle trails. It takes about as much effort to remove the rails and ties as it did to build the railroads over a century ago. After the rails and ties are removed, bridges are planked and guard rails are erected, crushed limestone is laid and graded and safety directional signs and mile markers are installed. There are ongoing costs to maintain the smooth trail surfaces, maintain the bridges, maintain the signs and pick up litter and debris.

To recover part of these costs, bicyclists along with other trail users age 18 and older must pay a daily or an annual trail admission fee. Write or call the address or phone number of the trail you're interested in for the current trail fees.

A Special Note for the State of Wisconsin

Remember to keep in mind that an annual admission fee can be used as a transfer on any of the Wisconsin State Trails during the year. You may buy admission cards by mail or in person from the Department of Natural Resources, each State Park trail headquarters or from the trail rangers along the trails. The trails are opened from 6 am to 11 pm daily. Pets are usually allowed, but must be on a leash no longer than eight feet.

For more information on the state parks, forests and trails, or to request campground reservation forms, call or write:

Wisconsin DNR
P.O. Box 7921, Madison, WI 53707
608-266-2181 or 608-267-2752 TDD
http://www.wiparks.net

A trail fee sign for the Mountain-Bay State Trail (WI)

Trail Descriptions

ASPHALT OR CONCRETE – suitable for bicycling, mountain bicycling, hiking, in-line skating and wheelchairs.

COARSE ASPHALT – suitable for bicycling, mountain bicycling, hiking and wheelchairs.

SMOOTH CRUSHED GRAVEL – suitable for bicycling, mountain bicycling, hiking and wheelchairs. During thawing and extremely wet weather, bicycles, mountain bicycles and wheelchairs should avoid using this trail surface because the soft surface can rut easily.

COARSE CRUSHED GRAVEL – suitable for mountain bicycling and hiking.

GRASS OR DIRT – suitable for mountain bicycling and hiking.

ORIGINAL BALLAST – difficult for most trail users due to the size of larger rocks.

CINDER – original crushed gravel from the railroad. This can range from very smooth for bicycling and mountain bicycling to very rough for all trail users.

WOOD CHIPS – suitable for walking & wheelchairs only.

Note: Trail users should check conditions for each trail by contacting the trail managers listed in this book.

The Gallipolis Bike Path in Ohio.

Legend

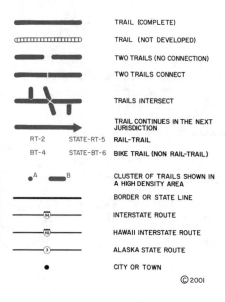

		TRAIL (COMPLETE)
		TRAIL (NOT DEVELOPED)
		TWO TRAILS (NO CONNECTION)
		TWO TRAILS CONNECT
		TRAILS INTERSECT
		TRAIL CONTINUES IN THE NEXT JURISDICTION
RT-2	STATE-RT-5	RAIL-TRAIL
BT-4	STATE-BT-6	BIKE TRAIL (NON RAIL-TRAIL)
A	B	CLUSTER OF TRAILS SHOWN IN A HIGH DENSITY AREA
		BORDER OR STATE LINE
		INTERSTATE ROUTE
		HAWAII INTERSTATE ROUTE
		ALASKA STATE ROUTE
		CITY OR TOWN

© 2001

Trail Use Symbols

Darker symbols: trail use allowed

Lighter symbols: trail use not allowed

- 🚲 Bicycling
- 🚲 Mountain Bicycling
- 🐎 Bridle Path
- In-line Skating
- Snowmobiling

- 🚶 Hiking
- ♿ Handicap Accessible
- 🎿 Cross-Country Skiing
- All Terrain Vehicles
- $ Trail fee required

State-RT-#: Major rail-trail (greater than 1 mile and/or smooth surface trail following a former railroad)

State-BT-#: Bike trail (smooth trail not following a former railroad)

Throughout the 50 state maps, these trails are labeled as either "RT" or "BT" with a hyphenated number following it.

Biking U.S.A.'s Rail-Trails

Biking Alabama Rail-Trails

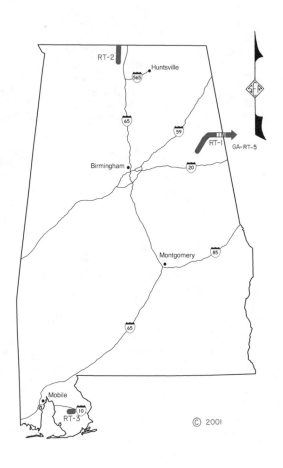

Trail Name:	Vicinity:
Chief Ladiga Trail	Anniston (Woodland Park) to Piedmont (Vigo Rd. & County Route-29)
Limestone Trail	Athens to AL-TN State Line
Robertsdale Trail	Robertsdale

Trail Listings

AL-RT-1	Chief Ladiga Trail
AL-RT-2	Limestone Trail
AL-RT-3	Robertsdale Trail

Alabama Highlights

CHIEF LADIGA TRAIL (AL-RT-1)

Built in 1996, Alabama's premier rail-trail is located near the Talladeqa National Forest. This Trail is named after Chief Ladiga (La-die-ga), an influential leader in this region during the early 1800s.

Chief Ladiga Trail.

Map:	Trail Length:	Surface											
(AL-RT-1)	24.5 miles	asphalt											
(AL-RT-2)	10.8 miles	smooth crushed gravel											
(AL-RT-3)	2.1 miles	concrete & asphalt											

Biking Alaska Rail-Trails

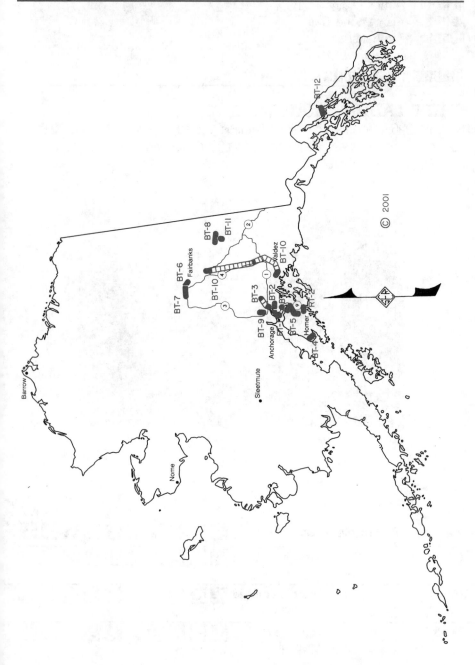

Trail Listings

Alaska Highlights

KNOWLES (TONY) COASTAL BICYCLE TRAIL (AK-RT-1)

Named after Alaska's governor, Tony Knowles, the trail follows both the Knik Arm and the Turnagain Arm Coasts and passes through Earthquake Park with a memorial to the 1964 Alaskan earthquake. Plans are to eventually extend this trail south to Seward using parts of the Old Seward Highway alignment. Beware of moose and bears!

SEWARD HIGHWAY BIKE PATH (AK-BT-11)

Declared on of the U.S.A.'s top scenic highways, sections of the original highway alignment are being transformed from "highways-to-bikeways" with the original concrete bridges still in place. Plans are to eventually make a bike path along the entire highway between Seward and Anchorage.

Alaska

Trail Name:	Vicinity:
Alaska Highway Bike Path	Tok to Tanacross (Mileposts 1314 to 1327)
Badger Road Bikeway	Ft. Wainwright to North Pole
Campbell Creek Bicycle Trail	Anchorage (W. Diamond Blvd. to Old Seward Highway)
Chester Creek Bicycle Trail	Anchorage (West Chester Lagoon to Russian Jack Springs Park & Tudor Rd.)
Fairbanks Bikeways	Fairbanks (Citywide Network)
Glen Highway Bicycle Trail	Anchorage (Davis Park) to North Birchwood Loop (Mileposts 3.0 to 20.4)
	Sutten (Mileposts 61 to 62)
Juneau Bike Path	Juneau (and surrounding area)
Knowles (Tony) Coastal Bicycle Trail	Anchorage (2nd Ave.) to Kinkaid Park
Parks Highway Bike Path	Wasilla to Houston Public Campground (Mileposts 42 to 57)
Richardson Highway Bike Path	Valdez to Old Valdez (Mileposts V-0 to V-4)
	Glennallen (Mileposts 110.8 to 111.8)
	Ft. Greely to Delta Junction (Mileposts 265.5 to 269.0)
Seward Highway Bike Path	Seward (Milepost 1.2 to 1.6)
	Moose Pass (Mileposts 28.6 to 30.0)
	Six Mile Creek to Granite Creek (Mileposts 58.5 to 64.0)
	Bird Point State Rec. Site (Bird to Gird Trail) (Mileposts 90.6 to 96.0)
	Bird Point to Indian (Mileposts 100.6 to 103.6)
Seward Rail-Trail	Seward (Seward Highway Mileposts 0 to 1)
Sterling Highway Bike Path	Homer (Mileposts 173.9 to 175.5)
Tok Cutoff Highway Bike Path	Tok (Mileposts 122.4 to 125.0)

Map:	Trail Length:	Surface	🚲	🛴	🐎	👶	✈	🚶	♿	⛷	🔭	$
(AK-BT-8)	13.0 miles	asphalt	🚲	🛴				🚶	♿	⛷		
(AK-BT-6)	10.5 miles	asphalt	🚲	🛴				🚶	♿	⛷		
(AK-BT-1)	3.8 miles	asphalt	🚲	🛴				🚶	♿	⛷		
(AK-BT-2)	10.5 miles	asphalt	🚲	🛴				🚶	♿	⛷		
(AK-BT-7)	30.0 miles	asphalt	🚲	🛴				🚶	♿	⛷		
(AK-BT-3)	17.4 miles	asphalt	🚲	🛴				🚶	♿	⛷		
	1.0 miles											
(AK-BT-12)	27.8 miles	asphalt	🚲	🛴		👶		🚶	♿	⛷		
(AK-RT-1)	10.5 Miles	asphalt	🚲	🛴	🐎	👶		🚶	♿			
(AK-BT-9)	15.0 miles	asphalt	🚲	🛴				🚶	♿	⛷		
(AK-BT-10)	4.0 miles	asphalt	🚲	🛴				🚶	♿	⛷		
	1.0 mile	asphalt										
	3.5 miles	asphalt										
(AK-BT-11)	0.4 miles	asphalt	🚲	🛴				🚶	♿	⛷		
	1.4 miles	asphalt										
	5.5 miles	asphalt										
	6.5 miles	asphalt										
	3.0 miles	asphalt										
(AK-RT-2)	1.0 mile	asphalt	🚲	🛴		👶		🚶	♿	⛷		
(AK-BT-4)	1.6 miles	asphalt	🚲	🛴				🚶	♿	⛷		
(AK-BT-11)	2.6 miles	asphalt	🚲	🛴				🚶	♿	⛷		

Biking Arizona's Rail-Trails

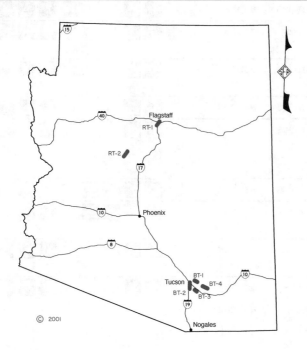

© 2001

Trail Name:	Vicinity:
Aviation Hwy-Golf Links Bike Path	Tucson: Park to Kolb
Prescott Peavine Trail	Prescott to U.S. Routes 89 & 89-A
Rillito River Bike Path	Tucson: La Cholla to Campbell Swan to Craycroft
Santa Cruz River Bike Path	Tucson: both sides from Grant to Silver Lake both sides from Ajo to Irvington
Spanish Trail Bike Path	Tucson: Broadway to Saguar National Park East
University Heights to Fort Tuthill Trail & Flagstaff Trail System	Flagstaff

Trail Listings

AZ-RT-1	University Heights to Ft. Tuthill Trail & Flagstaff Trail System
AZ-RT-2	Prescott Peavine Trail
AZ-BT-1	Rillito River Bike Path
AZ-BT-2	Santa Cruz River Bike Path
AZ-BT-3	Aviation Hwy-Golf Links Bike Path
AZ-BT-4	Spanish Trail Bike Path

Map:	Trail Length:	Surface
(AZ-BT-3)	8.5 miles	asphalt
(AZ-RT-2)	5.5 miles	coarse crushed gravel & ballast
(AZ-BT-1)	4.5 miles 1.5 miles	asphalt
(AZ-BT-2)	3.8 miles 1.0 mile	asphalt
(AZ-BT-4)	5.8 miles	asphalt
(AZ-RT-1)	3.0 miles	smooth crushed gravel, concrete

Biking Arkansas's Rail-Trails

Trail Name:	Vicinity:
Hot Springs Creek Greenway	Hot Springs
Levee Walking Trail	Helena
Marvell Bike Trail	Marvell (Parallels Main St.)

Trail Listings

Arkansas is still in its infancy of developing rail-trails.

Map:	Trail Length:	Surface	🚴	🚵	🐎	🛼	🏊	🚶	♿	⛷	🏄	$
(AR-BT-2)	4.5 miles	concrete	🚴	🚵		🛼		🚶	♿			
(AR-BT-1)	4.7 miles	asphalt	🚴	🚵		🛼		🚶	♿			
(AR-RT-1)	1.3 miles	asphalt	🚴	🚵		🛼		🚶	♿			

Biking California's Rail-Trails

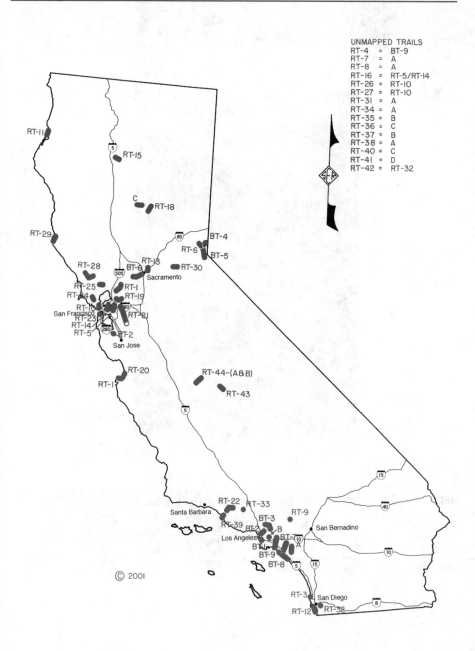

UNMAPPED TRAILS
RT-4	=	BT-9
RT-7	=	A
RT-8	=	A
RT-16	=	RT-5/RT-14
RT-26	=	RT-10
RT-27	=	RT-10
RT-31	=	A
RT-34	=	A
RT-35	=	B
RT-36	=	C
RT-37	=	B
RT-38	=	A
RT-40	=	C
RT-41	=	D
RT-42	=	RT-32

RT-11

RT-15

C RT-18

RT-29

RT-28   BT-6   RT-13   RT-30
RT-25
RT-24   RT-1   BT-4
RT-17   RT-19   RT-6   BT-5
San Francisco   RT-23   Sacramento
RT-14   RT-21
RT-5   BT-2
San Jose

RT-20

RT-1

RT-44-(A&B)

RT-43

© 2001

RT-22   RT-33   RT-9
Santa Barbara   BT-3
RT-39   BT-2   B   San Bernardino
Los Angeles   BT-1   A
BT-9
BT-8
RT-3   San Diego
RT-12   RT-38

Trail Listings

CA-RT-1	Fairfield Linear Park Trail
CA-RT-2	Bol Park Bike Path
CA-RT-3	Fay Avenue Bike Path
CA-RT-4	Seal Beach Regional Trail (Electric Avenue Median Park Trail)
CA-RT-5	Lafayette-Moraga Regional Trail
CA-RT-6	Tahoe City Truckee River Bike Trail
CA-RT-7	Tustin Branch Trail
CA-RT-8	Walnut Trail (Atchison, Topeka & Santa Fe Trail)
CA-RT-9	Duarte Bike Trail (Duarte Recreational Trail)
CA-RT-10	Mill Valley-Sausalito Path
CA-RT-11	Hammond Coastal Trail
CA-RT-12	Silver Strand Bikeway (Bayshore Bikeway)
CA-RT-13	Sacramento Northern Bike Trail
CA-RT-14	Ohlone Greenway (Santa Fe Greenway)
CA-RT-15	Sacramento River Trail
CA-RT-16	Shepherd Canyon Trail
CA-RT-17	Monterey Peninsula Recreational Trail
CA-RT-18	Paradise Memorial Trailway
CA-RT-19	Contra Costa Canal Regional Trail
CA-RT-20	Monterey Bay Coastal Trail
CA-RT-21	San Ramon Valley Iron Horse Regional Trail (Iron Horse Regional Trail)
CA-RT-22	Ojai Valley Trail
CA-RT-23	Lands End Trail
CA-RT-24	Sir Francis Drake Bikeway (Cross Marin Bike Trail)
CA-RT-25	Sonoma Bike Path
CA-RT-26	Tiburon Linear Park Trail
CA-RT-27	Larkspur Path
CA-RT-28	West County Trail & Joe Rodota Trail
CA-RT-29	Ten-Mile Coastal Trail (Mackerricher Haul Road Trail)
CA-RT-30	El Dorado Trail
CA-RT-31	Alton Bike Trail (Alton to Bristol Bike Trail)
CA-RT-32	Rose Canyon Bicycle Path
CA-RT-33	Fillmore Trail
CA-RT-34	Pacific Electric Bicycle Trail
CA-RT-35	Watts Towers Crescent Greenway
CA-RT-36	Midway Bike Path
CA-RT-37	Culver City Median Bikeway
CA-RT-38	Hoover Street Trail
CA-RT-39	Ventura River Trail

CA-RT-40	Chico Airport Bike Path
CA-RT-41	Durham Bike Path
CA-RT-42	King (Martin Luther) Promenade Trail
CA-RT-43	Reedley Rail-Trail Community Parkway
CA-RT-44-A	Clovis Old Town Trail
CA-RT-44-B	Fresno Sugar Pine Trail
CA-BT-1	Beach Bike Path; Los Angeles, CA
CA-BT-2	Ballona Creek Bike Path
CA-BT-3	Los Angeles River Bike Path
CA-BT-4	Tahoe City to Dollar Point Bike Path
CA-BT-5	Tahoe City to Tahoma Bike Path
CA-BT-6	Yolo Causeway / 2nd Street / Russell Blvd. Bike Paths
CA-BT-7	Santa Ana River Bikeway
CA-BT-8	Coast Highway Bikeway
CA-BT-9	San Gabriel River Bikeway

Seal Beach Regional Trail (Electric Avenue Median Park Trail).

California Highlights

SAN RAMON VALLEY IRON HORSE REGIONAL TRAIL (IRON HORSE REGIONAL TRAIL) (CA-RT-21)

Located in upscale Silicon Valley, the scenery along the trail varies from the urban and suburban setting on the northern end to the scenic oak trees in Alamo and Danville to the open grasslands on the south end. The trail passes through many parks and intersects with the Contra Costa Canal Regional Trail.

SILVER STRAND BIKEWAY (CA-RT-12)

This trails follows both the San Diego Bay and the Pacific Ocean Coast in southern California. The trail passes through Tidelands Park, the U.S. Naval Amphibious Base and the Silver Strand State Beach.

TEN-MILE COASTAL TRAIL (MACKERRICHER HAUL ROAD TRAIL) (CA-RT-29)

Opened in 1992, the Ten-Mile Coastal Trail follows the Pacific Ocean coast past the spectacular Ten-Miles Dunes & MacKerricher State Park in northern California.

TAHOE CITY TRUCKEE RIVER BIKE TRAIL (CA-RT-6)

Lake Tahoe is mostly known as a vacation and resort area in Eastern California and Western Nevada. The Tahoe City Truckee River Bike Trail also connects to the Tahoe City and Tahoma Bike Trails and also to the Tahoe City to Dollar Point Bike Trail, making the Tahoe City trail network approximately 20 miles long.

Trail Name:	Vicinity:
Alton Bike Trail (Alton to Bristol Bike Trail)	Santa Ana: Parallels Alton Ave. & Southern Pacific Railroad
Ballona Creek Bike Path	Los Angeles: Pacific Ave. to National Blvd.
Beach Bike Path; Los Angeles	Los Angeles: El Segundo Blvd. to Ballona Creek Washington St. to Santa Monica Ocean Ave. to Temescal Canyon Rd.
Bol Park Bike Path	Palo Alto (Hanover St. to Miranda Ave.)
Chico Airport Bike Path	Chico (Fortress St. to Esplanade & 11th Ave.)
Clovis Old Town Trail	Clovis to Fresno
Coast Highway Bikeway	Seal Beach to Newport Beach (trail follows Pacific Coast Highway / State Route 1)
Contra Costa Canal Regional Trail	Martinez to Pleasant Hill to Concord
Culver City Median Bikeway	Culver City to Los Angeles (trail follows center median of Culver Blvd.)
Duarte Bike Trail (Duarte Recreational Trail)	Duarte: Royal Oaks Park to Buena Vista St.
Durham Bike Path	Chico: State Route 99 to Jones Ave.
El Dorado Trail	Camino to Placerville
Fairfield Linear Park Trail	Fairfield: E Travis Blvd. to Chadbourne Rd.
Fay Avenue Bike Path	La Jolla: Prospect St. to Fay Ave.
Fresno Sugar Pine Trail	Fresno to Clovis
Fillmore Trail	Fillmore
Hammond Coastal Trail	McKinleyville: Mad River Rd. to Clam Beach County Park
Hoover Street Trail	Westminster (Bolsa Ave. to Garden Grove Freeway)
King (Martin Luther) Promenade Trail	San Diego (8th Ave. to Broadway)
Lafayette-Moraga Regional Trail	Lafayette to Moraga

Map:	Trail Length:	Surface	🚴 🚵 🐎 🛼 ✈ 🚶 ♿ ⛷ 🏍 $
(CA-RT-35)	1.8 miles	asphalt & concrete	
(CA-BT-2)	6.2 miles	asphalt	
(CA-BT-1)	3.2 miles 1.4 miles 1.2 miles	asphalt	
(CA-RT-2)	1.5 miles	asphalt	
(CA-RT-40)	3.5 miles	asphalt	
(CA-RT-44-A)	5.0 miles	asphalt	
(CA-BT-8)	12.0 miles	concrete & asphalt	
(CA-RT-19)	13.8 miles	asphalt	
(CA-RT-37)	2.0 miles	asphalt	
(CA-RT-9)	1.6 miles	asphalt	
(CA-RT-41)	2.5 miles	asphalt	
(CA-RT-30)	2.5 miles (Will be 8.0 miles)	asphalt	
(CA-RT-1)	5.5 miles	asphalt & concrete	
(CA-RT-3)	1.0 mile	asphalt	
(CA-RT-44-B)	3.0 miles	asphalt	
(CA-RT-33)	2.0 miles	asphalt	
(CA-RT-11)	3.0 miles	asphalt & smooth crushed gravel	
(CA-RT-38)	2.0 miles	asphalt	
(CA-RT-42)	1.5 miles	concrete & asphalt	
(CA-RT-5)	7.6 miles	asphalt & concrete	

California

Trail Name:	Vicinity:
Lands End Trail	San Francisco (Merry Way to El Camino Del Mar)
Larkspur Path	Corte Madera to Larkspur
Los Angeles River Bike Path	Los Angeles (Fletcher. Dr to Zoo Dr.)
Midway Bike Path	Chico (East Park Ave. to Jones Ave.)
Mill Valley-Sausalito Path	Mill Valley to Sausalito
Monterey Bay Coastal Trail	Monterey (Ocean View Blvd.) to Marina (Lapis Rd.)
Monterey Peninsula Recreational Trail	Pacific Grove to Seaside
Ohlone Greenway (Santa Fe Greenway)	Berkeley to Richmond
Ojai Valley Trail	Ojai (Fox St.) to Ventura (Foster Park)
Pacific Electric Bicycle Trail	Santa Ana (Parallels Maple St. & Rouselle St.)
Paradise Memorial Trailway	Paradise
Reedley Rail-Trail Community Parkway	Reedley (Manning Ave. to Dinuba Ave.)
Rose Canyon Bicycle Path	San Diego
Sacramento Northern Bike Trail	Sacramento & 18th Streets) to Rio Linda (M St.)
Sacramento River Trail	Redding (Court St. to Keswick Dam)
San Gabriel River Bikeway	Seal Beach (Pacific Coast Highway / State Route 1) to Cypress; trail follows San Gabriel River & Coyote Creek
San Ramon Valley Iron Horse Regional Trail (Iron Horse Regional Trail)	Concord (Monument Blvd.) to San Ramon (Alcosta Blvd.)
Santa Ana River Bikeway	Huntington Beach (Pacific Coast Highway / State Route 1) to Santa Ana (Villa Park Rd.)
Seal Beach Regional Trail (Electric Avenue Median Park Trail)	Seal Beach (6th St. to Seal Beach Blvd.)

Map:	Trail Length:	Surface	🚲	🚲	🐎	🛼	➡	🚶	♿	⛷	👓	$
(CA-RT-23)	2.0 miles	smooth crushed gravel	🚲	🚲	🐎			🚶	♿			
(CA-RT-27)	1.7 miles	asphalt	🚲	🚲	🐎	🛼		🚶	♿			
(CA-BT-3)	4.3 miles	asphalt	🚲	🚲		🛼		🚶	♿			
(CA-RT-36)	2.4 miles	asphalt	🚲	🚲	🐎	🛼		🚶	♿			
(CA-RT-10)	3.5 miles	asphalt	🚲	🚲	🐎	🛼		🚶	♿			
(CA-RT-20)	13.0 miles	asphalt (portions follow streets & bike lanes)	🚲	🚲	🐎	🛼		🚶	♿			$
(CA-RT-17)	4.8 miles	asphalt & concrete	🚲	🚲	🐎	🛼		🚶	♿	⛷		
(CA-RT-14)	2.5 miles	asphalt	🚲	🚲	🐎	🛼		🚶	♿			$
(CA-RT-22)	9.5 miles	asphalt	🚲	🚲	🐎	🛼		🚶	♿			$
(CA-RT-34)	2.1 miles	asphalt & concrete	🚲	🚲	🐎	🛼		🚶	♿			
(CA-RT-18)	5.5 miles	asphalt	🚲	🚲	🐎	🛼		🚶	♿			$
(CA-RT-43)	1.3 mile	asphalt & smooth crushed gravel	🚲	🚲	🐎	🛼		🚶	♿			
(CA-RT-32)	1.3 miles	asphalt	🚲	🚲		🛼		🚶	♿			
(CA-RT-13)	6.4 miles	asphalt	🚲	🚲		🛼		🚶	♿			
(CA-RT-15)	10.0 miles	asphalt & concrete	🚲	🚲	🐎	🛼		🚶	♿			$
(CA-BT-9)	6.0 miles	concrete & asphalt	🚲	🚲	🐎	🛼		🚶	♿			
(CA-RT-21)	23.0 miles	asphalt	🚲	🚲	🐎	🛼		🚶	♿	⛷		
(CA-BT-7)	12.0 miles	concrete & asphalt	🚲	🚲		🛼		🚶	♿			$
(CA-RT-4)	0.5 miles	asphalt, concrete & grass	🚲	🚲		🛼		🚶	♿			

Trail Name:	Vicinity:
Shepherd Canyon Trail	Oakland (Shepherd Canyon Rd. & Escher Dr. to Shepherd Canyon Park)
Silver Strand Bikeway	Coronado (Orange Ave.) to San Diego (Palm Ave.)
Sir Francis Drake Bikeway (Cross Marin Bike Trail)	Samuel P. Taylor State Park to Laquintas
Sonoma Bike Path	Sonoma (Sonoma Hwy. To 4th St. East)
Ten-Mile Coastal Trail (Mackerricher Haul Road Trail)	MacKerricher State Park to Ft. Bragg
Tiburon Linear Park Trail	Tiburon
Tahoe City to Dollar Point Bike Trail	Tahoe City to Dollar Point
Tahoe City to Tahoma Bike Trail	Tahoe City to Tahoma
Tahoe City Truckee River Bike Trail	Tahoe City (State Routes 89 & 28 near Lake Tahoe) to Squaw Valley; trail follows both the Truckee River and State Route 89
Tustin Branch Trail	Tustin to Villa Park Esplanade Section
	Newport Ave. Section Wanda Rd. Section
Ventura River Trail	Ventura (Olive St. to Foster Park)
Walnut Trail (Atchison, Topeka & Santa Fe Trail)	Irvine (parallels AT & SF railroad between Harvard Ave. & Sand Canyon Ave.)
Watts Towers Crescent Greenway	Los Angeles (Willowbrook near Watts Towers)
West County Trail & Joe Rodota Trail	Sebastopol to Santa Rosa and Granton
Yolo Causeway / 2nd Street / Russell Blvd. Bike Paths	West Sacramento (Interstate 80 & West Capitol Ave.) to Davis (Interstate 80 & Road 32-A)
	Davis (Road 32-A & Road 105 to Russell Blvd. & Cassidy Ln.); the trail follows both 2nd St. and Russell Blvd.

Map:	Trail Length:	Surface	🚲	🚵	🐎	🛼	✈	🥾	♿	⛷	🛻	$
(CA-RT-16)	3.0 miles	asphalt	●	●		●		●	●			
(CA-RT-12)	9.0 miles	concrete & asphalt	●	●	●	●		●	●	●		●
(CA-RT-24)	4.5 miles	asphalt & ballast	●	●	●	●		●	●			●
(CA-RT-25)	1.5 miles	asphalt	●	●		●		●				
(CA-RT-29)	8.0 miles	asphalt & wet sand	●	●	●	●		●	●	●		
(CA-RT-26)	2.7 miles	asphalt	●	●		●		●	●			
(CA-BT-4)	4.0 miles	asphalt	●	●		●		●	●			
(CA-BT-5)	10.0 miles	asphalt	●	●	●	●		●	●			
(CA-RT-6)	5.0 miles	asphalt	●	●	●	●		●	●			
(CA-RT-7)	1.0 mile	smooth crushed gravel	●	●		●		●	●			
	1.0 mile	asphalt										
	0.5 mile	asphalt										
(CA-RT-39)	6.3 miles	asphalt	●	●		●		●	●	●		
(CA-RT-8)	3.0 miles	asphalt	●	●	●	●		●	●			
(CA-RT-35)	0.2 miles	asphalt	●	●		●		●	●			
(CA-RT-28)	5.5 miles	asphalt	●	●	●	●		●	●			
(CA-BT-6)	3.2 miles	asphalt & concrete	●	●	●	●		●	●	●		
	9.0 miles	asphalt & concrete										

Biking Colorado's Rail-Trails

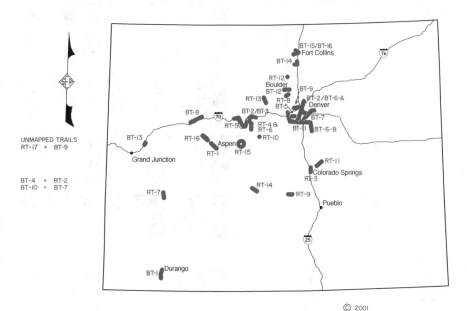

© 2001

Trail Listings

CO-RT-1	Rio Grande Trail
CO-RT-2	Platte River Greenway
CO-RT-3	Shooks Run Trail
CO-RT-4	Blue River Pathway
CO-RT-5	Ten-Mile Canyon Recreation Trail (Vail Pass Trail)
CO-RT-6	Frisco-Farmer's Korner Recreation Trail (Dillon Dam Trail)
CO-RT-7	Uncompahgre River Trail
CO-RT-8	Fowler Trail
CO-RT-9	Arkansas Riverwalk Trail
CO-RT-10	Narrow Gauge Trail
CO-RT-11	Rock Island Regional Trail
CO-RT-12	Corridor Trail
CO-RT-13	Fraser River Trail
CO-RT-14	Salida Trail System
CO-RT-15	Mineral Belt Trail
CO-RT-16	Roaring Fork Trail

CO-RT-17	Union Pacific Trail
CO-BT-1	Animas River Trail
CO-BT-2	Snake River Pathway (Keystone-Summit Cove Recreation Trail)
CO-BT-3-A	Dillon-Keystone Recreation Trail
CO-BT-3-B	Dillon Dam Trail
CO-RT-3-C	Frisco Lakefront Trail
CO-BT-4	Sanderson Gulch Trail
CO-BT-5	Bear Creek Trail
CO-BT-6-A	Cherry Creek Trail (Denver to Cherry Creek State Recreation Area)
CO-BT-6-B	Cherry Creek Trail (Parker)
CO-BT-7	Highline Canal Trail
CO-BT-8	Glenwood Canyon Recreational Trail
CO-BT-9	Clear Creek Bikeway
CO-BT-10	Creek Trail
CO-BT-11	C-470 Bikeway
CO-BT-12	Boulder Creek Bike Path
CO-BT-13	Interstate-70 Beaver Tunnels Alternate Bike Path
CO-BT-14	Loveland-Greeley Canal Bike Path
CO-BT-15	Spring Creek Bikeway
CO-BT-16	Cache La Poudre Bikeway

Colorado Highlights

GLENWOOD CANYON RECREATIONAL TRAIL (CO-BT-8)

This spectacular trail follows the Colorado River through Glenwood Canyon with breathtaking views of the canyon and the mountains. The Hanging Lake Trail and Spouting Rock Trail (both for hiking only) are highly recommended for seeing the natural wonders of Glenwood Canyon.

TEN-MILE CANYON RECREATION TRAIL (VAIL PASS TRAIL) (CO-RT-5)

This trail offers both the spectacular views of the Rocky Mountains and a very physical challenge of climbing mountains through thin air to this trail's highest point at Vail Pass, 10,550 feet above sea level. Vail Pass is the continental divide between the Atlantic and Pacific Oceans. This trail is both a "railway-to-trailway" and a "highway-to-bikeway" conversion. In Frisco, this trail connects to the blue River Pathway, the Frisco-Farmer's Korner Recreation Trail, the Snake River Pathway, the Dillon-Keystone Recreation Trail, the Dillon Dam Trail and the Frisco Lakefront Trail.

Trail Name:	Vicinity:
Animas River Trail	Durango
Arkansas Riverwalk Trail	Canon City
Bear Creek Trail	Lakewood (Kipling Pkwy.) to Denver (Federal Blvd. & Platte River Greenway)
Blue River Pathway	Breckenridge to Dillon Reservoir (Farmer's Corner); trail follows State Route 9
Boulder Creek Bike Path	Boulder (State Route 119 & Four-Mile Canyon Dr. to State Route 7/Agrapahoe Ave.); trail follows Boulder & S Boulder Creeks
C-470 Bikeway	Denver Area; bike path follows State Route 470 from Interstate-70 to Jordan Rd. & Cherry Creek (Trail incomplete)
	Interstate-70 to W Morrison Rd. W. Quincy Ave. to Platte Canyon Rd. U.S. Route 85/S. Santa Fe Dr. to Jordan Rd. & Cherry Creek
Cache La Poudre Bikeway	Fort Collins (Taft Hill Rd. to Prospect Rd. & Riverside Ave.)
Cherry Creek Trail (Denver to Cherry Creek State Rec. Area)	Denver (Speer Blvd. & Platte River to Cherry Creek State Recreation Area & Parker Rd.)
Cherry Creek Trail (Parker)	Parker (County Route 34 north of State Route 470 to State Route 83 south of Stroh Rd.)
Clear Creek Bikeway	Wheat Ridge (McIntyre St.) to Commerce City (74th Ave.)
Corridor Trail	Lyons
Creek Trail	Cherry Creek State Recreation Area (Parker Rd.) to Aurora (Alameda Ave.)
Dillon-Keystone Recreation Trail	Dillon (Lake Dillon Dr.) to Summit Cove (U.S. Route 6 & Montezuma Rd.)
Dillon Dam Trail	Frisco (Ten Mile Dr.) to Dillon (Lake Dillon Dr.)

Map:	Trail Length:	Surface	🚲	🚴	🐎	🛼	✈	🚶	♿	⛷	🔭	$
(CO-BT-1)	6.0 miles	asphalt & concrete										
(CO-RT-9)	3.5 miles	smooth crushed gravel										
(CO-BT-5)	6.0 miles	asphalt										
(CO-RT-4)	9.5 miles	asphalt										
(CO-BT-12)	8.0 miles	asphalt										
(CO-BT-11)	4.5 miles / 9.5 miles / 15.5 miles	asphalt										
(CO-BT-16)	5.0 miles	asphalt										
(CO-BT-6-A)	25.0 miles	asphalt										
(CO-BT-6-B)	8.0 miles	asphalt										
(CO-BT-9)	14.0 miles	asphalt										
(CO-RT-12)	0.8 miles	concrete, smooth crushed gravel & ballast										
(CO-BT-10)	5.0 miles	asphalt										
(CO-BT-3-A)	3.0 miles	asphalt										
(CO-BT-3-B)	4.0 miles	asphalt										

Colorado

Trail Name:	Vicinity:
Fowler Trail	El Dorado Canyon State Park (along South Boulder Creek)
Fraser River Trail	Fraser to Winter Park
Frisco-Farmer's Korner Recreation Trail	Frisco (Main St. & Interstate-70) to Dillon Reservoir (State Route 9)
Frisco Lakefront Trail	Frisco (Ten Mile Dr. to Peninsula Rd.)
Glenwood Canyon Recreational Trail	Glenwood Springs to Dotsero; trail follows Interstate-70 between mile posts 116 & 130
Highline Canal Trail	Chatfield Reservoir (S. Santa Fe Dr./U.S. Route 85 & State Route 470) to Denver (Colorado Blvd.) to Aurora (Environmental Park & State Route 30/6th Ave.)
Interstate-70 Beaver Tunnels Alternate Bike Path	Interstate-70 (Between mileposts 49 & 50)
Loveland-Greeley Canal Bike Path	Loveland (U.S. Route 34/Eisenhower Blvd. next to Lake Loveland to Lemay Ave. & Boyd Lake)
Mineral Belt Trail	Leadville (Circular Trail)
Narrow Gauge Trail	Jefferson (Pine Valley Ranch Park)
Platte River Greenway	Thornton (104th Ave.) to Denver (W. Colfax Ave.) to Chatfield Reservoir (U.S. Route 85/S. Santa Fe Dr. & State Route 470)
Rio Grande Trail	Ewing to Aspen
Roaring Fork Trail	Basalt to Woody Creek
Rock Island Regional Trail	Falcon to Payton
Salida Trail System	Salida

Map:	Trail Length:	Surface	🚲	🚴	🐎	inline skate	✈	🚶	♿	⛷	🏍	$
(CO-RT-8)	0.7 miles	smooth crushed gravel	●	●				●	●			$
(CO-RT-13)	6.3 miles	asphalt	●	●		●		●	●			
(CO-RT-6)	2.5 miles	asphalt	●	●		●		●	●	●		
(CO-RT-3-C)	2.0 miles	asphalt	●	●		●		●	●	●		
(CO-BT-8)	16.2 miles	asphalt	●	●		●		●	●	●		
(CO-BT-6)	35.0 miles	asphalt	●	●		●		●	●	●		
(CO-BT-13)	2.0 miles	asphalt	●	●		●		●	●	●		
(CO-BT-14)	6.0 miles	asphalt	●	●		●		●	●	●		
(CO-RT-15)	12.0 miles	asphalt	●	●	●	●		●	●	●		
(CO-RT-10)	2.0 miles	smooth crushed gravel	●	●		●		●	●			
(CO-RT-2)	28.5 miles	concrete	●	●		●		●	●			
(CO-RT-1)	12.0 miles	asphalt & smooth crushed gravel	●	●	●	●		●	●	●		
(CO-RT-16)	12.0 miles	asphalt & gravel	●	●	●	●		●	●			
(CO-RT-11)	9.2 miles	smooth-coarse crushed gravel & concrete	●	●		●		●	●			
(CO-RT-14)	7.0 miles	asphalt & concrete	●	●		●		●	●			

Colorado

Trail Name:	Vicinity:
Sanderson Gulch Trail	Denver (Xavier St. to Santa Fe Drive)
Shooks Run Trail	Colorado Springs
Snake River Pathway (Keystone-Summit Cove Recreation Trail)	Summit Cove to Keystone Resort
Spring Creek Bikeway	Fort Collins (Drake Rd. to Prospect Rd. & Riverside Ave.)
Ten-Mile Canyon Recreation Trail (Vail Pass Trail)	Dowd (Interstate-70 & U.S. Route 6 & 24) to Vail (South Frontage Rd.) to Vail Pass to Frisco (Interstate-70 & Main St.); trail follows Interstate-70 between mile posts 171 & 201
Uncompahgre River Trail	Montrose (E. Oak Grove & Rio Grande Rd. to US-Route 550)
Union Pacific Trail	Thornton

Ten-Mile Canyon Recreation Trail (Vail Pass Trail).

Map:	Trail Length:	Surface	🚴	🚵	🐎	🛼	🚣	🚶	♿	⛷	🏍	$
(CO-BT-4)	4.0 miles	asphalt										
(CO-RT-3)	4.2 miles	asphalt										
(CO-BT-2)	2.0 miles	asphalt										
(CO-BT-15)	4.0 miles	asphalt										
(CO-RT-5)	24.0 miles	asphalt										
(CO-RT-7)	4.5 miles	concrete										
(CO-RT-17)	0.5 miles	asphalt										

The Rocky Mountains make most of the scenery along the Ten-Mile Canyon Recreation Trail.

Biking Connecticut's Rail-Trails

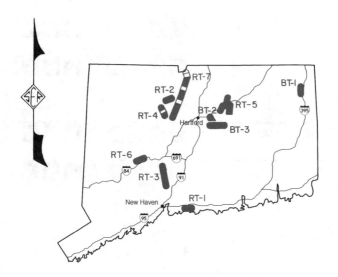

© 2001

Trail Listings

CT-RT-1	Trolley Trail (Branford, CT)
CT-RT-2	Stratton Brook State Park-Town Forest Trail
CT-RT-3	Farmington Canal Linear State Park Trail
CT-RT-4	Farmington River Trail
CT-RT-5	Vernon Rail-Trail (Town of Vernon Rails-to-Trails System)
CT-RT-6	Middlebury Greenway
CT-RT-7	Farmington Valley Greenway
CT-BT-1	Putnam River Trail
CT-BT-2	Captain John Bissell Greenway
CT-BT-3	Charter Oak Greenway

Connecticut Highlights

FARMINGTON CANAL LINEAR STATE PARK TRAIL
(CT-RT-3)
Both a "railway-to-trailway" and a "towpath-to-bikepath," the Farmington Canal Linear State Park Trail passes by neighborhoods, historic buildings, historic canal locks, steel bridges and stone arches which were all part of the canal era. The scenery consists mostly of woodlands and farmlands in the gently rolling hills of Connecticut.

FARMINGTON VALLEY GREENWAY (CT-RT-7)
Both a "railway-to-trailway" and a "towpath-to-bikepath," the Farmington Valley Greenway passes by the neighborhoods, historic buildings, historic canal locks, steel bridges and stone arches which were all part of the canal era.

Farmington Canal Linear State Park Trail.

Trail Name:	Vicinity:
Captain John Bissell Greenway	South Windsor (State Route 291 & the Connecticut River) to Manchester (State Route 384)
Charter Oak Greenway	Manchester (Forbes St. to State Route 83 & Charter Oak St.)
Farmington Canal Linear State Park Trail	Cheshire (Cornwall & Willow Streets.) to Mt. Carmel (State Route 10 & Todd Rd.)
Farmington River Trail	Farmington (Red Oak Hill Rd.) to Collinsville to Stratton Brook State Park (Some sections incomplete)
Farmington Valley Greenway	Farmington to Newgate State Wildlife Area Farmington, Hwy. 4 to Simsbury, Sand Hill Rd. Simsbury, Town Forest Rd. to Wolcott Rd. Granby, Hwy. 189 to Copper Hill Rd.
Middlebury Greenway	Middlebury
Putnam River Trail	Putnam (Downtown area; trail follows the eastern shore of the Quinsburg River.)
Stratton Brook State Park-Town Forest Trail	Stratton Brook State Park; near Simsbury
Trolley Trail (Branford, CT)	Pine Orchard (Totoket Rd.) to Stony Creek (Thimble Islands Rd.)
Vernon Rail-Trail (Town of Vernon Rails-to-Trails System)	Vernon Vernon (Phoenix St.) to Manchester (Progress Dr.) Vernon (Phoenix St.) to Bolton Notch & Williamantic Vernon (Warren Ave. to Vernon Ave.)

Map:	Trail Length:	Surface	🚲	🚵	🐎	🛼	➡	🚶	♿	⛷	🔭	$
(CT-BT-2)	8.0	asphalt (3.0 miles are bike lanes along Chapel St.)	●	●		●		●	●	●		
(CT-BT-3)	6.0 miles	asphalt	●	●		●		●	●	●		
(CT-RT-3)	8.0 miles	asphalt	●	●		●		●	●			
(CT-RT-4)	12.5 miles	asphalt, smooth crushed gravel & gravel	●	●	●	●		●				
(CT-RT-7)	20.0 miles 7.5 miles 3.5 miles 2.5 miles	asphalt	●	●		●		●	●	●		
(CT-RT-6)	8.0 miles	concrete, asphalt & smooth crushed gravel	●	●				●	●	●		
(CT-BT-1)	2.0 miles	concrete & asphalt	●	●		●		●	●	●		
(CT-RT-2)	2.5 miles	asphalt & gravel	●	●				●	●	●		
(CT-RT-1)	0.8 mile	concrete, smooth crushed gravel & gravel	●	●				●	●	●		
(CT-RT-5)	9.1 miles 1.8 miles 3.3 miles 4.0 miles	smooth crushed gravel	●	●	●			●	●	●		

Biking Delaware's Rail-Trails

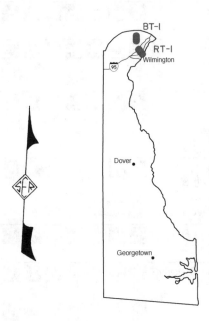

© 2001

Trail Name:	Vicinity:
Brandywine Park Trail	Wilmington (Brandywine Park); trail parallels the Brandywine Creek from Van Buren St. to the north.
Creek Road Trail	Wilmington (Creek Park); trail parallels the east side of the Brandywine Creek from Rockland Rd. to State Route 2/Thompson Bridge Rd.

Trail Listings

DE-RT-1	Brandywine Park Trail
DE-BT-1	Creek Road Trail

The Creek Road Trail follows the Brandywine Creek (DE).

Map:	Trail Length:	Surface	🚲	🚵	🐎	🛷	🛶	🥾	♿	⛸	🏍	$
(DE-RT-1)	1.0 mile	smooth crushed gravel	🚲	🚵				🥾	♿			
(DE-BT-1)	1.0 mile	asphalt	🚲	🚵		🛷		🥾	♿			

Biking the District of Columbia's Rail-Trails

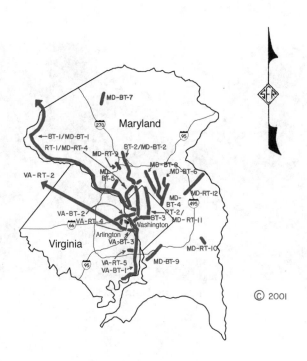

© 2001

Trail Listings

DC-RT-1	Capital Crescent Trail
DC-RT-2	Metropolitan Branch Trail
DC-BT-1	Chesapeake & Ohio Canal National Historic Park Trail
DC-BT-2	Rock Creek Park Trail
DC-BT-3	Potomac River & Reflection Pool Bike Paths

District of Columbia Highlights

CAPITAL CRESCENT TRAIL (DC-RT-1/MD-RT-4)

Built in 1993, this trail connects historic Georgetown and Washington, D.C. to Bethesda, MD. This trail goes through a 1910 brick tunnel and two office buildings with "air rights" above the railroad tunnel right-of-way. This trail connects to other bicycle trails throughout the DC area including the Chesapeake & Ohio Canal National Historic Park Trail, the Potomac River & Reflection Pool Bike Paths and the Rock Creek Park Trail.

CHESAPEAKE & OHIO CANAL NATIONAL HISTORIC PARK TRAIL (DC-BT-1/MD-BT-1)

Converted in 1973 to a biking and hiking trail, this is believed to be the United State's first "towpath-to-bikepath." Parts of the trail are suitable for standard bicycles: mostly the eastern portion toward Georgetown and Washington, D.C.

POTOMAC RIVER & REFLECTION POOL BIKE PATHS (DC-BT-3)

Many of these bike paths are part of the original large sidewalks which traverse the center of Washington, D.C. These trails connect many landmarks including the Lincoln Memorial, the Washington Monument, the Jefferson Memorial, the White House, the U.S. Capitol Building, numerous museums and many other famous memorials. These bike paths are a hub and connection to the Chesapeake & Ohio Canal National Historic Park Trail, the Capital Crescent Trail, the Mount Vernon Trail (VA) and the Custis Trail (VA).

Trail Name:	Vicinity:
Capital Crescent Trail	Washington, D.C. (Key Bridge) to Silver Spring, MD (Stewart Ave.)
Chesapeake & Ohio Canal National Historic Park Trail	Cumberland, MD (Visitor's Center) to Washington, D.C. (Georgetown & Rock Creek Park).
Metropolitan Branch Trail	Silver Spring, MD (Colesville Rd. & Wayne Ave.) to Washington, D.C. (Union Station on Massachusetts Ave. & Louisiana Ave.)
Potomac River & Reflection Pool Bike Paths	Washington DC (A trail follows the Potomac River between Georgetown & Interstate-395. Other trails traverse the historical Reflection Pool park area offering access to many of the United States' historical landmarks).
Rock Creek Park Trail	Washington DC (Pennsylvania Ave. & M St.) to DC-MD State Line

Bike paths traverse around Washington, D.C.'s Reflection Pool.

Map:	Trail Length:	Surface	🚲 🚲 🐎 🛼 ➰ 🚶 ♿ ⛷ 🔭 $
(DC-RT-1 / MD-RT-4)	11.0 miles	asphalt & smooth crushed gravel	
(DC-BT-1 / MD-BT-1)	184.5 miles	smooth crushed gravel, gravel, & dirt (many sections very rough)	
(DC-RT-2 or MD-RT-11)	8.0 miles	asphalt (portion follows streets)	
(DC-BT-3)	10.0 miles (network of city bike paths)	asphalt & concrete	
(DC-BT-2)	8.5 miles	asphalt	

The Capital Crescent Trail.

Biking Florida's Rail-Trails

Trail Listings

FL-RT-1	Tallahassee-St. Marks Historic Railroad State Trail
FL-RT-2	Gasparilla Island Trail (Boca Grande Bike Path)
FL-RT-3	Pinellas Trail (Fred Marquois Pinellas Trail)
FL-RT-4	Gainesville-Hawthorne State Trail
FL-RT-5	Withlacoochee State Trail
FL-RT-6	Van Fleet (General James A.) State Trail
FL-RT-7	West Orange Trail
FL-RT-8	Cady Way Trail
FL-RT-9	Overseas Heritage Trail
FL-RT-10	Stadium Drive Bike Path
FL-RT-11	South Dade Trail
FL-RT-12	Upper Tampa Bay Trail
FL-RT-13-A	Waldo Road Rail-Trail
FL-RT-13-B	Depot Avenue Rail-Trail
FL-RT-14	Branford Trail
FL-RT-15	Blackwater Heritage State Trail (Military Heritage Trail)
FL-RT-16	Cross Seminole Trail
FL-RT-17	Lake Minneola Scenic State Trail (Clermont Trail)
FL-RT-18	Cape Haze Pioneer Trail
FL-RT-19	Jacksonville-Baldwin Rail-Trail
FL-RT-20	Nature Coast State Trail-Fanning Springs (Nature Coast Trail State Park or Dixie-Levy-Gilchrest Greenway)
FL-RT-21	Suwannee River Greenway
FL-BT-1	State Route A1A Bike Path
FL-BT-2	Black Creek Trail
FL-BT-3	Gandy Trail Bridge Bikeway
FL-BT-4	Fort Clinch State Park Bike Path
FL-BT-5	Dickinson (Jonathan) State Park Bike Path
FL-BT-6	Oleta River State Park Recreation Area Bike Paths

Florida Highlights

GAINESVILLE-HAWTHORNE STATE TRAIL (FL-RT-4)

Opened in 1992, this rail-trail contains beautiful landscape scenery and traverses the Paynes Prairie State Preserve and the Lochloosa Wildlife Management Area.

OVERSEAS HERITAGE TRAIL (FL-RT-9)

This is the southernmost rail-trail in the 48 mainland states. This east-west trail follows the islands that divide the Atlantic Ocean from the Gulf of Mexico. This trail is a "railway-to-highway-to-bikeway" conversion using many of the original railroad trestles that were converted in 1938 to narrow highway bridges for the original U.S. Route 1. Today, most of U.S. Route 1 has been modernized and rerouted to newer and wider bridges, leaving the original ones for recreational use. The scenery includes ocean, tropical sea land and sea grass. Key West is a major tropical paradise for vacationers and tourists.

PINELLAS TRAIL (FRED MARQUOIS PINELLAS TRAIL) (FL-RT-3)

Built in the early 1990s, this urban-suburban rail-trail follows the Gulf of Mexico and crosses over Lake Seminole. There are also connector bike paths to both Clearwater Beach and Honeymoon Island State Park. The scenery along this state's most heavily-used rail-trail consists of neighborhoods, palm trees and parks. Many parts of this trail have a second asphalt strip running parallel to separate cyclists and rollerbladers from walkers.

TALLAHASSEE-ST. MARKS HISTORIC RAILROAD STATE TRAIL (FL-RT-1)

Florida's first rail-trail goes through a rural setting of small towns, woods and wetlands from the south edge of Tallahassee to the St. Marks River where the San Marcos de Apalache State Historic Site can be visited. In Tallahassee, this trail continues north as the Stadium Drive Bike Path, giving trail users access into Tallahassee, Florida's state capital.

VAN FLEET (GENERAL JAMES A.) STATE TRAIL (FL-RT-6)

This trail is considered to be Florida's most rural rail-trail. It traverses citrus groves and cattle ranches, and remnants of the Great Green Swamp are visible along the trail.

The Tallahassee-St. Marks Historic Railroad State Trail (FL).

Trail Name:	Vicinity:
Black Creek Trail	Orange Park (Holy Point) to Black Creek Park (U.S. Route 17)
Blackwater Heritage State Trail (Military Heritage Trail)	Milton (U.S. Route 90 & State Route 87) to Whiting Field U.S. Naval Air Station-South
Branford Trail	Branford (U.S. Route 27 to County Route 248)
Cady Way Trail	Orlando (Colonial Dr. & Orlando Fashion Square Mall) to Winter Park (Cady Way)
Cape Haze Pioneer Trail	Charlotte Beach (State Route 776 & County Route 771 to Harness Rd.)
Cross Seminole Trail	Oviedo (State Route 434) to Winter Springs (Gardena St.)
Depot Avenue Rail-Trail	Gainesville (Parallels Depot Ave. between Williston Dr/ State Route 331 & Archer Rd/State Route 24) (U.S. Route 441 & State Route 24 to University Ave.)
Dickinson (Jonathan) State Park Bike Path	Jonathan Dickinson State Park
Fort Clinch State Park Bike Path	Fort Clinch State Park
Gainesville-Hawthorne State Trail	Gainesville (SE 15th St.) to Hawthorne (SW 2nd Ave.)
Gandy Trail Bridge Bikeway	Tampa Bay (follows Gandy Blvd.)
Gasparilla Island Trail (Boca Grande Bike Path)	Gasparilla Island
Jacksonville-Baldwin Rail Trail	Jacksonville (Ingram Rd.) to Baldwin (Brandy Ranch Rd.)
Lake Minneola Scenic State Trail (Clermont Trail)	Minneola (Mohawk Rd.) to Clermont
Nature Coast State Trail-Fanning Springs (Nature Coast Trail State Park or Dixie-Levy-Gilchrest Greenway)	Fanning Springs to Old Town
Oleta River State Park Recreation Area Bike Path	Oleta River State Recreation Area (State Routes A1A & 826)

Map:	Trail Length:	Surface
(FL-BT-2)	7.5 miles	asphalt
(FL-RT-15)	9.2 miles	asphalt
(FL-RT-14)	4.7 miles	asphalt
(FL-RT-8)	3.5 miles	asphalt
(FL-RT-18)	7.2 miles	asphalt
(FL-RT-16)	3.7 miles	asphalt
(FL-RT-13-B)	2.1 miles	asphalt
(FL-BT-5)	1.5 miles	asphalt
(FL-BT-4)	3.5 miles	asphalt
(FL-RT-4)	16.0 miles	asphalt
(FL-BT-3)	5.9 miles	asphalt
(FL-RT-2)	6.5 miles	asphalt
(FL-RT-19)	14.7 miles	asphalt
(FL-RT-17)	3.5 miles	asphalt
(FL-RT-20)	4.0 miles	asphalt
(FL-BT-6)	7.0 miles	asphalt & smooth crushed gravel

Trail Name:	Vicinity:
Overseas Heritage Trail	Lower Matecumbe Key to Key West
Mile Posts 1.0 to 5.5; Key West Bike Paths	Key West (follow Truman Ave., S Roosevelt Blvd. and U.S. Route 1)
Mile Posts 12.0 to 13.0; Channel 5 Fishing Bridge-Pedestrian Path	Fiesta Key to Craig Key
Mile Posts 21.0 to 23.0; Cudjoe Key Pedestrian Path	Cudjoe Key
Mile Posts 29.5 to 31.5; Big Pine Key Path	Big Pine Key (Ships Way Crossing to 3rd St.)
Mile Posts 37.0 to 41.0; Bahia Honda to Little Duck Key	Bahia Honda State Park Area
Mile Posts 45.0 to 54.0; Pegeon Key to Marathon Path	Pigeon Key to Marathon
Mile Posts 54.5 to 59.5; Tom's Harbor Walkway Path	Grass Key to Walker's Island
Mile Posts 63.0 to 68.3; Conch Key to Long Key & Layton Path	Conch Key to Layton
Mile Posts 73.0 to 83.8; Lower Matecumbe Boardwalk & Islamorda Path	Lower Matecumbe Key to Islamorada
Mile Posts 89.0 to 107.0; Plantation to State Route 905 Path	Plantation to Key Largo (U.S. Route 1 & State Route 905)
Pinellas Trail (Fred Marquois Pinellas Trail)	St. Petersburg (34th St. N.) to Seminole (Park Blvd.) to Largo (East Bay Dr.) to Clearwater (Gulf to Bay) to Tarpon Springs (U.S. Route 19)
South Dade Trail	Kendall (72nd Ave.) to Peters (SW 112th Ave.); Trail parallels U.S. Route 1.
Stadium Drive Bike Path	Tallahassee (Florida State University Campus)
State Route A1A Bike Path	Marineland (Old State Route A1A) to Flager-Volusia County Line
Suwannee River Greenway	Brandford to Little River Springs

Map:	Trail Length:	Surface	🚴 🚵 🐎 🛼 ➡ 🚶 ♿ ⛷ 🔭 $
(FL-RT-9)	107.0 miles (trail incomplete; some sections open)	asphalt & concrete (portions follow back streets and parts of U.S. Route 1)	
	8.5 miles		
	1.0 mile		
	2.0 miles		
	2.0 miles		
	4.0 miles		
	9.0 miles		
	5.0 miles		
	5.3 miles		
	10.8 miles		
	18.0 miles		
(FL-RT-3)	47.0 miles	asphalt	
(FL-RT-11)	8.3 miles	asphalt	
(FL-RT-10)	1.5 miles	asphalt	
(FL-BT-1)	17.5 miles	asphalt	
(FL-RT-21)	8.0 miles	asphalt & dirt	

Florida

Trail Name:	Vicinity:
Tallahassee-St. Marks Historic Railroad State Trail	Tallahassee (Seaboard & Gamble Streets) to St. Marks (Riverfront).
Upper Tampa Bay Trail	Oldsmar (Old Memorial Hwy. to Veteran's Expressway)
Van Fleet (General James A.) State Trail	Mabel (State Route 50) to Polk City (State Route 33)
Waldo Road Trail	Gainesville (University Ave. to N 39th Ave.)
West Orange Trail	Oakland (State Route 50) to Apopka (U.S. Route 441)
Withlacoochee State Trail	Citrus Springs (U.S. Route 41) to Trilby (U.S. Route 98/301)

Gasparilla Island Trail (Dr. Jack McDonald).

Map:	Trail Length:	Surface	🚲 🚵 🐎 🛼 ✈ 🥾 ♿ ⛷ 🏍 $
(FL-RT-1)	16.5 miles	asphalt	🚲 🚵 🐎 🛼 🥾 ♿
(FL-RT-12)	3.0 miles	asphalt	🚲 🚵 🛼 🥾 ♿
(FL-RT-6)	29.2 miles	asphalt	🚲 🚵 🐎 🛼 🥾 ♿
(FL-RT-13-A)	2.6 miles	asphalt	🚲 🚵 🛼 🥾 ♿
(FL-RT-7)	19.0 miles	asphalt & concrete	🚲 🚵 🐎 🛼 🥾 ♿
(FL-RT-5)	46.0 miles	asphalt	🚲 🚵 🐎 🛼 🥾 ♿

The Gainesville-Hawthorne State Trail. (Dr. Jack McDonald)

Biking Georgia's Rail-Trails

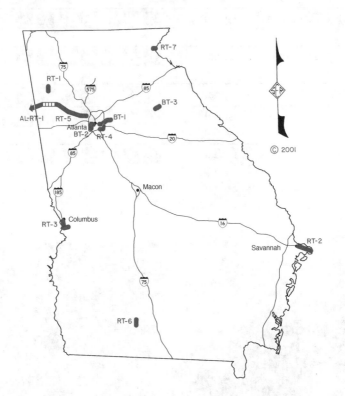

Trail Listings

GA-RT-1	Heritage Park Trail (Heritage Riverways Trail System)
GA-RT-2	McQueen's Island Multi-Use Historic-Scenic Trail (Old Savannah-Tybee Rail-Trail)
GA-RT-3	Chattahoochee River Walk Trail
GA-RT-4	Trolley Line Greenway Trail
GA-RT-5	Silver Comet Trail
GA-RT-6	Tallulah Falls Rail-Trail (Short Line Trail)
GA-RT-7	Tom "Babe" White Linear Park
GA-BT-1	Stone Mountain-Atlanta Greenway Trail
GA-BT-2	Westside Trail (Atlanta, GA)
GA-BT-3	North Oconee Greenway

Georgia Highlights

CHATTAHOOCHEE RIVER WALK TRAIL (GA-RT-3)

Country singer Alan Jackson sings about the romance and recreation along the Chattahoochee. Attractions along this trail include historic uptown Columbus, South Commons, Rotary Park, Bull Creek, Rigdon Park, Oxbow Meadows and the National Infantry Museum.

MCQUEEN'S ISLAND MULTI-USE HISTORIC-SCENIC TRAIL (OLD SAVANNAH-TYBEE RAIL-TRAIL) (GA-RT-2)

Opened in 1992, this easternmost trail became Georgia's second rail-trail. This trail follows the south channel of the Savannah River; scenery includes parks and wetlands with tropical plant life.

NORTH OCONEE GREENWAY (GA-BT-3)

This small trail will become part of an even larger trail network throughout the Athens Area. The old Murmur Trestle, well-known to R.E.M. fans, will become part of the Athens Bike Trail Network.

SILVER COMET TRAIL (GA-RT-5)

Built in 1998, the Silver Comet Trail traverses farmland and woodland with an abundance of magnolia trees and kudzu. Highlights along the trail include the Georgia Wildlife Management Area, a 700-foot long lighted tunnel, Coot's Lake, Powder Springs Park, Wild Horse Park, Heritage Park and numerous scenic views.

Georgia

Trail Name:	Vicinity:
Chattahoochee Riverwalk Trail	Columbus to Ft. Benning
Heritage Park Trail (Heritage Riverways Trail System)	Rome (A section parallels 2nd Ave. and both sides of Oostanaula River; another section goes from E Main St. to East 4th St.)
McQueen's Island Multi-Use Historic-Scenic Trail (Old Savannah-Tybee Rail-Trail)	Savannah to Tybee Island
North Oconee Greenway	Athens (Oak & Poplar Streets to Thomas St.)
Silver Comet Trail	Smyrna (Mavell Rd.) to Rockmart (Euharlee Creek & Downtown Area)
	Cedartown to GA-AL State Line
Stone Mountain-Atlanta Greenway Trail	Atlanta (5th & Fowler Streets) to Stone Mountain (Stone Mountain St. & Stone Mountain Memorial Park)
Tallulah Falls Rail-Trail (Short Line Trail)	Tallulah Gorge State Park near Tallulah Falls
Tom "Babe" White Linear Park	Moultrie (Lower Meigs Rd. to Municipal Airport); trail follows U.S. Route 319
Trolley Line Greenway Trail	Atlanta (Freedom Pkwy. & Jackson St) to Decatur (College Ave. & McDonough St.) passing through Wesley Coan Park.
Westside Trail (Atlanta, Ga)	East Point (Headline Dr. & Mt. Gilead Rd.) to Atlanta (Magnolia St. & Northside Dr.) passing through Anderson Park

Map:	Trail Length:	Surface	🚲	🚵	🐎	🛼	✈	🚶	♿	⛷	🐕	$
(GA-RT-3)	14.2 miles	asphalt & concrete										
(GA-RT-1)	2.0 miles (Trail Network)	asphalt										
(GA-RT-2)	21.0 miles (6.5 miles developed)	asphalt & smooth crushed gravel										
(GA-BT-3)	1.0 mile	asphalt										
(GA-RT-5)	37.6 miles	asphalt & concrete										
	8.3 miles	asphalt & concrete										
(GA-BT-1)	18.0 miles	asphalt (most of route follows streets)										
(GA-RT-6)	1.7 miles	asphalt										
(GA-RT-7)	5.0 miles	asphalt & smooth crushed gravel										
(GA-RT-4)	7.0 miles	asphalt & concrete (most of route follows streets)										
(GA-BT-2)	10.6 miles	asphalt (most of route follows streets)										

Biking Hawaii's Rail-Trails

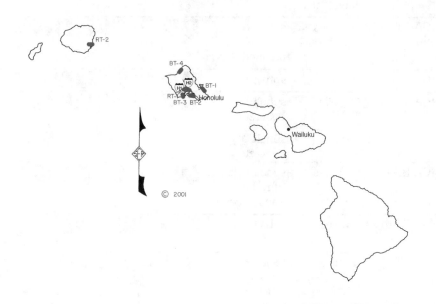

Trail Name:	Vicinity:
Kapa's Bike Path	Kauai
Ke Ala Pupukea Bike Path	Waimea Bay
Lanikai Bike Path	Kailua
Nimitz Bike Path	Pearl Harbor to Honolulu
Pearl Harbor Bike Path	Pearl Harbor to Ewa
West Loch Bike Path	Ewa (Follows bay near Ft. Weaver Rd.)

Trail Listings

The Pearl Harbor Bike Path in Honolulu, Hawaii. (Robyn Blanpied)

Hawaii Highlights

PEARL HARBOR BIKE PATH (HI-RT-1)

This is Hawaii's first rail-trail. It goes by the site of the infamous Pearl Harbor attack on December 7, 1941. This event was key in bringing the U.S. into WWII. Today, a memorial featuring the U.S.S. Arizona can be visited.

Map:	Trail Length:	Surface											
(HI-RT-2)	2.0 miles	asphalt											
(HI-BT-4)	1.8 miles	asphalt											
(HI-BT-1)	1.5 miles	asphalt											
(HI-BT-2)	3.8 miles	asphalt											
(HI-RT-1)	10.5 miles	asphalt											
(HI-BT-3)	1.6 miles	asphalt											

Biking Idaho's Rail-Trails

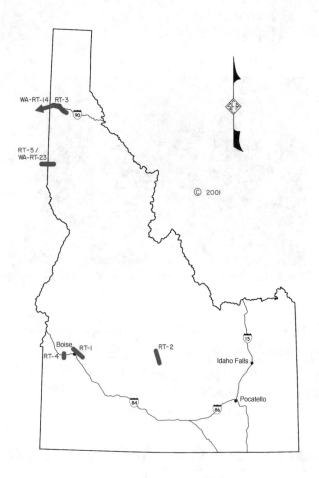

WA-RT-14 RT-3

RT-5 /
WA-RT-23

© 2001

Boise RT-1
RT-4

RT-2

Idaho Falls

Pocatello

Trail Listings

ID-RT-1	Ada County Ridge to Rivers Bikeway (Greenbelt Trail)
ID-RT-2	Wood River Trails
ID-RT-3	North Idaho Centennial Trail
ID-RT-4	Nampa to Stoddard Trail
ID-RT-5	Palouse (Bill Chipman) Trail

Idaho Highlights

ADA COUNTY RIDGE TO RIVERS BIKEWAY (GREENBELT TRAIL) (ID-RT-1)

This trail, built in the late 1960s, follows the Boise River through southwestern Idaho. Attractions along this trail include the Boise Art Museum, The Western Idaho State Fairgrounds, various riverside parks and the Idaho State Capitol Building.

NORTH IDAHO CENTENNIAL TRAIL (ID-RT-3)

Parts of this trail follow the Spokane River and the Lake Coeur d'Alene shore through the forested mountain region of northern Idaho. This trail connects to the Spokane River Centennial Trail in Washington state making a continuous 63-mile trail.

WOOD RIVER TRAILS (ID-RT-2)

This trail runs the entire length of the spectacular desert Wood River Valley with numerous views of the beautiful mountains. Highlights along this trail include Bellevue, the Blaine County Aquatic Center, Hailey, Bald Mountain, Ketchum and Sun Valley. This trail connects to a network of bike paths in Ketchum.

Trail Name:	Vicinity:
Ada County Ridge to Rivers Bikeway (Greenbelt Trail)	North side of Boise River: Boise (Glenwood) to Lucky Peak Reservoir (State Route 21)
	South side of Boise River: Boise (Ann Morrison Park to Eckert Rd.)
	South side of Boise River: Boise (Amity Rd. to State Route 21 / Gowen Rd.)
Nampa to Stoddard Trail	Nampa to Stoddard
North Idaho Centennial Trail	Parallel to Interstate-90 from ID-WA State Line to Coeur d'Alene (Cour d'Alene Lake Dr.)
Palouse (Bill Chipman) Trail	Moscow, ID to Pullman, WA
Wood River Trails	Hulen Meadows to Ketchum to Bellevue (Gannett Rd.); trail Parallels State Route 75

Ada County Ridge to Rivers Bikeway (Greenbelt Trail). (Dr. Jack McDonald)

Map:	Trail Length:	Surface	🚴	🚵	🐎	🛼	🏊	🚶	♿	⛷	🏍	$
(ID-RT-1)	18.0 miles	asphalt (sections incomplete)	●	●	●	●	●	●	●	●		
	8.5 miles											
	2.2 miles											
(ID-RT-4)	1.8 miles	asphalt & smooth crushed gravel	●	●	●	●		●	●			
(ID-RT-3)	24.0 miles	asphalt	●	●		●		●	●	●		
(ID-RT-5 / WA-RT-23)	7.5 miles	asphalt	●	●		●		●	●	●		
(ID-RT-2)	22.0 miles	asphalt	●	●	●	●		●	●	●		

Cyclists enjoy the Wood River Trails System.

Biking Illinois's Rail-Trails

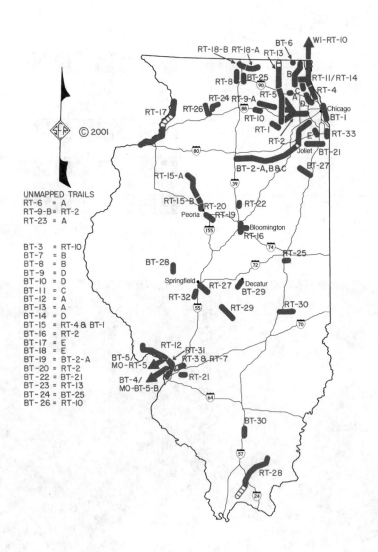

RT-18-B RT-18-A BT-6 RT-13 WI-RT-10

RT-8 BT-25 B RT-11/RT-14

RT-24 RT-9-A RT-5 RT-4

RT-17 RT-26 RT-10 A

© 2001 RT-1 Chicago BT-1

RT-2 E RT-33

80 Joliet BT-21

RT-15-A BT-2-A, B & C BT-27

39

RT-15-B RT-20 RT-22

Peoria RT-19

155 Bloomington

RT-16

74

RT-25

72

BT-28

Springfield RT-27 Decatur

RT-32 BT-29

55 RT-30

RT-29 70

RT-12

BT-5/ BT-31 RT-3 & RT-7

MO-RT-5

BT-4/ RT-21

MO-BT-5-B 64

BT-30

57

RT-28

24

UNMAPPED TRAILS
RT-6   = A
RT-9-B= RT-2
RT-23 = A

BT-3   = RT-10
BT-7   = B
BT-8   = B
BT-9   = D
BT-10 = D
BT-11 = C
BT-12 = A
BT-13 = A
BT-14 = D
BT-15 = RT-4 & BT-1
BT-16 = RT-2
BT-17 = E
BT-18 = E
BT-19 = BT-2-A
BT-20 = RT-2
BT-22 = BT-21
BT-23 = RT-13
BT-24 = BT-25
BT-26 = RT-10

Trail Listings

IL-RT-1	Gilman (Virgil L.) Trail
IL-RT-2	Illinois Prairie Path
IL-RT-3	Delyte Morris Bikeway
IL-RT-4	Green Bay Trail
IL-RT-5	Fox River Trail
IL-RT-6	Palatine Trail
IL-RT-7	Madison County Transit's Nature Trail (Sam Vadalabene Nature Trail or Madison County Nature Trail)
IL-RT-8	Rock River Recreation Path/Bauer Memorial Path
IL-RT-9-A	Great Western Trail (St. Charles to Sycamore)
IL-RT-9-B	Great Western Trail (West Chicago to Villa Park)
IL-RT-10	Dekalb Nature Trail
IL-RT-11	Libertyville Trail
IL-RT-12	Vadalabene (Sam) Great River Road Bike Trail
IL-RT-13	McHenry County Prairie Trail
IL-RT-14	North Shore Path (Robert McClorey Bike Path)
IL-RT-15-A	Rock Island Trail State Park
IL-RT-15-B	Pioneer Parkway Trail (Rock Island Trail Ext.)
IL-RT-16	Constitution Trail
IL-RT-17	Great River Trail
IL-RT-18-A	Long Prairie Trail
IL-RT-18-B	Stone Bridge Trail
IL-RT-19	River Trail of Illinois
IL-RT-20	Pimiteoui Bike Trail
IL-RT-21	Foster (Ronald J.) Heritage Trail (Glen Carbon Heritage Trail)
IL-RT-22	El Paso Walking Trail
IL-RT-23	Village Bike Path
IL-RT-24	Lowell Parkway Path
IL-RT-25	O'Mally's Alley Trail
IL-RT-26	Stengel (Joe) Trail
IL-RT-27	Lost Bridge Trail
IL-RT-28	Tunnel Hill State Trail
IL-RT-29	Lincoln Prairie Trail
IL-RT-30	Lincoln Prairie Grass Trail
IL-RT-31	Confluence Bikeway
IL-RT-32	Interurban Trail
IL-RT-33	Burnham Greenway
IL-BT-1	Chicago Lakefront Bike Path
IL-BT-2-A	I & M Canal Trail State Park; Cook County
IL-BT-2-B	I & M Canal Trail State Park; Will County

IL-BT-2-C	I & M Canal Trail State Park; La Salle, Grundy & Will Counties
IL-BT-3	Dekalb-Sycamore Trail
IL-BT-4	Old Chain of Rocks Bridge Bikeway
IL-BT-5	West Alton Trail
IL-BT-6	Chain O'Lakes State Park Trail
IL-BT-7	Grant Woods Forest Preserve Trail
IL-BT-8	Des Plaines River Trail
IL-BT-9	Zion Bike Trail
IL-BT-10	Illinois Beach State Park Trail
IL-BT-11	Skokie Valley Bikeway
IL-BT-12	Poplar Creek Trail
IL-BT-13	Busse Woods Bicycle Trail
IL-BT-14	North Branch Trail
IL-BT-15	North Shore Channel Trail
IL-BT-16	Salt Creek Trail
IL-BT-17	Tinley Creek Trail
IL-BT-18	Thorn Creek Trail
IL-BT-19	Waterfall Glen Multipurpose Trail
IL-BT-20	Danada, Herrick Lake & Blackwell Trails
IL-BT-21	Old Plank Road Trail
IL-BT-22	University Park Trail
IL-BT-23	Moraine Hills State Park Trail
IL-BT-24	Willow Creek-Rock Cut State Park Trail
IL-BT-25	Perryville Path
IL-BT-26	Kishwaukee Kiwanis Pathway
IL-BT-27	Kankakee River State Park Trail
IL-BT-28	Jim Edgar Panther Creek State Fish & Wildlife Area Bike Route
IL-BT-29	Rock Springs-Fairview Bikeway
IL-BT-30	Rend Lake Bike Trail

The Chicago Lakefront Bike Path (IL).

Cyclists enjoy the Illinois Prairie Path.

Illinois Highlights

CHICAGO LAKEFRONT BIKE PATH (IL-BT-1)

This spectacular urban trail follows the Lake Michigan coast in front of Chicago's picturesque skyline. This trail passes through Grant Park (featuring the Field Museum of Natural History, Soldier Field and the Shedd Aquarium) and many other lakeside parks.

FOX RIVER TRAIL (IL-RT-5)

This trail meanders along both sides of the Fox River in the Western Metropolitan area of Chicago. In Batavia, visit the trolley museum. Connections to this trail include the McHenry Country Prairie Trail to the north and the Illinois Prairie Path to the east.

GREAT RIVER TRAIL (IL-RT-17)

Built in 1990, this trail follows the famous Mississippi River through the towns of northwestern Illinois. Constant picturesque views of the river can be enjoyed while traveling along this trail.

ILLINOIS & MICHIGAN CANAL TRAIL STATE PARK; LA SALLE, GRUNDY & WILL COUNTIES (IL-BT-2-C)

Developed in 1980, this "towpath-to-bikepath" follows the historic Illinois & Michigan Canal and parts of the Illinois River. In addition to the canal villages, attractions include the locks, Des Plains Conservation Area, Gebhard Wood State Park, Illini State Park, Pecumsaugan Creek Blackball Mines National Park and Split Rock. Plans are to eventually connect this trail to other trails along the canal in both directions to reach Chicago and Bureau Junction.

ILLINOIS PRAIRIE PATH (IL-RT-2)

One of the first major "railway-to-trailway" conversions in the United States, this path was created in 1966. Today, the Illinois Prairie Path traverses a great portion of the suburbs west of Chicago and connects to many other major trails including the Fox River Trail and the Great Western Trail which runs from West Chicago to Villa Park.

OLD CHAIN OF ROCKS BRIDGE BIKEWAY
(IL-BT-4/MO-BT-5-B)
This unique short "highway-to-bikeway" goes over a steel span bridge. This bridge over the Mississippi River was once part of the old U.S. Route 66 that ran from Chicago, Illinois to Los Angeles, California.

ROCK ISLAND TRAIL STATE PARK (IL-RT-15-A)
Jesse James once robbed a train on this railway before it was turned into the Rock Island Trail State Park. The open country boasts farmland, prairie grass and wildflowers.

TUNNEL HILL STATE TRAIL (IL-RT-28)
This is the only rail-trail in the state of Illinois with a 543 foot long (originally 800 feet) railroad tunnel. This trail traverses the hilliest region of southern Illinois with 21 picturesque trestles.

Prairie flowers along the Rock Island Trail State Park.

Trail Name:	Vicinity:
Burnham Greenway	Calumet City (106th St. & William Powers Conservation Area to 142nd St. & Little Calumet River)
Busse Woods Bicycle Trail	Ned Brown Forest Preserve (near Shaumburg & Elk Grove Village)
Chain O'Lakes State Park Trail	Chain O'Lakes State Park (near Fox Lake, IL)
Chicago Lakefront Bike Path	Chicago (71st St. to Bryn Mawr); trail follows Lake Shore Dr.
Confluence Bikeway	Granite City to Alton (follows the Mississippi River East Levee)
Constitution Trail	Bloomington (Jefferson St. & Robinson to Vernon Rd. & Linden St.) to Normal (Airport Rd. & General Electric Rd.)
Danada, Herrick Lake & Blackwell Trails	Wheaton (Danada Forest Preserve on Naperville Rd.) to Warrenville (Herrick Lake Forest Preserve on Herrick Rd.) to Winfield (Blackwell Forest Preserve on Gary's Mill Rd.)
Dekalb Nature Trail	Dekalb
Dekalb-Sycamore Trail	Dekalb to Sycamore
Des Plaines River Trail	River Forest (Washington Blvd.) to Lake-Cook County Line (Lake-Cook Rd .); trail mostly follows the Des Plaines River
	Lincolnshire (State Route 22) to Russell (Russell Rd.); trail mostly follows the Des Plaines River
El Paso Walking Trail	El Paso
Foster (Ronald J.) Heritage Trail (Glen Carbon Heritage Trail)	Glen Carbon
Fox River Trail	Aurora (U.S. Route 30) To St. Charles to Algonquin (Kane-McHenry County line)
Gilman (Virgil L.) Nature Trail	Montgomery to Blisswoods Forest Preserve
Grant Woods Forest Preserve Trail	Grant Wood Forest Preserve (near Fox Lake, IL)

Map:	Trail Length:	Surface										
(IL-RT-33)	4.0 miles	asphalt										
(IL-BT-13)	11.2 miles	asphalt										
(IL-BT-6)	6.0 miles	smooth crushed gravel										
(IL-BT-1)	18 miles	concrete & asphalt										
(IL-RT-31)	21.0 miles	asphalt										
(IL-RT-16)	6.9 miles	asphalt										
(IL-BT-20)	9.3 miles	smooth crushed gravel & gravel										
(IL-RT-10)	1.3 miles	asphalt										
(IL-BT-3)	6.0 Miles	asphalt										
(IL-BT-8)	16.0 miles	smooth crushed gravel										
	24.0 miles											
(IL-RT-22)	5.0 miles	smooth crushed gravel										
(IL-RT-21)	3.2 miles	coarse asphalt										
(IL-RT-5)	35.0 miles	asphalt										
(IL-RT-1)	10.5 miles	asphalt & smooth crushed gravel										
(IL-BT-7)	6.0 miles	smooth crushed gravel										

Trail Name:	Vicinity:
Great River Trail	Rock Island to Savanna (some sections incomplete)
Great Western Trail (West Chicago to Villa Park)	West Chicago to Villa Park
Great Western Trail (St. Charles to Sycamore)	St. Charles (Randall Rd. / County Route 34) to Sycamore (State Route 64 east of Sycamore)
Green Bay Trail	Highland Park (Waukegan Ave.) to Wilmette (Forest Ave.)
Illinois & Michigan Canal Trail State Park; Cook County	Justice (La Grange Rd.) to Romeoville (135th St.)
Illinois & Michigan Canal Trail State Park; Will County (Heritage-Donnelley Trail)	Romeoville (135th St.) to Lockport to Joliet
Illinois & Michigan Canal Trail State Park; La Salle, Grundy & Will Counties	Joliet (U.S. Route 6) to La Salle (State Route 351)
Illinois Beach State Park Trail	Illinois Beach State Park (Near Waukegan & Zion, IL)
Illinois Prairie Path	Wheaton (Roosevelt Rd.) to Maywood (First Ave.), Wheaton (Roosevelt Rd.) to Elgin (Raymond Rd.), Wheaton (Roosevelt Rd.) to Aurora (Aurora Ave.) Batavia (Kirk Rd. & Indian Pkwy.), and West Chica (Geneva Rd.) to Geneva (State Route 25)
Interurban Trail	Chatham (Walnut St.) to Springfield
Jim Edgar Panther Creek State Fish & Wildlife Area Bike Route	Jim Edgar Panther Creek State Fish & Wildlife Area (near Chandlerville)
Kankakee River State Park Trail	Kankakee River State Park (follows Kankakee River Northwest of Bourbonnais)
Kishwaukee Kiwanis Pathway	DeKalb (7th Ave. to Green Valley Park)

Map:	Trail Length:	Surface	🚲	🚵	🏇	🛼	🏊	🚶	♿	⛷	🔭	$
(IL-RT-17)	59.5 miles	asphalt & smooth crushed gravel (parts follow streets & roads)	●	●		●		●	●	●		
(IL-RT-9-B)	11.8 miles	smooth crushed gravel	●	●	●			●		●		
(IL-RT-9-A)	18.0 miles	asphalt & smooth crushed gravel	●	●		●	●	●	●	●		
(IL-RT-4)	10.0 miles	asphalt & smooth crushed gravel	●	●	●	●		●	●			
(IL-BT-2-A)	14.0 miles	asphalt & smooth crushed gravel	●	●	●	●		●	●	●		
(IL-BT-2-B)	7.0 miles	asphalt	●	●	●	●		●	●	●		
(IL-BT-2-C)	55.5 miles	smooth crushed gravel	●	●	●			●		●		
(IL-BT-10)	12.0 miles	asphalt & smooth crushed gravel	●	●		●		●	●	●		
(IL-RT-2)	55.0 miles	smooth crushed gravel & asphalt	●	●				●	●	●		
(IL-RT-32)	7.0 miles	asphalt	●	●		●		●	●			
(IL-BT-28)	9.0 miles	coarse asphalt (part follow park roads)	●	●				●	●	●		
(IL-BT-27)	10.5 miles	smooth crushed gravel	●	●				●	●	●		
(IL-BT-26)	6.0 miles	asphalt	●	●		●		●	●	●		

Trail Name:	Vicinity:
Libertyville Trail	Libertyville
Lincoln Prairie Grass Trail	Mattoon (Northeast section) to Charleston (County Route 2)
Lincoln Prairie Trail	Taylorville (State Routes 29 & 48) to Pana (State Route 29 & County Route 12)
Long Prairie Trail	Boone-Winnebago Co. Line to Boone-McHenry Co. Line
Lost Bridge Trail	Springfield (Dirksen Parkway & IL-DOT Bldg.) to Rochester (Walnut St.)
Lowell Parkway Path	Dixon (Washington Ave. & Bradshaw St.) to Polo
McHenry County Prairie Trail	McHenry-Kane Co. Line to IL-WI State Line
Madison County Transit's Nature Trail (Sam Vadalabene Nature Trail or Madison County Nature Trail)	Pontoon Beach (Lake Dr.) to Edwardsville (State Route 159)
Moraine Hills State Park Trail	Morain Hills State Park (Near McHenry & Lakemore, IL)
Morris (Delyte) Bikeway	Edwardsville (Randle St.) to Madison (Bluff Rd. & South University Dr.)
North Branch Trail	Chicago (Devon Ave.) to Lake-Cook County Line (Lake-Cook Rd.); mostly follows North Branch River
North Shore Channel Trail	Chicago: California Ave. to Peterson Ave.
	Chicago: Devon Ave. to Evanston (Green Bay Rd.)
North Shore Path (Robert McClorey Bike Path)	Highland Park (Lake-Cook Rd.) to IL-WI State Line (Russell Rd.)

Map:	Trail Length:	Surface	🚲	🚵	🐎	🛼	🛷	🚶	♿	⛷	🏍	$
(IL-RT-11)	3.0 miles	smooth curshed gravel	🚲	🚵				🚶	♿	⛷		
(IL-RT-30)	12.6 miles	asphalt	🚲	🚵		🛼		🚶	♿	⛷		
(IL-RT-29)	15.0 miles	asphalt	🚲	🚵		🛼		🚶	♿	⛷		
(IL-RT-18-A)	14.6 miles	asphalt	🚲	🚵		🛼		🚶	♿	⛷		
(IL-RT-27)	5.0 miles	asphalt	🚲	🚵		🛼		🚶	♿	⛷		
(IL-RT-24)	6.5 miles	asphalt & gravel	🚲	🚵		🛼	🛷	🚶	♿	⛷		
(IL-RT-13)	25.0 miles	asphalt & ballast	🚲	🚵	🐎	🛼	🛷	🚶	♿	⛷		
(IL-RT-7)	7.9 miles	asphalt	🚲	🚵	🐎		🛷	🚶	♿	⛷		
(IL-BT-23)	10.0 miles	smooth crushed gravel	🚲	🚵				🚶	♿	⛷		
(IL-RT-3)	2.6 miles	asphalt, smooth crushed gravel, gravel & dirt	🚲	🚵		🛼		🚶	♿	⛷		
(IL-BT-14)	27.1 miles	asphalt	🚲	🚵		🛼		🚶	♿	⛷		
(IL-BT-15)	1.5 miles / 4.5 miles	asphalt	🚲	🚵		🛼		🚶	♿	⛷		
(IL-RT-14)	22.0 miles	smooth crushed gravel & asphalt	🚲	🚵				🚶	♿	⛷		

Trail Name:	Vicinity:
Old Chain of Rocks Bridge Bikeway	St. Louis, MO (Riverview Dr. & Interstate-270) to Granite City, IL (Chain of Rocks Rd./Old U.S. Route 66)
Old Plank Road Trail	Joliet (County Route 52) to Park Forest (Western Ave.)
O'Malley's Alley Trail	Champaign
Palatine Trail	Palatine
Perryville Path	Rockford (East Side)
Pimiteoui Bike Trail	Peoria (Robert Michel Bridge & Illinois River to Grant St. & Glen Oak Park).
Pioneer Parkway Trail (Rock Island Trail Extension)	Peoria (County Route D 38) to Alta (Allen Rd.)
Poplar Creek Trail	Poplar Creek Forest Preserve (Near Schaumburg & Hoffman Estates)
Rend Lake Bike Trail	Ina (next to Rend Lake & Wayne Fitzgerrell State Park)
River Trail of Illinois	East Peoria (Robert Michael Bridge & Illinois River) to Morton (Hawthorne Ave.)
Rock Island Trail State Park	Alta (Allen Rd.) to Toulon (State Route 91)
Rock River Recreation Path/Bauer Memorial Path	Rockford (Walnut) to Machesney Park (Harlem Rd.)
Rock Springs-Fairview Bikeway	Decatur (Main & Eldorado Streets to Rock Springs Center)
Salt Creek Trail	Oak Brook (York Rd.) to Brookfield (31st St. & Brookfield Zoo); trail mostly follows Salt Creek.

Map:	Trail Length:	Surface
(IL-BT-4 / MO-BT-5-B)	1.5 miles	concrete
(IL-BT-21)	20.0 miles	asphalt
(IL-RT-25)	0.5 miles	concrete
(IL-RT-6)	28.0 miles	asphalt
(IL-BT-25)	7.0 miles	asphalt & gravel
(IL-RT-20)	5.0 miles	asphalt (portion follows streets)
(IL-RT-15-B)	2.5 miles	smooth crushed gravel
(IL-BT-12)	9.7 miles	asphalt
(IL-BT-30)	8.0 miles	asphalt & smooth crushed gravel
(IL-RT-19)	5.0 miles	asphalt
(IL-RT-15-A)	27.0 miles	smooth crushed gravel
(IL-RT-8)	10.0 miles	asphalt & smooth crushed gravel
(IL-BT-29)	5.0 miles	asphalt
(IL-BT-16)	11.6 miles	asphalt

Illinois

Trail Name:	Vicinity:
Skokie Valley Bikeway	Lake-Cook County Line (Lake-Cook Rd.) to Lake Bluff (State Route 176); trail parallels U.S. Route 41.
Stengel (Joe) Trail	Polo (Judson Rd.) to Dixon (Washington Ave.)
Stone Bridge Trail	Roscoe (Mc Curry Rd. to Long Prairie Trail)
Thorn Creek Trail	South Chicago Heights (Stenger Rd. & Western Ave.) to South Holland (162nd Ave. & Torence Ave.) and to Lynwood & Lansing (Torrence Ave.)
Tinley Creek Trail	Middlothian (Middlothian Meadows near 159th St. & Cicero Ave.) to Oak Forest (Rubio Woods near 143rd St.) to Palos Heights (Calumet Sag Rd.-State Route 83).
Tunnel Hill State Trail	Harrisburg to Karnak
University Park Trail	University Park (Governors State University to Western Ave.)
Vadalabene (Sam) Great River Road Bike Trail	Alton to Pere Marquette State Park (trail parallels State Route 100)
Village Bike Path	Northbrook (Dundee Rd.)
Waterfall Glen Multipurpose Trail	Waterfall Glen Forest Preserve near Darien on Cass Ave. (Circular Trail)
West Alton Trail	West Alton, MO to Alton, IL (Trail follows U.S. Route 67)
Willow Creek-Rock Cut State Park Trail	Rock Cut State Park near Machesney Park (follows west side of Willow Creek)
Zion Bike Trail	Zion (Circular Route)

Map:	Trail Length:	Surface	🚴 🚵 🏇 🛼 ✈ 🚶 ♿ ⛷ 🏍 $
(IL-BT-11)	8.2 miles	asphalt	
(IL-RT-26)	11.0 miles	smooth crushed gravel (parts follow back roads)	
(IL-RT-18-B)	5.0 miles	asphalt	
(IL-BT-18)	18.0 miles	asphalt	
(IL-BT-17)	22.1 miles	asphalt	
(IL-RT-28)	47.0 miles	smooth crushed gravel	
(IL-BT-22)	6.0 miles	asphalt	
(IL-RT-12)	22.0 miles	asphalt (parts are bike lanes along State Route 100)	
(IL-RT-23)	1.1 miles	asphalt	
(IL-BT-19)	9.5 miles	smooth crushed gravel & gravel	
(IL-BT-5 / MO-RT-5)	2.9 miles (1.5 miles is rail-trail)	smooth crushed gravel, asphalt & concrete	
(IL-BT-24)	7.0 miles	asphalt	
(IL-BT-9)	6.2 miles	asphalt (parts follow streets)	

Biking Indiana's Rail-Trails

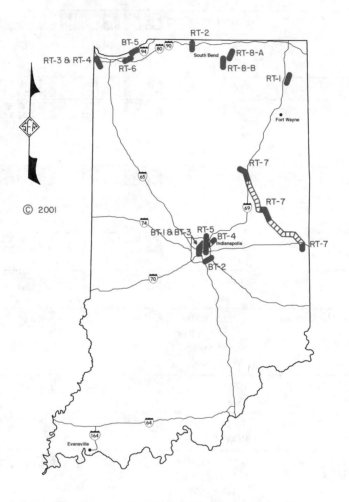

Trail Listings

IN-RT-1	Auburn to Waterloo Bike Trail
IN-RT-2	East Bank Trail
IN-RT-3	Cross-town Trail
IN-RT-4	Hammond-Erie-Lackawanna Bike Trail (Erie Trail Linear Park)
IN-RT-5	Monon Rail-Trail
IN-RT-6	Lake Michigan Heritage Greenway (Prairie-Duneland Trail or Oak Savannah Trail)
IN-RT-7	Cardinal Greenway
IN-RT-8-A	Pumpkinvine Nature Trail
IN-RT-8-B	Mill Race Trail (Maple City Greenway)
IN-BT-1	White River Wapahani Trail
IN-BT-2	Pleasant Run Trail
IN-BT-3	Central Canal Towpath Trail
IN-BT-4	Fall Creek Trail
IN-BT-5	Calumet Trail

Indiana Highlights

CARDINAL GREENWAY (IN-RT-7)

The Cardinal Greenway takes its name from the Cardinal Railroad Line which once followed this corridor. Today, the bike trail runs through the east-central region of Indiana over flat to gently-rolling farmland. This trail is part of the coast-to-coast American Discovery Trail.

MONON RAIL-TRAIL (IN-RT-5)

The Monon Rail-Trail gets its name from the Monon Railroad that once operated this corridor. Today, this north-south trail is Indianapolis's major spine to the Indy Parks Greenway trail network. City parks and the State Fairgrounds are along this trail; it also connects to the Central Canal Towpath which goes by the Indiana State Capitol Building.

Trail Name:	Vicinity:
Auburn to Waterloo Bike Trail	Auburn to Waterloo (follows State Route 427)
Calumet Trail	Dune Acres & Indiana Dunes National Lakeshore (Mineral Springs Rd.) to Porter-La Porte County Line (U.S. Route 12)
Cardinal Greenway	Richmond to Muncie to Marion
	Richmond in Downtown area north of U.S. Route 40
	Prairie Creek Reservoir on 550E to Muncie on Wysor
	Jonesboro on 10th St. to Marion on Miller Ave.
Central Canal Towpath Trail	Indianapolis (30th St. to Broad Ripple)
Cross-Town Trail	Griffith to Highland
East Bank Trail	South Bend (Cedar St. & Niles Ave. to Holy Cross College)
Fall Creek Trail	Indianapolis (Seth St. to Keystone Ave.)
Hammond-Erie-Lackawanna Bike Trail (Erie Trail Linear Park)	Hammond
Lake Michigan Heritage Greenway (Prairie-Duneland Trail or Oak Savannah Trail)	Lake-Porter County Line (County Line Rd.) to Portage to to Porter & Chesterton (State Route 149)
Mill Race Trail (Maple City Greenway)	Goshen (2nd St. & Clinton St. to Westwood Rd.)
Monon Rail-Trail	Indianapolis (10th St. & Mass Ave.) to Carmel (146th St.)
Pleasant Run Trail	Indianapolis (Garfield Park to Ellenberger Park)
Pumpkinvine Nature Trail	Goshen (Abshire Park on Lincoln Ave.) to Shipshewana (County Route 28)
White River Wapahani Trail	Indianapolis (30th St. to White River S.P. & Zoo)

Map:	Trail Length:	Surface	🚲 🚵 🐎 ⛸ ✈ 🥾 ♿ ⛷ 🔭 $
(IN-RT-1)	4.0 miles	concrete	
(IN-BT-5)	9.2 miles	coarse asphalt	
(IN-RT-7)	Will be 60.0 miles when complete 1.0 miles 10.3 miles 7.5 miles	asphalt	
(IN-BT-3)	5.5 miles	smooth crushed gravel	
(IN-RT-3)	4.0 miles	asphalt	
(IN-RT-2)	0.8 miles	asphalt	
(IN-BT-4)	3.2 miles (9.2 miles in 2002)	asphalt	
(IN-RT-4)	10.0 miles	asphalt	
(IN-RT-6)	5.8 miles	asphalt	
(IN-RT-8-B)	2.8 miles	smooth crushed gravel	
(IN-RT-5)	12.5 miles	asphalt	
(IN-BT-2)	6.9 miles	asphalt	
(IN-RT-8-A)	2.0 miles (Will be 16.0 miles)	asphalt & smooth crushed gravel	
(IN-BT-1)	7.0 miles	asphalt	

Biking Iowa's Rail-Trails

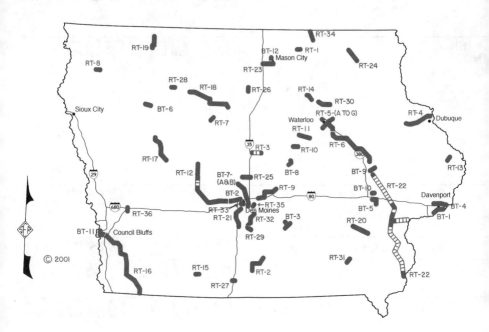

Trail Listings

IA-RT-1	Cook (Harry) Nature Trail
IA-RT-2	Cinder Path
IA-RT-3	"Praeri" Rail-Trail
IA-RT-4	Heritage Trail
IA-RT-5-A	Cedar Valley Trail Network; Cedar Prairie Trail
IA-RT-5-B	Cedar Valley Trail Network; Evansdale Trail
IA-RT-5-C	Cedar Valley Trail Network; South Riverside Trail
IA-RT-5-D	Cedar Valley Trail Network; Sergeant Road Trail
IA-RT-5-E	Cedar Valley Trail Network; Cedar Valley Lakes Trail
IA-RT-5-F	Cedar Valley Trail Network; Dr. Martin Luther King, Jr. Trail
IA-RT-5-G	Cedar Valley Trail Network; Trolley Trail
IA-RT-6	Cedar Valley Nature Trail
IA-RT-7	Fort Dodge Nature Trail
IA-RT-8	Puddle Jumper Trail

IA-RT-9	Chichaqua Valley Trail
IA-RT-10	Comet Trail
IA-RT-11	Pioneer Trail
IA-RT-12	Raccoon River Valley Trail
IA-RT-13	Jackson County Recreational Trail
IA-RT-14	Butler County Nature Trail (Shell Rock River Trail)
IA-RT-15	Maple Leaf Pathway
IA-RT-16	Wabash Trace Nature Trail
IA-RT-17	Sauk Rail-Trail
IA-RT-18	Three Rivers Trail
IA-RT-19	Dickinson County Trail (Great Lakes Spine Trail)
IA-RT-20	Kewash Nature Trail
IA-RT-21	Great Western Trail
IA-RT-22	Hoover Nature Trail
IA-RT-23	Trolley Trail (Clear Lake-Mason City)
IA-RT-24	Prairie Farmer Recreational Trail (Winneshiek County Trail)
IA-RT-25	Heart of Iowa Nature Trail
IA-RT-26	Franklin Grove Heritage Trail
IA-RT-27	Little River Nature Trail (Little River Scenic Pathway)
IA-RT-28	Laurens Trail
IA-RT-29	McVay Trail
IA-RT-30	Waverly Rail-Trail
IA-RT-31	Cedar View Trail (Jefferson County Park Bike Trail)
IA-RT-32	Carlisle-Indianola-WCCB Trail (Summerset Trail)
IA-RT-33	Jordan Creek Trail
IA-RT-34	Wapsi-Great Western Trail
IA-RT-35	Four-Mile Creek Greenway Trail
IA-RT-36	Rock Island-Old Stone Arch Nature Trail
IA-BT-1	Davenport Riverfront Trail
IA-BT-2	Clive Greenbelt Trail
IA-BT-3	Volksweg Trail
IA-BT-4	Duck Creek Parkway Bike Path
IA-BT-5	Iowa River Corridor Trail
IA-BT-6	Storm Lake's, Lake Trail
IA-BT-7-A	Dorrian (John Pat) Trail (Saylorville Trail)
IA-BT-7-B	Saylorville-Des Moines River Trail
IA-BT-8	Linn Creek Greenbelt Parkway Bike Trail
IA-BT-9	Sac & Fox Trail
IA-BT-10	North Ridge-North Liberty Trail
IA-BT-11	Western Historic Trail Center Trail
IA-BT-12	River City Greenbelt & Winnebago Trails

Iowa Highlights

CEDAR VALLEY NATURE TRAIL (IA-RT-6)
Opened in 1984, this trail roughly follows the Cedar River Valley through the bottomlands and scenic rolling farmlands of eastern Iowa. This trail connects to the Cedar Valley Trail Network in Cedar Falls, offering extra mileage for trail travel.

DORRIAN (JOHN PAT) TRAIL (SAYLORVILLE TRAIL) (IA-BT-7-A)
This urban trail follows the Des Moines River through the center of Des Moines, not far from the Iowa State Capitol Building. To the north, this trail connects to the Saylorville-Des Moines River Trail, giving trail users passage through the norther suburbs of Des Moines to Saylorville Lake and Polk City.

HERITAGE TRAIL (IA-RT-4)
With picturesque limestone bluffs and rugged woodlands with river overlooks, this trail passes through northeastern Iowa near the Mississippi River. The *Field of Dreams* farm where the move was made is just north of Dyersville.

RACCOON RIVER VALLEY TRAIL (IA-RT-12)
Built in 1989, this trail follows the Raccoon River Valley watershed just west of Des Moines in central Iowa. This trail passes through small towns, farming areas, prairie and wooded bottomlands.

SAUK RAIL-TRAIL (IA-RT-17)
This trail offers plenty of nature to enjoy in the western region of Iowa. Black Hawk Lake State Park, Breda's Rail Depot, Hazelbrush Wildlife Area, Mid-Prairie Park and Swan Lake State Park are the major attractions.

SAYLORVILLE-DES MOINES RIVER TRAIL (IA-BT-7-B)
This trail follows both the east side of Saylorville Lake and the east bank of the Des Moines River. It connects Polk City and Saylorville Lake to the city of Des Moines through the northern suburbs. To the south, it connects to the Dorrian (John Pat) Trail which takes trail users through the center of Des Moines near the Iowa State Capitol Building.

THREE RIVERS TRAIL (IA-RT-18)

The Three Rivers Trail gets its name from the three rivers that the trail follows: the West Fork Des Moines River, the East Fork Des Moines River and the Boone River. The west half of the trail consists of beautiful woodland scenery along the West Fork Des Moines River, while the east half of the trail goes through open prairie grasslands. From Dakota City, a trail spur goes south to Gotch State Park.

WABASH TRACE NATURE TRAIL (IA-RT-16)

This rail-trail traverses diagonally through the southwestern section of Iowa and gets its name from the Wabash Railroad. Highlights along this trail include the Dodge House National Landmark in Council Bluffs and the scenic countryside dotted with original small-town railroad depots.

Cedar Valley Nature Trail.

Trail Name:	Vicinity:
Butler County Nature Trail (Shell Rock River Trail)	Clarksville (C-33) to Shell Rock (T-63)
Carlisle-Indianola-WCCB Trail (Summerset Trail)	Carlisle (State Route 5) to Indianola (E. Euclid Ave.)
Cedar Valley Nature Trail	Hiawatha (Boyson Rd.) to Evansdale (Grand Blvd.)
Cedar Valley Trail Network; Cedar Prairie Trail	Cedar Falls (Ridgeway Ave. & S Main St. to State Route 58 & Cedar River)
Cedar Valley Trail Network; Cedar Valley Lakes Trail	Cedar Falls (Black Hawk Park on Lone Tree Rd.) to Waterloo (Cedar Bend Park on Parker St.)
Cedar Valley Trail Network; Dr. Martin Luther King, Jr. Trail	Waterloo (Franklin St. to Idaho St.)
Cedar Valley Trail Network; Evansdale Trail	Evansdale (N. Evans Rd. to Gilbert Dr. & Cedar Valley Nature Trail)
Cedar Valley Trail Network; Sergeant Road Trail	Waterloo (University Ave.) to Hudson (Eldora Rd.); trail follows Sergeant Rd./US-Route 63.
Cedar Valley Trail Network; South Riverside Trail	Cedar Falls (State Route 58 & Cedar River) to Waterloo (Green Hill Rd. & U.S. Route 218)
Cedar Valley Trail Network; Trolley Trail	Cedar Falls (Green Hill Rd. to Grand Blvd.)
Cedar View Trail (Jefferson County Park Bike Trail)	Fairfield (Jefferson County Park) to Libertyville (Hemlock Ave.)
Chichaqua Valley Trail	Bondurant (88th St.) to Baxter (F-17)
Cinder Path	Chariton (U.S. Route 34) to Humeston
Clive Greenbelt Trail	Clive (U.S. Route 6/Hickman Rd. to ?)
Comet Trail	Conrad to Beaman & Wolf Creek Park

Map:	Trail Length:	Surface	🚲	🚵	🐎	🛼	🛶	🚶	♿	⛷	🏍	$
(IA-RT-14)	5.4 miles	smooth crushed gravel	●	●				●	●	●		
(IA-RT-32)	11.0 miles	asphalt	●	●		●		●	●	●		
(IA-RT-6)	53.7 miles	smooth crushed gravel & asphalt	●	●		●		●	●	●		●
(IA-RT-5-A)	5.2 mile	asphalt & concrete	●	●		●		●	●	●		
(IA-RT-5-E)	10.0 miles	asphalt & concrete	●	●		●		●	●	●		
(IA-RT-5-F)	1.0 miles	concrete	●	●		●		●	●	●		
(IA-RT-5-B)	1.0 miles	asphalt	●	●		●		●	●	●		
(IA-RT-5-D)	8.8 miles	coarse asphalt	●	●		●		●	●	●		
(IA-RT-5-C)	2.4 miles	asphalt	●	●		●		●	●	●		
(IA-RT-5-G)	0.5 miles	asphalt & smooth crushed gravel	●	●				●	●	●		
(IA-RT-31)	5.0 miles	smooth crushed gravel	●	●				●	●	●		
(IA-RT-9)	20.0 miles	asphalt	●	●		●		●	●	●		
(IA-RT-2)	14.3 miles	smooth-coarse crushed gravel, cinders & concrete	●	●			●	●		●		
(IA-BT-2)	7.0 miles	asphalt	●	●	●	●		●	●	●		
(IA-RT-10)	6.0 miles	smooth crushed gravel	●	●	●			●	●	●		

Trail Name:	Vicinity:
Cook (Harry) Nature Trail	Osage to Spring Park
Davenport Riverfront Trail	Davenport (Credit Island Park to 18th St.); trail follows the Mississippi River
Dickinson County Trail (Great Lakes Spine Trail)	Milford (U.S. Route 71 & 230th St.) to Big Spirit Lake (State Route 327)
Dorrian (John Pat) Trail (Saylorville Trail)	Des Moines (SE 6th St. to Euclid Ave.); trail follows the Des Moines River
Duck Creek Parkway Bike Path	Davenport (Emeis Park on Wisconsin Ave.) to Bettendorf (State St./U.S. Route 67)
Fort Dodge Nature Trail	Ft. Dodge (Williams Dr. to D-14)
Four-Mile Creek Greenway Trail	Des Moines (Scott Ave. & Oakwood Dr.) to Altoona (NE Broadway Ave./U.S. Route 6 & 5th Ave.)
Franklin Grove Heritage Trail	Belmond (5th St., SE to 7th St. NE); follows R-65 between 7th & 8th Avenues
Great Western Trail	Des Moines (Valley Dr.) to Martensdale (Inwood St.)
Heart of Iowa Nature Trail	Slater to Melbourne
	Slater (First Ave. & Greene St.) to Huxley (535th Ave.)
	Huxley (5th Ave. to U.S. Route 69)
	Huxley (E. First St.) to Cambridge (585th Ave.)
	Maxwell (First St.) to Collins (690th Ave.)
	730th Ave. to Rhodes (Main St.)
Heritage Trail	Dubuque (U.S. Route 52 & Rupp Hollow Rd.) to Dyersville (State Route 136)
Hoover Nature Trail	Burlington to Cedar Rapids: Nichols to Conesville Burlington Cedar Rapids West Liberty

Map:	Trail Length:	Surface	🚲	🚴	🐎	🛼	➡	🚶	♿	⛷	🔭	$
(IA-RT-1)	2.0 miles	smooth crushed gravel	🚲	🚴	🐎			🚶	♿	⛷		
(IA-BT-1)	8.0 miles	asphalt	🚲	🚴		🛼		🚶	♿	⛷		
(IA-RT-19)	14.0 miles	asphalt	🚲	🚴		🛼	➡	🚶	♿	⛷		
(IA-BT-7-A)	5.7 miles	asphalt	🚲	🚴		🛼		🚶	♿	⛷		
(IA-BT-4)	15.1 miles	asphalt & concrete	🚲	🚴		🛼		🚶	♿	⛷		
(IA-RT-7)	3.0 miles	smooth crushed gravel	🚲	🚴		🛼		🚶				
(IA-RT-35)	8.0 miles	asphalt	🚲	🚴	🐎	🛼		🚶	♿	⛷		
(IA-RT-26)	1.8 miles	asphalt	🚲	🚴		🛼		🚶	♿			
(IA-RT-21)	17.8 miles	asphalt	🚲	🚴		🛼		🚶	♿	⛷		
(IA-RT-25)	32.0 miles (many sections incomplete) 3.0 miles 0.5 miles 3.0 miles 3.0 miles 4.5 miles	smooth crushed gravel (parts follow streets & back roads)	🚲	🚴	🐎		➡	🚶	♿	⛷		
(IA-RT-4)	26.0 miles	smooth crushed gravel	🚲	🚴	🐎		➡	🚶	♿	⛷		$
(IA-RT-22)	7.0 miles 4.0 miles 2.0 miles 5.0 miles	smooth crushed gravel	🚲	🚴	🐎			🚶	♿	⛷		$

Trail Name:	Vicinity:
Iowa River Corridor Trail	Iowa City (Gilbert St. to Rocky Shore Dr.)
Jackson County Recreational Trail	Spragueville to northeast of Spragueville (Z-34); trail follows the Maquoketa River
Jordan Creek Trail	Des Moines (S 60th St. to Grand Ave.); trail parallels E.P. True Parkway.
Kewash Nature Trail	Keota to Washington (Sesqui Park on W Main St. & North H Ave.)
Laurens Trail	Laurens (Parrel to State Route 10)
Linn Creek Greenbelt Parkway Bike Trail	Marshalltown (12th St. to Woodland); trail follows both Linn Creek & Iowa River
Little River Nature Trail (Little River Scenic Pathway)	Leon (NW 18th St. to Northwest Lake Rd.)
Maple Leaf Pathway	Diagonal
McVay Trail	Indianola (E Euclid Ave. & N 5th St. to E 2nd Ave. & 15th St.)
North Ridge-North Liberty Trail	Coralville (2nd St./U.S. Route 6) to North Liberty (Penn St.)(follows 5th St. & SR-965)
Pioneer Trail	Holland to Reinbeck (State Route 175)
"Praeri" Rail-Trail	Roland to Zearing
	Roland (Park St. to 620th Ave. & E-18)
	McCallsburg (E-18) to 670th Ave. & E-18
Prairie Farmer Recreational Trail (Winneshiek County Trail)	Calmar (U.S. Route 52) to Cresco (34th St.)
Puddle Jumper Trail	Orange City to Alton
Raccoon River Valley Trail	Jefferson (State Route 144) to Clive (U.S. Route 6/Hickman Rd.)
River City Greenbelt & Winnebago Trails	Mason City (19th St. & Coolidge to Nature Cut Rd.)

Map:	Trail Length:	Surface	🚲	🚲	🐎	🛼	➡	🚶	♿	⛷	🔭	$
(IA-BT-5)	6.0 miles	asphalt & concrete	●	●		●	●	●	●	●		
(IA-RT-13)	3.7 miles	smooth crushed gravel	●	●		●	●	●	●	●		
(IA-RT-33)	8.9 miles	asphalt & concrete	●	●		●	●	●	●	●		
(IA-RT-20)	13.8 miles	smooth crushed gravel	●	●		●	●	●	●	●		●
(IA-RT-28)	1.5 miles	smooth crushed gravel	●	●		●	●	●	●	●		
(IA-BT-8)	8.9 miles	asphalt	●	●		●	●	●	●	●		
(IA-RT-27)	2.0 miles	concrete	●	●		●	●	●	●	●		
(IA-RT-15)	2.5 miles	smooth crushed gravel, gravel (cinder) & dirt	●	●	●	●	●	●	●	●		
(IA-RT-29)	1.6 miles	asphalt & concrete	●	●		●	●	●	●	●		
(IA-BT-10)	5.0 miles	concrete	●	●		●	●	●	●	●		
(IA-RT-11)	12.0 miles	smooth crushed gravel	●	●	●		●	●	●	●		
(IA-RT-3)	10.5 miles (many sections incomplete) 1.5 miles 1.5 miles	smooth crushed gravel	●	●	●		●	●		●		
(IA-RT-24)	18.0 miles	smooth crushed gravel	●	●	●	●	●	●	●	●		
(IA-RT-8)	2.0 miles	smooth crushed gravel	●	●	●		●	●	●	●		
(IA-RT-12)	57.0 miles	asphalt	●	●		●	●	●	●	●		●
(IA-BT-12)	10.5 miles	concrete & smooth crushed gravel	●	●		●	●	●	●	●		

Trail Name:	Vicinity:
Rock Island-Old Stone Arch Nature Trail	Shelby to Interstate-80 (Exit-40)
Sac & Fox Trail	Cedar Rapids (Cole St. to E Post Rd.); trail follows Both Cedar River & Indian Creek
Sauk Rail-Trail	Carroll & Swan Lake State Park to Lake View (Black Hawk Lake State Park)
Saylorville-Des Moines River Trail	Des Moines (Euclid Ave.) to Saylorville Lake (State Route 415)
Storm Lake's Lake Trail	Storm Lake (State Route 110 & C-63 to Sunrise Park Rd.)
Three Rivers Trail	Eagle Grove (State Route 17) to Rolfe (C-26)
Trolley Trail (Clear Lake-Mason City)	Mason City (Coolidge & 19th St.) to Clear Lake (Grouse Ave. & B-35)
Volksweg Trail	Pella (T-15) to Red Rock Reservoir (Wallashuck Park & Campground off of G-28)
Wabash Trace Nature Trail	Council Bluffs (U.S. Route 275 & State Route 92) to Blanchard & IA-MO State Line
Wapsi-Great Western Trail	Riceville (T-68) to McIntyre & IA-MN State Line
Waverly Rail-Trail	Waverly (Bremer Ave.) to Denver (North of Denver on U.S. Route 63)
Western Historic Trail Center Trail	Council Bluffs (National Western Historic Trails Center on Downing Ave. to Iowa West Trailhead Park on U.S. Route 275 & 192nd St.)

Map:	Trail Length:	Surface
(IA-RT-36)	4.0 miles	asphalt
(IA-BT-9)	8.0 miles	smooth crushed gravel
(IA-RT-17)	33.0 miles	concrete, asphalt & smooth crushed gravel
(IA-BT-7-B)	23.6 miles	asphalt
(IA-BT-6)	5.0 miles	concrete (parts follow streets)
(IA-RT-18)	37.8 miles	smooth crushed gravel
(IA-RT-23)	8.0 miles	asphalt
(IA-BT-3)	13.5 miles	asphalt
(IA-RT-16)	64.3 miles	smooth crushed gravel
(IA-RT-34)	12.0 miles	smooth crushed gravel
(IA-RT-30)	7.5 miles	asphalt
(IA-BT-11)	6.0 miles	asphalt

Biking Kansas's Rail-Trails

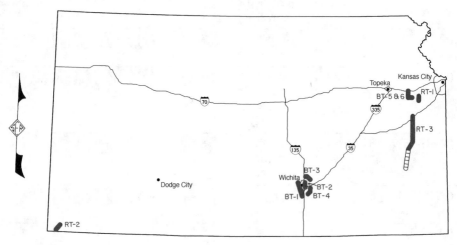

© 2001

Trail Listings

KS-RT-1	Haskell Rail-Trail (Lawrence Rail-Trail)
KS-RT-2	Whistle Stop Park Trail
KS-RT-3	Prairie Spirit Rail-Trail
KS-BT-1	Arkansas River Bike Trail
KS-BT-2	Interstate-135 Bike Trail
KS-BT-3	K-96 Bike Path
KS-BT-4	Gypsum Creek Bike Path
KS-BT-5	South Lawrence Trafficway Bike Path
KS-BT-6	Clinton Parkway Bike Path

The Prairie Spirit Rail-Trail in Garnett, Kansas.

Kansas Highlights

PRAIRIE SPIRIT RAIL-TRAIL (KS-RT-3)

This rail-trail became the longest trail in Kansas in 1996. This north-south trail in eastern Kansas goes through rural communities, farmlands, tallgrass prairies and even some woodlands. A wide variety of wildlife is abundant along this trail.

Trail Name:	Vicinity:
Arkansas River Bike Trail	Wichita (Broadway & Washington to 21st St. N & to Sedgwick County Park & Zoo on Ridge); trail follows the Arkansas River
Clinton Parkway Bike Path	Lawrence (South Lawrence Trafficway to Iowa St.); trail follows both sides of Clinton Parkway
Gypsum Creek Bike Path	Wichia (Turnpike Dr. to Douglas); trail mostly follows Interstate-35
Haskell Rail-Trail (Lawrence Rail-Trail)	Lawrence (E 23rd St. to E 29th St.)
Interstate-135 Bike Trail	Wichita (Stafford to 17th St. N.); trail follows Interstate-135
K-96 Bike Path	Wichita (Oliver to 127th St. E.); trail follows State Route 96 Expressway
Prairie Spirit Rail-Trail	Ottawa to Welda
South Lawrence Trafficway Bike Path	Lawrence (N1750 Rd. to Iowa St. & U.S. Route 59); trail follows South Lawrence Traffic Way/U.S. Route 10
Whistle Stop Park Trail	Elkhart (North Street Rd. to Boarder & Asmus Streets)

Map:	Trail Length:	Surface	🚴	🚵	🐎	🛼	✈	🚶	♿	⛷	🔭	$
(KS-BT-1)	12.0 miles	asphalt	🚴	🚵		🛼		🚶	♿	⛷		
(KS-BT-6)	4.0 miles and 4.0 miles	asphalt	🚴	🚵		🛼		🚶	♿	⛷		
(KS-BT-4)	6.5 miles	asphalt & concrete	🚴	🚵		🛼		🚶	♿	⛷		
(KS-RT-1)	1.1 miles	smooth crushed gravel	🚴	🚵				🚶	♿	⛷		
(KS-BT-2)	5.0 miles	asphalt	🚴	🚵		🛼		🚶	♿	⛷		
(KS-BT-3)	11.0 miles	concrete	🚴	🚵		🛼		🚶	♿			
(KS-RT-3)	33.5 miles	smooth crushed gravel & asphalt	🚴	🚵		🛼		🚶	♿	⛷	🔭	$
(KS-BT-5)	8.0 miles	asphalt	🚴	🚵		🛼		🚶	♿	⛷		
(KS-RT-2)	1.3 miles	asphalt	🚴	🚵	🐎	🛼		🚶	♿			

Biking Kentucky's Rail-Trails

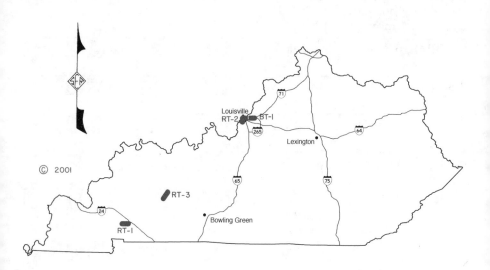

Trail Name:	Vicinity:
Cadiz Railroad Walking Trail	Cadiz (Jefferson St. to Commerce St.)
Louisville Beargrass Creek Trail	Louisville (River Rd. & Preston St. to Cherokee Park on Lexington Rd.)
Louisville Riverwalk Trail	Louisville (River Rd. & Preston St. to Shawnee Park on W Broadway & South Western Pkwy.)
Paradise Trail	Central City to Greenville

Trail Listings

KY-RT-1	Cadiz Railroad Walking Trail
KY-RT-2	Louisville River Walk Trail
KY-RT-3	Paradise Trail
KY-BT-1	Louisville Beargrass Creek Trail

Kentucky Highlights

LOUISVILLE BEARGRASS CREEK TRAIL (KY-BT-1)

This trail goes through the city where author Shawn E. Richardson lived from boyhood through college. Built in 1980, this trail connects Cherokee Park to downtown Louisville and the Louisville Riverwalk Trail. Together, these two trails are 12 miles long.

LOUISVILLE RIVERWALK TRAIL (KY-RT-2)

This trail follows the Ohio River from downtown Louisville to Shawnee Park. To the east, this trail connects to the Louisville Beargrass Creek Trail which goes through Cherokee Park. Both Cherokee Park and Shawnee Park were designed by Olmsted, the same man who designed New York's Central Park. Other attractions along this trail include the Louisville Skyline, the Belle of Louisville and the McAlpine Locks.

Map:	Trail Length:	Surface										
(KY-RT-1)	1.5 miles	asphalt										
(KY-BT-1)	3.6 miles	asphalt (parts follow streets)										
(KY-RT-2)	8.5 miles	asphalt										
(KY-RT-3)	5.8 miles	asphalt										

Biking Louisiana's Rail-Trails

© 2001

Trail Name:	Vicinity:
Jefferson Lakefront Linear Park Path	Kenner (Jefferson-St. Charles Parish Line) to Metairie (Lake Ave. & Jefferson-Orleans Parish Line); trail follows the Lake Pontchartrain Coast.
Jefferson Parish Bicycle & Pedestrian Path	Kenner (Jefferson-St. Charles Parish Line) to Jefferson (Monticello Ave. & Jefferson-Orleans Parish Line); trail follows the Mississippi River.
Tammany Trace Trail	Abita Springs (State Routes 36 & 59) to Slidell (U.S. Route 190). A rotating drawbridge over Lacombe Bayou (just east of State Route 434) restricts trail passage during certain hours and on certain days; contact the address or phone numbers below for the latest information.

Trail Listings
LA-RT-1   Tammany Trace Trail
LA-BT-1   Jefferson Lakefront Linear Park Path
LA-BT-2   Jefferson Parish Bicycle & Pedestrian Path

Louisiana Highlights

TAMMANY TRACE TRAIL (LA-RT-1)
In 1994, this trail became Louisiana's first "railway-to-trailway" conversion. Located just north of Lake Pontchartrain, this trail passes through Spanish moss wetlands, dense oak woodlands and the Fontainebleau State Park. When complete, this trail will be 31 miles long from Covington to Slidell.

Map:	Trail Length:	Surface										
(LA-BT-1)	10.0 miles (some sections incomplete)	asphalt										
(LA-BT-2)	11.0 miles	asphalt										
(LA-RT-1)	28.0 miles	asphalt										

Biking Maine's Rail-Trails

Trail Name:	Vicinity:
Androscoggin River Bike Path	Brunswick (Water St. to Old Bath Rd.)
Back Cove Trail	Portland (Back Cove; Circular trail follows Interstate-295 and Baxter Blvd.)
Calais Waterfront Walkway Trail	Calais (Pike's Park to Todd St.)
Eastern Promenade Trail	Portland (Fore & India Streets to Back Cove & Interstate-295); trail follows the Casco Bay Coast
St. John Valley Heritage Trail	Fort Kent (Market St.) to St. Francis
South Portland Greenbelt Walkway	South Portland (Spring Point Marina to Barberry Creek); trail parallels within a block of Broadway
Spring Point Shoreway	South Portland (Spring Point Marina to Fisherman Point); trail follows the Casco Bay Coast

Trail Listings

ME-RT-1	South Portland Greenbelt Walkway
ME-RT-2	Calais Waterfront Walkway Trail
ME-RT-3	St. John Valley Heritage Trail
ME-BT-1	Spring Point Shoreway
ME-BT-2	Back Cove Trail
ME-BT-3	Eastern Promenade Trail
ME-BT-4	Androscoggin River Bike Path

The South Portland Greenbelt Walkway.

Map:	Trail Length:	Surface	
(ME-BT-4)	5.0 miles	asphalt	
(ME-BT-2)	3.5 miles	smooth crushed gravel	
(ME-RT-2)	2.0 miles	smooth crushed gravel	
(ME-BT-3)	2.1 miles	asphalt	
(ME-RT-3)	16.6 miles	smooth crushed gravel	
(ME-RT-1)	2.5 miles	asphalt	
(ME-BT-1)	1.0 miles	asphalt	

Biking Maryland's Rail-Trails

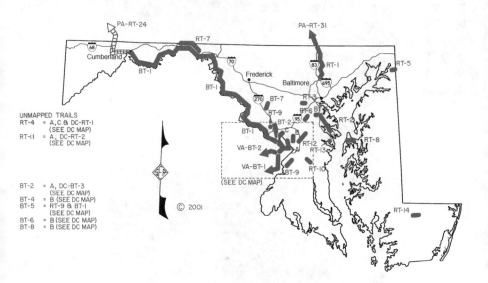

Trail Listings

MD-RT-1	Northern Central Railroad Trail
MD-RT-2	Baltimore & Annapolis Trail Park
MD-RT-3	Number 9 Trolley Line Trail
MD-RT-4	Capital Crescent Trail
MD-RT-5	Chesapeake & Delaware Canal Trail
MD-RT-6	Mill Trail
MD-RT-7	Western Maryland Rail-Trail
MD-RT-8	Cross Island Trail
MD-RT-9	Bethesda Trolley Trail
MD-RT-10	Chesapeake Beach Railroad Trail
MD-RT-11	Metropolitan Branch Trail
MD-RT-12	Washington, Baltimore & Annapolis Recreational Trail
MD-RT-13	Poplar Trail
MD-RT-14	Winterplace Park Trail
MD-BT-1	Chesapeake & Ohio Canal National Historic Park Trail
MD-BT-2	Rock Creek Stream Valley Park Trail
MD-BT-3	B.W.I. Trail
MD-BT-4	Anacostia Tributary Trail System

MD-BT-5	Little Falls Branch Hiker-Biker Trail
MD-BT-6	Paint Branch Hiker-Biker Trail
MD-BT-7	Magruder Branch Hiker-Biker Trail
MD-BT-8	Sligo Creek Hiker-Biker Trail
MD-BT-9	Henson Creek Biker Trail

Maryland Highlights

BALTIMORE & ANNAPOLIS TRAIL PARK (MD-RT-2)
This rail-trail gets its name from the former Baltimore & Annapolis Railroad which once ran from Glen Burnie (near Baltimore) to Annapolis. This trail is part of the East Coast Greenway which goes from Florida to Maine. On the north end, this trail connects to the 12 mile-long B.W.I. Trail. To the south, this trail will eventually extend into Annapolis, the state capital of Maryland.

CAPITAL CRESCENT TRAIL (MD-RT-4/DC-RT-1)
Built in 1993, this trail connects the historic Georgetown and Washington, D.C. areas to Bethesda, MD. This trail goes through a 1910 brick tunnel and near two office buildings with "air rights" above the railroad right-of-way. This trail connects to other bicycle trails throughout the DC area including the Chesapeake & Ohio Canal National Historic Park Trail, the Potomac River & Reflection Pool Bike Paths and the Rock Creek Park Trail.

CHESAPEAKE & OHIO CANAL NATIONAL HISTORIC PARK TRAIL (MD-BT-1/DC-BT-1)
Converted in 1973 to a biking and hiking trail, this is believed to be the first "towpath-to-bikepath" in the United States. Parts of the trail are suitable for standard bicycles, especially the eastern portion toward Georgetown and Washington, D.C.

NORTHERN CENTRAL RAILROAD TRAIL (MD-RT-1)
Abraham Lincoln rode the train to deliver the Gettysburg Address on this former railroad line. After his assassination, his body made the final journey on this same railroad line before he was taken home to Illinois. This trail is Maryland's first rail-trail, and opened in 1983. Attractions along this trail include Loch Raven Reservoir and Gunpowder Falls State Park. This trail connects to the 20-mile Heritage Rail-Trail County Park in Pennsylvania, making the total length of both trails 40 miles.

Maryland

Trail Name:	Vicinity:
Anacostia Tributary Trail System	Hyattsville (U.S. Route 1-A) to Berwyn Heights (State Route 193/Greenbelt Rd.); Hyattsville (U.S. Route 1-A) to Oakview Park (Oakview Dr. off of State Route 650/New Hampshire Ave.)
Baltimore & Annapolis Trail Park	Arnold (Boulters Way & Summers Run Rd. near State Route 450) to Glen Burnie (Dorsey Rd.); trail approximately follows State Route 2.
Bethesda Trolley Trail	Bethesda to Rockville
B.W.I. Trail	Baltimore-Washington International Airport near Linthicum (Circular trail around B.W.I. Airport)
Capital Crescent Trail	Silver Spring, MD (Stewart Ave.) to Washington, D.C. (Key Bridge)
Chesapeake Beach Railroad Trail	Upper Marlboro (Dunkirk Dr. to Harrogate Way); trail will eventually go from Seat Pleasant to Chesapeake Beach
Chesapeake & Delaware Canal Trail	Chesapeake City to MD-DE state line
Chesapeake & Ohio Canal National Historic Park Trail	Cumberland, MD (Visitor's Center) to Washington, D.C. (Georgetown & Rock Creek Park)
Cross Island Trail	Kent Island
Henson Creek Bike Trail	Indian Queens (Old Fort Rd. N) to Temple Hills (Temple Hill Rd. & Henderson Rd.)
Little Falls Branch Hiker-Biker Trail	MD-DC State Line Boundary (Macarthur Blvd., C & O Canal National Historic Park Trail & Little Falls Park) to Bethesda, MD (Bradley Blvd./State Route 191)

Map:	Trail Length:	Surface	🚲	🚵	🐴	🛼	✈	🚶	♿	⛷	👓	$
(MD-BT-4)	13.5 miles	asphalt										
(MD-RT-2)	13.3 miles	asphalt										
(MD-RT-9)	1.3 miles	asphalt										
(MD-BT-3)	12.5 miles	asphalt										
(MD-RT-4 / DC-RT-1)	11.0 miles	asphalt & smooth crushed gravel										
(MD-RT-10)	1.0 mile (trail will be 35.0 miles)	asphalt										
(MD-RT-5)	3.0 miles	smooth crushed gravel & dirt										
(MD-BT-1 / DC-BT-1)	184.5 miles	smooth crushed gravel, gravel, & dirt (many sections very rough)										
(MD-RT-8)	6.0 mile	asphalt										
(MD-BT-9)	6.0 miles	asphalt										
(MD-BT-5)	4.5 miles	asphalt										

Maryland

Trail Name:	Vicinity:
Magruder Branch Hiker-Biker Trail	Cedar Heights (King Valley Rd.) to Damascus (Woodfield Rd./State Route 124); trail follows Magruder Branch Creek.
Metropolitan Branch Trail	Washington, D.C. (Union Station on Massachusetts Ave. & Louisiana Ave.) to Silver Spring, MD (Colesville Rd. & Wayne Ave.)
Mill Trail	Savage Park
Northern Central Railroad Trail	Ashland (Paper Mill Rd.) to Oakland (MD-PA State Line)
Number 9 Trolley Line Trail	Ellicott City (Frederick Rd. & Oella Ave. to Chalfonte Dr.)
Paint Branch Hiker-Biker Trail	Berwyn Heights (Rhode Island Ave. & Lake Artemesia) to College Park (Cherry Hill Rd.); trail follows Paint Branch Creek
Poplar Trail	Annapolis (Admiral Dr. to Taylor Ave.)
Rock Creek Stream Valley Park Trail	Rockville, MD (Lake Needwood Regional Park) to MD-DC State Line
Sligo Creek Hiker-Biker Trail	Takoma Park (16th Ave. & Cypress Creek Dr.) To Arcola (Wheaton Ragional Park); trail follows Sligo Creek
Washington, Baltimore & Annapolis Recreational Trail	Lincoln (State Route 450/Annapolis Rd.) to Rockledge (Patuxent River Park)
Western Maryland Rail-Trail	Fort Frederick State Park (State Route 56) to Hancock (State Route 144 & Pennsylvania Ave.)
Winterplace Park Trail	Salisbury to Walston Switch

Map:	Trail Length:	Surface
(MD-BT-7)	3.5 miles	asphalt
(MD-RT-11 / DC-RT-2)	8.0 miles	asphalt (parts follow streets)
(MD-RT-6)	8.0 miles	smooth crushed gravel, gravel & ballast
(MD-RT-1)	19.7 miles	smooth crushed gravel
(MD-RT-3)	1.3 miles	asphalt
(MD-BT-6)	3.5 miles	asphalt
(MD-RT-13)	0.5 miles	asphalt
(MD-BT-2)	14.0	asphalt
(MD-BT-8)	11.0 miles	asphalt
(MD-RT-12)	5.6 miles	asphalt
(MD-RT-7)	14.0 miles	asphalt
(MD-RT-14)	2.0 miles	smooth crushed gravel & gravel

Biking Massachusetts's Rail-Trails

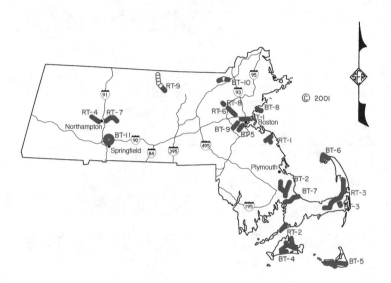

Trail Listings

MA-RT-1	Wompatuck State Park Bike Trails
MA-RT-2	Falmouth Shining Sea Trail (Shining Sea Bikeway)
MA-RT-3	Cape Cod Rail-Trail
MA-RT-4	Northampton Bike Path
MA-RT-5	Southwest Corridor Park Trail
MA-RT-6	Minuteman Commuter Bikeway
MA-RT-7	Norwottuck Rail-Trail (Five Colleges Bikeway)
MA-RT-8	North Central Pathway
MA-RT-9	Bedford Narrow Gauge Rail-Trail
MA-BT-1	Charles River Reservation Bikeway
MA-BT-2	Myles Standish State Forest Bike Paths
MA-BT-3	Nickerson State Park Bike Paths
MA-BT-4	Roadside Bike Paths (Martha's Vineyard)
MA-BT-5	Roadside Bike Paths (Nantucket)
MA-BT-6	Province Lands Bicycle Trail
MA-BT-7	Cape Cod Canal Bicycle Trail

Massachusetts Highlights

CAPE COD RAIL-TRAIL (MA-RT-3)

Opened in 1979, this is the longest rail-trail in Massachusetts. Following the Cape Cod Peninsula, scenery includes pine and oak trees, lakes, sand dunes, beaches and picturesque villages. Nickerson State Park and the Cape Cod National Seashore are two attractions along the way. This trail connects to the Nickerson State Park Bike Paths, offering eight additional miles of bike paths.

MINUTEMAN COMMUTER BIKEWAY (MA-RT-6)

This trail is located in the northwestern section of the Boston metropolitan area. Attractions along this trail include Alewife Station, Spy Pond, Wittemore Park, Arlington Reservoir and Mill Brook. This trail is only seven miles away from the highly-recommended Freedom Trail in downtown Boston (walking only) where Bunker Hill, the U.S.S. Constitution (Old Ironsides) and Paul Revere's home and grave can be visited.

ROADSIDE BIKE PATHS (MARTHA'S VINEYARD)

(MA-BT-4)

Martha's Vineyard is a very well-known vacation paradise where visitors can see State Beach, South Beach and the New England cottage communities of Vineyard Haven, Oak Bluffs and Edgartown. Most of the bike paths follow the main roads around Martha's Vineyard; the ferryboat system from this island takes trail users to both the Cape Cod Peninsula and Nantucket Island.

Trail Name:	Vicinity:
Bedford Narrow Gauge Rail-Trail	Bedford (Loomis St.) to Bedford-Billerica Town Line (Spring Rd.)
Cape Cod Rail-Trail (Bike Route-1)	Dennis (U.S. Route 6 & State Route 134) to Wellfleet (U.S. Route 6 & LeCount Hollow Rd.)
Cape Cod Canal Bicycle Trail	Buzzards Bay to Sagamore & Scusset Beach State Reservation; two trails follow the Cape Cod Canal on each side.
Charles River Reservation Bikeway	Boston (Path follows both sides of Charles River)
Chicopee Memorial State Park Bike Path	Chicopee Memorial State Park
Falmouth Shining Sea Trail (Shining Sea Bikeway)	Falmouth (Woods Hole Rd. & Mill Rd. to Church St.) Woods Hole (Woods Hole Rd. on Nantucket Sound)
Lowell Canalway System Trails	Lowell (Pawtucket Blvd. & Rourke Bridge to Hunt Falls Bridge & State Route 110)
Lynn-Nahant Beach Reservation Bike Path	Lynn (Lynn Shore Dr.) to Nahant (Nahant Beach Pkwy.)
Minuteman Commuter Bikeway	Arlington (Varnum St. & Margaret) to Bedford (South St. & Railroad Ave.)
Myles Standish State Forest Bike Paths	Myles Standish State Forest
Nickerson State Park Bike Paths	East Brewster (State Route 6A & Deer Park Rd. & Cape Cod Rail-Trail) to Nickerson State Park (Nook Rd.)
North Central Pathway	Gardner
Northampton Bike Path	Northampton (State & Standard Streets to Bridge Rd. & Look Memorial Park)
Norwottuck Rail-Trail (Five Colleges Bikeway)	Northampton (King St.) to Amherst (Warren Wright Rd.)
Olmstead Park & The Riverway	Boston (Jamaica Pond to Back Bay Fens Park); trail follows Jamaica Way, River Way, Fenway, and Park Dr.
Province Lands Bicycle Trail	Provincetown (Province Lands Rd. to Race Point Rd.)

Map:	Trail Length:	Surface	🚴	🛴	🐎	⛸	➡	🚶	♿	⛷	🔭	$
(MA-RT-9)	3.0 miles	asphalt & smooth crushed gravel										
(MA-RT-3)	25.0 miles	asphalt										
(MA-BT-7)	7.5 miles & 7.5 miles	asphalt										
(MA-BT-1)	16.0 miles	asphalt										
(MA-BT-11)	2.0 miles	asphalt										
(MA-RT-2)	4.0 miles	asphalt										
(MA-BT-10)	4.8 miles	asphalt & concrete										
(MA-BT-8)	2.5 miles	asphalt										
(MA-RT-6)	10.5 miles	asphalt										
(MA-BT-2)	15.0 miles	asphalt										
(MA-BT-3)	8.0 miles	asphalt										
(MA-RT-8)	2.5 miles	asphalt										
(MA-RT-4)	3.0 miles	asphalt										
(MA-RT-7)	10.0 miles	asphalt										
(MA-BT-9)	7.0 miles (sections incomplete)	asphalt										
(MA-BT-6)	7.5 miles	asphalt										

Massachusetts

Trail Name:	Vicinity:
Roadside Bike Paths (Martha's Vineyard)	Martha's Vinyard Island
Roadside Bike Paths (Nantucket)	Nantucket Island
Southwest Corridor Park Trail	Boston area; Backbay (Dartmouth St.& Columbus Ave.) to Forest Hills (Arbor Way & Washington St.).
Wompatuck State Park Bike Trails	Wompatuck State Park (Near Hingham)

Scenery along the Cape Cod Rail-Trail.

Map:	Trail Length:	Surface	🚲	🛼	🐎	🚋	✈	🚶	♿	⛷	🛷	$
(MA-BT-4)	25.0 miles network	asphalt	🚲	🛼		🚋		🚶	♿	⛷		
(MA-BT-5)	15.0 mile network	asphalt	🚲	🛼		🚋		🚶	♿	⛷		
(MA-RT-5)	5.0 miles	asphalt	🚲	🛼		🚋		🚶	♿	⛷		
(MA-RT-1)	6.0 miles	asphalt	🚲	🛼	🐎	🚋	✈	🚶	♿	⛷	🛷	

Cyclists enjoy the Cape Cod Rail-Trail.

Biking Michigan's Rail-Trails

RT-28
RT-22

Marquette • RT-29

Iron Mountain

Sault Ste Marie

RT-12

BT-1

BT-4

RT-17

RT-14-B

RT-14-A ⟨75⟩

RT-32

RT-19   RT-16   RT-20

BT-8

RT-24

RT-4   RT-31

© 2001   RT-30   RT-7

RT-6   BT-5   BT-8

RT-18   ⟨96⟩   RT-1   RT-13   RT-3   ⟨94⟩   BT-11

BT-9   RT-23

RT-9/   RT-25-   BT-12   BT-6
RT-27   (A&B)   RT-33   Pontiac

RT-5 ⟨196⟩ Kalamazoo   Lansing   BT-7   BT-1

RT-2   RT-15   BT-3   BT-2   Detroit

RT-21   Detroit

RT-34   RT-10   BT-13

⟨69⟩ RT-26   RT-11   BT-10

Grand Rapids

Trail Listings

MI-RT-1	Lansing River Trail
MI-RT-2	Battle Creek Linear Park Trail
MI-RT-3	Paint Creek Trail
MI-RT-4	Hart-Montague Bicycle Trail State Park
MI-RT-5	Kal-Haven Trail State Park
MI-RT-6	Lakeside Trail Linear Park
MI-RT-7	Trolley Line Trail (Clio Area Bike Path)
MI-RT-8	Bay Hampton Rail-Trail (Bay City Loop Rail-Trail)
MI-RT-9	Kent Trails
MI-RT-10	West Campus Bicycle Path
MI-RT-11	Kiwanis Trail
MI-RT-12	St. Ignace to Trout Lake Trail
MI-RT-13	West Bloomfield Trail Network
MI-RT-14-A	Traverse Area Recreation Trail (T.A.R.T.)
MI-RT-14-B	Leelanau Trail
MI-RT-15	Lakelands Trail State Park
MI-RT-16	Pere Marquette Rail-Trail of Mid-Michigan
MI-RT-17	Little Traverse Wheel Way
MI-RT-18	Grand Haven Boardwalk Trail
MI-RT-19	White Pine Trail State Park (Includes Crossroads Trail)
MI-RT-20	Anderson (Frank N.) Nature Trail
MI-RT-21	Ann Arbor's Huron River Trail (Gallup Park Trail)
MI-RT-22	Houghton Waterfront Trail
MI-RT-23	Portland River Trail (River Trail Park)
MI-RT-24	Harbor Beach Pedestrian-Bike Path
MI-RT-25-A	Henry (Paul) Thornapple Trail (Kentwood)
MI-RT-25-B	Henry (Paul) Thornapple Trail (Middleville)
MI-RT-26	Baw Beese Trail
MI-RT-27	Grand River Edges Trail
MI-RT-28	Hancock-Calumet Trail
MI-RT-29	Mattson Lower Harbor Park Trail
MI-RT-30	Musketawa Trail
MI-RT-31	Meijer (Fred) Heartland Trail
MI-RT-32	Betsie Valley Trail
MI-RT-33	Huron Valley Trail (South Lyon Rail-Trail)
MI-RT-34	Vicksburg Recreation Area Trailway
MI-BT-1	Mackinac Island Bikeways
MI-BT-2	Middle Route Bike Path (Hines Drive Bike Trail)
MI-BT-3	Interstate-275 Bike Path
MI-BT-4	Rogers City Trail

MI-BT-5	Iona River Trail
MI-BT-6	Harrison Township Bike Trail
MI-BT-7	Six-Mile Bike Path (Northville Twp-Wayne County, MI)
MI-BT-8	Flint River Trail
MI-BT-9	Lakeshore Trail
MI-BT-10	Lake Huron, Willow & Oakwoods Metroparks Bike Paths
MI-BT-11	Bridge to Bay Trail
MI-BT-12	Freedom Trail (Kensington Hike-Bike Trail)
MI-BT-13	Grosse Ile Trail System (John Neidhart Memorial Bike Path)

Michigan Highlights

HART-MONTAGUE BICYCLE TRAIL STATE PARK
(MI-RT-4)
This trail opened in 1989 and became Michigan's first long distance rail-trail to be managed by the Michigan Department of Natural Resources. The trail goes through small towns and gently rolling forests and farmland.

INTERSTATE-275 BIKE PATH (MI-BT-3)
Constructed during the 1970s, this was one of the first long distance bike paths built through southeastern Michigan. It follows Interstate 275 through southwestern Detroit and connects to the Middle Route Bike Path (Hines Drive Bike Trail) and the Lake Huron, Willow & Oakwood Metroparks Bike Paths.

KAL-HAVEN TRAIL STATE PARK (MI-RT-5)
This east-west trail in southwestern Michigan takes trail users through flat and gently rolling terrain of farmlands, woodland and cherry orchards. Wildlife is abundant along this trail.

MACKINAC ISLAND BIKEWAYS (MI-BT-1)
The movie Somewhere in Time was filmed here in the early 1980s. Automobiles were never introduced to Mackinac Island, so horse and buggy, walking and bicycles are still the only means of transportation. The bike trails on this island are probably the oldest in the United States, dating at least back to the 1920s.

MUSKETAWA TRAIL (MI-RT-30)
Opened in 1999, this trail traverses southwest Michigan. The scenery is dominated by creek crossings, small villages, farmland and wetland.

PERE MARQUETTE RAIL-TRAIL OF MID-MICHIGAN (MI-RT-16)

This rail-trail opened in 1993 and travels through the middle of the Lower Peninsula. Highlights include Emerson Park, Duck Hunters Memorial, Sanford Lake and Arbutus Bog

A covered bridge along the Kal-Haven Trail State Park.

Trail Name:	Vicinity:
Anderson (Frank N.) Nature Trail	Kawkawlin (State Route 247 & Saginaw Bay Visitor Center) to Bay City State Park
Ann Arbor's Huron River Trail (Gallup Park Trail)	Ann Arbor (Parker Mill Park to Fuller Rd.)
Battle Creek Linear Park Trail	Battle Creek (mostly follows Kalamazoo & Battle Creek Rivers from Dickman Rd. to Jackson St., Wagner Dr., Roosevelt Ave., and Goodale Ave.)
Baw Beese Trail	Osseo to Hillsdale
Bay Hampton Rail-Trail (Bay City Loop Rail-Trail)	Bay City to Hampton Township
Betsie Valley Trail	Frankfort
Bridge to Bay Trail	Marine City to St. Clair
Flint River Trail	Flint (Trail parallels Flint River from Longway/5th. Ave. & U. M.-Flint to Dort Highway & Johnson School)
Freedom Trail (Kensington Hike-Bike Trail)	Mt. Clemens to Metropolitan Beach
Grand Haven Boardwalk Trail	Grand Haven (Harbor Island & Jackson St. to Harbor Dr. & Grand Haven State Park)
Grand River Edges Trail	Grand Rapids
Grosse Ile Trail System (John Neidhart Memorial Bike Path)	Grosse Ile (follows Meridian Rd. & Groh Rd.)
Hancock-Calumet Trail	Hancock to Calumet
Harbor Beach Pedestrian-Bike Path	Harbor Beach (Huron Ave. & Garden St. to Ritchie Dr. & Municipal Marina and to State Route 25 & North Park Campground)
Harrison Township Bike Trail	Harrison Township (Jefferson Rd. & Tucker Park to Metropolitan Pkwy. & Metropolitan Beack)
Hart-Montague Bicycle Trail State Park	Hart (Water St.) to Montague (Dowling & Colby Roads.)
Henry (Paul) Thornapple Trail (Kentwood Section)	Kentwood (60th & Wing Streets to 44th & Kalamazoo Streets)
Henry (Paul) Thornapple Trail (Middleville Section)	Middleville

Map:	Trail Length:	Surface	Bicycling	Mountain Biking	Horseback Riding	Inline Skating	Canoeing	Walking/Hiking	Wheelchair Access	Cross-Country Skiing	Wildlife Viewing	Fees
(MI-RT-20)	1.0 mile	asphalt	●	●		●		●	●	●		
(MI-RT-21)	4.6 miles	asphalt	●	●		●		●	●	●		
(MI-RT-2)	18.0 miles	asphalt	●	●		●		●	●	●		
(MI-RT-26)	2.0 miles	asphalt & ballast	●	●		●		●	●	●		
(MI-RT-8)	8.5 miles	asphalt	●	●		●		●	●	●		
(MI-RT-32)	1.0 mile	asphalt	●	●		●	●	●	●	●		
(MI-BT-11)	6.5 miles	asphalt	●	●		●		●	●	●		
(MI-BT-8)	9.0 miles	asphalt	●	●		●		●	●			
(MI-BT-12)	9.0 miles	asphalt	●	●		●		●	●	●		
(MI-RT-18)	2.5 miles	asphalt	●	●		●		●	●	●		
(MI-RT-27)	0.5 miles	asphalt	●	●		●		●	●			
(MI-BT-13)	8.6 miles	asphalt	●	●		●		●	●	●		
(MI-RT-28)	13.0 miles	asphalt, gravel & dirt	●	●	●		●	●				
(MI-RT-24)	0.8 miles	asphalt	●	●		●		●	●			
(MI-BT-6)	2.5 miles	asphalt	●	●		●		●	●	●		
(MI-RT-4)	22.5 miles	asphalt	●	●	●	●	●	●	●	●		
(MI-RT-25-A)	2.7 miles	asphalt	●	●		●		●	●	●		
(MI-RT-25-B)	5.2 miles	gravel		●	●			●		●		

Trail Name:	Vicinity:
Houghton Waterfront Trail	Houghton
Huron Valley Trail (South Lyon Rail-Trail)	South Lyon (Dixboro Rd.) to Wixom (Pontiac Trail & Wixom Rd.)
Interstate-275 Bike Path	Northville (Haggerty Rd. & Ann Arbor Trail) to Monroe (Interstate-75 & Post Rd.)
Iona River Trail	Iona
Kal-Haven Trail State Park	Kalamazoo (10th St.) to South Haven (U.S. Route 31)
Kent Trails	Grand Rapids (O'Brien St. & Butterworth Dr. to Wilson Ave. & Johnson Park) and to Byron Center (84th St. & Douglas Walker Park)
Kiwanis Trail	Adrian to Tecumseh
Lake Huron, Willow & Oakwoods Metroparks Bike Paths	Rolumus Area (Hannan Rd. to Oakwoods Nature Center)
Lakelands Trail State Park	Pickney (Pickney Rd.) to Stockbridge (Clinton St.)
Lakeshore Trail	Grand Haven (Franklin & 5th Streets) to Holland (Lakeshore Dr. & Lake Macatawa) and to Butternut Dr. & James St.)
Lakeside Trail Linear Park	Spring Lake (follows State Route 104 between Cutler Rd. & Fruitport Rd.)
Lansing River Trail	Lansing (trail parallels the Grand River from North St. to Elm St. and the trail parallels the Red Cedar River from Elm St. to Clippert St. & Michigan Ave.)
Leelanau Trail	Greilickville
	Suttons Bay
Little Traverse Wheel Way	Petoskey to Harbor Springs
	Bay Harbor
	Charlevoix to Bay Shore
Mackinac Island Bikeways	Mackinac Island
Mattson Lower Harbor Park Trail	Harvey to Marquette

Map:	Trail Length:	Surface
(MI-RT-22)	4.5 miles	asphalt
(MI-RT-33)	11.0 miles	asphalt
(MI-BT-3)	44.1 miles	asphalt
(MI-BT-5)	18.0 miles	asphalt
(MI-RT-5)	34.0 miles	smooth crushed gravel
(MI-RT-9)	15.0 miles	asphalt
(MI-RT-11)	7.0 miles	asphalt
(MI-BT-10)	15.0 miles	asphalt
(MI-RT-15)	12.7 miles	smooth crushed gravel
(MI-BT-9)	22.0 miles	asphalt
(MI-RT-6)	1.1 miles	asphalt
(MI-RT-1)	8.0 miles	asphalt
(MI-RT-14-B)	2.0 miles	asphalt
	1.0 mile	asphalt
(MI-RT-17)	5.5 miles	asphalt
	5.5 miles	asphalt
	2.0 miles	asphalt
(MI-BT-1)	8.0 miles	asphalt
(MI-RT-29)	8.0 miles	asphalt

Michigan

Trail Name:	Vicinity:
Meijer (Fred) Heartland Trail	Sidney to Stanton
Middle Route Bike Path (Hines Drive Bike Trail)	Northville to Dearborn
Musketawa Trail	Marne (8th Ave. & Garfield) to Muskegon (Sherman & Black Creek Roads)
Paint Creek Trail	Rochester (Main St. & City Park) to Orien Township (State Route 24, Atwater & Newton)
Pere Marquette Rail-Trail of Mid-Michigan	Midland to Coleman
Portland River Trail (River Trail Park)	Portland (Portland High School & Lyons Rd. to Rowe and to Market & Canal)
Rogers City Trail	Rogers City
St. Ignace to Trout Lake Trail	St. Ignace to Trout Lake
Six-Mile Bike Path (Northville Twp-Wayne County, MI)	Northville (7-Mile & Northville Roads to Haggerty Rd. & Hines Dr.)
Traverse Area Recreation Trail (T.A.R.T.)	Traverse City (State Routes 22 & 72) to Acme (Bunker Hill Rd.)
Trolley Line Trail (Clio Area Bike Path)	Clio (Vienna Rd./State Route 57 & Jennings Rd. to Wilson Rd. & Neff Rd.; trail follows Pine Run Creek.
Vicksburg Recreation Area Trailway	Vicksburg
West Bloomfield Trail Network	West Bloomfield (Arrowhead Rd. & West Bloomfield Nature Preserve to Woodrow Wilson Rd. & Sylvan Manor Park)
West Campus Bicycle Path	Ypsilanti (Eastern Michigan University)
White Pine Trail State Park (includes Crossroads Trail)	Cadillac to Howard City
	Big Rapids to Reed City
	Belmont to Rockford

Map:	Trail Length:	Surface
(MI-RT-31)	6.5 miles	asphalt
(MI-BT-2)	17.5 miles	asphalt
(MI-RT-30)	26.0 miles	asphalt
(MI-RT-3)	8.5 miles	smooth crushed gravel
(MI-RT-16)	21.0 miles	asphalt
(MI-RT-23)	3.6 miles	asphalt
(MI-BT-4)	4.0 miles	asphalt
(MI-RT-12)	26.0 miles	smooth crushed gravel
(MI-BT-7)	3.0 miles	asphalt
(MI-RT-14-A)	10.0 miles	asphalt
(MI-RT-7)	5.0 miles	asphalt
(MI-RT-34)	1.8 miles	asphalt
(MI-RT-13)	4.3 miles	smooth crushed gravel
(MI-RT-10)	1.0 mile	asphalt
(MI-RT-19)	92.0 miles (trail incomplete)	
	12.0 miles	asphalt
	7.5 miles	asphalt

Biking Minnesota's Rail-Trails

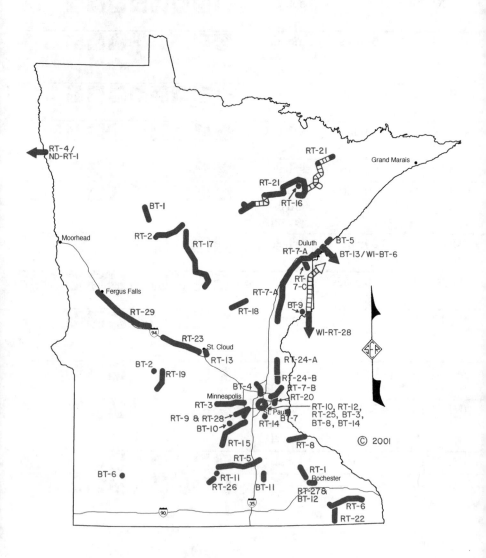

RT-4 /
ND-RT-1

RT-21

Grand Marais

RT-21

RT-16

BT-1

RT-2

RT-17

Moorhead

Duluth
RT-7-A

BT-5

BT-13 / WI-BT-6

RT-7-A

RT-7-C

Fergus Falls

RT-29

RT-18

BT-9

WI-RT-28

94

RT-23

St. Cloud

RT-13

BT-2

RT-19

RT-24-A

RT-24-B
BT-7-B
RT-20

BT-4

Minneapolis

RT-3

St. Paul

RT-9 & RT-28
BT-10

RT-14

RT-7

RT-10, RT-12,
RT-25, BT-3,
BT-8, BT-14

© 2001

RT-15

RT-8

RT-5

BT-6

RT-11
RT-26

BT-11

RT-1
Rochester

RT-27 &
BT-12

RT-6

35

RT-22

90

Trail Listings

MN-RT-1	Douglas State Trail
MN-RT-2	Heartland State Trail
MN-RT-3	Luce Line State Trail
MN-RT-4	Grand Forks-East Grand Forks Bikeway
MN-RT-5	Sakatah Singing Hills State Trail
MN-RT-6	Root River State Trail
MN-RT-7-A	Willard Munger State Trail (Hinckley Fire Trail)
MN-RT-7-B	Gateway State Trail
MN-RT-7-C	Alex Laveau Memorial Trail
MN-RT-8	Cannon Valley Trail
MN-RT-9	Minnetonka Loop Trail System
MN-RT-10	Minnehaha Trail
MN-RT-11	West Mankato Trail
MN-RT-12	St. Anthony Falls Heritage Trail (Stone Arch Bridge)
MN-RT-13	Beaver Island Trail (Tileston Mill Spur)
MN-RT-14	Big Rivers Regional Trail
MN-RT-15	Minnesota Valley State Trail
MN-RT-16	Virginia Trails
MN-RT-17	Paul Bunyan State Trail
MN-RT-18	Soo Line Trail
MN-RT-19	Glacial Lakes State Trail
MN-RT-20	Burlington Northern Regional Trail
MN-RT-21	Mesabi Trail
MN-RT-22	Harmony-Preston Valley State Trail (Root River Trail)
MN-RT-23	Lake Wobegon Trail
MN-RT-24-A	Sunrise Prairie Trail
MN-RT-24-B	Hardwood Creek Regional Trail
MN-RT-25	Cedar Lake Trail
MN-RT-26	Red Jacket Trail
MN-RT-27	Silver Creek Bike Trail
MN-RT-28-A	Southwest Regional L.R.T. Trail; Hopkins to Victoria
MN-RT-28-B	Southwest Regional L.R.T. Trail; Hopkins to Chaska
MN-RT-29	Central Lake Trail
MN-BT-1	Itasca State Park Bike Trail (Wilderness Drive)
MN-BT-2	Sibley State Park Bike Path
MN-BT-3	West River Parkway Trail
MN-BT-4	Mississippi River Regional Trail
MN-BT-5	Lakewalk Trail-Duluth
MN-BT-6	Currie-Lake Shetek State Park Bike Trail
MN-BT-7	Afton State Park Bike Path

MN-BT-8	Fort Snelling State Park Bike Path
MN-BT-9	St. Croix State Park Bike Path
MN-BT-10	Minnesota Valley State Park Bike Path
MN-BT-11	Owatonna Bike Path
MN-BT-12	Rochester Bike Paths
MN-BT-13	U.S. Route 2 Duluth-Superior Bike Trail
MN-BT-14	Grand Rounds Parkway System Trail

Minnesota Highlights

CANNON VALLEY TRAIL (MN-RT-8)

Opened in 1986, this trail takes its name from the Cannon River which it follows. Highlights along this trail include Tangential Wildlife Management Area, River Terrace Prairie State Natural Area, Cannon River Turtle Preserve State Natural Area, Red Wing Archaeological Preserve and both the Upper and Lower Anderson Parks.

DOUGLAS STATE TRAIL (MN-RT-1)

This trail is Minnesota's first rail-trail, and opened in 1974. Farmland and woodland make up most of the scenery on the southern end of the trail; the northern end passes through the Richard J. Dorer Memorial Hardwood State Forest. It connects to the Rochester Bike Paths Network.

GATEWAY STATE TRAIL (MN-RT-7-B)

This trail is located in the northeastern section of the St. Paul area. It opened to trail users in 1990, and passes through urban, suburban and rural areas. Highlights include Phalen-Keller Regional Park, Robin Hood Park, Flicek Park, Silver Lake Park, Lake De Montreville Park and Pine Point Park. Eventually, this trail will continue north to connect with the Willard Munger State Trail.

GRAND ROUNDS PARKWAY SYSTEM TRAIL (MN-BT-14)

Known as America's first urban scenic byway, this circular route gives trail users an opportunity to explore the area on both lightly-traveled park roads and bike paths. This trail system includes the Minnehaha Trail, Cedar Lake Trail, St. Anthony Falls Heritage Trail, West River Parkway Trail and Fort Snelling State Park Bike Path.

HEARTLAND STATE TRAIL (MN-RT-2)
This trail is located in northwestern Minnesota and opened as the state's second rail-trail in 1976. It passes through forests and offers an abundance of wildlife.

ITASCA STATE PARK BIKE TRAIL (WILDERNESS DRIVE) (MN-BT-1)
This is where the great river begins! The Mississippi River starts out as a small creek from Lake Itasca; it's narrow enough to walk across. Cyclists can enjoy both the bike trail and the park roads.

LAKE WOBEGON TRAIL (MN-RT-23)
A fictitious place in Minnesota, Lake Wobegon was popularized by Garrison Keillor on his radio program *A Prairie Home Companion*. This trail passes through the lakelands and prairies of central Minnesota.

PAUL BUNYAN STATE TRAIL (MN-RT-17)
This trail in northern Minnesota opened in 1995. It passes through northwoods forests and offers an abundance of wildlife.

ST. ANTHONY FALLS HERITAGE TRAIL (STONE ARCH BRIDGE) (MN-RT-12)
This beautiful stone arch bridge over the Mississippi River in downtown Minneapolis opened to trail users in 1994. This corridor connects to parks along the river and is also part of the Grand Rounds Parkway System Trail.

SAKATAH SINGING HILLS STATE TRAIL (MN-RT-5)
This east-west rail-trail in southeastern Minnesota opened in 1980 and winds through gently rolling farmland and prairie. A wooded section of the trail goes through Sakatah Lake State Park.

Minnesota

Trail Name:	Vicinity:
Afton State Park Bike Path	Hastings
Alex Laveau Memorial Trail	Carlton (State Route 45 & County Route 1) to Wrenshall (State Route 23 & County Route 4)
Beaver Island Trail (Tileston Mill Spur)	St. Cloud
Big Rivers Regional Trail	Mendota Heights (State Route 13 & Mendota Heights Rd.) to Lillydale (Lillydale Rd.); trail follows the Minnesota & the Mississippi Rivers
Burlington Northern Regional Trail	St. Paul (E 7th St.) to Maplewood (Beam Ave.)
Cannon Valley Trail	Cannon Falls (3rd St.) to Red Wing (Old W Main St.)
Cedar Lake Trail	Minneapolis
Central Lake Trail	Fergus Falls to Osakis (To be complete in 2004)
Currie-Lake Shetek State Park Bike Trail	Currie (County Route 38) to Lake Shetek State Park (County Route 37)
Douglas State Trail	Rochester (County Route 4) to Pine Island (Pine Island City Park)
Fort Snelling State Park Bike Path	St. Paul & Mendota (Ft. Snelling State Park)
Gateway State Trail	St. Paul (Cayuga St.) to Stillwater (Pine Point County Park along County Route 55/Norrel Ave. N.)
Glacial Lakes State Trail	Willmar (Civic Center Rd.) to Hawick Willmar to New London New London to Hawick
Grand Forks-East Grand Forks Bikeway	Grand Forks, ND to East Grand Forks, MN

Map:	Trail Length:	Surface	🚲	🚵	🐎	🛼	⛺	🏊	🚶	♿	⛷	🔭	$
(MN-BT-7)	4.0 miles	asphalt											
(MN-RT-7-C)	6.0 miles	asphalt (parts follow back roads)											
(MN-RT-13)	2.5 miles	asphalt											
(MN-RT-14)	4.2 miles	asphalt											
(MN-RT-20)	6.0 miles	asphalt											
(MN-RT-8)	19.7 miles	asphalt											
(MN-RT-25)	3.6 miles	asphalt											
(MN-RT-29)	55.0 miles	asphalt											
(MN-BT-6)	6.0 miles	asphalt											
(MN-RT-1)	12.5 miles	asphalt											
(MN-BT-8)	5.0 miles	asphalt											
(MN-RT-7-B)	18.3 miles	asphalt, coarse asphalt & smooth crushed gravel											
(MN-RT-19)	22.0 miles 12.0 miles 6.0 miles	asphalt smooth crushed gravel											
(MN-RT-4 / ND-RT-1)	25.0 miles for entire network	concrete & asphalt (trail network includes streets & bike lanes)											

Trail Name:	Vicinity:
Grand Rounds Parkway System Trail	Minneapolis & St. Paul (circular route); trail follows the Mississippi River, Stinson Blvd., St. Anthony Pkwy., Memorial Pkwy., Cedar Lake, Lake of the Isles, Lake Calhoun, Lake Harriet, Lake Nokomis and Minnehaha Creek
Hardwood Creek Regional Trail	Forest Lake (240th St. & Chisago-Washington County Line) to Hugo (Forest Blvd./U.S. Route 61 & Frenchman Rd./County Route 8)
Harmony-Preston Valley State Trail (Root River State Trail)	Root River State Trail to Preston (U.S. Route 52) to Harmony (U.S. Route 52 & County Route 22)
Heartland State Trail	Park Rapids (State Route 34) to Walker (State Route 371)
Itasca State Park Bike Trail (Wilderness Drive)	Itasca State Park; trail follows County Route 122
Lake Wobegon Trail	Avon to Albany to Sauk Centre & Albany to Holdingford
Lakewalk Trail-Duluth	Duluth (5th Ave. W & Bayfront Festival Park to London Rd. & 26th Ave. E.) (Canal Park Museum to 26th Ave East & London Rd.)
Luce Line State Trail	Plymouth (13th Ave.) to Winsted (County Route 9)
Mesabi Trail	Grand Rapids (3rd Ave. NE & Itasca County Fairgrounds) to Taconite (State Route 15)
	Nashwauk (Central Ave./County Route 86) to Gilbert (State Route 37/Broadway & State Route 135)
	Gilbert (State Route 37/Broadway & State Route 135) to Eveleth (U.S. Route 53 & State Route 37)
	Biwabik (State Routes 4 & 135 to Giants Ridge Golf & Ski Resort on State Route 138)
	Aurora (State Route 135 to Pine Grove Park on State Route 100/110)
	Tower to Soudan (U.S. Route 169)
	Ely (U.S. Route 169/State Route 1/Sheridan St.) to International Wolf Center.

Map:	Trail Length:	Surface	🚲 🛼 🐎 🚃 🛶 🥾 ♿ ⛷ 🔭 $
(MN-BT-14)	43.6 miles	asphalt (follow streets)	
(MN-RT-24-B)	9.5 miles	asphalt	
(MN-RT-22)	18.0 miles	asphalt	
(MN-RT-2)	27.0 miles	asphalt	
(MN-BT-1)	5.8 miles	asphalt	
(MN-RT-23)	37.0 miles	asphalt & smooth crushed gravel	
(MN-BT-5)	3.5 miles	asphalt	
(MN-RT-3)	28.0 miles	smooth crushed gravel & asphalt	
(MN-RT-21)	13.0 miles	asphalt	
	46.5 miles		
	4.0 miles		
	3.0 miles		
	3.0 miles		
	3.0 miles		
	3.0 miles		

Minnesota

Trail Name:	Vicinity:
Minnehaha Trail	Minneapolis (Minnehaha Ave. & Minnehaha Park) to Fort Snelling State Park (State Route 5 & Post Rd.)
Minnesota Valley State Park Bike Path	Shakopee to Chaska
Minnesota Valley State Trail	Minneapolis to Le Sueur
Minnetonka Loop Trail System	Minnetonka (trail system follows Interstate-494, Minnetonka Blvd., County Route 101, Townline Rd. & County Route 62; the trail system connects the Civic Center, Meadow Park, Big Willow Park, Purgatory Park, and Lone Lake Park)
Mississippi River Regional Trail	Coon Rapids (Coon Rapids Dam) to Fridley (University Ave.) to Minneapolis (St. Anthony Parkway); trail follows the Mississippi River
Owatonna Bike Path	Owatonna (18th St. to Mineral Springs Park)
Paul Bunyan State Trail	Baxter (State Route 371) to Hackensack (State Route 371)
Red Jacket Trail	Mankato to Rapidan
Rochester Bike Paths	Rochester (Citywide Network)
Root River State Trail	Fountain (County Route 8) to Houston (State Route 16)
St. Anthony Falls Heritage Trail (Stone Arch Bridge)	Minneapolis (Main St. SE. & 6th Ave. SE to Hennepin Ave. & Merriam Street Bridges)
St. Croix State Park Bike Path	Hinckley
Sakatah Singing Hills State Trail	Mankato to Faribault
Sibley State Park Bike Path	Sibley State Park
Silver Creek Bike Trail	Rochester
Soo Line Trail	Onamia to Isle
Southwest Regional L.R.T. Trail; Hopkins to Victoria	Hopkins (8th Ave. S & Main St.) to Victoria (Steiger L. Lane & Carver Park Reserve)

Map:	Trail Length:	Surface	(activity icons)
(MN-RT-10)	5.0 miles	asphalt	
(MN-BT-10)	6.5 miles	asphalt	
(MN-RT-15)	75.0 miles	asphalt & smooth crushed gravel	
(MN-RT-9)	32.0 miles	asphalt & smooth crushed gravel (parts follow streets	
(MN-BT-4)	10.5 miles	asphalt	
(MN-BT-11)	5.8 miles	asphalt	
(MN-RT-17)	46.4 miles	asphalt	
(MN-RT-26)	5.6 miles	asphalt & smooth crushed gravel	
(MN-BT-12)	26.0 miles	asphalt	
(MN-RT-6)	42.3 miles	asphalt	
(MN-RT-12)	1.5 miles	concrete	
(MN-BT-9)	5.5 miles	asphalt	
(MN-RT-5)	39.0 miles	asphalt	
(MN-BT-2)	2.0 miles	asphalt	
(MN-RT-27)	1.3 miles	asphalt	
(MN-RT-18)	11.0 miles	asphalt	
(MN-RT-28-A)	15.5 miles	asphalt & smooth crushed gravel	

Trail Name:	Vicinity:
Southwest Regional L.R.T. Trail; Hopkins to Chaska	Hopkins (8th Ave. S & Excelsior) to Chaska (Bluff Creek Dr. & U.S. Route 212)
Sunrise Prairie Trail	North Branch (Forest Blvd./County Route 30 & Maple) to Forest Lake (240th St. & Chisago-Washington County Line)
U.S. Route 2 Duluth-Superior Bike Trail	Duluth, MN (46th Ave. W & Michigan St.) to Superior, WI (Belknap & Susquehanna Ave.); trail follows U.S. Route 2)
Virginia Trails	Virginia
West Mankato Trail	Mankato City
West River Parkway Trail	Minneapolis (4th St. & West River Pkwy. to Godfrey Pkwy.); trail follows the Mississippi River.
Willard Munger State Trail (Hinckley Fire State Trail)	Hinkley (County Route 18) to Duluth (Michigan St./ State Route 23) & Sandstone (trail parallels County Route 61)

Cyclists enjoy the Willard Munger State Trail near Carlton.

Map:	Trail Length:	Surface	🚲	🛼	🐎	🛷	✈	🚶	♿	⛷	🏍	$
(MN-RT-28-B)	11.5 miles	smooth crushed gravel	🚲	🛼				🚶	♿	⛷		
(MN-RT-24-A)	15.5 miles	asphalt	🚲	🛼	🐎	🛷	✈	🚶	♿			
(MN-BT-13 / WI-BT-6)	2.0 miles	concrete	🚲	🛼		🛷	✈	🚶	♿			
(MN-RT-16)	1.0 mile	smooth crushed gravel & gravel	🚲	🛼			✈	🚶	♿			
(MN-RT-11)	1.5 miles	asphalt	🚲	🛼		🛷	✈	🚶	♿	⛷	🏍	
(MN-BT-3)	4.6 miles	asphalt & concrete	🚲	🛼		🛷	✈	🚶	♿			
(MN-RT-7-A)	72.0 miles	asphalt	🚲	🛼	🐎	🛷	✈	🚶	♿	⛷	🏍	

Author Shawn E. Richardson pauses
along the Root River State Trail.

Biking Mississippi's Rail-Trails

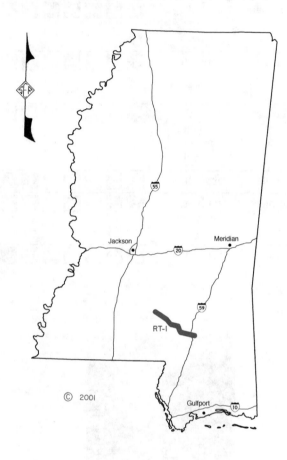

Jackson

Meridian

Gulfport

RT-I

© 2001

Trail Name:

Longleaf Trace Trail

Vicinity:

Hattiesburg (W 4th St. & University
of Southern Mississippi) to Prentiss
(U.S. Route 84)

Trail Listings

MS-RT-1   Longleaf Trace Trail

Mississippi Highlights

LONGLEAF TRACE TRAIL (MS-RT-1)

This trail is Mississippi's first rail-trail and opened in 2000. This cross-state trail has an abundance of thick pine woods, which is a great place to be on a hot day. It goes through woodland, farmland, occasional wetlands and small Mississippi towns complete with southern hospitality.

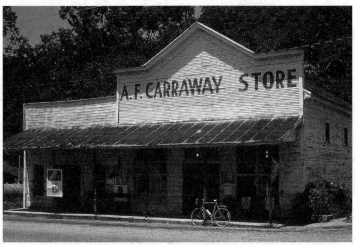

An old fashion general store along the Longleaf Trace Trail.

Map:	Trail Length:	Surface	
(MS-RT-1)	41.0 miles	asphalt	

Biking Missouri's Rail-Trails

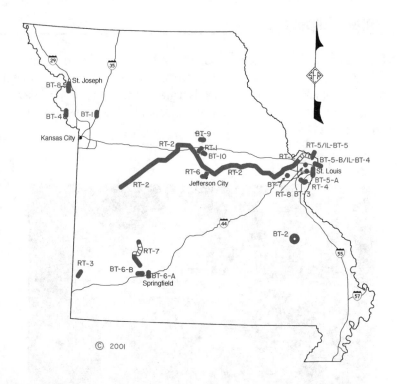

© 2001

Trail Listings

MO-RT-1	M.K.T. Nature/Fitness Trail
MO-RT-2	Katy Trail State Park
MO-RT-3	Frisco Greenway Trail
MO-RT-4	Grant's Trail
MO-RT-5	West Alton Trail
MO-RT-6	Jefferson City Greenway
MO-RT-7	Frisco Highline Trail
MO-RT-8	Jones (Ted & Pat) Trail (St. Louis, MO)
MO-BT-1	Watkins Mill State Park Bike Path
MO-BT-2	St. Joe State Park Bike Path
MO-BT-3	Forest Park Bike Paths
MO-BT-4	Weston Bend State Park Bike Path
MO-BT-5-A	St. Louis Riverfront Trail
MO-RT-5-B	Old Chain of Rocks Bridge Bikeway

MO-BT-6-A	Galloway Creek Greenway
MO-BT-6-B	South Creek/Wilson Creek Greenway
MO-BT-7	Babler (Dr. Edmund A.) Memorial State Park Bike Path
MO-BT-8	St. Joseph Urban Trail
MO-BT-9	Bear Creek Trail
MO-BT-10	Hinkson Creek Trail

Missouri Highlights

FRISCO HIGHLINE TRAIL (MO-RT-7)

Located in southwestern Missouri and opened in 1999, this is the state's second longest rail-trail. In Greene County, the terrain is flat to gently rolling; in Polk County, the terrain is hilly with many trestles. Most of the scenery is dominated by farmland and woodland.

GRANT'S TRAIL (MO-RT-4)

Grant's Trail is named after President Ulysses S. Grant who established the country's first national park. Located in the southern neighborhoods outside St. Louis, this trail opened in 1994. Highlights include Union Park, Clydesdale Park, Whitecliff Park and the Grant National Historic Site.

KATY TRAIL STATE PARK (MO-RT-2)

Currently, this trail is the longest in the nation. Originally opened in 1990, it was at that time only five miles long in Rocheport. 164 miles of the 235 miles follows the Missouri River, traveled by the Lewis and Clark expedition in 1804. Today, the Katy Trail is part of both the cross-country American Discovery Trail and the cross-country Lewis and Clark National Historic Trail. The scenery along the trail varies from wetlands and bluffs along the Missouri River to hilly, rolling farmland. Highlights include First Capital Park in St. Charles, Weldon Spring Wildlife Area, Howell Island Wildlife Area, the 243-foot Rocheport Tunnel and Windsor's Amish community. The trail also runs by Hermann, Jefferson City with a view of the Missouri State Capitol Building skyline, Hartsburg, Rocheport, Boonville, Sedalia and Clinton. This trail connects to both the M.K.T. Nature / Fitness Trail and the Jefferson City Greenway.

OLD CHAIN OF ROCKS BRIDGE BIKEWAY (MO-BT-5-B/IL-BT-4)

This unique short "highway-to-bikeway" goes over a steel span bridge. This bridge over the Mississippi River was once part of the old U.S. Route 66 that ran from Chicago, Illinois to Los Angeles, California.

Missouri

Trail Name:	Vicinity:
Babler (Dr. Edmund A.) Memorial State Park Bike Path	Dr. Edmund A. Babler Memorial State Park near Chesterfield
Bear Creek Trail	Columbia (Columbia Cosmopolitan Recreation Area & Creasy Springs Rd. to Oakland Park & Blue Ridge Rd.)
Forest Park Bike Paths	St. Louis (Forest Park)
Frisco Greenway Trail	Joplin (St. Louis Ave.) to Webb City (Mc Arthur Dr.)
Frisco Highline Trail	Willard (Jackson & Miller Streets) to Walnut Grove (Greene-Polk County Line)
	Bolivar (County Route T to Oakland)
Galloway Creek Greenway	Springfield (181 & Timbercrest to Seminole St. & Pershing School)
Grant's Trail	St. Louis (Hoffmeister to Pardee Rd.)
Hinkson Creek Trail	Columbia (Old U.S. Route 63 & Grindstone Nature Area to Providence Rd. & M.K.T. Nature/Fitness Trail)
Jefferson City Greenway	Jefferson City (Area) S. Country Club Dr. to Hessinger Rd. Washington Park to Dunklin St. Cedar City Dr. to Katy Rd. & Katy Trail State Park
Jones (Ted & Pat) Trail (St. Louis)	St. Louis Area; Normandy (Florissant Rd.) to Ferguson (Paul Ave.)
Katy Trail State Park	St. Charles (Tecumseh) to Jefferson City (Katy Rd.) to Sedalia (Griessen Rd, Engineer Ave., & 3rd St.) to Clinton (Sedalia St.)
M.K.T. Nature/Fitness Trail	Columbia (4th St. & University of Missouri) to McBaine (Katy Trail State Park)

Map:	Trail Length:	Surface	🚲	🚵	🐎	🛼	⛵	🚶	♿	⛷	🏍	$
(MO-BT-7)	2.0 miles	asphalt	●	●		●		●	●	●		
(MO-BT-9)	4.3 miles	smooth crushed gravel	●	●				●	●	●		
(MO-BT-3)	7.5 miles	asphalt	●	●		●		●	●	●		
(MO-RT-3)	3.8 miles	smooth crushed gravel	●	●		●		●	●	●		
(MO-RT-7)	11.7 miles 1.0 miles	smooth crushed gravel asphalt	●	●	●			●	●	●		
(MO-BT-6-A)	4.5 miles	asphalt & smooth crushed gravel	●	●				●	●	●		
(MO-RT-4)	6.2 miles	asphalt	●	●		●		●	●	●		
(MO-BT-10)	2.0 miles	smooth crushed gravel	●	●		●		●	●	●		
(MO-RT-6)	1.5 miles 0.5 miles 1.0 miles	asphalt, concrete & smooth crushed gravel	●	●		●		●	●	●		
(MO-RT-8)	2.0 miles	asphalt	●	●		●		●	●	●		
(MO-RT-2)	235.0 miles	smooth crushed gravel (parts follow streets through Boonville & Sedalia)	●	●	●			●	●	●		
(MO-RT-1)	8.9 miles	smooth crushed gravel	●	●		●		●	●	●		

Trail Name:	Vicinity:
Old Chain of Rocks Bridge Bikeway	St. Louis, MO (Riverview Dr. & Interstate-270) to Granite City, IL (Chain of Rocks Rd./Old U.S. Route 66)
St. Joe State Park Bike Path	St. Joe State Park near Farmington
St. Joseph Urban Trail	St Joseph (4th Ave. & Mason Rd. to Joseph Ave.)
St. Louis Riverfront Trail	St. Louis (Sullivan Blvd. & Gateway Arch to Riverview Dr. & North Riverfront Park; trail follows Mississippi River)
South Creek/Wilson Creek Greenway	Springfield (Battlefield Rd. to Campbell Ave.)
Watkins Mill State Park Bike Path	Watkins Mill State Park (near Lawson & Excelsior Springs)
West Alton Trail	West Alton, MO to Alton, IL (Trail follows U.S. Route 67)
Weston Bend State Park Bike Path	Weston Bend State Park near Weston

A birdseye view of the Katy Trail
State Park along the Missouri River.

Map:	Trail Length:	Surface	🚲 🚵 🐎 🛼 ✈ 🚶 ♿ ⛷ 🏍 $
(MO-BT-5-B / IL-BT-4)	1.5 miles	concrete	
(MO-BT-2)	14.0 miles	asphalt	
(MO-BT-8)	9.2 miles	concrete	
(MO-BT-5-A)	10.0 miles	asphalt	
(MO-BT-6-B)	5.0 miles	concrete & smooth crushed gravel	
(MO-BT-1)	3.8 miles	asphalt	
(MO-RT-5 / IL-BT-5)	2.9 miles (1.5 miles is rail-trail)	smooth crushed gravel, asphalt & concrete	
(MO-BT-4)	3.0 miles	asphalt	

Bluffs line the Katy Trail State Park near Rocheport.

Biking Montana's Rail-Trails

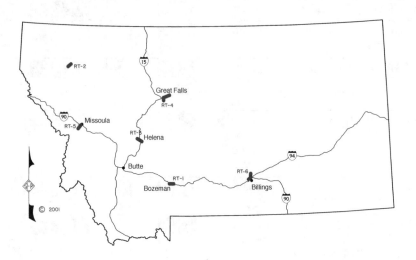

Trail Name:	Vicinity:
Bitterroot Branch Trail (Southside Trail)	Missoula (Russel St. to Hickory St. & Hickory St. to North Ave.)
Centennial Park Trail (Spring Meadows Lake & Centennial Park Trail)	Spring Meadows Lake State Park (Country Club Ave.) to Helena (Centennial Park & Last Chance Gulch St.)
Gallagator Linear Trail	Bozeman (Kagy Blvd. & 3rd Ave. to Story St. & Church Ave.)
Great Northern Historical Trail	Kalispell to Marion
Kiwanis Bike Trail (Heights Bike Trail)	Billings (Interstate 90 & Coulson Park to Mary St.)
River's Edge Trail	Great Falls (River Dr. & Broadwater to Rainbow Dam & Falls)

Trail Listings

MT-RT-1	Gallagator Linear Trail
MT-RT-2	Great Northern Historical Trail
MT-RT-3	Centennial Park Trail (Spring Meadows Lake & Centennial Park Trail)
MT-RT-4	River's Edge Trail
MT-RT-5	Bitterroot Branch Trail (Southside Trail)
MT-RT-6	Kiwanis Bike Trail (Heights Bike Trail)

Montana Highlights

RIVER'S EDGE TRAIL (MT-RT-4)

This trail follows the Missouri River that the Lewis and Clark expedition traveled in 1804. Today, it's part of the cross-country Lewis & Clark National Historic Trail. Highlights along this urban and rural trail include Black Eagle Falls and Dam Overlook, Lewis & Clark Interpretive Center, Giant Springs and the Great Falls.

Map:	Trail Length:	Surface										
(MT-RT-5)	2.3 miles	asphalt, gravel & ballast										
(MT-BT-3)	2.0 miles	smooth crushed gravel										
(MT-RT-1)	1.2 miles	smooth crushed gravel										
(MT-RT-2)	2.5 miles	smooth crushed gravel										
(MT-RT-6)	5.0 miles	concrete										
(MT-RT-4)	8.5 miles	asphalt & concrete										

Biking Nebraska's Rail-Trails

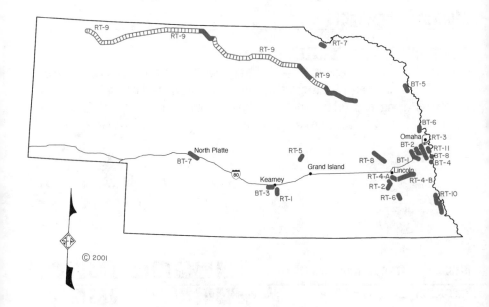

© 2001

Trail Listings

NE-RT-1	Ft. Kearney Hike-Bike Trail
NE-RT-2	Rock Island Trail
NE-RT-3	Keystone Trail
NE-RT-4-A	Mopac Trail
NE-RT-4-B	Mopac East Trail
NE-RT-5	Dannebrog Rail-Trail
NE-RT-6	Hickman Linear Path
NE-RT-7	Niobrara Trail
NE-RT-8	Oak Creek Trail
NE-RT-9	Cowboy Recreation & Nature Trail
NE-RT-10	Steamboat-Trace Trail
NE-RT-11	Field Club Trail
NE-BT-1	West Papio Trail
NE-BT-2	Big Papio Trail
NE-BT-3	Cottonmill Hike-Bike Trail
NE-BT-4	Bellevue Loop Trail
NE-BT-5	Blackbird Trail
NE-BT-6	Desoto Bend Trail
NE-BT-7	North Platte Trails
NE-BT-8	Back to the River Trail

Nebraska Highlights

COWBOY RECREATION & NATURE TRAIL (NE-RT-9)

When complete, this rail-trail will cross more than 221 bridges and go through 29 communities in 321 miles. The first sections were opened in 1996. On the eastern end, farmland, ranches and rivers lined with trees are common sights; in the middle, prairie dominates. On the western end, there is one oasis spot in Valentine and the rest of the trail travels through the open Sandhill Region.

MOPAC EAST TRAIL (NE-RT-4-B)

Opened in 1991, this trail goes through the prairies of eastern Nebraska. Elmwood, a town along the way, is home to the author Bess Streeter Aldrich (1881-1954) who wrote about pioneering in Nebraska. In Lincoln, this trail connects to the Mapac Trail and the city's trail network.

Nebraska

Trail Name:	Vicinity:
Back to the River Trail	Omaha (Missouri Ave. to Heartland of America Park); trail follows the Missouri River
Bellevue Loop Trail	Bellevue (36th St. to Harlan Lewis Rd. to Haworth Park); trail follows the Missouri River & Big Papillion Creek.
Big Papio Trail	Ralston (Seymour L. Smith Park on Harrison St. to State Route 38/W. Center Rd.)
Blackbird Trail	Macy
Cottonmill Hike-Bike Trail	Kearney
Cowboy Recreation & Nature Trail	Chadron to Valentine to O'Neill to Norfolk
	Valentine
	Ainsworth
	Long Pine
	O'Neil
	Neligh to Norfolk
Dannebrog Rail-Trail	Dannebrog (State Route 58 & 5th St. to Oak Creek to Pioneer St.)
Desoto Bend Trail	Blair
Field Club Trail	Omaha (Leavenworth St. to Center St.)
Ft. Kearney Hike-Bike Trail	Ft. Kearney State Recreation Area to Platte River
Hickman Linear Path	Hickman (7th St. to Chestnut St/S. 68th St.)
Keystone Trail	Bellevue (36th St.) to Omaha (Fort & 87th Streets); trail follows the Big & Little Papillion Creeks

Map:	Trail Length:	Surface	🚴	🛼	🐎	🚶	✈	🚶	♿	🎿	👓	$
(NE-BT-8)	2.8 miles	concrete										
(NE-BT-4)	10.0 miles	concrete										
(NE-BT-2)	4.0 miles	concrete										
(NE-BT-5)	7.1 miles	smooth crushed gravel & asphalt										
(NE-BT-3)	3.1 miles	concrete										
(NE-RT-9)	321.0 miles (trail incomplete) 6.0 miles 1.3 miles 1.5 miles 9.0 miles 35.2 miles	concrete & smooth crushed gravel										
(NE-RT-5)	3.5 miles	concrete, asphalt & wood chips										
(NE-BT-6)	5.5 miles	concrete & smooth crushed gravel										
(NE-RT-11)	1.3 miles	asphalt & concrete										
(NE-RT-1)	1.8 miles	smooth crushed gravel & cinder										
(NE-RT-6)	0.8 miles	asphalt										
(NE-RT-3)	12.0 miles	concrete										

Trail Name:	Vicinity:
Mopac East Trail	Lincoln (84th & Mopac Trail) to Wabash (346th)
Mopac Trail	Lincoln (30th & W St. to 84th & Hazelwood Dr.)
Niobrara Trail	Niobrara State Park (near Niobrara)
North Platte Trails	North Platte
Oak Creek Trail	Brainard to Valparaiso
Rock Island Trail	Lincoln (14th & Old Cheney to 27th & A St.)
Steamboat-Trace Trail	Nebraska City (OPPD Rd.) to Brownville (U.S. Route 136)
West Papio Trail	Girls and Boys Town (Blondo St.) to Zorinsky Lake; trail follows West Papillion Creek

A high spectacular trestle along the Cowboy Recreation & Nature Trail. (Dr. Jack McDonald)

Map:	Trail Length:	Surface	🚲	🚵	🐎	🛼	✈	🥾	♿	⛷	🛷	$
(NE-RT-4-B)	24.0 miles	smooth crushed gravel	🚲	🚵	🐎			🥾	♿	⛷		
(NE-RT-4-A)	3.7 miles	concrete	🚲	🚵		🛼		🥾	♿			
(NE-RT-7)	2.1 miles	smooth crushed gravel	🚲	🚵	🐎		✈	🥾	♿	⛷		
(NE-BT-7)	22.0 miles	concrete & smooth crushed gravel	🚲	🚵				🥾	♿	⛷		
(NE-RT-8)	12.0 miles	smooth crushed gravel	🚲	🚵				🥾	♿	⛷		
(NE-RT-2)	5.0 miles	concrete	🚲	🚵		🛼		🥾	♿			
(NE-RT-10)	21.0 miles	smooth crushed gravel	🚲	🚵				🥾	♿	⛷		
(NE-BT-1)	5.0 miles	concrete	🚲	🚵		🛼		🥾	♿	⛷		

Cyclists enjoy the Nebraska countryside along the Mopac East Trail.

Biking Nevada's Rail-Trails

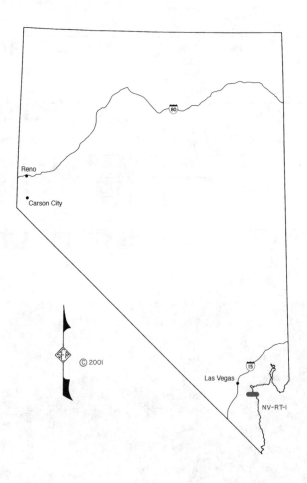

Trail Name: **Vicinity:**

Historic Railroad Hiking Trail   Lake Mead National Recreation Area (near
                                    Boulder City north of US Route-93) Trail
                                    connects to Boulder City Bike Paths

Trail Listings
NV-RT-1   Historic Railroad Hiking Trail

The Historic Railroad Hiking Trail in Nevada. (Dr. Jack McDonald)

The Historic Railroad Hiking Trail in Southern Nevada.
(Dr. Jack McDonald)

Map:	Trail Length:	Surface	
(NV-RT-1)	6.0 miles	smooth crushed gravel	

Biking New Hampshire's Rail-Trails

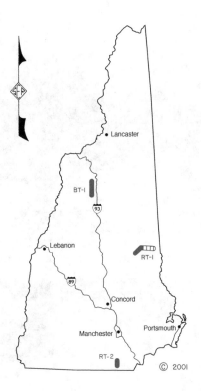

Trail Name:	Vicinity:
Cotton Valley Trail (Wolfeboro-Sanbornville Recreational Trail)	Wolfeboro to Sandbornville (Railroad tracks) & Wolfeboro (Railroad Ave. & Depot Square) to Cotton Valley Station (State Route 109)
Franconia Notch State Park Recreation Trail	Franconia Notch State Park (Skoocumchuck Brook to the Flume)
Nashua-Worcester Rail-Trail	Nashua

Trail Listings

NH-RT-1	Cotton Valley Trail (Wolfeboro-Sanbornville Recreational Trail)
NH-RT-2	Nashua-Worcester Rail-Trail
NH-BT-1	Franconia Notch State Park Recreation Trail

New Hampshire Highlights

COTTON VALLEY TRAIL (WOLFEBORO-SANBORNVILLE RECREATIONAL TRAIL) (NH-RT-1)

This rail-trail is one of a kind. The railroad tracks are still in place with the smooth trail surface right next to or in the middle of the track. Members of the Cotton Valley Rail-Trail Club are railroad hobbyists who share the trail with typical users and operate motorized railroad carts on the existing tracks. This trail meanders through the backwoods of Cotton Valley and goes right between several spectacular lakes. Sandbornville and Wolfeboro are both New England resort communities.

Map:	Trail Length:	Surface										
(NH-RT-1)	4.0 miles (will be 12.0 miles)	smooth crushed gravel & railroad track										
(NH-BT-1)	8.8 miles	asphalt										
(NH-RT-2)	1.3 miles	asphalt & dirt										

Biking New Jersey's Rail-Trails

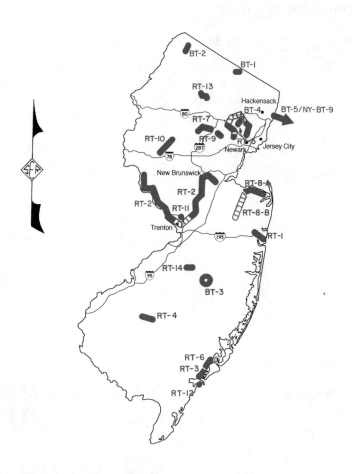

Trail Listings

NJ-RT-1	Felix (Edgar) Bike Path
NJ-RT-2	Delaware & Raritan Canal State Park Trail
NJ-RT-3	Somers Point Bike Path
NJ-RT-4	Monroe Township Bike Path
NJ-RT-5	West Essex Trail
NJ-RT-6	Linwood Bike Path (George K. Francis Bike Path)
NJ-RT-7	Patriots' Path
NJ-RT-8-A	Hudson (Henry) Trail; Atlantic Highlands to Matawan
NJ-RT-8-B	Hudson (Henry) Trail (Formerly Monmouth Heritage Trail); Matawan to Free Hold
NJ-RT-9	Traction Line Recreation Trail
NJ-RT-10	Columbia Trail
NJ-RT-11	Johnson Trolley Line Trail
NJ-RT-12	Ocean City Trail
NJ-RT-13	Edison Branch Rail-Trail
NJ-RT-14	Pemberton Rail-Trail
NJ-BT-1	Ringwood State Park Bike Path
NJ-BT-2	High Point State Park Bike Path
NJ-BT-3	Lebanon State Forest Bike Path
NJ-BT-4	Lenape Trail
NJ-BT-5	Washington (George) Bridge Bikeway

New Jersey Highlights

DELAWARE & RARITAN CANAL STATE PARK TRAIL
(NJ-RT-2)

This trail, opened in 1974, is the longest in New Jersey. It is both a "railway-to-trailway" and "towpath-to-bikepath" conversion. Remnants of the old canal locks, stone spillways and stone-arched culverts are evidence of the canal era. Water still flows through most of the canal, making canoe travel possible. Attractions along this trail include Prallsville Mills in Stockton, Griggstown, Blackwells Mill and Bull's Island Natural Area.

WASHINGTON (GEORGE) BRIDGE BIKEWAY (NJ-BT-5/NY-BT-9)

Although very short, this is the only trail across the Hudson River between Lower New York State (Manhattan) and the state of New Jersey. On the New York side, this trail connects to the Hudson River Greenway which follows the Hudson River from George Washington Bridge to the south tip of Manhattan where the Statue of Liberty can be seen.

Trail Name:	Vicinity:
Columbia Trail	High Bridge to Hunderdon-Morris Co. Line
Delaware & Raritan Canal State Park Trail	Frenchtown (12th St.) to Trenton (Parkside Ave.)
	Trenton (Bakers Basin Rd.) to New Brunswick (Demott Ln. & foot bridge)
Edison Branch Rail-Trail	Woodport & Milton (Mahlon Dickerson Reservation)
Felix (Edgar) Bike Path	Manasquan (Main St.) to Allaire State Park (Hospital Rd.)
Hudson (Henry) Trail; Atlantic Highlands to Matawan	Atlantic Highlands (Avenue D) to Aberdeen (Broadway & Gerard Ave.)
Hudson (Henry) Trail (Formerly Monmouth Heritage Trail); Matawan to Freehold	Matawan (Girard Ave.) to Freehold
Johnson Trolley Line Trail	Lawrence Township
Lebanon State Forest Bike Path	Lebanon State Park
Lenape Trail	South Mountain Reservation
Linwood Bike Path (George K. Francis Bike Path)	Linwood to Somers Point
Monroe Township Bike Path	Monroe
Ocean City Trail	Ocean City
Patriots' Path	East Hanover to Washington
Pemberton Rail-Trail	Pemberton
Ringwood State Park Bike Path	Ringwood State Park
Somers Point Bike Path	Somers Point (bike path follows Atlantic Ave. from Maryland Ave. to Ocean Heights Ave.)
Traction Line Recreation Trail	Morristown (Morris Ave.) to Madison (Danforth Rd.)
Washington (George) Bridge Bikeway	Fort Lee, NJ to Manhattan, NY; trail follows Interstate-95
West Essex Trail	Verona (Arnold Way) to Cedar Grove (Essex-Passaic County Line)

Map:	Trail Length:	Surface	🚴	🚵	🐎	🛼	✈	🚶	♿	🎿	🏍	$
(NJ-RT-10)	8.0 miles	asphalt & smooth crushed gravel	●	●	●			●	●	●		
(NJ-RT-2)	29.3 miles / 32.0 miles	smooth crushed gravel	●	●	●			●	●	●		
(NJ-RT-13)	2.5 miles	smooth crushed gravel & cinders	●	●	●			●				
(NJ-RT-1)	3.6 miles	asphalt	●	●	●	●		●	●	●		
(NJ-RT-8-A)	9.0 miles	asphalt	●		●	●		●	●	●		
(NJ-RT-8-B)	12.0 miles	asphalt (trail to open in 2002)	●	●								
(NJ-RT-11)	2.5 miles	asphalt, gravel & dirt	●	●				●	●			
(NJ-BT-3)	10.0 miles	asphalt	●	●	●			●	●	●		
(NJ-BT-4)	8.0 miles	asphalt	●	●	●			●	●	●		
(NJ-RT-6)	4.5 miles	asphalt	●	●		●		●	●	●		
(NJ-RT-4)	4.0 miles	asphalt	●	●		●		●	●	●		
(NJ-RT-12)	0.9 miles	asphalt	●	●		●		●	●	●		
(NJ-RT-7)	6.0 miles	asphalt	●	●	●			●	●	●		
(NJ-RT-14)	2.5 miles	asphalt	●	●		●		●	●	●		
(NJ-BT-1)	10.0 miles	asphalt	●	●				●	●	●		
(NJ-RT-3)	1.0 mile	asphalt	●	●		●		●	●	●		
(NJ-RT-9)	3.0 miles	asphalt	●	●		●		●	●	●		
(NJ-BT-5 / NY-BT-9)	1.0 mile	concrete	●	●				●	●			
(NJ-RT-5)	2.8 miles	smooth crushed	●	●				●				

Biking New Mexico's Rail-Trails

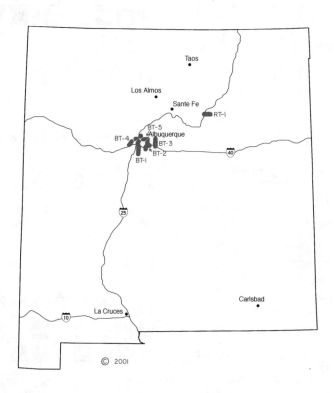

© 2001

Trail Name:	Vicinity:
Gillinas Hiking Trail	Las Vegas
Mariposa-Riverview Bike Trail	Albuquerque (Dellyne Ave. to La Luz Del Cielo)
Paseo Del Bosque-Atvisco Riverside Drain Bike Trail	Albuquerque (Follows Rio Grande River from Heather Lane to Paseo Del Norte)
Paseo Del Nordeste Bike Trail	Albuquerque (Yale Blvd. To Pennsylvania St. & Paseo Del Norte)
Paseo Del Norte Bike Trail	Albuquerque (Coors Blvd. to 2nd St.)
Tramway Boulevard Bike Trail	Albuquerque (follows Tramway Blvd. from Central Ave. to Paseo Del Norte)

Trail Listings

NM-RT-1	Gillinas Hiking Trail
NM-BT-1	Paseo Del Bosque-Atvisco Riverside Drain Bike Trail
NM-BT-2	Paseo Del Nordeste Bike Trail
NM-BT-3	Tramway Boulevard Bike Trail
NM-BT-4	Mariposa-Riverview Bike Trail
NM-BT-5	Paseo Del Norte Bike Trail

New Mexico Highlights

PASEO DEL BOSQUE-ATVISCO RIVERSIDE DRAIN BIKE TRAIL (NM-BT-1)

Built in 1976 to celebrate the U.S.A.'s 200th birthday, this urban and suburban bike path follows the Rio Grande River through the center of Albuquerque. Features along this trail include the Rio Grande Zoo, Rio Grande Nature Preserve and Albuquerque skyline and neighborhoods.

Map:	Trail Length:	Surface
(NM-RT-1)	1.5 miles	asphalt
(NM-BT-4)	2.7 miles	asphalt
(NM-BT-1)	16.0 miles	asphalt
(NM-BT-2)	9.0 miles	asphalt
(NM-BT-5)	3.0 miles	asphalt
(NM-BT-3)	10.0 miles	asphalt

Biking New York's Rail-Trails

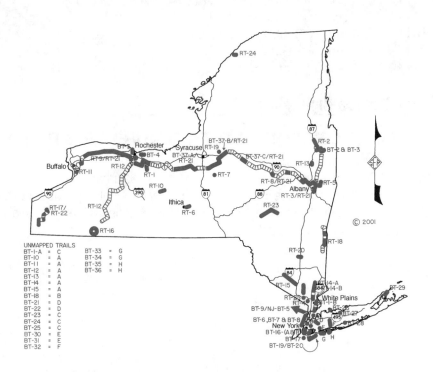

UNMAPPED TRAILS
BT-I-A = C   BT-33 = G
BT-IO = A   BT-34 = G
BT-II = A   BT-35 = H
BT-I2 = A   BT-36 = H
BT-I3 = A
BT-I4 = A
BT-I5 = A
BT-I8 = B
BT-2I = D
BT-22 = D
BT-23 = C
BT-24 = C
BT-25 = C
BT-30 = E
BT-3I = E
BT-32 = F

© 2001

Trail Listings

NY-RT-1	Rochester, Syracuse, & Eastern Trail
NY-RT-2	Warren County Bikeway
NY-RT-3	Mohawk-Hudson Bikeway Hike-Bike Trail
NY-RT-4	Esposito (Raymond G.) Memorial Trail
NY-RT-5	Uncle Sam Bikeway
NY-RT-6	East Ithaca Recreation Way
NY-RT-7	Gorge Trail
NY-RT-8	Canalway Trail (Montgomery County)
NY-RT-9	Erie Canal Heritage Trail
NY-RT-10	Outlet Trail
NY-RT-11	Lehigh Memory Trail

NY-RT-12	Genesee Valley Greenway
NY-RT-13	Saratoga Springs Bicycle System & Pedestrian Path
NY-RT-14-A	North County Trailway
NY-RT-14-B	South County Trailway
NY-RT-15	Heritage Trail (Orange Heritage Trail)
NY-RT-16	Allegheny River Valley Trail
NY-RT-17	Wells (Alison) Ney Nature Trail
NY-RT-18	Harlem Valley Rail-Trail
NY-RT-19	Verona Beach Trail System
NY-RT-20	Hudson Valley Trailway
NY-RT-21	New York State Canalway Trail System
NY-RT-22	Chautauqua Rails to Trails
NY-RT-23	Catskill Scenic Trail
NY-RT-24	Maple City Trail
NY-RT-25	Clarke (Joseph B.) Rail-Trail
NY-BT-1-A	Bronx River Parkway Bikeway
NY-BT-1-B	Bronx River Pathway
NY-BT-2	Feeder Canal Park Heritage Trail (Glen Falls-Hudson Falls)
NY-BT-3	Old Champlain Canal Towpath (Fort Edward)
NY-BT-4	State Route 104 Bike Path
NY-BT-5	State Route 390 Bike Path
NY-BT-6	Hudson River Greenway
NY-BT-7	East River Greenway
NY-BT-8	Wagner (Bobby) Walkway
NY-BT-9	Washington (George) Bridge Bikeway
NY-BT-10	Tri-Boro Bridge Bikeway
NY-BT-11	Queensboro Bridge Bikeway
NY-BT-12	Roosevelt Island Bikeway
NY-BT-13	Williamsburg Bridge Bikeway
NY-BT-14	Manhattan Bridge Bikeway
NY-BT-15	Brooklyn Bridge Bikeway
NY-BT-16-A	Shore Parkway Path (West)
NY-BT-16-B	Shore Parkway Path (East)
NY-BT-17	Coney Island Boardwalk
NY-BT-18	Ocean Parkway Bikeway
NY-BT-19	Flat Bush & Marine Parkway Bridge Bikeway
NY-BT-20	Rockaway Boardwalk
NY-BT-21	Flushing Bay Promenade Bikeway
NY-BT-22	Cross Island Parkway Bikeway
NY-BT-23	Pelham Parkway Bikeway
NY-BT-24	Mosholu Parkway Bikeway

NY-BT-25	Clemente (Roberto) State Park Bikeway
NY-BT-26	Caumsett State Park Bike Paths
NY-BT-27	Sunken Meadow State Park Bike Path
NY-BT-28	Heckscher State Park Bike Path
NY-BT-29	Orient Beach State Park Bike Path
NY-BT-30	Valley Stream State Park Bike Path
NY-BT-31	Hempstead Lake State Park Bike Path
NY-BT-32	Massapequa County Preserve to Bethpage State Park Bike Path
NY-BT-33	Lawrence to Atlantic Beach Bike Path
NY-BT-34	Long Beach Park Bike Path
NY-BT-35	Jones Beach State Park Bike Path
NY-BT-36	Jones Beach State Park to Cedar Creek County Park Bike Path
NY-BT-37-A	Old Erie Canal Trail (Port Byron to Solvay)
NY-BT-37-B	Old Erie Canal Trail (East Syracuse to Rome)
NY-BT-37-C	State Canal Park Trail; Lock 20
NY-BT-38	Tallman Mountain State Park Bike Path
NY-BT-39	Hook Mount/Nyack Beach Bikeway
NY-BT-40	Jones Point Path

New York Highlights

BROOKLYN BRIDGE BIKEWAY (NY-BT-15)
This bike path crosses over one of the most popular historic span bridge in the United States.

ERIE CANAL HERITAGE TRAIL (NY-RT-9)
This trail is part of the east-west cross-state New York Canalway Trail System. This trail is both a rail-rail and a "towpath-to-bikepath" where mules once pulled cargo from Buffalo to New Albany and Hudson Falls. In Rochester, this trail connects to the Genesee Valley Greenway. Other sections along this canal have also been converted to bikepaths; for a complete list, see the New York Canalway Trail System on page 165.

HUDSON RIVER GREENWAY (NY-BT-6)
This north-south trail follows the Hudson River through Manhattan. Attractions along this trail include Riverbank State Park, Hudson River Park, Battery Park, the Statue of Liberty, the New York skyline and Memorial World Trade Center, scene of the September 11, 2001 "Attack on America."

MOHAWK-HUDSON BIKEWAY HIKE-BIKE TRAIL
(NY-RT-3)
This trail is part of the east-west cross-state New York Canalway Trail System. Attractions along this trail include Plotterkill Aqueduct, Shaker Miller's house, Cornelius Reynold's house, parks and New York's State Capitol Building in Albany. Other sections along this canal have also been converted to bikepaths; for a complete list, see the New York Canalway Trail System on page 165.

NEW YORK STATE CANALWAY TRAIL SYSTEM
(NY-RT-21)
Traveling along the Erie Canal during the 1800s was described in the early American folksong "Fifteen Miles on the Erie Canal." Today, the New York State Canalway Trail System is making the effort to restore and preserve the active and abandoned canal corridors from Buffalo to New Albany to Hudson Falls for both recreational water travel and trail users. The list below shows which sections have been converted for biking and hiking. When complete, this trail will be 524 miles long.

Erie Canal Heritage Trail (NY-RT-9)
Old Erie Canal Trail (Port Byron to Solvay) (NY-BT-37-A)
Old Erie Canal Trail (East Syracuse to Rome) (NY-BT-37-B)
State Canal Park Trail; Lock 20 (NY-BT-37-C)
Canalway Trail (Montgomery County) (NY-RT-8)
Mohawk-Hudson Bikeway Hike-Bike Trail (NY-RT-3)
Feeder Canal Park Heritage Trail (Glen Falls-Hudson Falls) (NY-BT-3)
Warren Country Bikeway (NY-RT-2)

NORTH COUNTY TRAILWAY (NY-RT-14-A)
This trail is part of the former Putnam Division of the New York Central Railroad which commuters used to refer to as The Old Put. Parks along this suburban and rural trail include Keogel Park, Railroad Park, J.R. Lake Park, Turkey Mountain Park, Kitchawan Preserve, Gedney Park, Graham Chills Park and Tarrytown Lakes County Park. Several railroad stations still stand along the trail as well. On the south end, this trail connects to the 1.2 mile Tarrytown Lakes Extension Trail. Eventually, this trail will be extended south and connect to the South County Trailway.

OLD ERIE CANAL TRAIL (EAST SYRACUSE TO ROME) (NY-BT-37-B)

This trail is part of the east-west cross-state New York Canalway Trail System. Attractions on this trail include Green Lakes State Park, the Canal Education Center, the Canastota Canal Town Museum and the Erie Canal Village. Other sections along this canal have also been converted to bikepaths; for a complete list, see the New York Canalway Trail System on page 165.

OLD ERIE CANAL TRAIL (PORT BYRON TO SOLVAY) (NY-BT-37-A)

This trail is part of the east-west cross-state New York Canalway Trail System. One attraction along this trail is the New York State Fairgrounds in Solvay, just west of Syracuse. Other sections along this canal have also been converted to bikepaths; for a complete list, see the New York Canalway Trail System on page 165.

ROCHESTER, SYRACUSE, & EASTERN TRAIL

(NY-RT-1)

This trail in the canal town of Fairport was New York state's first "railway-to-trailway" conversion. Built in 1975, this trail is only a few blocks from the Erie Canal Heritage Trail.

STATE CANAL PARK TRAIL; LOCK 20 (NY-BT-37-C)

This trail is part of the east-west cross-state New York Canalway Trail System. Attractions along this trail include Lock 20 and Utica Marsh State Wildlife Management Area. Other sections along this canal have also been converted to bikepaths; for a complete list, see the New York Canalway Trail System on page 165.

WASHINGTON (GEORGE) BRIDGE BIKEWAY

(NY-BT-9/NJ-BT-5)

Although very short, this is the only trail across the Hudson River between Lower New York State (Manhattan) and the state of New Jersey. On the New York side, this trail connects to the Hudson River Greenway which follows the Hudson River from George Washington Bridge to the south tip of Manhattan where the Statue of Liberty can be seen.

The Erie Canal Heritage Trail (NY).

Trail Name:	Vicinity:
Allegheny River Valley Trail)	Allegheny to Olean (Circular trail crosses State Route 417/College and follows the Allegheny River)
Bronx River Parkway Bikeway	The Bronx: Leland & Obrien to Lafayette; Pelham Pkwy N & Bronx Park E to E 233rd; trail follows the Bronx River.
Bronx River Pathway	Mt. Vernon Bronxville to Tuckahoe Hartsdale to Valhalla (Taconic State Pkwy.); trail follows Bronx River & Bronx River Pkwy.
Brooklyn Bridge Bikeway	Manhattan (Centre) to Brooklyn (Adams)
Canalway Trail (Montgomery County)	Fort Plain (Lock 15) to Canajoharie (Lock 14) Fort Hunter (Lock 12) to Amsterdam (Eastern city limits & Lock 11)
Catskill Scenic Trail	Bloomville (State Route 10) to Grand Gorge (State Route 23)
Caumsett State Park Bike Paths	Caumsett State Park (near Huntington on Lloyd Harbor Rd.)
Chautauqua Rails to Trails	Sherman (Titus Rd. to Summerdale Rd.) Mayville (Bentley Rd. to State Route 430 & State Route 27) Mayville (State Route 29/Plank Rd.) to Brocton (Thayer Rd.) Brocton (Webster Rd. to State Route 20)
Clarke (Joseph B.) Rail-Trail	Tappan (Oak Tree Rd.) to Blauvelt (Western Highway)
Clemente (Roberto) State Park Bikeway	The Bronx in Roberto Clemente State Park (W 176th St.); trail follows the Harlem River
Coney Island Boardwalk	Brooklyn (E 15th St. to W 37th St.); trail follows the Atlantic Ocean Coast. Hours are restricted from 5 AM to 10 AM.

Map:	Trail Length:	Surface
(NY-RT-16)	5.6 miles	asphalt
(NY-BT-1-A)	1.2 miles 2.6 miles	asphalt
(NY-BT-1-B)	1.0 mile 3.6 miles 5.0 miles	asphalt
(NY-BT-15)	1.5 miles	concrete & asphalt
(NY-RT-8)	4.0 miles 8.0 miles	asphalt
(NY-RT-23)	19.0 miles	smooth crushed gravel
(NY-BT-26)	4.5 miles	asphalt
(NY-RT-22)	5.5 miles 4.0 miles 5.0 miles 2.0 miles	smooth crushed gravel & gravel
(NY-RT-25)	3.0 miles	smooth crushed gravel, gravel & cinder
(NY-BT-25)	0.7 miles	asphalt
(NY-BT-17)	2.5 miles	asphalt, concrete & boardwalk

Trail Name:	Vicinity:
Cross Island Parkway Bikeway	Queens (Utopia to Northern Blvd.); trail follows the Little Neck Bay Coast and Cross Island Pkwy.
East Ithaca Recreation Way	Ithaca to Dryden
East River Greenway	Manhattan (F.D.R. Dr. & Pier 9 to F.D.R. Dr. & Avenue C) trail follows the East River.
Erie Canal Heritage Trail	East of North Tonawanda (State Route 270 to Tonawanda Creek) Lockport (Cold Springs Rd.) to Rochester to Palmyra (State Route 31 & Aqueduct Park)
Esposito (Raymond G.) Memorial Trail	South Nyack to Sparkill
Feeder Canal Park Heritage Trail (Glen Falls-Hudson Falls)	Glen Falls (Haviland Ave. to Glen St./U.S. Rooute-9) Glen Falls (Shermantown Rd.) to Hudson Falls (Burgoyne Ave./County Route 37 & Old Champlain Canal Towpath)
Flat Bush & Marine Parkway Bridge Bikeway	Brooklyn (Flatbush & Avenue W to Marine Pkwy. Bridge & Jacob Riis Park)
Flushing Bay Promenade Bikeway	Queens (31st Dr. & LaGuardia Airport to 34th Ave. & Shea Stadium); trail follows the Flushing Bay Coast.
Genesee Valley Greenway	Rochester: Exchange Blvd./State Route 383 to Genesee Valley Park & Scottsville Rd./State Route 383 Court St. & South Ave. to Genesee Valley Park; trail follows both sides of the Genesee River
Gorge Trail	Cazenovia
Harlem Valley Rail-Trail	Wassaic to Millerton (Main St.) Ancram (Under Mountain Rd.) to Taconic State Park & Copake Falls (State Route 344)
Heckscher State Park Bike Path	East Islip (River Rd.) to Heckscher State Park (South Bay)

Map:	Trail Length:	Surface	🚲	🚲	🐎	👟	⛵	🥾	♿	⛷	🔭	$
(NY-BT-22)	3.0 miles	asphalt	●	●		●		●	●			
(NY-RT-6)	2.2 miles	asphalt & gravel (cinders)	●	●	●			●	●	●		
(NY-BT-7)	3.5 miles	asphalt	●	●		●		●	●			
(NY-RT-9)	3.0 miles 70.0 miles	smooth crushed gravel & asphalt	●	●		●		●	●	●		
(NY-RT-4)	3.0 mile	smooth crushed gravel & gravel	●	●				●	●	●		
(NY-BT-2)	2.0 miles 4.3 miles	smooth crushed gravel	●	●		●		●	●			
(NY-BT-19)	6.0 miles	asphalt & concrete	●	●		●		●	●			
(NY-BT-21)	1.8 miles	asphalt	●	●		●		●	●			
(NY-RT-12)	2.0 miles 2.0 miles (will be 90 miles)	asphalt	●	●	●	●	●	●	●	●		
(NY-RT-7)	2.2 miles	smooth crushed gravel (cinder) & ballast	●	●	●			●	●	●		
(NY-RT-18)	11.5 miles 4.0 miles	asphalt	●	●	●			●	●	●		
(NY-BT-28)	2.5 miles	asphalt	●	●		●		●	●			

Trail Name:	Vicinity:
Hempstead Lake State Park Bike Path	Hempstead Lake State Park (near Hempstead and Rockville Centre); most of the trail follows N Village Ave. between De Mott Ave. & Southern State Parkway
Heritage Trail (Orange Heritage Trail)	Goshen (Hartley Rd.) to Monroe (County Route 17M/Airplane Park)
Hook Mount/Nyack Beach Bikeway	Hook Mount Nyack Beach State Park; trail follows the Hudson River
Hudson River Greenway	Manhattan (W 181st St. & Henry Hudson Pkwy./State Route 9-A next to the George Washington Bridge to Battery Park & Henry Hudson Pkwy./ State Route 9-A); trail follows the Hudson River
Hudson Valley Trailway	Ohioville (State Route 299 & County Route 22) to Highland (U.S. Route 9-W)
Jones Beach State Park Bike Path	Jones Beach State Park (trail follows the Atlantic Ocean Coast west from Ocean Pkwy. & Wantagh State Pkwy.)
Jones Beach State Park to Cedar Creek County Park Bike Path	Jones Beach State Park to Seaford (Cedar Creek County Park); trail parallels Wantagh State Pkwy.
Jones Point Path	Bear Mount State Park (Jones Point); trail follows both U.S. Route 9-W and the Hudson River
Lawrence to Atlantic Beach Bike Path	Lawrence (State Route 878) to to Atlantic Beach (Along the Atlantic Ocean Coast)
Lehigh Memory Trail	Amherst
Long Beach Park Bike Path	Long Beach (Long Beach Park and the trail follows the Atlantic Ocean Coast)
Manhattan Bridge Bikeway	Manhattan (Bowery) to Brooklyn (Jay)
Maple City Trail	Ogdensburg
Massapequa County Preserve to Bethpage State Park Bike Path	Massapequa Park (Massapequa County Preserve on Merrick Rd.) to Bethpage (Bethpage State Park)
Mohawk-Hudson Bikeway Hike-Bike Trail	Albany (Quay St. & Broadway) to Rotterdam Junction (State Route 5-S & Scafford La.) and Troy (Middleburgh & 8th Streets) to Lansinburg (State Route 142/Northern Dr.)

Map:	Trail Length:	Surface
(NY-BT-31)	3.5 miles	asphalt
(NY-RT-15)	11.0 miles	asphalt & smooth crushed gravel
(NY-BT-39)	4.9 miles	asphalt
(NY-BT-6)	11.5 miles	asphalt
(NY-RT-20)	2.4 miles	asphalt
(NY-BT-35)	1.8 miles	asphalt
(NY-BT-36)	4.3 miles	asphalt & concrete
(NY-BT-40)	1.9 miles	asphalt
(NY-BT-33)	3.0 miles	asphalt & concrete
(NY-RT-11)	0.8 miles	asphalt
(NY-BT-34)	2.0 miles	asphalt
(NY-BT-14)	1.5 miles	concrete
(NY-RT-24)	1.8 miles	asphalt
(NY-BT-32)	7.5 miles	asphalt
(NY-RT-3)	41.0 miles	asphalt (parts follow streets)

Trail Name:	Vicinity:
Mosholu Parkway Bikeway	The Bronx (Bronx Park E & Bronx River Pkwy. to Van Cortland Park S.); trail follows Mosholu Pkwy.
New York State Canalway Trail System	Buffalo to Rochester to Syracuse to Albany to Hudson Falls. Existing trails are being connected to form a continuous trail. For more details, see these existing trails: Erie Canal Heritage Trail Old Erie Canal Trail State Canal Park Trail; Lock 20 Canalway Trail (Montgomery County) Feeder Canal Park Heritage Trail Mohawk-Hudson Bikeway Hike-Bike Trail Glen Falls Feeder Canal Trail Warren County Bikeway
North County Trailway	Pleasantville & Eastview (State Route 100-C & Saw Mill River Pkwy.) to Yorktown Heights on the Westchester-Putnam County Line
Ocean Parkway Bikeway	Brooklyn (Brighton Beach Ave. to Church)
Old Champlain Canal Towpath (Fort Edward)	Fort Edward (McIntyre St.) to Feeder Canal Park Heritage Trail and to the northeast.
Old Erie Canal Trail (East Syracuse to Rome)	East Syracuse & Minoa to Rome (Erie Canal Village Area)
Old Erie Canal Trail (Port Byron to Solvay)	Port Byron to Solvay (State Fairgrounds)
Orient Beach State Park Bike Path	Orient Beach State Park (Orient Point on State Route 25 to Ben's Point along Gardiners Bay)
Outlet Trail	Pen Yan to Dresden
Pelham Parkway Bikeway	Bronx (Pelham Parkway N & Bronx Park E to Pelham Shore, Pelham Pay Park, & the Bronx-Westchester County Line)
Queensboro Bridge Bikeway	Manhattan (E 59th St. & First Ave.) to Queens (Queens Blvd. & Crescent)

Map:	Trail Length:	Surface										
(NY-BT-24)	2.0 miles	asphalt										
(NY-RT-21)	524.0 miles when all trails are completed	asphalt & smooth crushed gravel										
(NY-RT-14-A)	22.1 miles	asphalt										
(NY-BT-18)	5.0 miles	asphalt & concrete										
(NY-BT-3)	2.8 miles	smooth crushed gravel & gravel										
(NY-BT-37-B)	36.0 miles	smooth crushed gravel										
(NY-BT-37-A)	22.0 miles	smooth crushed gravel										
(NY-BT-29)	2.5 miles	asphalt										
(NY-RT-10)	7.5 miles	asphalt & ballast										
(NY-BT-23)	8.0 miles	asphalt										
(NY-BT-11)	1.3 miles	concrete										

Trail Name:	Vicinity:
Rochester, Syracuse, & Eastern Trail	Fairport & surrounding area (Baird Rd. & Midvale Dr. to NY State Erie Canal & Watson Rd. to Pannell Rd.)
Rockaway Boardwalk	Brooklyn (B 126th St. to B 19th St.); trail follows the Atlantic Ocean Coast. Hours are restricted from 5 AM to 10 AM.
Roosevelt Island Bikeway	Roosevelt Island (circular trail around island)
Saratoga Springs Bicycle System & Pedestrian Path	Saratoga Springs (Franklin & West Circular Streets to Congress Ave.)
Shore Parkway Path (West)	Brooklyn (Bay Ridge Ave. to Bay Pkwy.); trail follows the Upper New York Bay Coast, Lower New York Bay Coast, and Shore Pkwy.
Shore Parkway Path (East)	Brooklyn (Knapp St. & Emmons) to Queens (91st St.); trail follows the Rockaway Inlet Coast, Jamaica Bay Coast, and Shore Pkwy.
South County Trailway	Bronx-Westchester County Line (Mill River Pkwy. & Farragut Ave.) to Pleasantville & Eastview (State Route 100-C & Saw Mill River Pkwy.)
State Canal Park Trail; Lock 20	Whitesboro (Lock 20) to Utica
State Route 104 Bike Path	West Webster (Bay Dr.) to Webster (Salt Rd.); trail parallels State Route 104
State Route 390 Bike Path	Greece (Ridge Rd./State Route 104 to Lake Ontario State Pkwy.); trail parallels State Route 390
Sunken Meadow State Park Bike Path	Kings Parks (Salonga Rd.) to Sunken Meadow State Park on Smithtown Bay.
Tallman Mountain State Park Bike Path	Piermont (Tallman Mountain State Park near U.S. Route 9-W)
Tri-Boro Bridge Bikeway	Manhattan (E 125th St.) to Queens (Grand Central Pkwy. & 27th St.) & Bronx Bruckner Expressway & E 132nd St.)
Uncle Sam Bikeway	Troy

Map:	Trail Length:	Surface	🚲	🚵	🐎	🛼	➡	🥾	♿	⛷	👓	$
(NY-RT-1)	8.0 miles	smooth crushed gravel (parts follow streets)	🚲	🚵	🐎		➡	🥾		⛷		
(NY-BT-20)	4.5 miles	asphalt, concrete & Boardwalk	🚲	🚵		🛼		🥾	♿			
(NY-BT-12)	4.0 miles	asphalt	🚲	🚵		🛼		🥾	♿			
(NY-RT-13)	39.6 miles (trail system) & 1.0 mile (path)	asphalt	🚲	🚵		🛼		🥾	♿			
(NY-BT-16-A)	4.5 miles	asphalt	🚲	🚵		🛼	➡	🥾	♿			
(NY-BT-16-B)	7.5 miles	asphalt	🚲	🚵		🛼	➡	🥾	♿			
(NY-RT-14-B)	14.1 miles	asphalt	🚲	🚵		🛼	➡	🥾	♿			
(NY-BT-37-C)	4.5 miles	smooth crushed gravel	🚲	🚵		🛼		🥾	♿	⛷		
(NY-BT-4)	6.0 miles	asphalt	🚲	🚵		🛼		🥾	♿	⛷		
(NY-BT-5)	4.0 miles	asphalt	🚲	🚵		🛼		🥾	♿	⛷		
(NY-BT-27)	1.5 miles	asphalt	🚲	🚵		🛼		🥾	♿			
(NY-BT-38)	2.1 miles	asphalt	🚲	🚵		🛼		🥾	♿			
(NY-BT-10)	7.0 miles	asphalt & concrete	🚲	🚵		🛼		🥾	♿			
(NY-RT-5)	3.5 miles	asphalt	🚲	🚵	🐎	🛼		🥾	♿			

Trail Name:	Vicinity:
Valley Stream State Park Bike Path	Valley Stream State Park near Valley Stream (Valley Stream Blvd. to Hendrickson Ave. & Southern State Parkway
Verona Beach Trail System	Verona Beach State Park
Wagner (Bobby) Walkway	Manhattan (E 62nd St. & F.D.R. Dr. to E 125th St. & Tri-Boro Bridge); trail follows the East River & the Hudson River
Warren County Bikeway	Lake George (Southern end of Lake George) to Glens Falls (Platt & McDonald Streets)
Washington (George) Bridge Bikeway	Manhattan, NY to Fort Lee, NJ; trail follows Interstate 95
Wells (Alison) Ney Nature Trail	Brocton (Thayer Rd. to Bliss Rd.)
Williamsburg Bridge Bikeway	Manhattan (Delancey & Clinton) to Brooklyn (Broadway & Bedford)

Fifteen Miles on the Erie Canal.

Map:	Trail Length:	Surface	🚲	🚴	🐴	🛼	🛷	🚶	♿	⛷	🏍	$
(NY-BT-30)	3.0 miles	asphalt	🚲	🚴		🛼		🚶	♿			
(NY-RT-19)	15.0 miles	smooth crushed gravel & packed sand	🚲	🚴	🐴			🚶		⛷		
(NY-BT-8)	3.5 miles	asphalt	🚲	🚴		🛼		🚶	♿			
(NY-RT-2)	10.0 miles	asphalt	🚲	🚴		🛼		🚶	♿	⛷		
(NY-BT-9 / NJ-BT-5)	1.0 mile	concrete	🚲	🚴		🛼		🚶	♿			
(NY-RT-17)	5.0 miles	smooth crushed gravel	🚲	🚴				🚶		⛷		
(NY-BT-13)	1.3 miles	concrete	🚲	🚴		🛼		🚶	♿			

Natural Wildlife along the Erie Canal Heritage Trail.

Biking North Carolina's Rail-Trails

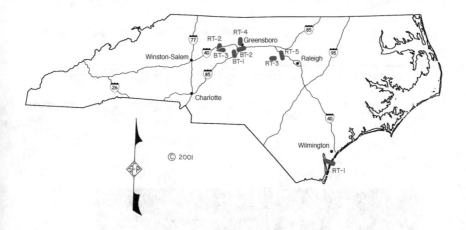

Trail Listings

NC-RT-1	River to the Sea Bikeway (Bike Route 1)
NC-RT-2	Stroll Way
NC-RT-3	Libba Cotton Trail
NC-RT-4	Lake Brandt Greenway
NC-RT-5	American Tobacco Trail
NC-BT-1	Bicentennial Greenway
NC-BT-2	North Buffalo Creek Greenway
NC-BT-3	Salem Creek Trail

The American Tobacco Trail (NC).

North Carolina Highlights

AMERICAN TOBACCO TRAIL (NC-RT-5)

This north-south trail gets its name from the former railroad line that used to haul tobacco through this area. It connects the Durham Bulls Athletic Park to North Carolina Central University and Elmira Park.

LAKE BRANDT GREENWAY (NC-RT-4)

Opened in 1997, this trail connects Jaycee Park, Country Park, Guilford Courthouse National Military Park, Bur-Mil Park and Lake Brandt through the northern neighborhoods of Greensboro.

Trail Name:	Vicinity:
American Tobacco Trail	Durham (Durham Expressway & South St. to Cornwallis Rd.)
Bicentennial Greenway	Highpoint (Penny Rd. to Gallimore Dairy Rd.)
Lake Brandt Greenway	Greensboro (Jaycee Park Dr. & Jaycee Park to Strawberry Rd. (Bur-Mil Park)
Libba Cotton Trail	Carrboro (Roberson St. to Merritt Mill Rd. & Camero)
North Buffalo Creek Greenway	Greenville (Ashland Dr. to Elm St.) Ashland Dr. to W Market St. W Friendly Ave. Elm St.; trail follows North Buffalo Creek.
River to the Sea Bikeway (Bike Route 1)	Wilmington (Market & Front Streets) to Wrightsville Beach (Lumina Ave.); short sections of separate bike paths parallel Park Ave. between Castle St. & Greenville Loop
Salem Creek Trail	Winston-Salem (Peters Creek Pkwy. to Salem Ave. to Salem Lake Rd.); trail parallels Salem Creek
Stroll Way	Winston-Salem (4th St to Salem Ave.); trail follows Old Salem Rd.

The Stroll Way in Winston-Salem.

Map:	Trail Length:	Surface	🚲	🛴	🐎	🛼	✈	🚶	♿	⛷	🏍	$
(NC-RT-5)	3.0 miles	asphalt	🚲	🛴	🐎			🚶	♿			
(NC-BT-1)	6.1 miles	asphalt	🚲	🛴		🛼		🚶	♿	⛷		
(NC-RT-4)	3.6 miles	asphalt & concrete	🚲	🛴		🛼		🚶	♿			
(NC-RT-3)	0.4 miles	asphalt	🚲	🛴		🛼		🚶	♿			
(NC-BT-2)	0.7 miles 3.3 miles	asphalt	🚲	🛴		🛼		🚶	♿	⛷		$
(NC-RT-1)	12.0 miles	asphalt & concrete (most follows streets)	🚲	🛴	🐎	🛼		🚶	♿			
(NC-BT-3)	4.5 miles	asphalt	🚲	🛴		🛼		🚶	♿	⛷		
(NC-RT-2)	1.2 mile	asphalt, coarse asphalt, & concrete	🚲	🛴		🛼		🚶	♿			

A trestle along the Lake Brandt Greenway.

Biking North Dakota's Rail-Trails

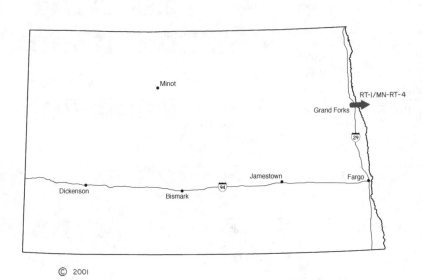

© 2001

Trail Name:	Vicinity:
Grand Forks-East Grand Forks Bikeway	Grand Forks, ND (Columbia Rd. & U.S. Route 2/Gateway Dr.) to East Grand Forks, MN (Red River Bridge)

Trail Listings

The Original Train Station along the Grand Forks-East Grand Forks Bikeway in North Dakota (Floyd Hickok).

Map:	Trail Length:	Surface	🚴 🚲 🐎 🛼 ➘ 🚶 ♿ ⛷ 🐾 $
(ND-RT-1 / MN-RT-4)	2.5 miles (part of 8.0 miles in Grand Forks, ND & 5.0 miles in East Grand Forks, MN trail network)	concrete & asphalt	🚴 🚲 🐎 🛼 ➘ 🚶 ♿ ⛷ 🐾 $

Biking Ohio's Rail-Trails

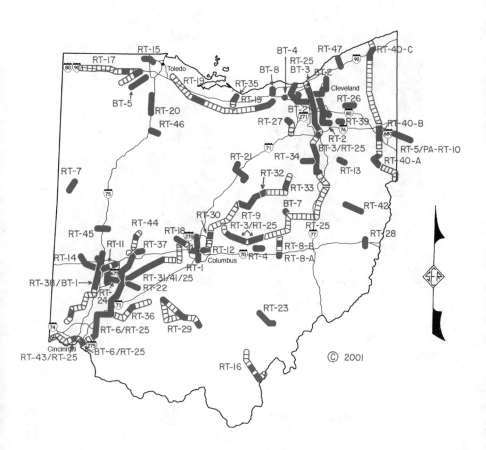

Trail Listings

OH-RT-1	Olentangy/Lower Scioto Bikeways (Bike Route 47)
OH-RT-2	Bike & Hike Trail
OH-RT-3-A	Evans (Thomas J.) Bike Path (Johnstown to Newark)
OH-RT-3-B	Evans (Thomas J.) Bike Path (Newark to Hanover or Panhandle Trail)
OH-RT-4	Blackhand Gorge Trail
OH-RT-5	Stavich Bicycle Trail
OH-RT-6-A	Little Miami Scenic Trail
OH-RT-6-B	Bike Route 1 (Little Miami Scenic Trail)
OH-RT-7	Celina-Coldwater Bikeway
OH-RT-8-A	Zane's Landing Trail
OH-RT-8-B	Muskingum Recreational Trail
OH-RT-9	Kokosing Gap Trail
OH-RT-11-A	Mad River Bikeway
OH-RT-11-B	Kauffman Avenue Bike Path
OH-RT-12	Interstate-670 Bikeway
OH-RT-13	Nickelplate Trail
OH-RT-14	Wolf Creek Rail-Trail
OH-RT-15	University-Parks Hike-Bike Trail
OH-RT-16-A	Gallipolis Bike Path
OH-RT-16-B	Bidwell to Kerr Bike Path
OH-RT-17	Wabash Cannonball Trail
OH-RT-18	Heritage Rail-Trail
OH-RT-19	North Coast Inland Bike Path
OH-RT-20	Slippery Elm Trail
OH-RT-21	Richland B & O Trail
OH-RT-22	Bike Route 3 (Xenia to Jamestown)
OH-RT-23-A	Hockhocking-Adena Bikeway
OH-RT-23-B	Riverside Bikeway
OH-RT-24	Bike Route 2; Creekside Trail
OH-RT-25	Ohio to Erie Trail
OH-RT-26	Headwater Trail
OH-RT-27	Lester Rail Trail
OH-RT-28	National Road Bikeway
OH-RT-29	Tri County Triangle Trail
OH-RT-30	Westerville Bikeway
OH-RT-31	Bike Route 4 (Prairie Trail)
OH-RT-32	Mohican Valley Trail
OH-RT-33	Holmes County Rail-Trail
OH-RT-34	Sippo Valley Trail

OH-RT-35	Huron River Greenway
OH-RT-36	Clinton Rail-Trail
OH-RT-37	Buck Creek Bike Path (Bike Route 1)
OH-RT-38	Great Miami River Trail (Taylorsville Metropark; Bike Route 25)
OH-RT-39	Towner's Woods Rail-Trail
OH-RT-40-A	Great Ohio Lake to River Greenway; Little Beaver Creek Greenway Trail
OH-RT-40-B	Great Ohio Lake to River Greenway; Mahoning Bikeway
OH-RT-40-C	Great Ohio Lake to River Greenway; Western Reserve Greenway
OH-RT-41	Wilberforce Spur Trail
OH-RT-42	Harrison County Conotton Creek Trail
OH-RT-43	Cincinnati Riverfront Bike Path
OH-RT-44	Simon-Kenton Trail
OH-RT-45	Piqua Activity Trail for Health (P.A.T.H.)
OH-RT-46	Blanchard River Rail-Trail (Findlay, OH)
OH-RT-47	Lake Metroparks Greenway Trail
OH-BT-1-A	Great Miami River Trail (River Corridor Bikeway; Bike Route 25)
OH-BT-1-B	Stillwater River Trail (River Corridor Bikeway)
OH-BT-1-C	Hamilton Bikeway
OH-BT-2	Emerald Necklace Trail
OH-BT-3	Towpath Trail (Ohio & Erie Canal)
OH-BT-4	Interstate-480 Bikeway
OH-BT-5	Miami & Erie Canal Towpath Trail
OH-BT-6	Lunken Airport Bike Path
OH-BT-7	Coshocton-Lake Park Bike Path
OH-BT-8	Black River Bridgeway Trail

Ohio Highlights

BIKE & HIKE TRAIL (OH-RT-2)

This trail became Ohio's second rail-trail in 1972. This trail connects Cleveland's Emerald Necklace Trail and park system to the Cuyahoga Valley National Park Towpath Trail and the city of Kent.

BIKE ROUTE 2; CREEKSIDE TRAIL (OH-RT-24)

This east-west trail goes from the eastern neighborhoods of Dayton to the replica of Xenia's Hub Station. In Dayton, this trail connects to the Mad River Bikeway. In Xenia, this trail connects to the Little Miami Scenic Trail (Bike Route 1), Bike Route 3 and Bike Route 4 (Prairie Trail).

BLACKHAND GORGE TRAIL (OH-RT-4)

This short but very scenic trail follows the heavily-wooded Licking River Valley through the Blackhand Gorge near Toboso. It takes its name from the Blackhand rock that it cuts through.

EMERALD NECKLACE TRAIL (OH-BT-2)

This trail winds through a series of Cleveland's Metroparks on the east, south and west edges of the city. It connects to both the Towpath Trail (a section of the Ohio to Erie Trail) and the Bike and Hike Trail.

EVANS (THOMAS J.) BIKE TRAIL (JOHNSTOWN TO NEWARK) (OH-RT-3-A)

Opened in 1975, this east-west trail in central Ohio is the state's third rail-trail and is part of the Ohio to Erie Trail. Most of this scenic trail follows the Raccoon River through gently rolling farmland and hilly woodlands. Historic Granville is a major attraction along this trail and is home to Dennison University. In Newark, this trail connects to a network of trails on the O.S.U. Newark campus.

GREAT MIAMI RIVER TRAIL (RIVER CORRIDOR BIKEWAY; BIKE ROUTE 25) (OH-BT-1-A)

This north-south trail follows the Great Miami River from Miamisburg to the center of Dayton. Parts of this trail follow the river levee, and others follow the Miami and Erie Canal Towpath. It connects to both the Stillwater River Trail and the Mad River Bikeway.

HOCKHOCKING-ADENA BIKEWAY/RIVERSIDE BIKEWAY (OH-RT-23)

Opened in 1996, this rail-trail follows the Hocking River through the mountains of southeastern Ohio. Attractions along the trail include the Ohio University Campus in Athens, Wayne National Forest and Hocking College in Nelsonville.

KOKOSING GAP TRAIL (OH-RT-9)

Opened in 1991, this rail-trail follows the Koskosing River through the forested hills and rolling farmlands of central Ohio. Between Mt. Vernon and Danville, this trail passes through Gambier (Kenyon College) and Howard, which has a beautiful stone arch underpass. This trail connects to the Mohican Valley Trail and is also part of the Ohio to Erie Trail.

LITTLE MIAMI SCENIC TRAIL/BIKE ROUTE 1
(OH-RT-6)
This rail-trail follows the Little Miami River through southwestern Ohio. Currently, this is one of Ohio's longest rail-trails and is also part of the Ohio to Erie Trail. The scenery varies from wooded valleys on the southern end to rolling farmland on the northern end. Highlights along this trail include Milford, Miamiville, Loveland, Fort Ancient State Park, Oregonia, Historic Waynesville, Xenia (replica of the original Xenia Station Hub), Yellow Springs (Antioch College & Glen Helen Nature Center) and Springfield.

NATIONAL ROAD BIKEWAY (OH-RT-28)
Opened in 1998, this is Ohio's only rail-trail to have a lighted railroad tunnel. North of St. Clairsville, this trail crosses a curved trestle through the Appalachian Mountains in eastern Ohio.

NORTH COAST INLAND BIKE PATH (OH-RT-19)
This east-west trail follows Lake Erie ten miles inland across northern Ohio. The land varies from flat to rolling farmlands. One attraction is the home of American writer Sherwood Anderson in Clyde. Another attraction is the famous Underground Railroad in Oberlin used between 1850 and the mid-1860s by Harriet Tubman and others to help slaves escape from the southern states.

OHIO TO ERIE TRAIL (OH-RT-25)
Existing trails from southwest, central and northeast Ohio are being connected to form a continuous trail. For more details, see these existing trails:

Cincinnati Riverfront Bike Path
Lunken Airport Bike Path
Little Miami Scenic Trail/Bike Route 1
Bike Route 4
Heritage Rail-Trail
Lower Scioto/Olentangy Bikeways
Interstate-670 Bikeway
Evans (Thomas J.) Bike Path
Towpath Trail (Ohio & Erie Canal)
Westerville Bikeway
Kokosing Gap Trail
Mohican Valley Trail
Holmes County Rail-Trail

OLENTANGY/LOWER SCIOTO BIKEWAYS (BIKE ROUTE 47) (OH-RT-1)
This trail follows the river levees and banks of both the Olentangy River and the Scioto River through Columbus. Only the southernmost mile of this trail (opened in 1967) is a rail-trail, but it was Ohio's first. Attractions include the Ohio State Capitol Building, the Columbus city skyline, historic German Village neighborhood in Columbus, O.S.U. campus, Antrim Lake and historic Worthington.

RICHLAND B & O TRAIL (OH-RT-21)
This trail forms a crescent through the rolling hills and farmlands of Central Ohio. This trail is near Malabar Farm State Park and Gorman Nature Center. Mansfield is known for both its carousel museum and historic 1895 reformatory where movies such as "The Shawshank Redemption" were filmed.

TOWPATH TRAIL (OHIO & ERIE CANAL) (OH-BT-3)
The Towpath Trail follows part of the former Ohio & Erie Canal through northeastern Ohio. Attractions along this trail include Massillon, Crystal Lake, Canal Fulton, Summit Lake Park, downtown Akron Cuyahoga Valley National Park, Peninsula, the Canal Visitor Center and the city of Cleveland. In the Cuyahoga Valley National Park, this trail connects to both the Emerald Necklace Trail and the Bike and Hike Trail.

UNIVERSITY-PARKS HIKE-BIKE TRAIL (OH-RT-15)
This east-west trail traverses the western neighborhoods of Toledo. Opened in 1995, this rail-trail takes its name from the two major attractions along its route: the University of Ohio and the Wildwood Preserve Metroparks. This rail-trail parallels an active railroad; however, a thick stand of trees separates these two corridors.

WOLF CREEK RAIL-TRAIL (OH-RT-14)
This trail goes through flat and gently rolling meadows and farmlands of western Ohio. It is just west of the city of Dayton, and attractions include Sycamore State Park and Golden Gate Park in Brookville.

Trail Name:	Vicinity:
Bidwell to Kerr Bike Path	Bidwell (State Route 554) to Kerr (Kerr Rd.)
Bike & Hike Trail	Walton Hills near Cleveland (Alexander Rd.) to Cuyahoga Falls (Hudson Dr.) to Silver Lake (Kent Rd. & Church) to Kent (Monroe Falls-Kent Rd) and to Stow (Young Rd. & Silver Springs Park)
Bike Route 1	See Little Miami Scenic Trail & Simon-Kenton Trail
Bike Route 2; Creekside Trail	Dayton (Springfield Pike & Smithville Rd.) and Dayton (Woodbine Ave.) to Xenia (Miami Ave.)
Bike Route 3	Xenia (Miami Ave.) to Jamestown (State Route 72)
Bike Route 4 (Prairie Trail)	Xenia (Miami Ave. & Detroit St.) to South Charleston (Jamestown Rd./C-383)
Bike Route 7	See Stillwater River Recreation Trail
Bike Route 8	See Mad River Recreation Trail
Bike Route 25	See Great Miami River Trail
Bike Route 38	See Wolf Creek Recreation Trail
Bike Route 47	See Olentangy/Lower Scioto Bikeways
Black River Bridgeway Trail	Elyria (Ford Rd. under Interstate-90) to Lorain (31st St.)
Blackhand Gorge Trail	Claylick (Brownsville & Brushy Fork Roads) to Toboso (Toboso Rd.)
Blanchard River Rail-Trail	Findlay (Broad Ave. & Howard St. to N Cory & High Streets)
Buck Creek Bike Path	Springfield (Plum St. & Cliff Park Dr.) to Buck Creek State Park (Croft Rd.)
Celina-Coldwater Bikeway	Celina U.S. Route 127 & Schnuck Rd.) to Coldwater (4th St.)
Cincinnati Riverfront Bike Path	Cincinnati (Clay Wade Bailey Bridge to Roebling Suspension Bridge); trail follows the Ohio River
Clinton Rail-Trail	Wilmington (Nelson Ave. to Mulberry St.)

Map:	Trail Length:	Surface	🚲	🚵	🐎	🛼	✈	🚶	♿	🎿	🔭	$
(OH-RT-16-B)	4.5 miles	smooth crushed gravel										
(OH-RT-2)	29.0 miles	smooth crushed gravel & asphalt (parts follow streets & roads)										
(OH-RT-24)	15.9 miles	asphalt										
(OH-RT-22)	1.2 miles (will be 11.0 miles)	asphalt										
(OH-RT-31)	17.7 miles	asphalt										
(OH-BT-1 / OH-RT-38)												
(OH-RT-1)												
(OH-BT-8)	3.5 miles	asphalt										
(OH-RT-4)	4.5 miles	asphalt										
(OH-RT-46)	1.0 mile	asphalt										
(OH-RT-37)	4.1 miles	asphalt										
(OH-RT-7)	4.5 miles	asphalt										
(OH-RT-43)	0.5 miles	concrete										
(OH-RT-36)	1.5 miles (will be 30.0 miles)	asphalt										

Trail Name:	Vicinity:
Coshocton to Lake Park Bike Path	Coshocton (Bridge St. to Lake Park)
Emerald Necklace Trail	Cleveland Area:
	Lakewood (Detroit Ave.) to Brooklyn (State Route 17/Brookpark Rd. & Net Park Blvd.) and to Strongsville (Valley Pkwy. & W 130th St.) (Lakewood to Middleburg Heights) (Middleburg Heights to Strongsville) (Parma to Strongsville)
	Brecksville (State Route 21/Brecksville Rd. & Valley Creek Pkwy. to Cuyahoga River & Towpath Trail)
	Walton Hills (Alexander Rd.) to Bentleyville (Miles Rd.)
	Mayfield (Buttermilk Falls Pkwy.) to Willoughby Hills (U.S. Route 6/Chardon Rd. & Buttermilk Falls Pkwy.)
Evans (Thomas J.) Bike Trail (Johnstown to Newark)	Johnstown (Douglas Ave.) to Newark (Church St. & YMCA)
Evans (Thomas J.) Bike Trail (NEwark to Hanover or Panhandle Trail)	Newark (E. Main St. & Buena Vista) to Hanover (Fellumee Rd.)
Gallipolis Bike Path	Gallipolis (Mill Creek Rd. to U.S. Route 35 & Old U.S. Route 35)
Great Miami River Recreation Trail (River Corridor Bikeway; Bike Route 25	Montgomery-Warren County Line (Cincinnati Pike) to Dayton (Helena St. & Island Park))
Great Miami River Recreation Trail (Taylorsville Metropark; Bike Route 25)	Dayton (York Rd. & Rip Rap Rd.) to Vandalia (Taylorsville Metropark on U.S. Route 40)
Great Ohio Lake to River Greenway; Western Reserve Greenway	Ashtabula (West Ave.) to Austinburg (Lampson Rd.)
Great Ohio Lake to River Greenway; Mahoning Bikeway	Mineral Ridge (W Mahoning-Trumbull County Line Rd.) to Canfield (Western Reserve Rd.)
Great Ohio Lake to River Greenway; Little Beaver Creek Greenway Trail	Leetonia (State Route 358 & County Route 414A to Lisbon (State Route 164/Lincoln Ave.)

Map:	Trail Length:	Surface										
(OH-BT-7)	3.0 miles	asphalt										
(OH-BT-2)		asphalt										
	13.5 miles & 8.0 miles & 7.5 miles											
	4.0 miles											
	14.0 miles											
	4.0 miles											
(OH-RT-3-A)	18.8 miles	asphalt										
(OH-RT-3-B)	8.5 miles	asphalt										
(OH-RT-16-A)	3.3 miles	smooth crushed gravel										
(OH-BT-1-A)	26.0 miles	asphalt										
(OH-RT-38)	3.0 miles	asphalt										
(OH-RT-40-C)	9.0 miles	asphalt										
(OH-RT-40-B)	12.0 miles	asphalt										
(OH-RT-40-A)	8.5 miles	asphalt										

Trail Name:	Vicinity:
Hamilton Bikeway	Hamilton (Neilen & Court to Forest Lake Ln (Joyce Park)
Harrison County Conotton Creek Trail	Bowerston to Jewett; trail follows Conotton Creek
Headwaters Trail	Mantua Mennonite Rd.) to Garrettsville (State Route 88 & Village Park Library)
Heritage Rail-Trail	Hilliard (Main & Center Streets) to Plain City (Cemetery Pike)
Hockhocking-Adena Bikeway/Riverside Bikeway	Athens (State St. east of U.S. Route 33) to Nelsonville (Hocking Pkwy. & Hocking College)
Holmes County Rail-Trail	Holmes-Knox Co. Line (U.S. Route 62) to Millersburg to Holmes-Wayne Co. Line (C-192 Rd.)
Huron River Greenway	Huron (River Rd. south of State Route 2 to Mason Rd.)
Interstate-480 Bikeway	North Olmsted (Stearns Rd. to Great Northern Blvd.); trail parallels Interstate 480.
Interstate-670 Bikeway	Columbus (Cleveland Ave./State Route 3 to Airport Dr.); trail parallels Interstate-670.
Kauffman Avenue Bike Path	Fairborn (Wright Brothers Memorial near National Rd. to Central & Wright Avenues); trail parallels Kauffman Ave.
Kokosing Gap Trail	Mt. Vernon (Liberty St.) to Danville (Washington & Richards Streets)
Lake Metroparks Greenway Trail	Painesville (U.S. Route 20/Mentor Ave. to Painesville-Ravenna Rd.)
Lester Rail-Trail	Lester (State Route 252) to Medina (Abbeyville Rd.)
Lewis Trail	Wilberforce (Bike Route 4 to Central State University on U.S. Route 42)
Little Miami Scenic Trail/Bike Route 1	Milford (U.S. Route 50 & State Route 125) to Xenia (Miami Ave.) to Springfield (Jefferson & Center Streets)

Map:	Trail Length:	Surface	🚲	🚵	🐎	🛼	🛶	🚶	♿	⛷	🔭	$
(OH-BT-1-C)	3.6 miles	asphalt	●	●		●		●	●	●		
(OH-RT-42)	11.4 miles	asphalt	●	●		●		●	●	●		
(OH-RT-26)	7.0 miles	smooth crushed gravel	●	●				●	●	●		
(OH-RT-18)	6.5 miles	asphalt	●	●	●	●		●	●	●		
(OH-RT-23)	16.5 miles	asphalt	●	●		●		●	●	●		
(OH-RT-33)	29.0 miles	asphalt & smooth crushed gravel	●	●	●	●		●	●	●		
(OH-RT-35)	12.8 miles (trail incomplete)	smooth crushed gravel	●	●				●	●	●		
(OH-BT-4)	3.0 miles	asphalt	●	●		●		●	●	●		
(OH-RT-12)	3.0 miles	asphalt	●	●		●		●	●	●		
(OH-RT-11-B)	4.0 miles	asphalt & concrete	●	●		●		●	●	●		
(OH-RT-9)	13.2 miles	asphalt	●	●		●		●	●	●		
(OH-RT-47)	4.5 miles	asphalt	●	●	●	●		●	●	●		
(OH-RT-27))	3.2 miles	smooth crushed gravel	●	●	●	●		●	●	●		
(OH-RT-41)	0.8 miles	asphalt	●	●		●		●	●	●		
(OH-RT-6)	68.0 miles	asphalt with parallel dirt	●	●	●	●		●	●	●		

Trail Name:	Vicinity:
Lunken Airport Bike Path	Cincinnati (Circular trail around Lunken Airport following both Wilmer Ave. & Little Miami River)
Mad River Recreation Trail (Bike Route 8)	Dayton (Webster St. to Eastwood Metropark & Springfield Pike)
Miami & Erie Canal Towpath Trail	Providence (U.S. Route 24 & Jeffers Rd.) to Waterville (U.S. Route 24 & River Rd.)
Mohican Valley Trail	Danville (North St.) to Knox-Holmes County Line (U.S. Route 62)
Muskingum Recreational Trail	Ellis (Ellis Dam Rd. to Muskingum River Trestle) Dresden (Rock Cut Rd. to Main St.)
National Road Bikeway	St. Clairsville (State Route 9 & 278 to 435 & Baseball Fields)
Nickelplate Trail	Louisville (S. Chapel St & Ravenna Ave. to Dellbrook & Belfort Avenues)
North Coast Inland Bike Path	Fremont (St. Joseph & East Side Park) to Clyde (Maple St.) Kipton (Baird Rd.) to Elyria (2nd & 3rd Streets)
Ohio to Erie Trail	Cincinnati to Columbus to Cleveland
Olentangy/Lower Scioto Bikeways (Bike Route 47)	Columbus (Interstate-71 & State Route 104/Frank Rd.) to Worthington (W. Wilson Bridge Rd.); trail follows both the Scioto & Olentangy Rivers.
Piqua Activity Trail for Health (P.A.T.H.)	Piqua (Spiker Rd. to Troy-Sidney Rd.)
Richland B & O Trail	Mansfield (6th St. & Rowland in North Lake Park to Butler (State Routes 95 & 97)
Simon-Kenton Trail	Urbana (State Route 55) to Cedar Swamp (Woodburn Rd.)

Map:	Trail Length:	Surface	🚴	🚵	🐎	🛼	🏊	🚶	♿	⛷	🔭	$
(OH-BT-6)	5.0 miles	asphalt										
(OH-RT-11-A)	2.9 miles	asphalt										
(OH-BT-5)	10.1 miles	dirt (mostly), concrete, gravel & smooth crushed gravel										
(OH-RT-32)	4.6 miles	smooth crushed gravel										
(OH-RT-8-B)	0.5 miles 4.5 miles	asphalt										
(OH-RT-28)	2.5 miles	asphalt										
(OH-RT-13)	1.5 miles	asphalt										
(OH-RT-19)	6.4 miles 13.1 miles	asphalt										
(OH-RT-25)	450.0 miles when complete	asphalt & smooth crushed gravel										
(OH-RT-1)	20.2 miles	asphalt & concrete										
(OH-RT-45)	5.5 miles	asphalt										
(OH-RT-21)	18.3 miles	asphalt										
(OH-RT-44)	2.0 miles	asphalt										

Trail Name:	Vicinity:
Sippo Valley Trail	Dalton (N Freet St.) to Massillon (W 6th St. & Water)
Slippery Elm Trail	Bowling Green (Maple St.) to North Baltimore (Broadway)
Stavich Bicycle Trail	Lowellville, OH (State Route 289/Wood St.) to New Castle, PA (Washington St.)
Stillwater River Recreation Trail (Bike Route 7)	Dayton (Helena St. & Island Park to Shoup Mill Rd. & Sinclair Park)
Towners Woods Rail-Trail	Kent (Towner's Woods Park on Rockwell Rd. & Ravenna Rd.) to Ravenna (Redbrush Rd.)
Towpath Trail (Ohio & Erie Canal)	Navarre (Hudson Dr.) to Cleveland (Harvard. Ave.); certain sections are complete Navarre Navarre to Massillon Massillon to Clinton Summit Lake Park to Akron Akron Akron to Cleveland
Tri-County Triangle Trail	Washington C.H. (Court & Water Streets) to Chillicothe (Poplar St.); trail is incomplete: Washington, C.H. Frankfort to Anderson Chillicothe
University-Parks Hike-Bike Trail	Toledo (Secor Rd. & Toledo University to King Road)
Wabash Cannonball Trail	Maumee to Liberty & Maumme to Montpelier: Oak Openings Metropark White House
Westerville Bikeway	Westerville (State Route 3/State St. to Maxtown Rd.)
Wolf Creek Recreation Trail (Bike Route 38)	Trotwood (Olive Rd.) to Verona (Preble County Line Rd. & Montgomery-Preble County Line)
Zanes Landing Trail	Zanesville (Market St. to Park & north city limits on State Route 666)

Map:	Trail Length:	Surface	🚲	⛸	🐎	🛷	✈	🚶	♿	⛷	🏍	$
(OH-RT-34)	9.0	asphalt & smooth crushed gravel										
(OH-RT-20)	12.0 miles	asphalt with parallel dirt										
(OH-RT-5 / PA-RT-10)	11.0 miles	asphalt										
(OH-BT-1-B)	3.0 miles	asphalt										
(OH-RT-39)	1.2 miles	smooth crushed gravel										
(OH-BT-3)												
	1.0 miles	smooth crushed gravel										
	4.0 miles											
	15.0 miles											
	1.0 miles	asphalt & concrete										
	0.5 miles	concrete smooth crushed gravel										
	34.0 miles											
(OH-RT-29)		asphalt										
	1.0 miles											
	7.0 miles											
	2.3 miles											
(OH-RT-15)	6.2 miles	asphalt										
(OH-RT-17)	65.0 miles (trail incomplete)	asphalt										
	3.5 miles											
	1.0 miles											
(OH-RT-30)	2.3 miles	asphalt										
(OH-RT-14)	13.0 miles	asphalt										
(OH-RT-8-A)	3.0 miles	asphalt										

Biking Oklahoma's Rail-Trails

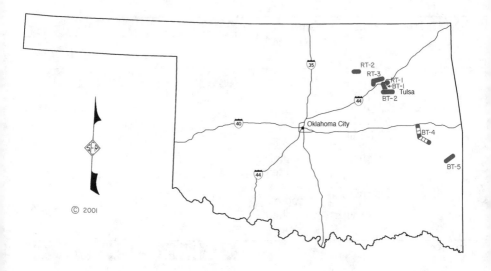

RT-2
RT-3
RT-1
BT-1
Tulsa
BT-2
Oklahoma City
BT-4
BT-5

© 2001

Trail Listings

OK-RT-1	Midland Valley Trail & River Parks Pedestrian Bridge
OK-RT-2	Cleveland Trail
OK-RT-3	Katy Trail
OK-RT-4	Indian Nations Recreation Trail
OK-RT-5	Old Frisco Trail
OK-BT-1	River Park Trail (Arkansas River)
OK-BT-2	Creek Turnpike Trail

Author Shawn E. Richardson takes a rest near the Midland Valley Trail & River Parks Pedestrian Bridge in Tulsa, Oklahoma.

Oklahoma Highlights

RIVER PARK TRAIL (ARKANSAS RIVER) (OK-BT-1)

This trail follows the Arkansas River through Tulsa. Attractions include downtown Tulsa's skyline and Riverside Drive Park. This trail connects to the Midland Valley Trail & River Parks Pedestrian Bridge (a former railroad trestle) and the Creek Turnpike Trail. From downtown Tulsa, streets can be followed for several blocks to reach the Katy Trail.

Oklahoma

Trail Name:	Vicinity:
Cleveland Trail	Cleveland (Jobo Rd.) to Osage (Arkansas River Bridge)
Creek Turnpike Trail	Jenks (Main St. Bridge) to Tulsa (U.S. Route 64/Memorial Dr.)
Indian Nations Recreation Trail	Warner Porum Stigler
Katy Trail	Tulsa (Denver Ave.) to Sand Springs (State Route 97 & Arkansas River)
Midland Valley Trail & River Parks Pedestrian Bridge	Tulsa (Cincinnati Ave. to Arkansas River)
Old Frisco Trail	Poteau to Wister
River Park Trail (Arkansas River)	Tulsa (Southwest Blvd.) to Jenks (Main St. Bridge)

Map:	Trail Length:	Surface
(OK-RT-2)	2.5 miles	asphalt
(OK-BT-2)	3.5 miles	asphalt
(OK-RT-4)	1.5 miles 1.5 miles 2.0 miles (will be 39.0 miles when complete & connected	asphalt
(OK-RT-3)	7.0 miles	asphalt
(OK-RT-1)	1.8 miles	asphalt
(OK-RT-5)	8.2 miles	smooth crushed gravel
(OK-BT-1)	8.7 miles	asphalt

Biking Oregon's Rail-Trails

Trail Listings

OR-RT-1	Fanno Creek Trail (Oregon Electric R.O.W. Trail & Linear Park)
OR-RT-2	Mill City Trail
OR-RT-3	Banks-Vernonia State Trail
OR-RT-4	Springwater Corridor Trail
OR-RT-5	Astoria River Trail
OR-RT-6	O.C. & E. Woods Line State Trail
OR-RT-7	Row River Trail
OR-BT-1	Columbia River Gorge Bikeway (Old U.S. Route 30)
OR-BT-2	Marine Drive Bike Path
OR-BT-3	Interstate-205 Bikeway
OR-BT-4-A	Bascom (Ruth) Riverbank Trail; North & East Bank (Willamette River Recreational Corridor Trail)
OR-BT-4-B	Bascom (Ruth) Riverbank Trail; West & South Bank (Willamette River Recreational Corridor Trail)
OR-BT-5	Interstate-84 Bikeway
OR-BT-6	Fort Stevens State Park Bike Paths

Oregon Highlights

BANKS-VERNONIA STATE TRAIL (OR-RT-3)

This trail opened in 1991 as Oregon's first rail-trail. It passes through mountains, fields and dense forests of northwestern Oregon, and also crosses several spectacular trestles. Eventually, the three sections will be joined to form a continuous 21 mile-long corridor.

COLUMBIA RIVER GORGE BIKEWAY (OLD U.S. ROUTE 30) (OR-BT-1)

This trail is a "highway-to-bikeway" conversion of old U.S. Route 30. Although most of this trail is shared with automobiles, the narrow sharp curves and speed limit enforcement keeps traffic down to 15-25 m.p.h. The scenery and attractions of the Columbia River Gorge include Shepperd's Dell, Mitchell Point, Horsetail Falls, Beacon Rock, the Vista House at Crown Point and the Maryhill Museum. The Mitchell Point tunnel is closed to automobiles, but not to trail users.

ROW RIVER TRAIL (OR-RT-7)

Opened in 1995, the Row River Trail traverses western Oregon near Interstate 5. The scenery consists of beautiful wooded hills and mountains near Row River and Dorena Lake. Highlights include the Mosby Creek covered bridge, Cerro Gordo, Dorena Dam, Row Point, Harms Park, Bake Stewart Park and Hawley Butte.

SPRINGWATER CORRIDOR TRAIL (OR-RT-4)

The east sections of this trail first opened in 1993. This scenic route traverses wetlands, buttes, farmlands, pastures, neighborhoods and industrial areas. Highlights include Tideman Johnson Nature Park, Bell Station, Beggars-Tick Wildlife Refuge, Powell Butte, Linneman Station, Cedarville Park and Gresham Main City Park.

Trail Name:	Vicinity:
Astoria River Trail	Astoria (Basin St. & U.S. Route 101/Marine Dr. to U.S. Route 30/Lief Erikson Dr. & 39th St.); trail follows the Columbia River.
Banks-Vernonia State Trail	Banks (Weed St. & Anderson Park) to Buxton (Pongratz Rd.) to Manning (Phil Rd. & Sell Rd.) to Vernonia (State Route 47 & West Fork Dairy Creek)
Bascom (Ruth) Riverbank Trail; North & East Bank (Willamette River Recreational Corridor Trail)	Eugene (Delta Hwy. & Green Acres to D St.)
Bascom (Ruth) Riverbank Trail; West & South Bank (Willamette River Recreation Corridor)	Eugene (Formac to Franklin Blvd.)
Columbia River Gorge Bikeway (Old U.S. Route 30)	Troutdale (NE Halsey St. & Historic Columbia River Highway) to The Dalles (U.S. Route 30 & U.S. Route 197); bikeway follows Historical U.S. Route 30 between mileposts 14 to 92
	Warrensdale to Cascade Locks (Mileposts 39.5 to 45.5)
	Hood River to Mosier (Mileposts 68.5 to 73.0)
Fanno Creek Trail (Oregon Electric R.O.W. Trail & Linear Park)	Tiagard (SW Scholls Ferry Rd.) to Beaverton (to Denney Rd.)
	Beaverton (SW 92nd Ave.) to Firlock (SW Oleson)
Fort Stevens State Park Bike Paths	Fort Stevens State Park (near Hammond)
Interstate-84 Bikeway	Portland (122nd Ave. to 182nd Ave.); bike path parallels Interstate-84.
Interstate-205 Bikeway	Portland, OR (State Route 213) to Vancouver, WA (State Route 14); bike path parallels Interstate-205
Marine Drive Bikeway	Portland (33rd to NE Sundial Rd. & Troutdale Airport); trail parallels Marine Dr.

Map:	Trail Length:	Surface
(OR-RT-5)	5.1 miles	asphalt & concrete
(OR-RT-3)	7.0 miles (Vernonia to Tophill), 1.5 miles (Buxton), & 4.0 miles (Manning to Banks)	asphalt
(OR-BT-4-A)	7.5 miles	asphalt
(OR-BT-4-B)	4.5 miles	asphalt
(OR-BT-1)		asphalt
	6.0 miles	
	4.5 miles	
(OR-RT-1)	2.5 miles	asphalt
	1.3 miles	asphalt
(OR-BT-6)	9.5 miles	asphalt
(OR-BT-5)	3.0 miles	asphalt
(OR-BT-3 / WA-BT-2)	16.9 miles	asphalt (parts follow streets)
(OR-BT-2)	12.4 miles	asphalt (parts follow streets)

Trail Name:	Vicinity:
Mill City Trail	Mill City (Linn Blvd. & SW 10th St. to NE Alder St.)
O.C. & E. Woods Line State Trail	Klamath Falls (Washburn Way to State Route 39)
Row River Trail	Cottege Grove (Main St.) to Culp Creek (Row River Rd.)
Springwater Corridor Trail	Portland (McLoughlin Blvd.) to Boring (Palmblad Rd.)

Banks-Vernonia State Trail

Map:	Trail Length:	Surface										
(OR-RT-2)	2.0 miles	asphalt & gravel										
(OR-RT-6-A)	4.0 miles	asphalt										
(OR-RT-7)	16.0 miles	asphalt & concrete										
(OR-RT-4)	16.8 miles	asphalt										

Pedestrians as well as cyclists can enjoy the Springwater Corridor Trail.

Biking Pennsylvania's Rail-Trails

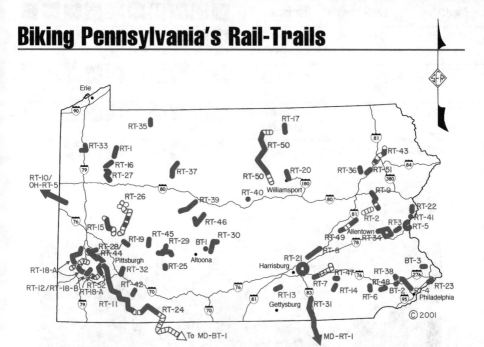

Trail Listings

PA-RT-1	Oil Creek State Park Trail
PA-RT-2	Switchback Railroad Trail
PA-RT-3	Nor-Bath Trail (Bath-Allen Trail)
PA-RT-4	Schuylkill River Trail (Philadelphia to Valley Forge Bikeway)
PA-RT-5	Palmer Township Bike Path (National Trails Towpath Bike Trail)
PA-RT-6	Struble Trail
PA-RT-7	Conewago Trail
PA-RT-8	Stony Valley Railroad Grade Trail
PA-RT-9	Lehigh Gorge State Park Trail
PA-RT-10	Stavich Bicycle Trail
PA-RT-11	Youghiogheny River Trail
PA-RT-12	Arrowhead Trail
PA-RT-13	Cumberland County Biker-Hiker Trail
PA-RT-14	Lancaster Junction Trail
PA-RT-15	Butler-Freeport Community Trail
PA-RT-16	Justus (Samuel) Recreation Trail
PA-RT-17	Lambs Creek Hike & Bike Trail

PA-RT-18-A	Montour Trail; Coraopolis to Thompsonville
PA-RT-18-B	Montour Trail; Bethel Branch
PA-RT-19	Roaring Run Trail
PA-RT-20	Lycoming Creek Bikeway
PA-RT-21	Capital Area Greenbelt Trail
PA-RT-22	Plainfield Township Recreation Trail
PA-RT-23	Bristol Spurline Park Trail
PA-RT-24	Allegheny Highlands Trail
PA-RT-25	Mayer (Jim) Rivers Walk
PA-RT-26	Armstrong Trail
PA-RT-27	Allegheny River Trail
PA-RT-28	Three Rivers Heritage Trail
PA-RT-29	Ghost Town Trail
PA-RT-30	Lower Trail (Pennsylvania Mainline Canal Trail)
PA-RT-31	Heritage Rail-Trail County Park (York County Heritage Rail-Trail)
PA-RT-32	Five Star Trail
PA-RT-33	French Creek Recreational Trail (Ernst Bike Trail)
PA-RT-34	Ironton Rail-Trail
PA-RT-35	Warren-North Warren Bike-Hike Trail
PA-RT-36	Back Mountain Trail
PA-RT-37	Clarion River-Little Toby Creek Trail
PA-RT-38	Betzwood Rail-Trail
PA-RT-39	Clearfield to Grampian Rail-Trail
PA-RT-40	Duncan Trail
PA-RT-41	Forks Township Recreation Trail
PA-RT-42	Indian Creek Valley Hiking & Biking Trail
PA-RT-43	Lackawanna River Heritage Trail
PA-RT-44	Eliza Furnace Trail
PA-RT-45	Hoodlebog Trail
PA-RT-46	Houtzdale Line Trail
PA-RT-47	Lititz-Warwick Trailway
PA-RT-48	Chester Valley Trail
PA-RT-49	Kennedy (John F.) Walking Trail
PA-RT-50	Pine Creek Trail
PA-RT-51	Luzerne County Rail-Trail
PA-RT-52	Steel Valley Trail
PA-BT-1	Canoe Creek State Park Bike Paths
PA-BT-2	Valley Forge National Historic Park Bike Paths
PA-BT-3	Tyler State Park Bike Paths

Pennsylvania Highlights

ALLEGHENY HIGHLANDS TRAIL (PA-RT-24)
Opened in 1994, this trail follows the Casselman River and Flaugherty Creek. It winds through the Appalachian Mountains, passes through two tunnels and goes past a train station. When complete, this trail will connect to both the Youghiogheny River Trail and the Chesapeake & Ohio Canal National Historic Park Trail in Maryland.

CAPITAL AREA GREENBELT TRAIL (PA-RT-21)
This trail gets its name from its close proximity to Pennsylvania's Capitol Building. It follows the Susquehanna River through the center of Harrisburg, then loops around to the east side to connect with Wildwood Lake and Reservoir Park.

HERITAGE RAIL-TRAIL COUNTY PARK (YORK COUNTY HERITAGE RAIL-TRAIL) (PA-RT-31)
Abraham Lincoln rode the train to deliver the Gettysburg Address on this former railroad line. After his assassination, his body made the final journey on this same railroad line before he was taken home to Illinois. This trail in south-central Pennsylvania opened in 1994 and is the United States' only rail-trail with both an active railroad and a tunnel. Attractions include Glen Rock, Hanover Junction, Howard Tunnel and York's Colonial Courthouse. This trail connects to the 20 mile-long Northern Central Railroad Trail in Maryland, making the trails 40 miles long together.

MONTOUR TRAIL; CORAOPOLIS-THOMPSONVILLE (PA-RT-18-A)
Opened in 1990, this trail wraps around the western and southern parts of the Pittsburgh metropolitan area. Highlights include the Enlow Tunnel, McDonald Trestle, Cecil Park, the National Tunnel and Greer Tunnel. When complete, this trail will connect to both the Arrowhead Trail and the Steel Valley Trail.

OIL CREEK STATE PARK TRAIL (PA-RT-1)
This scenic trail opened as Pennsylvania's first rail-trail in 1975. It follows Oil Creek through the beautiful wooded mountains of Oil Creek State Park.

PINE CREEK TRAIL (PA-RT-50)

This trail follows Pine Creek through north-central Pennsylvania. Mountains, waterfalls and rocky outcroppings dominate the scenery. Attractions include canoeing, whitewater rafting and the town of Blackwell.

SCHUYLKILL RIVER TRAIL (PHILADELPHIA TO VALLEY FORGE BIKEWAY) (PA-RT-4)

Opened in 1978, this rail-trail follows the Schuylkill River through northwestern Philadelphia and surrounds. Attractions include Valley Forge National Historic Park, Riverfront Park in Norristown, historic Spring Mill, Schuylkill Center for Environmental Education, Manayunk Canal Towpath and Philadelphia's Art Museum.

THREE RIVERS HERITAGE TRAIL (PA-RT-28)

Opened in 1994, this trail gets its name from the confluence of the Ohio, Allegheny and Monongahela Rivers. This trail follows the north branch of the Ohio and Allegheny Rivers, offering a view of downtown Pittsburgh's skyline. Plans are to eventually connect this trail to both the Eliza Furnace Trail and the Steel Valley Trail.

VALLEY FORGE NATIONAL HISTORIC PARK BIKE PATHS (PA-BT-2)

This trail forms a loop around the battlefield site of the Valley Forge National Historic Park. Attractions include the National Memorial Arch, Washington's Headquarters and the Visitor Center where George Washington's war tent is on display.

YOUGHIOGHENY RIVER TRAIL (PA-RT-11)

The first ten miles of the Youghiogheny River Trail opened in 1986 near Ohiopyle. Today, the trail has grown to 71 miles traveling through the mountains of southwestern Pennsylvania. The north section of the trail follows the Youghiogheny River from McKeesport to Connellsville and the south section follows the Youghiogheny River from Connellsville to Confluence. Highlights include Cedar Creek County Park, Ohiopyle State Park and the Falling Water Home designed by Frank Lloyd Wright (north of Ohiopyle). Plans are to connect the trail segments through Connellsville and then connect the entire trail to the Allegheny Highland Trail in Confluence. Currently, this trail connects to the Steel Valley Trail in McKeesport.

Trail Name:	Vicinity:
Allegheny Highlands Trail	Confluence to Meyersdale
Allegheny River Trail	Franklin (Bredinsburg Rd.) to Brandon (T-385) & Kennerdell Tunnel
Armstrong Trail	Ford City Kittanning (U.S. Route 422) to Manorville (State Route 128)
Arrowhead Trail	Thompsonville (U.S. Route 19 & Valley Brook Rd.) to Library Junction (Brush Run just west of Library)
Back Mountain Trail	Luzerne (Perry Rd.) to Trucksville (Carverton Rd.); trail follows U.S. Route 309.
Betzwood Rail-Trail	Valley Forge National Historic Park (U.S. Route 422 & Trooper Rd. to Perkiomen Creek); trail roughly follows U.S. Route 422.
Bristol Spurline Park Trail	Bristol (Bath Rd. to Green Lane Rd. & Radcliffe St.)
Butler-Freeport Community Trail	Herman to Sarver (Sarver Rd.)
Canoe Creek State Park Bike Paths	Canoe Creek State Park (near Hollidaysburg)
Capital Area Greenbelt Trail	Harrisburg (loop trail follows Front St. to Wildwood Lake, Elmerton Ave., Herr St., Reservoir Park & Paxton St.)
Chester Valley Trail	Exton (U.S. Route 30 to U.S. Route 202)
Clarion River-Little Toby Creek Trail	Brockway (7th Ave. & Taylor Park) to Ridgeway (Water St.)
Clearfield to Grampian Rail-Trail	Clearfield (Chester St.) to Grampian (State Route 729 & South St.)
Conewago Trail	Elizabethtown (State Route 230 on southeast side of Conewago Creek to Prospect Rd. & Lancaster-Lebanon County Line)
Cumberland County Biker-Hiker Trail	Pine Grove Furnace State Park (Quarry Rd.) to Toland (Hunters Run Rd.)

Map:	Trail Length:	Surface	🚲	🚵	🐎	🛼	🏊	🥾	♿	⛷	🔭	$
(PA-RT-24)	21.0 miles	smooth crushed gravel	●	●	●			●	●	●		
(PA-RT-27)	15.0 miles	asphalt	●	●	●	●		●	●	●		
(PA-RT-26)	1.4 miles 1.0 mile	asphalt smooth crushed gravel	●	●	●	●	●	●	●	●		
(PA-RT-12)	3.8 miles	asphalt	●	●	●	●		●	●	●	●	
(PA-RT-36)	2.2 miles	smooth crushed gravel	●	●		●		●	●	●		
(PA-RT-38)	2.0 miles	asphalt, smooth crushed gravel & dirt	●	●			●	●	●	●		
(PA-RT-23)	2.5 miles	asphalt	●	●		●		●	●		●	
(PA-RT-15)	10.0 miles	smooth crushed gravel	●	●				●	●	●		
(PA-BT-1)	1.5 miles	smooth crushed gravel	●	●				●	●	●		
(PA-RT-21)	20.0 miles (2.0 miles rail-trail)	asphalt & gravel (parts follow streets)	●	●				●	●	●		
(PA-RT-48)	1.4 miles	smooth crushed gravel	●	●				●	●	●		
(PA-RT-37)	18.0 miles	smooth crushed gravel & cinders	●	●				●	●	●		
(PA-RT-39)	10.5 miles	smooth crushed gravel	●	●	●			●	●	●		
(PA-RT-7)	5.0 miles	smooth crushed gravel & cinders	●	●	●		●	●	●	●		
(PA-RT-13)	7.0 miles	smooth crushed gravel (parts follow railroad bed road)	●	●				●	●	●		

Pennsylvania

Trail Name:	Vicinity:
Duncan Trail	Bald Eagle State Forest
Eliza Furnace Trail	Pittsburgh (Parkway East & Grant St. to Schenley Park); trail follows north bank of Monongahela River
Five Star Trail	Greensburg (U.S. Route 119) to Youngwood
Forks Township Recreation Trail	Forks Township to Palmer Township
French Creek Recreational Trail (Ernst Bike Trail)	Meadville (U.S. Route 322/Smock Hwy.) to Watson Run (U.S. Route 19 north of Semerad Rd.)
Ghost Town Trail	Nanty Glo (State Route 271) to Dilltown (State Route 403) & White Mill (U.S. Route 422)
Heritage Rail-Trail County Park (York County Heritage Rail-Trail)	PA-MD State Line & New Freedom (State Route 851) to York (Pershing Ave.)
Hoodlebog Trail	Indiana (Oakland Ave.) to north of Graceton Coral (U.S. Route 119)
Houtzdale Line Trail	Ramey to Houtzdale
Indian Creek Valley Hiking & Biking Trail	Indian Head to Champion
Ironton Rail-Trail	Ironton (Main St.& North Whitehall Ballfields) to Coplay (Saylor Park Cement Industry Museum & Lehigh River) & Hokendauqua (Lehigh River & Hokendauqua Playground)
Justus (Samuel) Recreation Trail	Franklin (Bredinsburg Rd.) to Oil City (W. First St.)
Kennedy (John F.) Walking Trail	Pottsville (Laurel Blvd. to York Farm Rd.)
Lackawanna River Heritage Trail	Scranton (N 7th Ave to Elm St.)
Lambs Creek Hike & Bike Trail	Mansfield (U.S. Route 6) to Lamb's Creek Village (U.S. Route 15); trail follows U.S. Route 15
Lancaster Junction Trail	Landisville (State Route 283/Champ Rd.) to Lancaster Junction (Auction Rd.)

Map:	Trail Length:	Surface	Bicycling	Mountain Biking	Horseback Riding	Inline Skating	Snowmobiling	Hiking	Wheelchair Accessible	Cross-Country Skiing	ATV	$
(PA-RT-40)	1.8 miles	smooth crushed gravel	●	●		●		●	●	●		
(PA-RT-44)	4.0 miles	asphalt & smooth crushed gravel	●	●		●		●	●	●		
(PA-RT-32)	7.5 miles	asphalt & smooth crushed gravel	●	●				●	●	●		
(PA-RT-41)	7.0 miles	asphalt & gravel	●	●	●	●		●	●			
(PA-RT-33)	5.0 miles	smooth crushed gravel	●	●	●			●	●	●		
(PA-RT-29)	16.0 miles	smooth crushed gravel	●	●				●	●	●		
(PA-RT-31)	20.1 miles	smooth crushed gravel	●	●	●			●	●	●		
(PA-RT-45)	6.0 miles	asphalt	●	●		●		●	●	●		
(PA-RT-46)	10.5 miles	smooth crushed gravel & cinders	●	●	●			●		●		
(PA-RT-42)	5.0 miles	smooth crushed gravel	●	●				●	●	●		
(PA-RT-34)	9.0 miles	smooth crushed gravel & asphalt	●	●	●			●	●	●		
(PA-RT-16)	5.8 miles	asphalt	●	●	●	●		●	●	●		
(PA-RT-49)	1.2 miles	asphalt	●	●		●		●	●			
(PA-RT-43)	1.5 miles	smooth crushed gravel & gravel	●	●		●	●	●				
(PA-RT-17)	3.7 miles	asphalt	●	●		●		●	●	●		
(PA-RT-14)	2.3 miles	smooth crushed gravel & cinders	●	●	●			●	●	●		

Trail Name:	Vicinity:
Lehigh Gorge State Park Trail	Jim Thorpe (Coalport Rd.) to Glen Onoko (Bridge & River Access Area)
	Penn Haven Junction to Rockport (SR-4014) to White Haven (State Route 940 & White Haven Shopping Center)
Lititz-Warwick Trailway	Lititz (Oak St. to Clay Rd.)
Lower Trail (Pennsylvania Mainline Canal Trail)	The Town of Water Street (SR-4014 east of U.S. Route 22) to Williamsburg (State Route 866) to Canoe Creek State Park
Luzerne County Rail-Trail	Pittston (Old Forge to Wilkes-Barre)
Lycoming Creek Bikeway	Williamsport (Memorial Dr.) to Cogan Station (W Creek Rd.); trail follows U.S. Route 15
Mayer (Jim) Rivers Walk	Johnstown (State Route 403/Bridge St. to Michigan Ave.)
Montour Trail; Coraopolis-Thompsonville	Coraopolis (State Route 51 & Montour Rd.) to McDonald (State Route 980) Venice (State Routes 50 & 980) to Hendersonville (Morganza Rd. & Greer Tunnel) South Park (Brownsville Rd.) Snowden (Snowden Rd. to Gill Hall Rd.)
Montour Trail; Bethel Branch	Library (Washington-Allegheny County Line near McMurray Rd. to Logan & Irishtown Rd.)
Nor-Bath Trail (Bath-Allen Trail)	Jacksonville (State Route 329) to Howertown (Sauage Rd.)
Oil Creek State Park Trail	Petroleum Center (T-617 & T-599) to Titusville (T-602)
Palmer Township Bike Path (National Trails Towpath Bike Trail)	Bethlehem & Palmer Townships; South Easton (Chain Dam Rd. & Riverview Park) to Prospect Park (Freemansburg Hwy.) to Wilsonboro (Columbia & 27th Streets) & Wilsonboro (William Penn Highway & 25th St. to 25th St. south of Freemansburg Hwy.)
Pine Creek Trail	Ansonia to Waterville

Map:	Trail Length:	Surface
(PA-RT-9)	1.5 miles 17.5 miles	smooth crushed gravel
(PA-RT-47)	1.4 miles	asphalt
(PA-RT-30)	16.5 miles	smooth crushed gravel
(PA-RT-51)	1.8 miles	smooth crushed gravel
(PA-RT-20)	5.0 miles	asphalt
(PA-RT-25)	1.2 miles	smooth crushed gravel
(PA-RT-18-A)	17.5 miles 4.5 miles 1.5 miles 0.9 miles	smooth crushed gravel
(PA-RT-18-B)	2.1 miles	smooth crushed gravel
(PA-RT-3)	5.2 miles	smooth crushed gravel
(PA-RT-1)	9.7 miles	asphalt
(PA-RT-5)	7.8 miles	asphalt
(PA-RT-50)	41.0 miles	smooth crushed gravel

Trail Name:	Vicinity:
Plainfield Township Recreation Trail	Stockertown (Sullivan Trail Rd.) to Pen Argyl (Pen Argyl Rd.)
Roaring Run Trail	Apollo (Kiski Ave. & Canal Rd. to Roaring Run); trail follows the Kiskiminetas River)
Schuylkill River Trail (Philadelphia to Valley Forge Bikeway)	Philadelphia (Spring Garden St. Bridge) to Valley Forge National Historic Park (U.S. Route 422 & Valley Forge Rd.); trail follows Schuylkill River.
Stavich Bicycle Trail	Lowellville, OH (State Route 289/Wood St.) to New Castle, PA (Washington St.)
Steel Valley Trail	McKeesport (Monongahela Ave.) to Clairton (New England Rd.)
Stony Valley Railroad Grade Trail	Dauphin (five miles northeast of Dauphin on Stony Creek Valley Rd.) to Indiantown Gap (Goldmine Rd.)
Struble Trail	Downingtown (Norwood Rd. south of U.S. Route 30 to Dowlin Forge Rd); trail follows Brandywine Creek.
Switchback Railroad Trail	Summit Hill (State Route 902) to Jim Thorpe (U.S. Route 209 & Center St.)
Three Rivers Heritage Trail	Pittsburgh (West End Bridge to Washington's Landing Island); trail follows the north bank of the Ohio & Allegheny Rivers.
Tyler State Park Bike Paths	Tyler State Park (near Newtown)
Valley Forge National Historic Park Bike Paths	Valley Forge National Historic Park (Circular Route)
Warren-North Warren Bike-hike Trail	Warren (4th Ave.) to North Warren (U.S. Route 62); trail parallels U.S. Route 62 & Conewango Creek.
Youghiogheny River Trail	McKeesport to Connellsville
	Connellsville to Confluence

Map:	Trail Length:	Surface	🚲	🚵	🐎	⛸	➡	🚶	♿	🎿	🛶	$
(PA-RT-22)	6.7 miles	smooth crushed gravel & asphalt	●	●				●	●			
(PA-RT-19)	2.0 miles	smooth crushed gravel			●			●				
(PA-RT-4)	22.0 miles	asphalt (parts follow streets & park roads)	●	●		●		●	●			
(PA-RT-10 / OH-RT-5)	11.0 miles	asphalt	●	●		●		●	●			
(PA-RT-52)	4.0 miles	asphalt & smooth crushed gravel	●	●		●		●	●			
(PA-RT-8)	18.0 miles	smooth crushed gravel, cinders & dirt	●	●	●		●	●	●	●		
(PA-RT-6)	2.6 miles	asphalt	●	●	●			●	●			
(PA-RT-2)	15.0 miles	smooth crushed gravel, gravel, & ballast	●	●		●		●	●	●		
(PA-RT-28)	5.5 miles	asphalt & smooth crushed gravel	●	●		●		●	●	●		
(PA-BT-3)	8.5 miles	asphalt	●	●		●		●	●	●		
(PA-BT-2)	5.5 miles	asphalt	●	●		●		●	●	●		
(PA-RT-35)	3.0 miles	asphalt	●	●		●		●	●			
(PA-RT-11)	43.0 miles	smooth crushed gravel	●	●	●			●	●	●		
	28.0 miles	smooth crushed gravel										

Biking Rhode Island's Rail-Trails

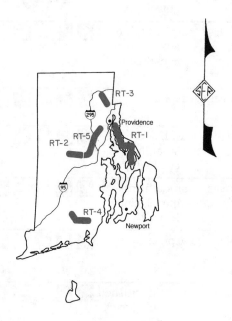

© 2001

Trail Name:	Vicinity:
Blackstone River Bike Path	Lincoln Area; Lonsdale (State Route 123/Front St.) to Quinnville (State Route 116/Washington Hwy.)
Coventry Greenway	Coventry Center (Town Farm Rd.) to Arctic (Read Ave.)
East Bay Bike Path	Bristol (Thames St. & Independence Park) to Providence (Washington Bridge & Gano St.)
South County Bike Path	West Kingston (Liberty Ln.) to Peacedale (High St.)
Washington Secondary Bicycle Path	Cranston to West Warwick

Trail Listings

RI-RT-1	East Bay Bike Path
RI-RT-2	Coventry Greenway
RI-RT-3	Blackstone River Bike Path
RI-RT-4	South County Bike Path
RI-RT-5	Washington Secondary Bicycle Path

Rhode Island Highlights

EAST BAY BIKE PATH (RI-RT-1)

This rail-trail opened in 1987 and is Rhode Island's first. It follows the east sides of the Providence River and Narragansett Bay and offers views of the Providence skyline. Highlights include Haines Park, Brickyard Pond, Bristol Harbor and Independence Park. On the north end, this trail crosses over the Providence River, giving trail users access to Providence, Rhode Island's capital.

Map:	Trail Length:	Surface										
(RI-RT-3)	3.5 miles	asphalt										
(RI-RT-2)	5.0 miles	asphalt & gravel										
(RI-RT-1)	14.5 miles	asphalt										
(RI-RT-4)	4.3 miles	asphalt										
(RI-RT-5)	4.5 miles	asphalt										

Biking South Carolina's Rail-Trails

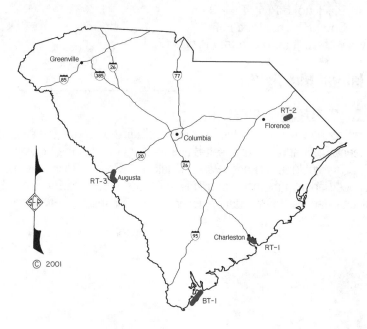

Greenville

85 385 26 77

RT-2
Florence

Columbia

20
26

RT-3 Augusta

95 Charleston
RT-1

© 2001

BT-1

Trail Name:	Vicinity:
Hilton Head Island Bike Paths	Hilton Head Island (most of the trail network follows U.S. Route 278)
Marion Hike & Bike Trail	Marion
North Augusta "Greeneway"	North Augusta (Detour Rd. & Railroad Ave. next to 13th St. Bridge to Pisgah Rd. & Five Notch Rd.
West Ashley Bikeway	Charleston (U.S. Route 17/Savannah Hwy. & Wappoo Rd. to State Route 61/Andrews Blvd.)

Trail Listings

SC-RT-1	West Ashley Bikeway
SC-RT-2	Marion Hike & Bike Trail
SC-RT-3	North Augusta "Greeneway"
SC-BT-1	Hilton Head Island Bike Paths

South Carolina Highlights

HILTON HEAD ISLAND BIKE PATHS (SC-BT-1)

Hilton Head Island is off the southeast edge of South Carolina. It is both a resort area and a tropical paradise. A network of bike paths, dating to the early 1970s, cross the northern two thirds of the island. The southern third of the island, which includes additional bike paths, South Beach and the famous Harbor Town Lighthouse are off-limits to non-residents.

NORTH AUGUSTA "GREENEWAY" (SC-RT-3)

The "Greeneway," named after former Mayor Thomas W. Greene, meanders from the upper wooded hills of North Augusta down to the riverfront of the Savannah. Highlights include Riverview Park, Crystal Lake, the golf course along the river and the Augusta, GA skyline across the Savannah River.

Map:	Trail Length:	Surface	🚲	🚵	🐎	🛼	✈	🚶	♿	⛷	🏍	$
(SC-BT-1)	11.0 miles	asphalt	🚲	🚵		🛼		🚶	♿			
(SC-RT-2)	0.3 miles	asphalt & dirt	🚲	🚵	🐎	🛼		🚶	♿			
(SC-RT-3)	5.2 miles	asphalt	🚲	🚵		🛼		🚶	♿			
(SC-RT-1)	2.0 miles	asphalt	🚲	🚵		🛼		🚶	♿			

Biking South Dakota's Rail-Trails

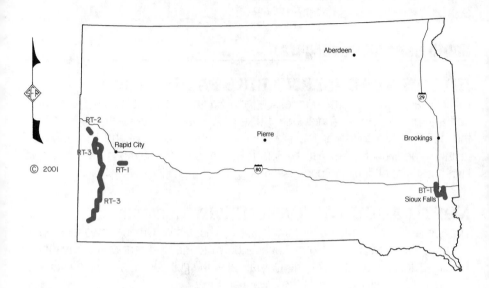

Trail Name:	Vicinity:
Mickelson (George S.) Trail	Edgemont (U.S. Route 18) to Custer (6th & Washington Streets) to Deadwood (U.S. Route 85/Charles St.)
Rapid City Recreational Path	Rapid City (State Route 44/Jackson Blvd. & Chapel Ln. to Cambell St.); trail follows Rapid Creek.
Spearfish Recreation Trail	Spearfish (Spearfish Canyon Rd. to Custer & 3rd Streets)
Yankton Trail	Sioux Falls: 60th St. N near the Airport to Interstate-229 & Western Ave. then to Southeastern Ave. Southeastern Ave. & 49th St. to Weber Ave. & Rice St.); both trail sections connect together.

Trail Listings

SD-RT-1	Rapid City Recreational Path
SD-RT-2	Spearfish Recreation Trail
SD-RT-3	Mickelson (George S.) Trail
SD-BT-1	Yankton Trail

South Dakota Highlights

MICKELSON (GEORGE S.) TRAIL (SD-RT-3)

This north-south trail is located in the Black Hills region of South Dakota. Spectacular trestles and four rock tunnels are part of the scenery. Attractions include Cicero Peak, Custer, Spring Creek, the Crazy Horse Monument, the railroad museum in Hill City, Custer Peak Lookout and several mining museums in Lead and Deadwood. Mount Rushmore is 11 miles east of Hill City on State Route 244.

Map:	Trail Length:	Surface
(SD-RT-3)	114.0 miles	smooth-coarse crushed gravel
(SD-RT-1)	7.2 miles	concrete & asphalt
(SD-RT-2)	2.8 miles	concrete (parts follow streets)
(SD-BT-1)	18.5 miles	asphalt

Biking Tennessee's Rail-Trails

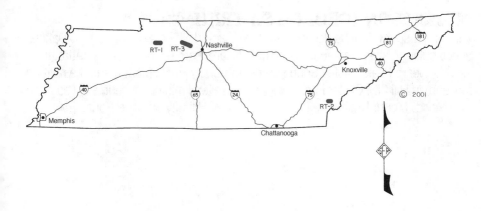

Trail Name:	Vicinity:
Cumberland River Bicentennial Trail	Ashland City (northwest end of town) to Sycamore Recreation Area; trail follows the north bank of the Cumberland River
Ligon (Betsy) Park & Walking Trail	Erin (McMillan & Hiett Streets to State Route 49/E Main & Elm Streets)
Tellico Plains Rail-Trail	Tellico Plains (Community Center); parallels Bank St.

Trail Listings

TN-RT-1	Ligon (Betsy) Park & Walking Trail
TN-RT-2	Tellico Plains Rail-Trail
TN-RT-3	Cumberland River Bicentennial Trail

Cumberland River Bicentennial Trail.

Map:	Trail Length:	Surface	🚲 🏍 🐎 🛼 🚣 🚶 ♿ 🏃 🛻 $
(TN-RT-3)	4.0 miles	asphalt, smooth crushed gravel & ballast	🚲 🏍 🐎 🛼 🚣 🚶 ♿ 🏃 🛻 $
(TN-RT-1)	2.0 miles	asphalt	🚲 🏍 🐎 🛼 🚣 🚶 ♿ 🏃 🛻 $
(TN-RT-2)	0.9 miles	asphalt	🚲 🏍 🐎 🛼 🚣 🚶 ♿ 🏃 🛻 $

Biking Texas's Rail-Trails

Trail Listings

TX-RT-1	Cargill Long Park Trail
TX-RT-2	Lake Mineral Wells State Trailway
TX-RT-3	Harrisburg-Sunset Rail-Trail (Houston, TX)
TX-RT-4	Katy Trail
TX-BT-1	Brazos Bend State Park Bike Path
TX-BT-2	Mckinney Falls State Park Bike Path
TX-BT-3	Ray Roberts Lake State Park Bike Path
TX-BT-4	Bachman Lake Park Trail
TX-BT-5	Crawford Park Trail
TX-BT-6	Fireside Park Trail
TX-BT-7	Glendale Park Trail
TX-BT-8	Phelps (John C.) Trail
TX-BT-9	Kiest Park Trail
TX-BT-10	Williams (Raymond W.) Hike & Bike Trail
TX-BT-11	Rochester Park Trail
TX-BT-12	White Rock Creek Trail
TX-BT-13	White Rock Lake Hike & Bike Trail

Texas Highlights

LAKE MINERAL WELLS STATE TRAILWAY (TX-RT-2)

In 1999, this trail opened in northeastern Texas and is currently the state's longest rail-trail. Mineral Wells, Lake Mineral Wells State Park, Garner and Weatherford are major attractions on this trail.

Trail Name:	Vicinity:
Bachman Lake Park Trail	Dallas (3500 W Northwest Highway)
Brazos Bend State Park Bike Path	Brazos Bend State Park
Cargill Long Park Trail	Longview (Marshall Ave. to Hollybrook Dr.)
Crawford Park Trail	Dallas (8740 Elam)
Fireside Park Trail	Dallas (8600 Fireside)
Glendale Park Trail	Dallas (1300 E Ledbetter)
Harrisburg-Sunset Rail-Trail (Houston)	Houston (Commerce St. & Mc Kee St. to Avenue R & Hidalgo Park)
Katy Trail	Dallas (3300 Harry Hines; follows east side of Turtle Creek)
Kiest Park Trail	Dallas (3012 South Hampton)
Lake Mineral Wells State Trailway)	Mineral Wells (U.S. Route 281) to Weatherford (Cartwright Park Rd.)
McKinney Falls State Park Bike Path	McKinney Falls State Park
Phelps (John C.) Trail	Dallas (3000 Tips)
Ray Roberts Lake State Park Bike Path	Ray Roberts Lake State Park
Rochester Park Trail	Dallas (3000 Rochester)
White Rock Creek Trail	Dallas (6900 Valley View)
White Rock Lake Hike & Bike Trail	Dallas (8300 Garland Rd.)
Williams (Raymond W.) Hike & Bike Trail	Dallas (Pentagon Pkwy.)

Map:	Trail Length:	Surface	🚴	🚵	🐎	🛼	➡	🚶	♿	⛷	🛶	$
(TX-BT-4)	3.1 miles	asphalt & concrete	●	●		●		●	●			
(TX-BT-1)	15.0 miles	smooth crushed gravel	●	●				●				
(TX-RT-1)	3.0 miles	asphalt	●	●		●		●	●			
(TX-BT-5)	2.1 miles	asphalt	●	●		●		●	●			
(TX-BT-6)	1.2 miles	concrete	●	●		●		●	●			
(TX-BT-7)	1.7 miles	asphalt	●	●		●		●	●			
(TX-RT-3)	5.9 miles	asphalt (parts follow streets)	●	●	●	●		●	●			
(TX-RT-4)	4.0 miles	concrete	●	●		●		●	●			
(TX-BT-9)	2.4 miles	asphalt	●	●		●		●	●			
(TX-RT-2	22.0 miles	asphalt & smooth crushed gravel	●	●	●			●	●	●		$
(TX-BT-2)	3.0 miles	asphalt	●	●		●		●	●			
(TX-BT-8)	1.3 miles	asphalt	●	●		●		●	●			
(TX-BT-3)	2.5 miles	concrete	●	●		●		●	●			
(TX-BT-11)	3.5 miles	concrete	●	●		●		●	●			
(TX-BT-12)	7.5 miles	asphalt	●	●		●		●	●			
(TX-BT-13)	11.8 miles	asphalt	●	●		●		●	●			
(TX-BT-10)	0.9 miles	asphalt	●	●		●		●	●			

Biking Utah's Rail-Trails

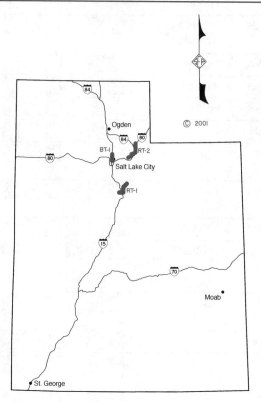

Trail Name:	Vicinity:
Historic Union Pacific Rail-Trail State Park	Park City (Bonanza Dr.) to Coalville (200 North)
Provo Jordan River Parkway Trail	Provo (Center St. in Utah Lake State Park) to Provo Canyon (Vivian Park on U.S. Route 189 & South Fork Rd.); trail mostly follows the Provo River & University Ave.
Provo River Bike Path (Salt Lake City)	Salt Lake City (1700 South to 700 North); trail follows the Jordan River)

Trail Listings

Utah Highlights

HISTORIC UNION PACIFIC RAIL-TRAIL STATE PARK (UT-RT-2)

This trail opened in 1993 and mostly follows Interstate 80 through the Rocky Mountains east of Salt Lake City. Part of this trail follows the Mormon Trail. The scenery along this trail consists of desert and scrublands. Highlights include Park City, Jordanelle Reservoir, Star Pointe, Wanship, Coalville and Echo Reservoir.

Map:	Trail Length:	Surface										
(UT-RT-2)	21.0 miles	smooth crushed gravel & asphalt										
(UT-RT-1)	15.1 miles	asphalt										
(UT-BT-1)	4.0 miles (some sections incomplete)	asphalt										

Biking Vermont's Rail-Trails

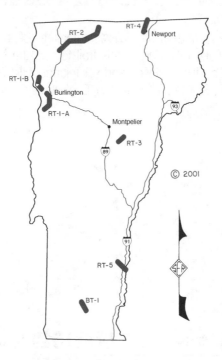

Trail Listings

VT-RT-1-A	Burlington Bike Path
VT-RT-1-B	Causeway Park Rail-Trail
VT-RT-2	Missisquoi Valley Rail-Trail
VT-RT-3	Graniteville Trails
VT-RT-4	Beebe Spur Recreation Trail
VT-RT-5	Toonerville Trail (Springfield Trail)
VT-BT-1	Valley Trail

Vermont Highlights

BEEBE SPUR RECREATION TRAIL (VT-RT-4)
Opened in 1999, this trail offers spectacular views of Lake Memphremagog. Although this is Vermont's fourth rail-trail, it is the nation's first rail-trail to touch an international border (Vermont, U.S.A. and Quebec, Canada). Some day, this trail may link to "La Route Verte" bike route system in the Canadian provinces.

BURLINGTON BIKE PATH (VT-RT-1-A)
Opened in 1986, this is Vermont's first rail-trail. The north-south trail mostly follows the Lake Champlain coastline through the center of Burlington. Features along this trail include Oakledge Park, Roundhouse Point, Perking Pier, College Street, Leddy Park, Bike Path Beach and the Winooski River. On the other side of the Winooski River, this trail continues north as the Causeway Park Rail-Trail.

MISSISQUOI VALLEY RAIL-TRAIL (VT-RT-2)
Opened in 1995, this trail follows the Missisquoi River through the northwestern region of Vermont. The scenery along the trail consists of farmlands, forests, meadows and wetlands. Highlights include St. Albans, Sheldon Springs, Enosburg Falls, East Berkshire and Richford.

Vermont

Trail Name:	Vicinity:
Beebe Spur Recreation Trail	Newport (State Route 5/N. Derby Rd. & Prouty Dr.) to USA-Canada Border (near John's River & Lake Memphregog)
Burlington Bike Path	Burlington (Austin Dr. to North Ave. & Winooski River)
Causeway Park Rail-Trail	Colchester (Airport Park on Colchester Point Rd. to Lake Champlain)

Lake Champlain to South Hero on Grand Isle (U.S. Route 2); a 200 foot gap exists in Lake Champlain |
Graniteville Trails	Websterville to Graniteville
Missisquoi Valley Rail-Trail	St. Albans City (U.S. Route 7 & State Route 105) to Richford (State Route 105/Troy St.)
Toonerville Trail (Springfield Trail)	Springfield (U.S. Route 11 behind Robert S. Jones Industrial Center) to Connecticut River (U.S. Routes-5 & 11)
Valley Trail	West Dover to Mount Snow Resort; trail roughly follows State Route 100

Map:	Trail Length:	Surface	🚲 🛴 🐎 🛼 🏊 🚶 ♿ ⛷ 🏍 $
(VT-RT-4)	4.0 miles	smooth crushed gravel	
(VT-RT-1-A)	7.6 miles	asphalt	
(VT-RT-1-B)	3.2 miles	smooth crushed gravel	
	1.0 mile		
(VT-RT-3)	1.4 miles	asphalt & ballast	
(VT-RT-2)	26.4 miles	smooth-coarse crushed gravel	
(VT-RT-5)	3.0 miles	asphalt	
(VT-BT-1)	5.0 miles	smooth crushed gravel & asphalt	

Biking Virginia's Rail-Trails

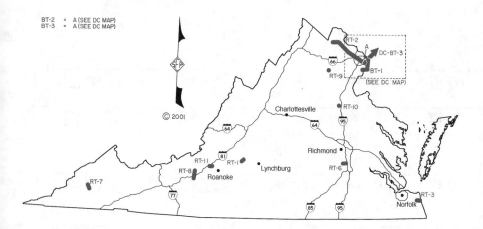

UNMAPPED TRAILS
RT-4 = A (SEE DC MAP)
RT-5 = BT-I (SEE DC MAP)

BT-2 = A (SEE DC MAP)
BT-3 = A (SEE DC MAP)

RT-2

A

DC-BT-3

66

BT-I

RT-9

(SEE DC MAP)

RT-IO

© 2001

Charlottesville

64

64

95

Richmond

RT-II

81

RT-I

Lynchburg

RT-6

RT-8

Roanoke

RT-7

77

85

95

RT-3

Norfolk

Trail Listings

VA-RT-1	Blackwater Creek Trail
VA-RT-2	Washington & Old Dominion (W. & O. D.) Railroad Regional Park Trail
VA-RT-3	Park Connector Bikeway
VA-RT-4	Bluemont Junction Trail
VA-RT-5	Orange & Alexandria Historical Trail
VA-RT-6	Chester Linear Park Trail
VA-RT-7	Guest River Gorge Trail
VA-RT-8	Huckleberry Trail
VA-RT-9	Warrenton Branch Greenway
VA-RT-10	Virginia Central Railway Trail
VA-RT-11	Hanging Rock Battlefield Trail
VA-BT-1	Mt. Vernon Trail
VA-BT-2	Custis Trail (Includes Interstate-66 Bikeway)
VA-BT-3	Four-Mile Run Trail (Includes Wayne F. Anderson Bikeway)

Virginia Highlights

MT. VERNON TRAIL (VA-BT-1)

Built in 1973, this trail follows the Potomac River from Washington, D.C. to Mount Vernon. Attractions along this trail include the Washington, D.C. skyline, the National Airport, Daingerfield Island, historic Alexandria, Dyke Marsh, Fort Hunt Park and Mount Vernon, which was President George Washington's home on the Potomac River. This trail connects to the Custis Trail, Four-Mile Run Trail, Orange and Alexandria Historic Trail and the Potomac River and Reflection Pool Bike Paths in Washington, D.C.

Virginia

Trail Name:	Vicinity:
Blackwater Creek Trail	Lynchburg
Bluemont Junction Trail	Arlington (Wilson Blvd. & N Manchester St. to State Route 237/Washington Blvd. & N Glebe Rd.)
Chester Linear Park Trail	Chester (State Route 10 to McAllister Dr.)
Custis Trail (Includes Interstate-66 Bikeway)	Arlington, VA (Patrick Henry Drive) to Washington, D.C.
Four-Mile Run Trail (Includes Wayne F. Anderson Bikeway)	Arlington (North Patrick Henry Dr. to Interstate-395)
Guest River Gorge Trail	Four miles south of Coeburn (State Route 72 & Access Road to trail); trail follows the Guest River
Hanging Rock Battlefield Trail	Salem to Hanging Rock
Huckleberry Trai	Blacksburg (Clay St.) to Christainsburg (NRV Mall on U.S. Route 460/N. Franklin St. & State Route 114)I
Mt. Vernon Trail	Washington, D.C. (Arlington Memorial Bridge) to Alexandria, VA (mostly Union & Green Streets) to Mt. Vernon, VA (George Washington's home on the Potomac River); trail follows George Washington Memorial Pkwy.
Orange & Alexandria Historical Trail	Alexandria (Wilkes St.; Union St. to Royal St.); trail is part of a bike route which follows streets
Park Connector Bikeway	Virginia Beach (follows Independence Blvd.)
Virginia Central Railway Trail	Spotsylvania (Salem Church Rd. to Gordon Rd.)
Warrenton Branch Greenway	Warrenton (4th St.)
Washington & Old Dominion (W. & O. D.) Railroad Regional Park Trail	Arlington (Shirlington Dr.) to Leesburg (U.S. Route 15/King St.) To Purcellville (21st St. & East St.)

Map:	Trail Length:	Surface	🚲	🛼	🐴	👶	✈	🚶	♿	⛷	🔭	$
(VA-RT-1)	18.0 miles	asphalt & gravel										
(VA-RT-4)	1.3 miles	asphalt										
(VA-RT-6)	1.0 mile	smooth-coarse crushed gravel										
(VA-BT-2)	5.8 miles	asphalt										
(VA-BT-3)	6.5 miles	asphalt										
(VA-RT-7)	5.8 miles	smooth crushed gravel (1.5 miles)										
(VA-RT-11)	1.6 miles	smooth crushed gravel & gravel										
(VA-RT-8)	5.8 miles	asphalt										
(VA-BT-1)	18.0 miles	asphalt (parts follow streets										
(VA-RT-5)	0.2 miles	asphalt										
(VA-RT-3)	4.9 miles	asphalt										
(VA-RT-10)	0.8 miles	asphalt										
(VA-RT-9)	1.5 miles	asphalt										
(VA-RT-2)	45.0 miles	asphalt & smooth crushed gravel										

Biking Washington's Rail-Trails

UNMAPPED TRAILS
RT-2 = A   RT-13 = C   BT-5 = RT-1 & B
RT-3 = B   RT-16 = D   BT-8 = BT-7
RT-5 = C   RT-17 = D   BT-9 = C
RT-7 = B   RT-19 = C
RT-9 = D   RT-20 = RT-4
RT-11 = C   RT-34 = RT-4

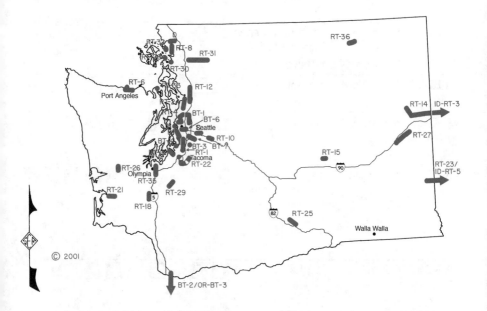

Trail Listings

WA-RT-1-A	King County Interurban Trail
WA-RT-1-B	Interurban Trail
WA-RT-2	Elliot Bay Trail (Myrtle Edwards Park Trail & Terminal-91)
WA-RT-3	Alki Trail (Seattle Waterfront Trail)
WA-RT-4	Burke-Gilman Trail
WA-RT-5	Preston-Snoqualmie Trail
WA-RT-6	Waterfront Trail (Port Angeles Waterfront Trail or Olympic Discovery Trail)
WA-RT-7	Duwamish Trail
WA-RT-8	Whatcom County & Bellingham Interurban Trail
WA-RT-9	South Bay Trail
WA-RT-10	North Bend-Tanner Trail (Northwest Timber Trail)
WA-RT-11	Corridor Trail
WA-RT-12	Snohomish-Arlington Centennial Trail
WA-RT-13	Rainer Multiple Use Trail (Issaquah Trail)
WA-RT-14	Spokane River Centennial Trail
WA-RT-15	Neppel Landing Trail
WA-RT-16	Lower Padden Creek Trail (Lanabee Trail)
WA-RT-17	Railroad Trail (Scudder Pond Trail)
WA-RT-18	Woodard Bay Trail
WA-RT-19	Snoqualmie Centennial Trail
WA-RT-20	Ship Canal Trail
WA-RT-21	Willapa Hills State Trail (Raymond to Southbend Riverfront Trail)
WA-RT-22	Foothills Trail
WA-RT-23	Palouse (Bill Chipman) Trail
WA-RT-24	Everett-Shoreline Interurban Trail
WA-RT-25	Lower Yakima Valley Pathway
WA-RT-26	Sylvia Creek Forestry Trail
WA-RT-27	Columbia Plateau Trail
WA-RT-28	Thompson (Tommy) Parkway Trail
WA-RT-29	Yelm-Tenino Trail
WA-RT-30	Burlington Rail-Trail
WA-RT-31	Cascade Trail
WA-RT-32	Dungeness River Bridge Trail
WA-RT-33	Scott (Larry) Memorial Trail
WA-RT-34	South Ship Canal Trail
WA-RT-35	Chehalis Western Trail
WA-RT-36	Republic Rail-Trail
WA-BT-1	Sammamish River Trail
WA-BT-2	Interstate-205 Bikeway

WA-BT-3	Soos Creek Trail
WA-BT-4	B. P. A. Trail
WA-BT-5	Green River Trail
WA-BT-6	Interstate-90 Bikeway
WA-BT-7	Cedar River Trail
WA-BT-8	Lake Washington Trail
WA-BT-9	Snoqualmie Ridge Trail
WA-BT-10	Commencement Bay Bike Path

Washington Highlights

BURKE-GILMAN TRAIL (WA-RT-4)
This rail-trail goes through northern Seattle, following the north bank of Lake Union and the west bank of Lake Washington. Highlights include Gas Works Park, Matthews Beach Park and the Tracy Owen Station. A view of the Seattle skyline, as well as a view of the *Sleepless in Seattle* house can be seen from the southwest bank of Lake Union across from Gas Works Park. On the north end, this trail connects to the Sammamish River Trail.

KING COUNTY INTERURBAN TRAIL (WA-RT-1)
Opened in 1972, this was Washington's first rail-trail. It runs north-south through southern King County, just south of Seattle. This trail passes through the cities of Pacific, Algona, Aubur, Kent and Tukwila. The scenery is mostly urban and suburban areas. The trail connects to the Green River Trail, giving users access into the southern neighborhoods of Seattle.

SAMMAMISH RIVER TRAIL (WA-BT-1)
This trail, combined with the Burke-Gilman Trail, forms a 24 mile crescent above Lake Washington from Seattle to Bothwell, Woodinville and Redmond. This trail follows the Sammamish River and goes through Northshore Athletic Fields, Sixty Acres Park and Marymoor Park, which has a veledrome race track for bicycles.

SNOHOMISH'S CENTENNIAL TRAIL (WA-RT-12)
Located in northwestern Washington, this north-south rail-trail opened in 1991. Scenery includes rolling farmlands, wetlands, wildlife and the peaks of the Cascade Mountains. Highlights along the trail include Monroe, Snohomish, Lake Stevens and Arlington.

SPOKANE RIVER CENTENNIAL TRAIL (WA-RT-14)

This trail follows the Spokane River through eastern Washington. Aside from Spokane, the scenery along this trail is mostly rural, offering views of the river and mountains. The section from Nine Mile Dam to Spokane is not a rail-trail and involves climbing hills; from Spokane to the Washington-Idaho state line, it is a gentle-grade rail-trail. Attractions include Riverside State Park, the Geologic Viewpoint, Spokane and Spokane Falls Community Colleges, Riverfront Park in Spokane, Gonzaga University, Minnehaha Rocks, Boulder Beach, Mirabeau Park, Walk-in-the-Wild Zoo, the Millstones, Greenacres, State Visitor Information Center and the Washington-Idaho state line. This trail connects to the North Idaho Centennial Trail, making the total length a continuous 63 miles.

The Burke-Gilman Trail in Seattle, Washington.

Trail Name:	Vicinity:
Alki Trail (Seattle Waterfront Trail)	Seattle (Alki Beach Park on 63rd Ave. SW to Lotus Ave. SW); trail follows both Alki & Harbor Avenues.
B. P. A. Trail	Federal Way (Panther Lake Park to Celebration Park on S 324th St. & to First Ave. S & 320th St.)
Burke-Gilman Trail	Seattle (8th Ave. NW & Leary Way NW) to Bothell (State Route 522 & Sammamish River)
Burlington Rail-Trail	Burlington (N. Regent St. to La Fayette Rd.)
Cascade Trail	Sedro-Woolley to Concrete
Cedar River Trail	Renton (Lake Washington & Cedar River Parking Area) to Cedar Grove (196th Ave. SE); trail follows the Cedar River.
Chehalis Western Trail	Lacey (103rd Ave. SE to Pacific Ave. SE)
Columbia Plateau Trail	Cheney (Fish Lake to Martin Rd. & Downs Lake)
Commencement Bay Bike Path	Tacoma (Ruston Way & N 49th St. to Schuster Pkwy. & S 9th St.); trail follows Commencement Bay.
Corridor Trail	Snoqualmie (Bruce St.) to Snoqualmie River
Dungeness River Bridge Trail	Sequim (Dungeness River to East Runnion Rd.)
Duwamish Trail	Seattle (Harbor Ave. & Don Armeni Park to West Marginal Place S & S 102nd St.); trail follows both W Marginal Way and the Duwamish River.
Elliot Bay Trail (Myrtle Edwards Park Trail & Terminal-91)	Seattle (Alaskan Way to W Galer St.)
Everett-Shoreline Interurban Trail	Everett to Mt. Lake Terrace

Map:	Trail Length:	Surface	🚲 🚵 🐎 ⛸ ✈ 🥾 ♿ ⛷ 🛻 $
(WA-RT-3)	4.2 miles	asphalt	
(WA-BT-4)	3.0 miles	asphalt	
(WA-RT-4)	14.1 miles	asphalt	
(WA-RT-30)	1.5 miles	smooth crushed gravel	
(WA-RT-31)	25.0 miles	asphalt & smooth crushed gravel	
(WA-BT-7)	8.0 miles	asphalt	
(WA-RT-35)	5.3 miles	asphalt	
(WA-RT-27)	24.0 miles	asphalt & smooth crushed gravel	
(WA-BT-10)	5.0 miles	asphalt	
(WA-RT-11)	0.4 miles	asphalt	
(WA-RT-32)	0.5 miles	asphalt & concrete	
(WA-RT-7)	9.4 miles	asphalt (parts follow streets)	
(WA-RT-2)	3.1 miles (two 1.5-mile trails)	asphalt	
(WA-RT-24)	8.5 miles	asphalt & gravel	

Foothills Trail	Puyallup (follows Puyallup River) McMillin (State Route 162 & Puyallup River) to South Prairie (trail follows State Route 162) & Buckley (trail follows State Route 165)
Green River Trail	Auburn (Brannan Park to North Green River Park) Kent (Horsehead Bend & 83rd Ave. SE to Tukwila (Cecil Moses Memorial Park on 102nd St. & Marginal Place S.); trail follows the Green River
Interstate-90 Bikeway	Seattle (12th Ave. S.) to Mercer Island (Island Creek Way) to Bellevue (118th Ave. SE & Mercer Slough Nature Park); trail follows Interstate-90
Interstate-205 Bikeway	Portland, OR (State Route 213) to Vancouver, WA (State Route 14); bike path parallels Interstate-205.
Interurban Trail (Snohomish County)	Edmonds (Lake Ballinger) to Everett
King County Interurban Trail	Pacific (3rd Ave. SE) to Kent (E. James St.) to Tuckwila (Interstate-405)
Lake Washington Trail	Renton (NE 7th St near Interstate-405) to New Castle (New Castle Beach Park near 118th Ave. SE & Interstate-405)
Lower Padden Creek Trail (Lanabee Trail)	Bellingham
Lower Yakima Valley Pathway	Sunnyside (Lower Yakima County Park); trail follows Yakima Valley Highway & Interstate-82
Neppel Landing Trail	Moses Lake (State Route 171/Broadway & Alder St.)
North Bend-Tanner Trail (Northwest Timber Trail)	North Bend (Railroad Depot) to Tanner (Tanner Rd.); trail follows Cedar Falls Way
Palouse (Bill Chipman) Trail	Moscow, ID to Pullman, WA
Preston-Snoqualmie Trail	Preston (87th Place near Interstate-90, Exit 22 to Snoqualmie Falls Overlook)

Code	Distance	Surface
(WA-RT-22)	0.5 miles 10.8 miles 2.0 miles	asphalt
(WA-BT-5)	1.0 mile 20.0 miles	asphalt (parts follow streets & roads)
(WA-BT-6)	8.0 miles	asphalt
(WA-BT-2 / OR-BT-3)	16.9 miles	asphalt (parts follow streets)
(WA-RT-1-B)	14.0 miles	asphalt
(WA-RT-1-A)	15.0 miles	asphalt (parts follow streets)
(WA-BT-8)	6.0 miles	asphalt (parts follow streets)
(WA-RT-16)	1.0 mile	smooth crushed gravel
(WA-RT-25)	6.3 miles	asphalt
(WA-RT-15)	0.5 miles	concrete
(WA-RT-10)	2.5 miles	asphalt & smooth crushed gravel
(WA-RT-23 / ID-RT-5)	7.5 miles	asphalt
(WA-RT-5)	6.2 miles	asphalt

Trail Name:	Vicinity:
Railroad Trail (Scudder Pond Trail)	Bellingham (E. North St. & King St. to Lake Whatcom on Electric Ave. & Northshore Ave.)
Rainer Multiple Use Trail (Issaquah Trail)	Issaquah (Gilman Blvd. to 2nd Ave.)
Republic Rail-Trail	Republic (State Route 21 & High School) to Sanpoil (Fairgrounds)
Sammamish River Trail	Bothwell (State Route 522 & the Burke-Gilman Trail over the Sammamish River) to Bellevue (Marymoor Park & West Lake Rd.)
Scott (Larry) Memorial Trail	Port Townsend (Boat St. to Cape George Rd.)
Ship Canal Trail	Seattle (Salmon Bay to Lake Union); trail follows the south side of the Ship Canal
Snohomish-Arlington Centennial Trail	Arlington to Snohomish-King County line
Snoqualmie Centennial Trail	Snoqualmie (trail parallels North Bend Blvd. N.)
Snoqualmie Ridge Trail	Snoqualmie (Trail parallels State Route 18)
Soos Creek Trail	Covington (Lake Meridian Park near State Route 516/SE 272nd St. to Gary Grant Soos Creek Park on SE 208th St.)
South Bay Trail	Bellingham (Mill Ave & 10th St. to Railroad Ave. & E Maple St.); trail follows State St.
South Ship Canal Trail	Seattle; follow Lake Washington Ship Canal (Fremont Bridge to 6th Ave. West)
Spokane River Centennial Trail	Spokane (Nine-mile Dam on Charles Rd. & Rutter Pkwy. to Downtown Spokane along Summit Blvd.) to WA-ID State Line next to Interstate-90
Sylvia Creek Forestry Trail	Montesano (Lake Sylvia north of Montesano)

Map:	Trail Length:	Surface
(WA-RT-17)	4.0 miles	smooth crushed gravel
(WA-RT-13)	2.0 miles	concrete
(WA-RT-36)	3.2 miles	asphalt & smooth crushed gravel
(WA-BT-1)	10.0 miles	asphalt
(WA-RT-33)	1.8 miles	smooth crushed gravel
(WA-RT-20)	0.8 miles	asphalt
(WA-RT-12)	17.0 miles	asphalt
(WA-RT-19)	0.5 miles	asphalt
(WA-BT-9)	3.5 miles	asphalt
(WA-BT-3)	4.0 miles	asphalt
(WA-RT-9)	4.0 miles	asphalt, concrete & smooth crushed gravel
(WA-RT-34)	0.5 miles	asphalt
(WA-RT-14)	39.0 miles	asphalt (parts follow streets & back roads)
(WA-RT-26)	2.3 miles	asphalt & dirt

Trail Name:	Vicinity:
Thompson (Tommy) Parkway Trail	Anacortes
Waterfront Trail (Port Angeles Waterfront Trail or Olympic Discovery Trail)	Port Angeles (Ediz Hook to Race St.)
Whatcom County & Bellingham Interurban Trail	Bellingham (Old Fairhaven Pkwy.) to Larrabee State Park & Clayton Beach (State Route 11/Chuckanut Dr.)
Willapa Hills State Trail (Raymond to Southbend Riverfront Trail)	Raymond (U.S. Route 101 & State Route 6) to South Bend (U.S. Route 101 & Jackson St.)
Woodard Bay Trail	Chehalis (Woodard Bay Natural Resource Conservation Area to Martin Way)
Yelm-Tenino Trail	Yelm to Rainer

Spokane River Centennial Trail.

Map:	Trail Length:	Surface	🚲	🚴	🐎	🛼	✈	🥾	♿	⛷	🔭	$
(WA-RT-28)	4.0 mile	asphalt										
(WA-RT-6)	5.8 miles	asphalt										
(WA-RT-8)	7.0 miles	smooth crushed gravel										
(WA-RT-21)	5.0 miles	asphalt										
(WA-RT-18)	6.0 miles	asphalt										
(WA-RT-29)	7.0 miles	asphalt										

The Seattle Skyline view along the Burke-Gilman Trail.

Biking West Virginia's Rail-Trails

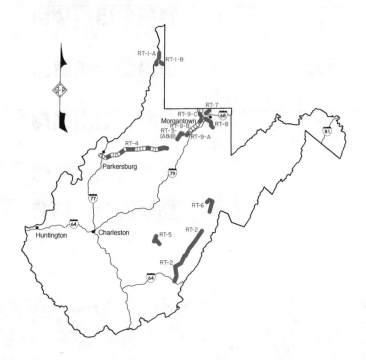

Trail Listings

WV-RT-1-A	Greater Wheeling Trail (North-South)
WV-RT-1-B	Greater Wheeling Trail (East-West)
WV-RT-2	Greenbrier River State Park Trail
WV-RT-3-A	Prickett's Fork Trail
WV-RT-3-B	West Fork River Trail
WV-RT-4	North Bend State Park Rail-Trail
WV-RT-5	Cranberry-Tri-Rivers Trail
WV-RT-6	West Fork Trail
WV-RT-7	Cheat Haven Trail
WV-RT-8	Deckers Creek Trail
WV-RT-9-A	McPark Trail (Marion County Trail)
WV-RT-9-B	Mon River Trail (South)
WV-RT-9-C	Caperton Trail

West Virginia Highlights

GREATER WHEELING TRAIL: EAST-WEST (WV-RT-1-B)
Opened in the late 1990s, this rail-trail follows Wheeling Creek through the Appalachian Mountains from downtown Wheeling to Elm Grove. Highlights include the Ohio River in downtown Wheeling, Wetzel's Cave and the curving brick railroad tunnel through east Wheeling. This trail connects to the Greater Wheeling Trail; North-South.

GREATER WHEELING TRAIL: NORTH-SOUTH
(WV-RT-1-A)
Opened in 1982 in northern West Virginia, this is the state's first rail-trail. It follows the Ohio River through the Appalachian Mountains from Wheeling to Pike Island Dam. Attractions include downtown Wheeling, the 1849 Wheeling Suspension Bridge, Wheeling Island and the Wheeling Waterfront Amphitheater. This trail connects to the Greater Wheeling Trail; East-West.

GREENBRIER RIVER STATE PARK TRAIL (WV-RT-2)
Opened in 1982, this is West Virginia's second and longest rail-trail. This trail follows the Greenbrier River through the Appalachian Mountains and farmland valleys. Attractions along the trail are Calvin Price State Forest, Watoga State Park, Marlington, Seneca State Forest, Cass Scenic Railroad State Park and two former railroad tunnels.

NORTH BEND STATE PARK RAIL-TRAIL (WV-RT-4)
This east-west rail trail opened during the 1990s and ranks number one out of all the nation's rail-trails for having the most former railroad tunnels. It has twelve tunnels, and the longest is 2,297 feet long. The Appalachian Mountains dominate the scenery; North Bend State Park is the major attraction. This trail is part of the American Discovery Trail.

Trail Name:	Vicinity:
Caperton Trail	Morgantown (White Park on U.S. Route 119) to Star City (Star City Riverfront Park on U.S. Route 19); trail follows Monongahela River
Cheat Haven Trail	Cheat Lake (Morgan Run Rd. off of County Route 857 to WV-PA State Line next to Cheat Lake Dam); trail follows east side of Cheat Lake
Cranberry-Tri-Rivers Trail	Monongahela Nation Forest Area (trail follows Cherry River & State Route 55 from Richwood to Gauley River; and Gauley River between Sara's Tunnel and Twin Streams Recreation)
Deckers Creek Trail	Morgantown (U.S. Route 119/University Ave. & Hazel Ruby McQuain Park) to Reedsville (Morgan Mine Rd.)
Greater Wheeling Trail: East-West	Wheeling (17th St.) to Elm Grove (Lava Ave)
Greater Wheeling Trail: North-South	Wheeling (Trail follows the Ohio River from 48th St. in south Wheeling to Pike Island Dam north of Wheeling)
Greenbrier River State Park Trail	North Caldwell (County Route 38/Stone House Rd.) to Cass Scenic Railroad Park (State Route 66)
McPark Trail (Marion County Trail)	Fairmont (State Route 73) to Pricketts Fort State Park
Mon River Trail (South)	Uffington (County Route 73) to Morgantown (White Park on U.S. Route 119); trail follows Monongahela River.
North Bend State Park Rail-Trail	Parkersburg to Walker: Walker to Eaton's Tunnel Cairo to North Bend S.P. Ellenboro to Pennsboro West Union to Smithburg Industrial to Wolf Summit

Map:	Trail Length:	Surface
(WV-RT-9-C)	5.9 miles	asphalt
(WV-RT-7)	4.5 miles	smooth crushed gravel
(WV-RT-5)	16.5 miles	smooth-coarse crushed gravel
(WV-RT-8)	18.8 miles	asphalt & smooth crushed gravel
(WV-RT-1-B)	4.0 miles	asphalt
(WV-RT-1-A)	8.5 miles	asphalt
(WV-RT-2)	77.6 miles	asphalt & smooth-coarse crushed gravel
(WV-RT-9-A)	2.0 miles	smooth crushed gravel
(WV-RT-9-B)	1.9 miles	smooth crushed gravel
(WV-RT-4)	72.0 miles 3.1 miles 3.1 miles 4.7 miles 2.9 miles 9.7 miles	ballast: smooth crushed gravel

Trail Name:	Vicinity:
Prickett's Fork Trail	Fairmont to Bricketts
West Fork River Trail	Fairmont & Norway (near US-Route 19/Chestnut Ave.) to Shinnston (U.S. Route 19); trail follows the West Fork River
West Fork Trail	Durbin to Bemis

Greater Wheeling Trail (East-West)

Map:	Trail Length:	Surface	🚴 🛼 🏇 🚂 ➡ 🚶 ♿ ⛷ 🏍 $
(WV-RT-3-A)	2.5 miles	smooth crushed gravel	🚴 🛼 🏇 🚂 ➡ 🚶 ♿ ⛷
(WV-RT-3-B)	16.0 miles	asphalt & smooth crushed gravel	🚴 🛼 🏇 🚂 🚶 ♿ ⛷
(WV-RT-6)	22.0 miles	asphalt & smooth crushed gravel	🚴 🛼 🏇 🚂 🚶 ♿ ⛷

One of the 12 tunnels along the North Bend State Park Trail.

Biking Wisconsin's Rail-Trails

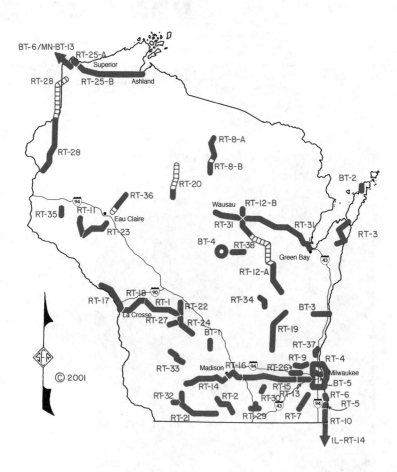

Trail Listings

WI-RT-1	Elroy-Sparta State Trail
WI-RT-2	Sugar River State Trail
WI-RT-3	Ahnapee State Trail
WI-RT-4	Oak Leaf Trail (Old-76 Bike Trail)
WI-RT-5-A	Racine County Bicycle Trail (North Shore Trail)
WI-RT-5-B	Racine County Bicycle Trail (Racine-Sturtevant Trail)
WI-RT-6	Racine County Bicycle Trail (M. R. K. Trail)
WI-RT-7	Racine County Bicycle Trail
WI-RT-8-A	Bearskin State Trail
WI-RT-8-B	Hiawatha State Trail
WI-RT-9	Bugline Recreation Trail
WI-RT-10	Kenosha County Bicycle Trail
WI-RT-11	Red Cedar State Trail
WI-RT-12-A	Wouwash State Trail (Oshkosh to Hortonville)
WI-RT-12-B	Wouwash State Trail (Split Rock to Aniwa)
WI-RT-13-A	New Berlin Recreation Trail
WI-RT-13-B	Waukesha Bike Trail
WI-RT-14	Military Ridge State Trail
WI-RT-15	Glacial Drumlin State Trail
WI-RT-16	Capital City State Trail
WI-RT-17	Great River State Trail
WI-RT-18	La Crosse River State Trail
WI-RT-19	Wild Goose State Trail
WI-RT-20	Pine Line Trail
WI-RT-21	Cheese Country Recreation Trail
WI-RT-22	Omaha Trail
WI-RT-23	Chippewa River State Trail
WI-RT-24	400 State Trail
WI-RT-25-A	Osaugie Trail
WI-RT-25-B	Tri-County Recreation Corridor Trail
WI-RT-26	Lake County Recreation Trail
WI-RT-27	Hillsboro State Trail
WI-RT-28	Gandy Dancer State Trail
WI-RT-29	Rock/Springbrook/Kiwanis Trails
WI-RT-30	Glacial River Trail
WI-RT-31	Mountain-Bay State Trail
WI-RT-32	Pecatonica State Trail
WI-RT-33	Pine River Recreation Trail
WI-RT-34	Mascoutin Valley State Trail
WI-RT-35	Wildwood Trail

WI-RT-36	Old Abe State Trail
WI-RT-37	Ozaukee Interurban Trail
WI-RT-38	Tomorrow River State Trail
WI-BT-1	Baraboo-Devils Lake State Park Trail
WI-BT-2	Sunset/Hidden Bluff Trails
WI-BT-3	Old Plank Road Trail
WI-BT-4	Green Circle Trail
WI-BT-5	Aaron (Henry) State Trail
WI-BT-6	U.S. Route 2 Duluth-Superior Bike Trail

Wisconsin Highlights

AHNAPEE STATE TRAIL (WI-RT-3)

Opened in 1973 in the northeastern peninsula of Wisconsin, this is the state's third rail-trail. It follows the Ahnapee River through farmland and wetland.

BEARSKIN STATE TRAIL (WI-RT-8-A)

In 1977, this trail opened in northern Wisconsin. Pine trees, lakes, colorful wetlands and plenty of wildlife set the trail's flavor.

CAPITAL CITY STATE TRAIL (WI-RT-16)

This trail winds through urban areas, suburbs and parks of Wisconsin's state capital right to the downtown area. Attractions include Dunns Marsh Park, Seminole Hills Park, Olin & Turville Park, Lake Monona, Ontario Park and the Wisconsin State Capitol Building. Eventually this trail will connect to both Military Ridge State Trail and Glacial Drumlin State Trail.

CHIPPEWA RIVER STATE TRAIL (WI-RT-23)

This east-west trail in northwestern Wisconsin opened in 1992. It follows the Chippewa River and passes from urban and suburban areas to rural settled farmland to wilderness and wetlands. Highlights include Eau Claire, Careyville, Meridean and the 800 foot-long trestle crossing over the Chippewa River to the Red Cedar State Trail.

ELROY-SPARTA STATE TRAIL (WI-RT-1)

In 1967, this trail became Wisconsin's first rail-trail. It goes through the unglaciated hills, valleys, farms and woodlands and Amish settlement of southwestern Wisconsin. This trail also goes through three former railroad tunnels; the longest is 3/4 mile long. In Elroy, this trail connects to both the 400 State Trail and Omaha Trail. In Sparta, it connects to the LaCrosse River State Trail.

GANDY DANCER STATE TRAIL (WI-RT-28)

Opened in 1995, this trail traverses northwestern Wisconsin. Scenery consists mostly of farmlands, woodlands and lakes. Highlights include St. Croix Falls, Frederic, Siren, Yellow Lake, Danbury and the St. Croix River on the Wisconsin-Minnesota state line.

GLACIAL DRUMLIN STATE TRAIL (WI-RT-15)

Opened in 1986, this trail traverses southeastern Wisconsin and connects the outside of Madison (Wisconsin's state Capital) to the outside of Milwaukee (Wisconsin's largest city). The terrain is gently rolling with a few hills on the east end; scenery is farmland and wetlands with plenty of wildlife. Highlights include Deerfield Community Park, Mills Wildlife Area, Rock Lake, the old train station headquarters in Lake Mills, Aztalan State Park and Pohmann Park.

GREAT RIVER STATE TRAIL (WI-RT-17)

This rail-trail, opened in 1988, follows the Mississippi River through southwestern Wisconsin. The scenery consists mostly of distant bluffs and rock outcroppings along the river. Attractions include the Upper Mississippi River Wildlife & Fish Refuge, Trempealeau Wildlife Area, Perrot State Park and Trempealeau National Wildlife Refuge. In La Crosse, this trail connects to La Crosse River State Trail.

MILITARY RIDGE STATE TRAIL (WI-RT-14)

Traversing southwestern Wisconsin, this trail opened in 1985. Scenery includes broad vistas, farmlands, wooded hillsides, glacial moraines and wildflowers. Attractions along the trail include Governor Dodge State Park, Blue Mounds State Park, Mounds View Park, Blue Mounds Caverns and the city of Madison. In Madison, this trail connects to the Capital City State Trail.

MOUNTAIN-BAY STATE TRAIL (DELLY TRAIL)
(WI-RT-31)
This trail takes its name from the small mountains near Wausau and the large Green Bay. Opened in 1996, it traverses northeastern Wisconsin and is the state's longest linear trail. Rolling dairy farm lands and woodlands dominate the scenery. Highlights include Norrie Lake, Stockbridge Indian Reservation, Shawano, Shawano Lake and the suburbs of Green Bay. In Eland, this trail connects to the northern section of the Wiouwash State Trail.

OAK LEAF TRAIL (OLD-76 BIKE TRAIL) (WI-RT-4)
This trail was originally started in 1939 as a circular 64-mile bikeway using lightly-traveled streets, roads and park roads around Milwaukee. Over the years, the trail slowly changed and grew longer; parts of the old route changed from roads to bike paths. First called the "Milwaukee 64," then the "Milwaukee 76," it is now known as the Oak Leaf Trail. Attractions are practically unlimited and include downtown Milwaukee, Lake Michigan and most of Milwaukee's parks and landmarks. In West Allis, this trail connects to the New Berlin Recreational Trail, taking trail users to Waukesha and Glacial Drumlin State Trail.

RED CEDAR STATE TRAIL (WI-RT-11)
Opened in 1981, this scenic rail-trail follows the Red Cedar River through north-western Wisconsin. Scenery varies from the wooded Red Cedar River Valley through Menomonie, Irvington and Downsville to a flood plain and Dunnville Wildlife Area on the south end. Here it crosses an 800-foot trestle over the Chippewa River and connects to the Chippewa River State Trail.

SUGAR RIVER STATE TRAIL (WI-RT-2)
This rail-trail, opened in 1972, is Wisconsin's second. The scenery consists of gently rolling hills, farms and wetlands in the Sugar River Valley. The main attraction along this route is New Glarus, a town settled by Swiss immigrants. The main street is built in Swiss architectural style. Other attractions along the way include Brodhead and New Glarus Woods State Park.

WILD GOOSE STATE TRAIL (WI-RT-19)
This trail in southeastern Wisconsin near Lake Winnebago opened in 1989. Farmlands and woodlands dominate the scenery. Attractions along the trail include Horicon National Wildlife Refuge and Horicon March Wildlife Area.

Bearskin State Trail.

Trail Name:	Vicinity:
Aaron (Henry) State Trail	Milwaukee (sections of trail follows Menomonee River from East Erie St. & Henry W Maier Festival Park to W Wells St. & Doyne Park)
Ahnapee State Trail	Casco Junction (Sunset Rd.) to Algoma (County Route-S)
	Algoma (County Route-M) to Sturgeon Bay (Neenah Ave.)
Baraboo-Devils Lake State Park Trail	Baraboo (State Route 123 & Walnut St.) to Devils Lake State Park (State Route 123 & County Route DL); trail follows State Route 123
Bearskin State Trail	Harshaw (County Route K) to Minocqua (west of U.S. Route 51)
Bugline Recreation Trail	Menomonee Falls (State Route 175/Appleton Ave.) to Merton (Main St.)
Capital City State Trail	Madison (U.S. Route 18/151 & County Route PD to Dempsey & Cottage Roads)
Cheese Country Recreation Trail	Mineral Point (Old Darlington Rd.) to Monroe (21st St.)
Chippewa River State Trail	Eau Claire (Short St.) to Red Cedar State Park Trail Mile 0-7 Mile 7-23
Elroy-Sparta State Trail	Elroy (State Route 71 & State Route 80/82/ 2nd St.) to Sparta (John St.)
400 State Trail	Reedsburg (Walnut St.) to Elroy (Cedar St.)
Gandy Dancer State Trail	St. Croix Falls (Pine St.) to Danbury & WI-MN State Line (State Route 77 & St. Croix River)
Glacial Drumlin State Trail	Cottage Grove (County Route N) to Waukesha (MacArthur Rd.)

Map:	Trail Length:	Surface	🚲	🛼	🐴	🚂	🏊	🚶	♿	⛷	🔭	$
(WI-BT-5)	7.0 miles (trail incomplete)	asphalt	●	●	○	●	○	●	●	●	○	○
(WI-RT-3)	12.4 miles / 15.3 miles	smooth crushed gravel	●	●	●	○	●	●	●	●	○	○
(WI-BT-1)	2.5 miles	asphalt	●	●	○	●	○	●	●	●	○	○
(WI-RT-8-A)	18.4 miles	smooth crushed gravel	●	●	●	○	●	●	●	○	○	●
(WI-RT-9)	12.2 miles	smooth crushed gravel	●	●	●	○	●	●	●	●	○	○
(WI-RT-16)	14.0 miles	asphalt	●	●	○	●	○	●	●	●	●	●
(WI-RT-21)	47.0 miles	smooth-coarse crushed gravel	●	●	●	○	●	●	●	●	●	●
(WI-RT-23)	23.5 miles	asphalt	●	●	○	●	●	●	●	●	●	●
(WI-RT-1)	32.5 miles	smooth crushed gravel	●	●	○	○	●	●	●	○	●	●
(WI-RT-24)	22.0 miles	smooth crushed gravel	●	●	○	○	●	●	●	○	●	●
(WI-RT-28)	48.0 miles	smooth crushed gravel	●	●	○	○	●	●	●	●	●	●
(WI-RT-15)	51.0 miles	smooth crushed gravel & asphalt	●	●	●	●	●	●	●	●	○	●

Wisconsin

Trail Name:	Vicinity:
Glacial River Trail	Fort Atkinson (Pond Rd. to Farmco Ln.); part of trail follows State Route 26 & Janesville Ave.
Great River State Trail	La Crosse (County Route B east of State Route 16) to Marshland (State Route 35)
Green Circle Trail	Stevens Point (Circular Trail); trail follows Hoover St., Plover River, Point Dr., Wisconsin River, and Tommy's Turnpike and passes through Plover River Park, Inverson Park, Schmeeckle Reserve, Bukolt Park, Whitling Park, Little Plover Park & Like Pacawa Park.
Hiawatha State Trail	Tomahawk (W. Somo Ave.) to Lincoln-Oneida County Line (County Route L)
Hillsboro State Trail	Hillsboro (Air Hill) to Union Center (State Route 33)
Kenosha County Bicycle Trail	WI-IL State Line (Russell Rd.) to Kenosha (directly follows the Lake Michigan coast from 91st St. to 35th St.) to Kenosha-Racine County Line (County Line Rd.)
La Crosse River State Trail	La Crosse (County Route B east of State Route 16) to Sparta (John St.)
Lake County Recreation Trail	Waukesha (Golf Club Rd. west of County Route T) to Delafield (Delafield Rd.)
Mascoutin Valley State Trail	Ripon (County Route E & Locust Rd.) to Rush Lake (County Route E) to Berlin (County Route F/Ripon Rd.)

Map:	Trail Length:	Surface	🚲 🚲 🐎 🛼 🏊 🚶 ♿ ⛷ 🐾 $
(WI-RT-30)	4.0 miles	asphalt & smooth crushed gravel (parts follow streets & roads)	
(WI-RT-17)	24.0 miles	smooth crushed gravel (parts follow streets)	
(WI-BT-4)	24.0 miles	smooth crushed gravel & asphalt (parts follow streets)	
(WI-RT-8-B)	6.2 miles	smooth crushed gravel	
(WI-RT-27)	4.3 miles	smooth crushed gravel	
(WI-RT-10)	16.0 miles	smooth crushed gravel & asphalt (parts follow streets through Kenosha)	
(WI-RT-18)	21.5 miles	smooth crushed gravel	
(WI-RT-26)	8.0 miles	asphalt & smooth crushed gravel (parts follows streets)	
(WI-RT-34)	10.5 miles	smooth crushed gravel	

Wisconsin

Trail Name:	Vicinity:
Military Ridge State Trail	Dodgeville (State Route 23 & County Route YZ) to Madison (U.S. Route 18/151 & County Route PD)
Mountain-Bay State Trail (Delly Trail)	Green Bay (Lakeview Dr.) to Kelley (east of Wausau on Schofield Ave. & Municipal)
New Berlin Recreation Trail	West Allis & Waukesha-Milwaukee Co. Line (124th St.) to Waukesha (Springdale Rd.)
Oak Leaf Trail (Old-76 Bike Trail)	Milwaukee (Lake Michigan Coast & Lincoln Memorial Dr. to Glendale (Milwaukee River Pkwy.) to River Hills (N. River Rd.) to Milwaukee (Bradley Rd. & 91st St.) to Wauwatosa (Menomonee River Pkwy.) to West Allis (Root River Pkwy.) to Greenfield (Root River Pkwy.) to Greendale (Root River Pkwy. & 68th St.) to Franklin (68th St. & Drexel Ave.) to Oak Creek (Drexel Ave.) to South Milwaukee (Oak Creek Pkwy.) to Cudahy (Lake Michigan Coast) to St. Francis (Lake Michigan Coast) to Milwaukee (Lake Michigan Coast & Lincoln Memorial Dr.); east-west connector route: Milwaukee (Logan & Superior Streets) to West Allis (Honey Creek Pkwy. & 84th St.) to Wauwatosa (Menomonee River Pkwy.)
Old Abe State Trail	Lake Wissota State Park (97th Ave. & County Routes-S & O) to Cornell (State Route 64/178 & Park Rd. in Mill Yard Park)
Old Plank Road Trail	Sheboygan (Erie Ave. next to Interstate-43) to Green Bush & Old Wade House State Park (Plank Rd.)
Omaha Trail	Elroy (2nd Main St.) to Camp Douglas (County Route H)
Osaugie Trail	Superior (E St. to Mocassin Bike Rd.); trail follows U.S. Route 2 & 53/ 2nd St.

Map:	Trail Length:	Surface	🚴 🚲 🐎 🛼 ✈ 🚶 ♿ ⛷ 🐾 $
(WI-RT-14)	42.0 miles	smooth crushed gravel & asphalt	
(WI-RT-31)	83.4 miles	smooth crushed gravel & asphalt (parts follow streets through Shawano)	
(WI-RT-13-A)	6.0 miles	smooth crushed gravel	
(WI-RT-4)	96.4 miles	asphalt (parts follow streets & roads)	
(WI-RT-36)	17.0 miles	asphalt	
(WI-BT-3)	17.5 miles	asphalt (parts follow streets)	
(WI-RT-22)	12.5 miles	coarse asphalt	
(WI-RT-25-A)	5.0 miles	asphalt	

Wisconsin

Trail Name:	Vicinity:
Ozaukee Interurban Trail	Ozaukee-Milwaukee County Line to Cedarburg to Port Washington to Ozaukee-Sheboygan County Line
Pecatonica State Trail	Calamine (County Route G & the Cheese Country Recreational Trail) to Belmont (U.S. Route 151)
Pine Line Trail	Medford (Allman Ave. & River Rd. to Pleasant Ave.)
Pine River Recreation Trail	Richland Center (U.S. Route 14 & State Route 80) to Lone Rock (Richland St.)
Racine County Bicycle Trail (Burlington to Waukesha County Line)	Burlington (Congress St.) to Racine-Waukesha County Line
Racine County Bicycle Trail (M.R.K. Trail)	Racine (Layard Ave. to 7 Mile Rd.); trail roughly follows State Route 32/Douglas Ave.
Racine County Bicycle Trail (North Shore Trail)	Racine-Kenosha County Line (County Line Rd.) to Racine (19th St. & West Blvd.)
Racine County Bicycle Trail (Racine-Sturtevant Trail)	Racine (19th St. & West Blvd.) to Sturtevant (State Route 31/Greenbay Rd.)
Red Cedar State Trail	Menomonie (State Route 29) to Chippewa River State Park Trail
Rock/Springbrook/Kiwanis Trail	Janesville First Section: Afton Rd. to Riverside St. & Franklin St. (following Rock River) Second section: Riverside St. & Franklin St. to Riverside Park (following Rock River) Third Section: Riverside St. & Franklin St. to U.S. Route 14
Sugar River State Trail	Brodhead (W 3rd Ave.) to New Glarus (6th Ave. & Railroad St.) & to New Glarus Woods State Park (State Route 39/69 & County Route NN)

Map:	Trail Length:	Surface	🚲	🚵	🐎	inline skate	🏊	🥾	♿	🎿	🔭	$
(WI-RT-37)	28.5 miles	asphalt & smooth crushed gravel	●	●		●		●	●			
(WI-RT-32)	10.5 miles	smooth crushed gravel	●	●	●		●	●	●		●	
(WI-RT-20)	3.0 miles	smooth crushed gravel	●	●	●		●	●	●			
(WI-RT-33)	14.6 miles	smooth crushed gravel	●	●			●	●	●	●		●
(WI-RT-7)	14.0 miles	smooth crushed gravel (some sections follow back roads)	●	●	●			●	●	●		
(WI-RT-6)	5.0 miles	smooth crushed gravel	●	●	●		●	●	●	●		
(WI-RT-5-B)	3.0 miles	smooth crushed gravel	●	●		●		●	●	●		
(WI-RT-5-A)	4.0 miles	smooth crushed gravel	●	●				●	●	●		
(WI-RT-11)	14.5 miles	smooth crushed gravel	●	●	●		●	●	●	●		●
(WI-RT-29)	14.8 miles	asphalt & smooth crushed gravel (parts follow streets)	●	●		●		●	●	●		
(WI-RT-2)	23.5 miles	smooth crushed gravel	●	●		●	●	●	●	●		●

Trail Name:	Vicinity:
Sunset/Hidden Bluff Trails	Peninsula State Park (near Sturgeon Bay on State Route 42)
Tomorrow River State Trail	Plover (Hoover Rd.) to Portage-Waupaca County Line
U.S. Route 2 Duluth-Superior Bike Trail	Duluth, MN (46th Ave. W & Michigan St.) to Superior, WI (Belknap & Susquehanna Ave.); trail follows U.S. Route 2)
Tri-County Recreation Corridor Trail	Superior (U.S. Route 2/51 & Moccasin Mike Rd.) to Ashland (State Routes 137 & 112)
Waukesha Bike Trail	Waukesha (MacArthur Rd. to the downtown area along the Fox River and to Springdale Rd.)
Wild Goose State Trail	Juneau (State Route 60 & County Route W) to Fond du Lac (County Route VVV)
Wildwood Trail	Spring Valley (Pierce-St. Croix County Rd.) to Woodville (County Route BB)
Wiouwash State Trail (Oshkosh to Hortonville)	Oshkosh to Hortonville
Wiouwash State Trail (Split Rock to Aniwa)	Split Rock to Aniwa

Wisconsin

Map:	Trail Length:	Surface	🚲	🚵	🐎	🛼	✈	🥾	♿	🎿	🔭	$
(WI-BT-2)	5.8 miles	smooth crushed gravel	●	●		●	●	●	●			
(WI-RT-38)	10.0 miles & 3.0 miles	smooth crushed gravel	●	●	●		●	●	●			
(WI-BT-6 / MN-BT-13)	2.0 miles	concrete	●	●		●		●	●			
(WI-RT-25-B)	61.8 miles	smooth crushed gravel	●	●	●		●	●	●		●	
(WI-RT-13-B)	7.5 miles	asphalt (parts follow streets)	●	●		●		●	●	●		
(WI-RT-19)	34.0 miles	smooth crushed gravel (parts follow back roads & streets)	●	●	●		●	●	●	●		
(WI-RT-35)	7.0 miles	smooth crushed gravel & gravel	●	●	●		●	●	●			
(WI-RT-12-A)	20.3 miles	smooth crushed gravel	●	●	●		●	●	●			
(WI-RT-12-B)	21.0 miles (sections incomplete)	smooth crushed gravel	●	●	●		●	●	●			

Biking Wyoming's Rail-Trails

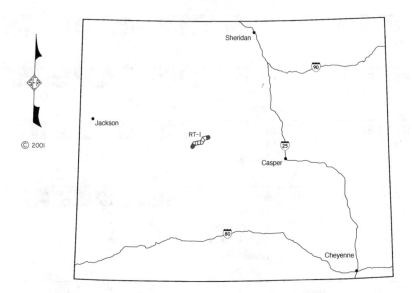

© 2001

Trail Name:	Vicinity:
Wyoming Heritage Trail	Riverton (Wind River & Monroe to Honor Farm Rd.) & Shoshoni (Poison Creek to First St.)

Trail Listings
WY-RT-1   Wyoming Heritage Trail

Wyoming Highlights

WYOMING HERITAGE TRAIL (WY-RT-1)
With the first sections open in 1996, this is Wyoming's first rail-trail. It mostly follows the Wind River across the rugged ranches and scrubland of western Wyoming. Riverton has a network of paved bike paths in addition to this trail. Plans are to eventually connect the two trail segments in Riverton and Shoshone to form a continuous 23-mile rail-trail.

Wyoming Heritage Trail.

Map:	Trail Length:	Surface									
(WY-RT-1)	3.5 miles (Riverton) & 1.5 miles (Shoshoni); 23.0 miles when complete	asphalt									

U.S.A.'s Cross Country Rail-Trails

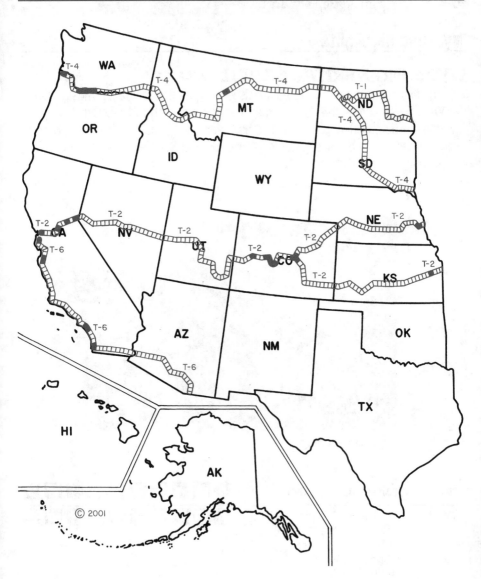

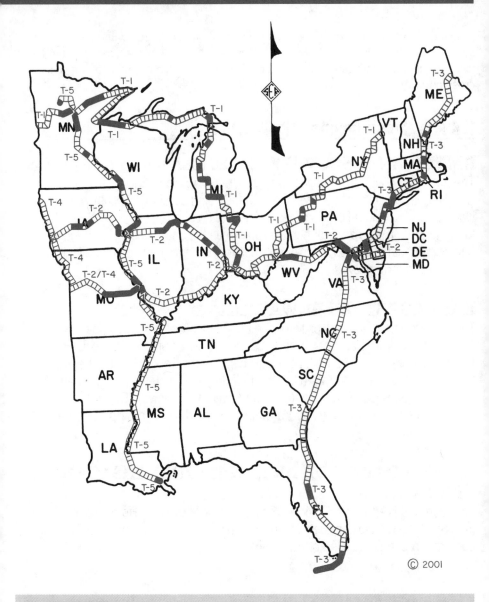

© 2001

Trail Listings

USA-T-1	North Country Trail
USA-T-2	American Discovery Trail
USA-T-3	East Coast Greenway
USA-T-4	Lewis & Clark National Historic Trail
USA-T-5	Mississippi River Trail
USA-T-6	Juan Bautista De Anza National Historic Trail

Imagine being able to bicycle or walk across the United States without ever having to share the trail with automobiles. Plans are in the works to connect the existing rail-trails and bike trails together so trail users can enjoy a continuous cross-country trail.

U.S.A.'s Cross Country Highlights

AMERICAN DISCOVERY TRAIL (USA-T-2)

The American Discovery Trail goes from the Pacific Coast in California to the Atlantic Coast in Delaware. Between Denver, CO and Cincinnati, OH there is a North Loop and South Loop in the trail. The North Loop goes through Nebraska, Iowa, northern Illinois and northern Indiana while the South Loop goes through Kansas, Missouri, southern Illinois and southern Indiana. Parts of the trail follow rail-trails and towpaths.

EAST COAST GREENWAY (USA-T-3)

The East Coast Greenway mostly follows the Atlantic Coast from Florida to Maine. This multi-use trail is an alternative to the well-known Appalachian Trail, which is limited to hiking only. The Baltimore & Annapolis Trail Park (MD), the Delaware & Raritan Canal State Park Trail (NJ), the Farmington Canal Linear State Park Trail (CT), the Charter Oak Greenway (CT), the Coventry Greenway (RI) and the South Portland Greenbelt Walkway (ME) are all designated to become part of the East Coast Greenway.

JUAN BAUTISTA DE ANZA NATIONAL HISTORIC TRAIL (USA-T-6)

The Juan Bautista De Anza National Historic Trail follows the California Pacific Coast from San Francisco to San Diego, then veers east and runs north of the U.S.-Mexico border from San Diego, CA and to Nogales, AZ.

LEWIS & CLARK NATIONAL HISTORIC TRAIL
(USA-RT-4)
This trail follows the historic route that the Lewis and Clark expedition traveled in 1804 along the Missouri and Columbia Rivers. Currently, Katy Trail State Park (MO), River's Edge Trail (MT) and Columbia River Gorge Bikeway (OR) are trails directly along the two rivers.

MISSISSIPPI RIVER TRAIL (USA-T-5)
The Mississippi River Trail follows the entire river from New Orleans, LA to Itasca State Park in Minnesota. Currently, Jefferson Parish Bicycle & Pedestrian Path (LA), Confluence Bikeway (IL), Vadalbene (Sam) Great River Road Bike Trail (IL), Great River Trail (IL), Great River State Park Trail (WI), Minnehaha Trail (MN), West River Parkway Trail (MN), St. Anthony Falls Heritage Trail (MN), Fort Snelling State Park Bike Path (MN), Grand Rounds Parkway System Trail (MN), Mississippi River Regional Trail (MN), Beaver Island Trail (MN) and Itasca State Park Bike Trail (MN) directly follow the Mississippi River.

NORTH COUNTRY TRAIL (USA-T-1)
From Minnesota to Ohio, this trail meanders through and around Lake Superior, Lake Michigan, Lake Huron and Lake Erie. Parts of the North Country Trail follow rail-trails and towpaths.

The Mississippi River Trail goes by the Arch of St. Louis, Missouri.

U.S.A.'s Cross Country Rail-Trails

Trail Name:	Vicinity:
American Discovery Trail	Point Reyes National Seashore, CA to NV to UT to CO to KS to MO to NE to IA to IL to IN to OH to KY to WV to MD to DC to Cape Henlopen State Park, DE
East Coast Greenway	Key West, FL to GA to SC to NC to VA to DC to MD to DE to PA to NJ to NY to CT to RI to MA to NH to Calais, ME
Juan Bautista De Anza National Historic Trail	San Francisco, CA to Nogales, AZ
Lewis & Clark National Historic Trail	Camp DuBois in Wood River, IL to MO to KS to IA to NE to SD to ND to MT to ID to WA to Les Shirley Park, OR
Mississippi River Trail	New Orleans, LA to MS to AR to TN to KY to MO to IL to IA to WI to Lake Itasca, MN
North Country Trail	Lake Sakakawea, ND to MN to WI to MI to OH to PA to Port Henry/Crown Point, NY

Map:	Trail Length:	Surface	🚲 🚵 🏇 ⛸ 🚣 🚶 ♿ ⛷ 🔭 $
(US-T-2)	Will be 6356 miles	asphalt & smooth crushed gravel	🚲 🚵 🏇 ⛸ 🚶 ♿ ⛷
(US-T-3)	Will be 2500 miles	asphalt & smooth crushed gravel	🚲 🚵 🏇 ⛸ 🚶 ♿ ⛷
(US-T-6)	Will be 1200 miles	asphalt & smooth crushed gravel	🚲 🚵 🏇 ⛸ 🚶 ♿ ⛷
(US-T-4)	Will be 3700 miles	asphalt & smooth crushed gravel	🚲 🚵 🏇 ⛸ 🚶 ♿ ⛷
(US-T-5)	Will be 2000 miles	asphalt & smooth crushed gravel	🚲 🚵 🏇 ⛸ 🚶 ♿ ⛷
(US-T-1)	Will be 4600 miles	asphalt & smooth crushed gravel	🚲 🚵 🏇 ⛸ 🚶 ♿ ⛷

U.S.A.'s Rail-Trail Facts

U.S.A.'s Longest Rail-Trails

In the past, most of the long distance cyclists outgrew the bike trails as a result of their limited distances and moved on to using the back roads. In recent times, bike trails are being built longer using the abandoned railroads & canal towpaths. As a result, the long distance cyclists are returning to the bike trails and use them in conjunction with the back roads. Below is a list of U.S.A.'s longest continuous rail-trails (trails more than 30.0 miles long); please note that some sections of these rail-trails may follow streets & back roads for a short distance.

U.S.A.'s Longest Rail-Trails (asphalt or concrete surface)

Length	State	Trail
72.0 mi.	MN	Willard Munger State Trail (Hinckley Fire State Trail)
68.0 mi.	OH	Little Miami Scenic Trail/Bike Route 1
47.0 mi.	FL	Pinellas Trail (Fred Marquois Pinellas Trail)
46.4 mi.	MN	Paul Bunyan State Trail
46.0 mi.	FL	Withlacoochee State Trail
45.0 mi.	VA	Washington & Old Dominion (W. & O. D.) Railroad Regional Park Trail
44.1 mi.	MI	Interstate-275 Bike Path (*)
42.3 mi.	MN	Root River State Trail
41.0 mi.	NY	Mohawk-Hudson Bikeway Hike-Bike Trail
41.0 mi.	MS	Longleaf Trace Trail
39.0 mi.	MN	Sakatah Singing Hills State Trail
39.0 mi.	WA	Spokane River Centennial Trail
37.6 mi.	GA	Silver Comet Trail
37.0 mi.	MN	Lake Wobegon Trail
35.0 mi.	IL	Fox River Trail

(*) Non Rail-Trails

The Little Miami Scenic Trail in Yellow Springs, Ohio.

U.S.A.'s Longest Rail-Trails (smooth crushed gravel surface)

Certain portions of these trails may consist of an asphalt or concrete surface.

Length	State	Trail
235.0 mi.	MO	Katy Trail State Park
184.5 mi.	MD-DC (*)	C. & O. Canal National Historic Park Trail (Trail also has a coarse crushed gravel & dirt surface)
114.0 mi.	SD	Mickelson (George S.) Trail
96.4 mi.	WI	Oak Leaf Trail
83.4 mi.	WI	Mountain-Bay State Trail (Delly Trail)
77.6 mi.	WV	Greenbrier River State Park Trail (Also has a coarse crushed gravel surface)
75.0 mi.	MN	Minnesota Valley State Trail
71.0 mi.	PA	Youghiogheny River Trail
64.0 mi.	IA	Wabash Trace Nature Trail
61.8 mi.	WI	Tri-County Recreation Corridor Trail (Also has a coarse crushed gravel surface)
59.5 mi.	IL	Great River Trail
57.0 mi.	IA	Raccoon River Valley Trail
55.5 mi.	IL (*)	Illinois & Michigan Canal Trail State Park, La Salle, Grundy, & Will Counties
55.0 mi.	IL	Illinois Prairie Path
53.7 mi.	IA	Cedar Valley Nature Trail
51.0 mi.	WI	Glacial Drumlin State Trail
48.0 mi.	WI	Gandy Dancer State Trail
47.0 mi.	IL	Tunnel Hill State Trail
47.0 mi.	WI	Cheese Country Recreation Trail (Also has a coarse crushed gravel surface)
44.0 mi.	WI	Military Ridge State Trail
37.8 mi.	IA	Three Rivers Trail
35.2 mi.	NE	Cowboy Recreation & Nature Trail (Neligh to Norfolk)
35.0 mi.	NY	D. & H. Canal Heritage Corridor (O. & W. Rail-Trail)
34.0 mi.	MI	Kal-Haven Trail State Park
34.0 mi.	WI	Wild Goose State Trail
34.0 mi.	OH (*)	Towpath Trail (Akron to Cleveland)
33.5 mi.	KS	Prairie Spirit Rail-Trail
33.0 mi.	IA	Sauk Rail-Trail
32.0 mi.	WI	Elroy-Sparta State Trail

(*) Non Rail-Trails

U.S.A.'s Bi-State Rail-Trails

Most rail-trails & bike trails fall into a jurisdiction of either a town, township, City, or County; many of the trails also traverse two or more counties within a given state. However, it is rare that a trail continues from one state into another or that even two trails connect to one another on state lines. With this, cyclists can have even longer trails to enjoy. These are U.S.A.'s Bi-State trails.

States	Joint Length	Trail(s) Joined Together
DC-MD	11.0 miles	Capital Crescent Trail (DC-MD)
DC-MD (*)	185.0 miles	Chesapeake & Ohio Canal National Historic Park Trail (DC-MD)
DC-MD (*)	22.5 miles	Rock Creek Park Trail (DC) Rock Creek Stream Valley Park Trail (MD)
ID-WA	63.0 miles	North Idaho Centennial Trail (ID) Spokane River Centennial Trail (WA)
ID-WA	7.5 miles	Palouse (Bill Chipman) Trail (ID-WA)
IL-MO (*)	1.1 miles	Old Chain of Rocks Bridge Bikeway (IL-MO)
IL-WI	38.0 miles	North Shore Path (Robert McClorey Bike Path) (IL) Kenosha County Bicycle Trail (WI)
IL-MO	2.9 miles	West Alton Trail (IL-MO)
MD-DC	11.0 miles	Capital Crescent Trail (MD-DC)
MD-DC (*)	185.0 miles	Chesapeake & Ohio Canal National Historic Park Trail (MD-DC)
MD-DC (*)	22.5 miles	Rock Creek Stream Valley Park Trail (MD) Rock Creek Park Trail (DC)
MD-PA	39.8 miles	Northern Central Railroad Trail (MD) Heritage Rail-Trail County Park (York County Heritage Rail-Trail) (PA)
MO-IL (*)	1.1 miles	Old Chain of Rocks Bridge Bikeway (MO-IL)
MO-IL	2.9 miles	West Alton Trail (MO-IL)
OH-PA	11.0 miles	Stavich Bicycle Trail (OH-PA)
PA-MD	39.8 miles	Heritage Rail-Trail County Park (York County Heritage Rail-Trail) (PA) Northern Central Railroad Trail (MD)
PA-OH	11.0 miles	Stavich Bicycle Trail (PA-OH)
WA-ID	7.5 miles	Palouse (Bill Chipman) Trail (WI-ID)
WA-ID	63.0 miles	Spokane River Centennial Trail (WA) North Idaho Centennial Trail (ID)
WI-IL	38.0 miles	Kenosha County Bicycle Trail (WI) North Shore Path (Robert Mcclorey Bike Path) (IL)

(*) Non Rail-Trails

The Spokane Centennial Trail meets the North Idaho Centennial Trail on the Washington-Idaho state line.

U.S.A.'s First Rail-Trails

When and where was the first abandoned railroad converted into a rail-trail? Most cyclists recognize the Illinois Prairie Path (IL) and the Elroy-Sparta State Park Trail (WI) as being the first two major rail-trails to be constructed between 1965 and 1967; to this very day with both trails being built in different stages, it is not clear which of the two trails opened first. However, the Fairfield Linear Park Trail (CA), the Gilman (Virgil L.) Trail (IL) and the Harry Cook Nature Trail (IA) are three shorter rail-trails and all three were built in 1961. Therefore, it is obvious that the first three smooth surfaced rail-trails for biking were built in 1961.

If you eliminate the use of bicycling and limit it to walking and hiking only, other rail-trails were built even earlier. Though these two rail-trails are not mentioned in this book since they both have a rough gravel and/or dirt surface, the Cathedral Aisle Trail (Aiken, SC) was constructed in 1939 and the Creek Trail (San Jose, CA) was constructed in 1932. Therefore, California was the first state to build their first rail-trail for walking.

The Gilman (Virgil L.) Trail in Illinois became one of U.S.A.'s first rails-to-trails conversion in 1961. (Dr. Jack McDonald).

U.S.A.'s Rail-Trails with Rails

Several of U.S.A.'s rail-trails have active railroads paralleling them with a safe separation between the two corridors. In many cases, there were two separate railroad corridors paralleling each other; when one of the corridors abandoned, there was an opportunity for a rails-to-trail conversion. In other cases, there was a multi-track railroad corridor where some of the tracks were removed; this also created an opportunity for a rails-to-trails conversion. These types of trails can be enjoyed by railroad buffs as well as the typical trail users. This list below consists of U.S.A.'s Rail-Trails with railroads.

STATE	U.S.A.'s Rail-Trails with Rails
AK	Knowles (Tony) Coastal Bicycle Trail
CA	Alton Bike Trail (Alton to Bristol Bike Trail)
CA	Fillmore Trail
CA	Hoover Street Trail
CA	King (Martin Luther) Promenade Trail
CA	Rose Canyon Bicycle Path
CA	Sacramento Northern Bike Trail
CA	Walnut Trail (Atchison Topeka & Santa Fe Bicycle Trail)
CA	Watts Towers Crescent Greenway
CO	Animas River Trail
CO	Mineral Belt Trail
CO	Platte River Greenway
CO	Rock Island Regional Trail
CO	Shooks Run Trail
GA	Chatahoochee River Walk Trail
ID	North Idaho Centennial Trail
IL	Foster (Ronald J.) Heritage Trail (Glen Carbon Heritage Bike Trail)
IL	Great River Trail
IL	Green Bay Trail
IL	Illinois Prairie Path
IL	Madison County Transit's Nature Trail (Sam Vadalabene Nature Trail or Madison County Nature Trail)
IL	North Shore Path (Robert McClorey Bike Path)
IL	Rock River Recreation Path/Bauer Memorial Path
IN	Lake Michigan Heritage Greenway (Prairie-Duneland Trail or Oak Savannah Trail)
IA	Heritage Trail
KY	Louisville River Walk Trail
MD	Western Maryland Rail-Trail
MA	Falmouth Shining Sea Trail (Shining Sea Bikeway)
MA	Southwest Corridor Park Trail

MI	Ann Arbor's Huron River Trail (Gallup Park Trail)
MI	Traverse Area Recreation Trail (T.A.R.T.)
MN	Cedar Lake Trail
MT	River's Edge Trail
NH	Cotton Valley Trail (Wolfeboro-Sanbornville Recreational Trail)
NJ	Traction Line Recreation Trail
NC	Libba Cotton Bike Path
OH	Celina-Coldwater Bikeway
OH	Evans (Thomas J.) Bike Trail (Newark to Hanover or Panhandle Trail)
OH	Muskingum Recreational Trail
OH	North Coast Inland Bike Path (Fremont to Clyde)
OH-PA	Stavich Bicycle Trail
OH	University-Parks Hike-Bike Trail
OH	Zane's Landing Trail
OK	Katy Trail
PA	Heritage Rail-Trail County Park (York County Heritage Rail-Trail)
PA	Lehigh Gorge State Park Trail
PA	Oil Creek State Park Trail
PA	Schuykill River Trail (Philadelphia to Valley Forge Bikeway)
PA-OH	Stavich Bicycle Trail
PA	Three Rivers Heritage Trail
VT	Burlington Bike Path
WA	Alki Trail (Seattle Waterfront Pathway)
WA	Corridor Trail
WA	Duwamish Trail
WA	Lower Yakima Valley Pathway
WA	Neppel Landing Trail
WA	Rainer Multiple Use Trail (Issaquah Trail)
WA	South Bay Trail
WV	Greater Wheeling Trail (North-South)
WI	Bugline Recreation Trail
WI	Capital City State Trail
WI	Glacial Drumlin State Trail
WI	Great River State Trail
WI	La Crosse River State Trail
WI	Mountain-Bay State Trail (Delly Trail)
WI	New Berlin Recreation Trail
WI	Racine County Bicycle Trail (M.R.K. Trail)
WY	Wyoming Heritage Trail

Part of the Glacial Drumlin State Trail (WI) has rails next to the trail.

The track that this 1940s-era passenger train ran along is the predecessor of many of the bike trails that exist today.

U.S.A.'s Rail-Trails with Tunnels

Most of U.S.A.'s converted rail-trails have bridges and trestles but do not have the original railroad tunnels. However, some of the rail-trails throughout the United States do have the original railroad tunnels making them a major feature along any rail-trail. Some tunnels have lights provided inside while others have no lights. Therefore, a trail user may want to bring a flashlight so one can see their way through the tunnels. Bicyclists should walk their bicycles through the longer tunnels without lights to avoid collisions with other trail users. These rail-trails listed below have at least one original railroad tunnel.

State	Tunnels	Longest	Rail-Trail
CA	1	620 ft.	Fairfield Linear Park Trail
CA	1	500 ft.	Sacramento River Trail
GA	1	780 ft.	Silver Comet Trail
IL	1	543 ft.	Tunnel Hill State Trail
MD	2	800 ft.	Capital Crescent Trail
MD	1	3118 ft.	Chesapeake & Ohio Canal National Historic Park Trail (*)
MO	1	243 ft.	Katy Trail State Park
NV	5	500 ft.	Historic Railroad Hiking Trail
OH	1	532 ft.	National Road Bikeway
OR	2	493 ft.	Columbia River Gorge Bikeway (Old Us Route 30) (*)
PA	1	3810 ft.	Allegheny River Trail
PA	2	3500 ft.	Allegheny Highlands Trail
PA	3	620 ft.	Montour Trail; Coraopolis-Thompsonville
PA	1	253 ft.	Heritage Rail-Trail County Park (York County Heritage Rail-Trail)
SD	4	270 ft.	Mickelson (George S.) Trail
VA	1	400 ft.	Orange & Alexandria Historical Trail
WA	1	1500 ft.	Interstate-90 Bikeway (*)
WV	1	620 ft.	Cranberry-Tri-Rivers Trail
WV	2	511 ft.	Greenbrier River State Park Trail
WV	1	1200 ft.	McPark Trail (Marion County Trail)
WV	12	2297 ft.	North Bend State Park Rail-Trail
WV	1	500 ft.	Greater Wheeling Trail; East-West
WI	3	3960 ft.	Elroy-Sparta State Trail
WI	1	875 ft.	Omaha Trail

(*) Historical tunnel was neither a railroad tunnel nor along a rail-trail.

"Tunnel #3" is the longest U.S.A. Rail-Trail tunnel (3960 feet) along the Elroy-Sparta State Trail in Wisconsin.

This tunnel near Rocheport is located along the Katy Trail State Park in Missouri.

U.S.A.'s Different Rail-Trail Regions

The United States of America is blessed with many different regions to visit rail-trails. Whether you visit the Great Lakes states in the Midwest, the east coast states next to the Atlantic Ocean, the west coast states next to the Pacific Ocean, the Appalachian Mountains in the eastern states, the Rocky Mountains in the western states, the tropical regions in the southeastern states, the arid deserts in the southwestern states, or even Alaska or Hawaii, each area offers its unique scenery and environment.

When planning a bicycle trip along one of U.S.A.'s rail-trails or bike trails, you may want to consider the conditions and environment of each state. As you can expect, the warm weather seasons are longer in the southeastern states than they are in the Midwestern & northeastern states; since most former railroads have a gentle grade, these trails, for the most part are easy to travel whether it's the Little Miami Scenic Trail (OH), the Cape Cod Rail-Trail (MA) the Tallahassee-St. Marks Historic Railroad State Trail (FL) or the Silver Comet Trail (GA). However, the Appalachian states tend to have longer & steeper rail-trail grades than the ones in the Great Lakes & Midwest; the Appalachian area also contains wildlife including bears. An example would include the Youghiogheny River Trail (PA).

The environment for the rail-trails in the states along the Mississippi River tend to be similar to both the Midwestern states and the southeastern states. These trails also tend to be pleasant to visit. Examples of these trails would include the Elroy-Sparta State Trail (WI), the Willard Munger State Trail (MN), the Katy Trail State Park (MO), the Longleaf Trace Trail (MS) and the Tammany Trace Trail (LA). However, in the southern states along the Gulf of Mexico, the reptile wildlife can be quite abundant including many species of snakes and alligators; make sure to keep a safe distance from the alligators before you pass by.

The trails in the western states tend to offer more challenges than all of the trails in the eastern states such as much longer mountain trail grades to climb, sparse communities, harsher climates, open desert lands, wildlife (such as bears and buffalo), and the lack of water facilities. It is very important to make sure that you carry even more water on your bicycle in the western states than the amount that you would normally carry in the eastern states. The wilderness trails in the western states are similar to the highways in the western states; the trail corridors tend to go through ranches among the livestock, pass through ranch gates and cross cattle grates. It is very important to not leave the trail until you come to a major road. Examples of these trails are Mickelson (George S.) Trail (SD), the River's Edge Trail (MT) and the Historic Union Pacific Rail-Trail State Park (UT). The Rocky Mountain states tend to be the most difficult region to bicycle as far as the extremes go in ground elevation. Colorado has elevations over 10,000 feet above sea level which makes the air becomes very thin for breathing. Therefore, it is very important to take frequent breaks in these climates to avoid passing out; you may also want to consider purchasing a portable oxygen tank to carry with you. An example of an extreme high elevation trail is the Ten-Mile Canyon Recreation Trail (Vail Pass Trail) (CO).

The climate of the western states next to the Pacific Ocean tend to be pleasant to travel as one might expect in the eastern states. Examples of this would be the Monterey Bay Coastal Trail (CA), the Banks-Vernonia State Trail (OR) and the Burke-Gilman Trail (WA).

Alaska offers its own challenges to bicycle in. The communities are extremely sparse and the vast wilderness contains a very high abundant wildlife such as elk, reindeer, mountain goats, dall sheep, black bears, brown bears, lynx and moose. If you encounter any of these animals, do not approach them; wait until they leave the trail corridor before passing by. No trails in this state are exempt from these conditions; not even the Knowles (Tony) Coastal Bicycle Trail (AK) in Anchorage.

Hawaii is a tropical paradise far removed from the other 49 states and can be one of the hardest states to reach in the U.S.A. for biking rail-trails. Since these spectacular islands are huge volcanic mountains, most of the roads and trails are located near the base of the islands where the oceans are. The roads tend to be very heavily traveled so use extreme caution. The most historical rail-trail in Hawaii is the Pearl Harbor Bike Path (HI) in Honolulu where the historic site of the 1941 attack on Pearl Harbor can be visited.

No matter which U.S.A. trail you visit, the setting is either urban, suburban, rural, wilderness, or some combination of the four. Many of these trails are patrolled by rangers and police. Most of these trails are closed during the dusk to dawn hours for safety reasons. Therefore, it is advisable to be off of the trails after dark.

Some of U.S.A.'s rail-trails cross ranches where gates must be opened, then closed to keep farm animals in their pasture.

U.S.A.'s Regional Map

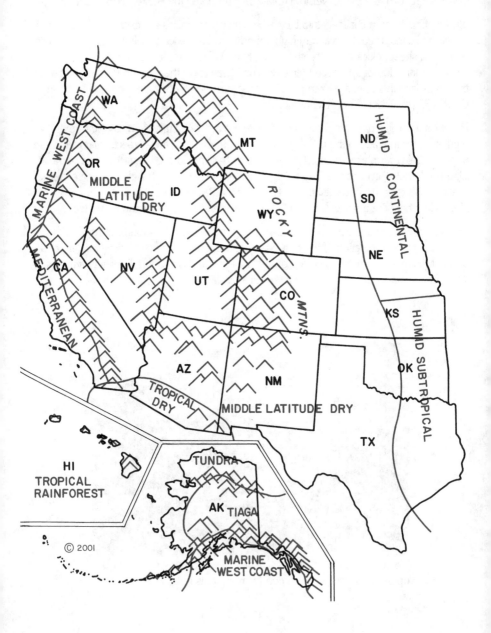

U.S.A.'s Regional Map

MN

WI

MI

IA

HUMID CONTINENTAL

IL IN OH

MO

KY

WV

VA

TN

APPALACHIAN MTNS.

NC

AR

SC

HUMID SUBTROPICAL

MS AL GA

LA

ME

VT

NH

NY

MA

CT

RI

PA

NJ
DC
DE
MD

FL

TROPICAL (WET & DRY)

© 2001

Further Bicycle Route Information

U.S.A.'s Published Bicycle Maps by State

Most of these bicycle maps show a combination of back roads (suggested routes), bike routes (Signed route along streets & back roads), bike lanes (separate lanes for bicycles along streets & back roads), and separate bike paths including rail-trails. Some of these maps are free while others require a fee; the prices and availability of these maps are subject to change without notice.

Arizona

Cycle Arizona, Map of Suitable Bicycle Routes on the State Highway System
1 in. = 22 miles
Arizona DOT, Planning Division
201 N Stone, P.O. Box 27210, Tucson, AZ 85726
520-791-4372

Colorado

Colorado Bicycling Map
1 in. = 10.5 miles
Bicycle Colorado
P.O. Box 698, Salida, CO 81201
719-530-0051
http://www.bicyclecolo.org

Connecticut

Connecticut Bicycle Map
1 in. = 3.5 miles
Connecticut DOT
2800 Berlin Turnpike, P.O. Box 317546, Newington, CT 06131

Delaware

Delaware Maps for Bicycle Users
1 in. = 0.75 miles & 1 in. = 1.75 miles
Delaware DOT
P.O. Box 778, Dover, DE 19903
302-760-2453
http://www.state.de.us/govern/agencies/ or
deldot/bike/welcome.htm

D.C.

Washington DC Regional Bike Map
2 in. = 1 mile & 1.25 in = 2 miles
Dept. of Public Works
2000 14th St., NW, 5th Floor, Washington, D.C. 20009

Georgia

Georgia Bicycle Touring Guide
1 in. = 13.5 miles
Georgia Tourism Division, Georgia Dept. of Industry, Trade & Tourism
P.O. Box 1776, Atlanta, GA 30301

404-656-3590
http://www.georgia.org/itt/tourism

Georgia Traffic Flow Map
1 in. = 1.1 miles
Georgia DOT
#2 Capitol Square, Room 347, Atlanta, GA 30334
404-656-3507

Idaho

Idaho Bicycling Guide
1 in. = 24 miles
Idaho DOT, Bike/Pedestrian Coordinator
P.O. Box 7129, Boise, ID 83707
208-334-8272
http://www2.state.id.us/itd/planning/ or abouttpd/ips/ip_staff.htm

Illinois

Illinois Official Bicycle Map (9-map Set)
1 in. = 3.7 miles
Illinois DOT, Map Sales, Room 121
2300 S Dirksen Parkway, Springfield, IL 62764

Indiana

Cross-State Bike Route Maps (12 Routes) Hoosier Bikeway System Guidebooks
1 in. = 0.75 miles
Indiana DNR Map Sales
402 W Washington St., Room 160, Indianapolis, IN 46204
317-232-4180
http://www.state.in.us/dnr/outdoor/trails.

Iowa

Iowa Transportation Map for Bicyclists
1 in. = 12 miles
Iowa DOT, Office of Project Planning, State Trails Program
800 Lincoln Way, Ames, IA 50010
515-239-1621
http://www.state.ia.us/government/dot/ sitemap.htm#travel

Kansas

Kansas 2000-2001 Bicycling Guide
1 in. = 28 miles
Kansas DOT, Thacher Building, 2nd Floor
217 SE 4th St., Topeka, KS 66603
913-296-7448

Kentucky

Cross-State Bike Route Maps (8 Routes) Kentucky Bicycle Tours
1 in. = 14 miles
Travel
P.O. Box 2011, Frankfort, KY 40602
800-225-8747 or 502-564-4930

http://www.kentuckytourism.com

Maine	**Maine Bike Map**

1 in. = 9 miles; 1 in. = 20 miles
Maine DOT
#16 House Station, Child St., Augusta, ME 04333
207-287-6600

Maryland **Maryland Bicycle Map**
1 in. = 6 miles
Maryland State Highway Administration
707 Calvert St., Mailstop C-502, Baltimore, MD 21202
800-252-8776

Massachusetts **Massachusetts Bicycle Map**
1 in. = 2 miles
Rubel Bike Maps
P.O. Box 401035, Cambridge, MA 02140
617-776-6567
http://www.bikemaps.com

Michigan **Biking in Michigan (83 County Map Set)**
1 in. = 2 miles
Intermodal Section, Michigan DOT
P.O. Box 30050, Lansing, MI 48909
517-335-2823 or 517-373-9049
http://www.mdot.state.mi.us/planning/mibike

Minnesota **Explore Minnesota Bikeways (6-map Set)**
1 in. = 6 miles
Minnesota Bookstore
117 University Ave., St. Paul, MN 55155
800-657-3757 or 612-297-3000

Missouri **Missouri Bicycle Suitability Map**
1 in. = 8 miles
Trails Coordinator, Missouri DNR
P.O. Box 176, Jefferson City, MO 65102
800-334-6946 or 573-751-2479

Montana **Bicycling the Big Sky: Montana Traffic Data for Bicyclists**
1 in. = 40 miles
Montana DOT, Transportation Planning Division
2701 Prospect Ave., Helena, MT 59620
800-714-7296
http://www.mdt.state.mt.us.

Nebraska   **Nebraska 1999 Bicycle Guide**
1 in. = 30 miles
State Bicycle Coordinator, Nebraska Dept. of Roads
P.O. Box 94759, Lincoln, NE 68509
402-479-4338

Nevada   **Nevada State Bicycle Network, 2000**
1 in. = 38 miles
State Bicycle/Pedestrian Coordinator, Nevada DOT
1263 S Stewart St., Carson City, NV 89712
775-888-7433

New Hampshire   **Statewide Bicycle Route System; State of NH**
New Hampshire Dept. of Transportation, Bicycle Pedestrian
Program,
P.O. Box 483, Concord, NH 03302
603-271-1622

New Mexico   **New Mexico Bicycle Map**
(To be available in 2002)
New Mexico Highway & Transportation Dept., Strategic Planning
Bureau, Long Range Planning Section
P.O. Box 1149, SB-1, Santa Fe, NM 87504
505-827-5248 or NM 800-827-5514

New York   **Cross-State Bike Route Maps (4 Routes) New York Bicycle**
Touring Guide Route Maps
1 in. = 4 miles
Hoffman, William
624-B Candlewyck Rd., Lancaster, PA 17601
717-560-3636

North Carolina   **Cross-State Bike Route Maps (10 Routes)**
North Carolina Bicycling Highways
1 in. = 4.5 miles
North Carolina DOT
P.O. Box 25201, Raleigh, NC 27611
919-733-2804
http://www.dot.state.nc.us/transit/bicycle/

Ohio   **Biking Ohio Map & List of Bikeways in Ohio**
Scale: 1 in. = 24 miles
Ohio DOT, Division of Multi Modal Planning & Programs,
Bicycle/Pedestrian Program
P.O. Box 899, Columbus, OH 43216
614-644-7095

http://www.dot.state.oh.us/bike

Cross-State Bike Route Maps (8 Routes) Bike Route Maps
Scale 1 in. = 2 miles
Columbus Outdoor Pursuits
P.O. Box 14384, Columbus, OH 43214
614-447-1006
http://www.outdoor-pursuits.org

Oregon

Oregon Bicycling Guide
1 in. = 15 miles
Oregon DOT, Transportation Building
Salem, OR 97310
503-986-3556
http://www.odot.state.or.us/techserv/bikewalk

Rhode Island

A Guide to Cycling in the Ocean State (RI)
1 in. = 2 miles
Rhode Island DOT, Intermodal Transportation Planning
2 Capitol Hill Providence, RI 02903
401-222-4203 (ext. 4034)
http://www.dot.state.ri.us

South Carolina

South Carolina Bicycle Touring Guide
1 in. = 12 miles
State Bicycle/Pedestrian Coordinator, Traffic Engineering, South
Carolina DOT
955 Park St., P.O. Box 191, Columbia, SC 29202
803-737-1052
http://www.dot.state.sc.us/

Tennessee

Cross-State Bike Route Maps (5 Routes) Cycling Tennessee's Highways
1 in. = 4 miles
State Bicycle Coordinator, Tennessee DOT
505 Deaderick St., Suite 900, James K. Polk Building, Nashville, TN
37243
615-741-5310

Vermont

Bicycle Touring Map of Vermont
1 in. = 5 miles
Green Mountain Cyclery
133 Strongs Ave., Rutland, VT 05701
802-7750869
http://www.travel-vermont.com.repage.bicycle.htm

Washington
(State)

Washington State Traffic Data for Bicyclists
1 in. = 13.5 miles & 1 in. = 3.25 miles
Washington State DOT, Bicycle & Pedestrian Program
P.O. Box 47393, Olympia, WA 98504
360-705-7277
http://www.wsdot.wa.gov

Wisconsin

Wisconsin State Bike Map
1 in. = 4 miles
Bicycle Federation of Wisconsin
104 King St., Suite 204, P.O. Box 1224, Madison, WI 3701
608-251-4456
http://www.perfectiondata.com.com

Wyoming

Wyoming Bicycle Guidance Map
1 in. = 16 miles
Wyoming Transportation Dept., WYDOT Planning
5300 Bishop Blvd., Cheyenne, WY 82009
307-777-4719
http://www.wydotweb.state.wy.us/Docs/Modes/Bicycle/Bicycle.html

A cyclist enjoys this rugged scenery in the Black Hills of
South Dakota along the Mickelson Trail.

U.S.A.'s Cross-Country Bike Route Maps

These bike routes are designed for the experienced long distance cyclist. The bike routes follow primarily lightly traveled back roads across the United States and parts of Canada. Selected sections of these bike routes are signed along the roadways to assist the cyclists. For more information, contact the address on the bottom of this page.

Bike Route Code #   Adventure Cycling Cross-Country Bike Route

#BC-10   Northern Tier Bicycle Route
                Anacortes, WA to Bar Harbor, ME
                4315 miles, 1 in. = 4 miles (11 map set)

#BC-12   Great Parks Bicycle Route
                Jasper, Alberta (Canada) to Durango, CO
                2455 miles, 1 in. = 4 miles (6 map set)

#BC-14   Atlantic Coast Route (USA-Bike Route 1)
                Bar Harbor, ME to Ft. Myers Beach, FL
                2525 miles, 1 in. = 4 miles (7 map set)

#BC-15   Trans America Bicycle Route (USA-Bike Route 76)
                Astoria, OR to Yorktown, VA
                4260 miles, 1 in. = 4 miles (12 map set)

#BC-16   Pacific Coast Bicycle Route
                Vancouver, BC (Canada) to Imperial Beach, CA
                1830 miles, 1 in. = 4 miles (5 map set)

#BC-17   Southern Tier Bicycle Route
                San Diego, CA to St. Augustine, FL
                3190 miles, 1 in. = 4 miles (7 map set)

#BC-18   Great River South Bicycle Route
                Muscatine, IA to St. Francisville, LA
                1335 miles, 1 in. = 4 miles (3 map set)

#BC-19   North Lakes Bicycle Route
                Osceola, WI to Monroeville, IN
                1095 miles, 1 in. = 4 miles (3 map set)

BC-21   Western Express Bicycle Route
                San Francisco, CA to Pueblo, CO
                1585 miles, 1 in. = 4 miles (4 map set)

For current prices, contact: Adventure Cycling Association (Bikecentennial)
150 E Pine St., P.O. Box 8308, Missoula, MT 59807
1-800-721-8719
http://www.adv-cycling.org.

U.S.A.'s Cross-Country Bike Route Maps

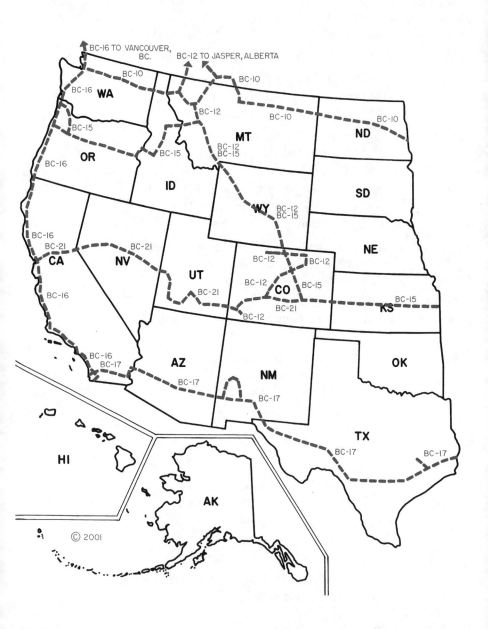

U.S.A.'s Cross-Country Bike Route Maps

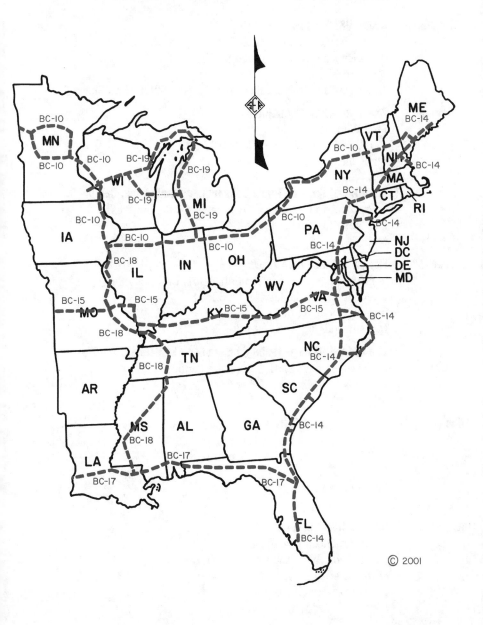

© 2001

U.S.A.'s Rails-to-Trails Guide Books

U.S. General **Biking USA'S Rail-Trails**
Shawn E. Richardson, 2002, Adventure Publications, Inc.
820 Cleveland St. S, Cambridge, MN 55008
800-678-7006
Trail Listings & Trail Location. Maps included for all 50 States.

California **Rail-Trail Guide to California**
Fred Wert, 1995, Infinity Press
P.O. Box 17883, Seattle, WA 98107
Maps Included

The Official Rails-to-Trails Conservancy Guidebook, California
Tracy Salcedo-Chourre, 2001, The Globe Pequot Press
P.O. Box 480, Guilford, CT 06437
Maps Included

Florida **Florida's Paved Bike Trails**
Jeff Kunerth & Gretchen Kunerth, 2001, University Press of Florida
15 NW 15th St. Gainesville, FL 32611
http://www.upf.com
Maps Included

The Official Rails-to-Trails Conservancy Guidebook, Florida
David Gluckman, 2001, The Globe Pequot Press
P.O. Box 480, Guilford, CT 06437
Maps Included

Illinois **Bicycle Trails of Illinois**
2002, American Bike Trails
610 Hillside Ave., Antioch, IL 60002
800-246-4627
http://www.abtrails.com
Maps Included

Iowa **Bicycle Trails of Iowa**
2003, American Bike Trails
610 Hillside Ave., Antioch, IL 60002
800-246-4627
http://www.abtrails.com
Maps Included

Massachusetts Bike Paths of Massachusetts
Stuart Johnstone, 1996, Active Publications
P.O. Box 716, Carlisle, MA 01741
Maps Included

Minnesota   **Biking in Vikingland**
Marlys Mickelson, 1999, Adventure Publications, Inc.
820 Cleveland St. S, Cambridge, MN 55008
800-678-7006
Maps included; book also shows some trails in Wisconsin.

Missouri   **Biking Missouri's Rail-Trails**
Shawn E. Richardson, 2004, Adventure Publications, Inc.
820 Cleveland St. S, Cambridge, MN 55008
800-678-7006
Maps Included

New Jersey   **24 Great Rail-Trails of New Jersey**
Craig Della Penna, 1999, New England Cartographics Inc.
P.O. Box 9369, North Amherst, MA 01059
888-995-6277 or 413-549-4124
Maps Included

New York   **Cycling along the Canals of New York**
Louis Russi, 1999, Vitesse Press
4431 Lehigh Rd., #288, College Park, MD 20740
301-772-5915.
http://www.acornpub.com
Maps Included

Ohio   **Biking Ohio's Rail-Trails**
Shawn E. Richardson, 2000, Adventure Publications, Inc.
820 Cleveland St. S, Cambridge, MN 55008
800-678-7006
Maps Included

Oregon   **The Official Rails-to-Trails Conservancy Guidebook, Washington & Oregon**
Mia Barbera, 2001, The Globe Pequot Press
P.O. Box 480, Guilford, CT 06437
Maps Included

U.S.A.'s Rails-to-Trails Guide Books

Pennsylvania   **Pennsylvania's Great Rail-Trails**
Rails-to-Trails Conservancy, 1998, RTC
1100 17th St. NW, 10th Floor, Washington, D.C. 20036
202-331-9696
Maps Included

Free Wheeling Easy in and Around Western Pennsylvania
Mary Shaw & Roy Weil, Associates
414 S Craig St., #307, Pittsburgh, PA 15213
http://www.spoke.compose.ce.cmu.edu/fwe/fwe.htm
Maps Included

Washington   **Washington's Rail-Trails**
State   Fred Wert, 2001, The Mountaineers
1011 SW Klickitat Way, Seattle, WA 98134
800-553-4453
http://www.mountaineers.org
Maps Included

The Official Rails-to-Trails Conservancy Guidebook, Washington & Oregon
Mia Barbera, 2001, The Globe Pequot Press
P.O. Box 480, Guilford, CT 06437
Maps Included

West Virginia   **Adventure Guide to West Virginia's Rail-Trails**
1995, West Virginia Rails-to-Trails Council
P.O. Box 8889, South Charleston, WV 25303
304-722-6558
Maps Included

Wisconsin   **Biking Wisconsin's Rail-Trails**
Shawn E. Richardson, 2004, Adventure Publications, Inc.
820 Cleveland St. S, Cambridge, MN 55008
800-678-7006
Maps Included

Atlantic States (DE, MD, VA, WV)

The Official Rails-to-Trails Conservancy Guidebook, MD, DE, VA, WV
Barbara A. Noe, 2000, The Globe Pequot Press
P.O. Box 480, Guilford, CT 06437
Maps Included

New England States   (CT, MA, ME, NH, RI & VT)

Great Rail-Trails of the Northeast
Craig Della Penna, 1995, New England Cartographics Inc.
P.O. Box 9369, North Amherst, MA 01059
888-995-6277 or 413-549-4124
Maps Included

The Official Rails-to-Trails Conservancy Guidebook, CT, RI, MA, VT, NH, ME
Cynthia Mascott, 2000, The Globe Pequot Press
P.O. Box 480,Guilford, CT 06437
Maps Included

Bikers & Hikers enjoy crossing this trestle on the Youghiogheny River Trail near Ohiopyle, Pennsylvania.

U.S.A.'s Bicycle Information Contact by State

U.S.A. Nationwide
General Information
Adventure Cycling Association • P.O. Box 8308 • Missoula, MT 59807 • 406-721-1776 • http://www.adv-cycling.org

American Bike Trails • 610 Hillside Ave. • Antioch, IL 60002 • 800-246-4627 • http://www.abtrails.com

American Youth Hostels (AYH) • P.O. Box 37613 • Washington, D.C. 20013 • 202-783-6161

Biking U.S.A.'s Rail-Trails (Rail-Trail & Bike Trail Maps) Adventure Publications, Inc. • 820 Cleveland St. S • Cambridge, MN 55008 • 800-678-7006 • http://www.BikingUSARailTrails.com

Government Agency Info (U.S. Parks/Forests & State Parks/Forests) • http://www.peakto-peak.net/park_us_sta.html

Rails to Trails Conservancy • 1100 17th St. NW, 10th Floor, Washington, D.C. 20036 • 202-331-9696 • http://www.railtrails.org

Tourism (U.S.A. & Worldwide) • http://www.mbnet.mb.ca/lucas/travel/tourism-offices.html

Trail Resources • 211 Spring St. • Batavia, IL 60510 • http://www.perfectiondata.com.com

U.S. DOT FHWA, HEPH-30 • Room 3301, 400 7th St. SW • Washington, D.C. 20590 • 202-366-5013

Trail Information
American Discovery Trail • American Discovery Trail • P.O. Box 20155 • Washington, D.C. 20041 • 800-663-2378 or 703-753-0149 • http://www.discoverytrail.org

East Coast Greenway • East Coast Greenway Alliance • 135 Main St. • Wakefield, RI 02879 • 401-789-1706 or 401-789-4625 • http://www.greenway.org

Juan Bautista De Anza National Historic Trail • Anza Trail Coalition of Arizona • P.O. Box 42612 • Tucson, AZ • 85733 520-325-0909 • http://www.therapure.com/anza-trail

Lewis & Clark National Historic Trail • Lewis & Clark Trail Heritage Foundation Inc. • P.O. Box 3434 • Great Falls, MT 59403 • http://www.lewisandclark.org

Mississippi River Trail • Mississippi River Trail • 7777 Walnut Grove Rd., P.O. Box 27 • Memphis, TN 38120 • 901-624-3600 • http://www.bicyclemrt.org

North Country Trail • North Country Trail Association • 229 E Main St. • Lowell, MI 49331 • 888-454-NCTA, 888-454-6282 or 616-897-5987 • http://www.northcountrytrail.org

Alabama
General Information
Alabama Bicycle Coordinator, Bureau of Multimodal Transortation, Alabama DOT • 1409 Coliseum Blvd. • Montgomery, AL 36103 • 334-242-6085

Alabama Bureau of Tourism & Travel • 401 Adams Ave., P.O. Box 4927 • Montgomery, AL 36103 • 800-ALABAMA, 800-252-2262 or 334-242-6085 • http://www.touralabama.org

Trail Information

Chief Ladiga Trail Trail • Manager, City of Piedmont • 109 N Center Ave., P.O. Box 112 • Piedmont, AL • 36272 256-447-9007 or 256-447-3363 • http://www.calhounconews.com

Limestone Trail • Coordinator for Rail-Trails, Limestone County Parks & Recreation Board, Athens Road Runners • P.O. Box 945, 310 Washington St. • Athens, AL 35612 • 205-230-9010

Robertsdale Trail • City of Robertsdale • P.O. Box 429 • Robertsdale, AL 36567 • 334-947-7354

Alaska

General Information

Alaska Bicycle/Pedestrian Coordinator, Alaska DOT & PF • 3132 Channel Dr., Suite 200 • Juneau, AK 99801 • 907-465-6989 • http://www.dot.state.ak.us/

Alaska Division of Tourism • P.O. Box 110801 • Juneau, AK 99811 • 800-862-5275 or 907-465-2012 • http://www.commerce.state.ak.us/tourism/homenew.htm

Alaska Marine Highway System (From Bellingham, WA to Alaska), Alaska DOT • 907-465-3900 for reservations • http://www.dot.state.ak.us/external/amhs/home.html

Trail Information

Alaska Highway Bike Path • Alaska DOT & PF, Bicycle/Pedestrian Coordinator • 3132 Channel Dr., Suite 200 • Juneau, AK 99801 • 907-465-6989 • http://www.dot.state.ak.us/

Campbell Creek Bicycle Trail • Anchorage Trails & Greenways Coalition • P.O. Box 92394 • Anchorage, AK 99509 • 907-566-ATGC or 907-566-2842

Chester Creek Bicycle Trail • Anchorage Trails & Greenways Coalition • P.O. Box 92394 • Anchorage, AK 99509 • 907-566-ATGC or 907-566-2842

Fairbanks Bikeways • Alaska DOT & PF, Bicycle/Pedestrian Coordinator • 3132 Channel Dr., Suite 200 • Juneau, AK 99801 • 907-465-6989 • http://www.dot.state.ak.us/

Glen Highway Bicycle Trail • Anchorage Trails & Greenways Coalition • P.O. Box 92394 • Anchorage, AK 99509 • 907-566-ATGC or 907-566-2842

Glen Highway Bicycle Trail • Alaska DOT & PF, Bicycle/Pedestrian Coordinator • 3132 Channel Dr., Suite 200 • Juneau, AK 99801 • 907-465-6989 • http://www.dot.state.ak.us/

Juneau Bike Paths • Juneau Parks & Recreation Dept. • 155 Seward St. • Juneau, AK 99801 • 907-586-5226 or 907-364-3388 or 907-364-2800

Knowles (Tony) Coastal Bicycle Trail • Municipality of Anchorage, Dept. of Culture & Recreation; Parks and Beautification Division • P.O. Box 196650 • Anchorage, AK 99519 907-343-4474

Knowles (Tony) Coastal Bicycle Trail • Anchorage Trails & Greenways Coalition • P.O. Box 92394 • Anchorage, AK 99509 • 907-566-ATGC or 907-566-2842

Parks Highway Bike Path • Alaska DOT & PF, Bicycle/Pedestrian Coordinator • 3132 Channel Dr., Suite 200 • Juneau, AK 99801 • 907-465-6989 • http://www.dot.state.ak.us/

Richardson Highway Bike Path • Alaska DOT & PF, Bicycle/Pedestrian Coordinator • 3132 Channel Dr., Suite 200 • Juneau, AK 99801 • 907-465-6989 • http://www.dot.state.ak.us/

Seward Highway Bike Path • Alaska DOT & PF, Bicycle/Pedestrian Coordinator • 3132

Channel Dr., Suite 200 • Juneau, AK 99801 • 907-465-6989 • http://www.dot.state.ak.us/

Seward Rail-Trail Alaska DOT & PF, Bicycle/Pedestrian Coordinator • 3132 Channel Dr., Suite 200 • Juneau, AK 99801 • 907-465-6989 • http://www.dot.state.ak.us/

Sterling Highway Bike Path • Alaska DOT & PF, Bicycle/Pedestrian Coordinator • 3132 Channel Dr., Suite 200 • Juneau, AK 99801 • 907-465-6989 • http://www.dot.state.ak.us/

Tok Cutoff Highway Bike Path • Alaska DOT & PF, Bicycle/Pedestrian Coordinator • 3132 Channel Dr., Suite 200 • Juneau, AK 99801 • 907-465-6989 • http://www.dot.state.ak.us/

Arizona
General Information
Arizona Bicycle/Pedestrian Planner Arizona DOT, Planning Division • 201 N Stone, P.O. Box 27210 • Tucson, AZ 85726 • 520-791-4372

Arizona Office of Tourism • 2702 N 3rd St., Suite 4015 • Phoenix, AZ 85009 • 800-279-7654 • http://www.arizonaguide.com

Trail Information
Aviation Hwy-Golf Links Bike Path • City of Tucson DOT, Alternate Modes Office • P.O. Box 27210 • Tucson, AZ 85726 • 602-791-4372

Prescott Peavine Trail • Trails & Open Space, City of Prescott • Prescott, AZ 86302 • 520-445-5880

Rillito River Bike Path • City of Tucson DOT • Alternate Modes Office • P.O. Box 27210 • Tucson, AZ 85726 • 602-791-4372

Santa Cruz River Bike Path • City of Tucson DOT • Alternate Modes Office • P.O. Box 27210 • Tucson, AZ 85726 • 602-791-4372

Spanish Trail Bike Path • City of Tucson DOT • Alternate Modes Office • P.O. Box 27210 • Tucson, AZ 85726 • 602-791-4372

University Heights to Fort Tuthill Trail • City of Flagstaff • 211 W Aspen Ave. • Flagstaff, AZ 86001 • 520-779-7632 or 520-774-9541

Arkansas
General Information
Arkansas Bicycle Coordinator Arkansas Highway & Transportation Dept. • P.O. Box 2261 • Little Rock, AR 72203 • 501-569-2020

Arkansas Dept. Of Parks & Tourism One Capitol Mall • Little Rock, AR 72201 • 800-NATUR-AL, 800-628-8725 or 501-682-7777 • http://www.arkansas.com

Trail Information
Hot Springs Creek Greenway • City of Hot Springs 111 Opera • P.O. Box 700 • Hot Springs National Park, AR 71902 • 501-321-6800

Levee Walking Trail • City of Helena • 226 Perry St. • Helena, AR 72342 • 870-338-9831

Marvell Bike Trail • City of Marvell • City Hall P.O. Box 837 • Marvell, AR 72366 • 870-829-2573

California

General Information

California Bicycle Coordinator Caltrans-Headquarters • P.O. Box 942874, M.S. #1 • Sacramento, CA 94274 • 916-653-0036 • http://www.dot.ca.gov

California Division of Tourism • P.O. Box 1499 Dept. TIA • Sacramento, CA 95812 • 800-GO-CALIF, 800-862-2543 or 916-322-2881 • http://www.gocalif.ca.gov

Rails to Trails Conservancy, California Field Office • http://www.railtrails.org/CA

Trail Information

Alton Bike Trail (Alton to Bristol Bike Trail) • City of Santa Ana Parks, Recreation & Community Services Agency • P.O. Box 1988, M-23 • Santa Ana, CA 92702 • 714-571-4211

Ballona Creek Bike Path • Metropolitan Transportation Authority, Customer Relations, Dept. 7170, One Gateway Plaza • Los Angeles, CA 90012 • 800-COMMUTE or 800-266-6883

Beach Bike Path • Los Angeles, CA Metropolitan Transportation Authority, Customer Relations, Dept. 7170, One Gateway Plaza • Los Angeles, CA 9001 • 2 800-COMMUTE or 800-266-6883

Chico Airport Bike Path • Assistant Director of Public Works, Municipal Services Dept. City of Chico • P.O. Box 4320 • Chico, CA 95927 • 530-895-4800

Clovis Old Town Trail • Coalition for Community Trails • P.O. Box 1313 • Clovis, CA 93613 • 559-323-0892

Coast Highway Bikeway • City of Seal Beach • 211 8th St. • Seal Beach, CA 90740 • 562-431-2527 • www.ci.seal-beach.ca.us

Contra Costa Canal Regional Trail • Trails Specialist, East Bay Regional Park District 2950 Peralta Oaks Court • P.O. Box 5381 • Oakland, CA 94605 • 510-544-2611 • http://www.ebparks.org

Culver City Median Bikeway • Bicycle Coordinator for the City of Los Angeles • 213-580-1199

Culver City Median Bikeway • Public Works Dept. • P.O. Box 507 • Culver City, CA 90232 • 310-253-6420

Duarte Bike Trail (Duarte Recreational Trail) • Duarte Parks & Recreation Dept. • 1600 E Huntington Dr. • Duarte, CA 91010 • 626-357-6118 Ext. 201

Durham Bike Path • Assistant Director of Public Works, Municipal Services Dept. City of Chico • P.O. Box 4320 • Chico, CA 95927 • 530-895-4800

El Dorado Trail • Recreation & Parks • City of Placerville 549 Main St. • Placerville, CA 95667 • 916-642-5232

Fairfield Linear Park Trail • Assistant Community Services • City of Fairfield 1000 Webster St. • Fairfield, CA 94533 • 707-428-7465 • http://www.ci.fairfield.ca.us

Fay Avenue Bike Path • Bicycle Coordinator • City of San Diego • 1010 2nd Ave., Suite 800 • San Diego, CA 92101 • 619-533-3110

Fresno Sugar Pine Trail • Fresno City Parks & Recreation Dept. • 1033 5th St. • Clovis, CA 93612 • 559-297-2354

Fillmore Trail City Engineer • City of Fillmore • 524 Sespe Ave. • Fillmore, CA 93015 • 805-524-3701

Hammond Coastal Trail • Parks Supervisor, Humbolt County Dept. of Public Works • 1106 Second St. • Eureka, CA 95501 • 707-839-2086

Hoover Street Trail • City of Westminster • 8200 Westminster Blvd. • Westminster, CA 92683 • 714-898-3311

King (Martin Luther) Promenade Trail • Bike Coordinator • City of San Diego • 1010 2nd Ave, Suite 800, MS609 • San Diego, CA 92101 • 619-533-3110

Lafayette-Moraga Regional Trail • East Bay Regional Park District • 2950 Peralta Oaks Ct. • P.O. Box 5381 • Oakland, CA 94605 • 510-544-2611 or 510-635-0135 • http://www.ebparks.org

Lands End Trail • Golden Gate National Recreation Area Fort Mason Building • 201 San Francisco, CA 94123 415-561-4511

Larkspur Path • Town of Corte Madera • 300 Tamalpais Dr. • Corte Madera, CA • 94925 415-927-5064

Los Angeles River Bike Path • Metropolitan Transportation Authority, Customer Relations • Dept. 7170, One Gateway Plaza • Los Angeles, CA 9001 • 2 800-COMMUTE or 800-266-6883

Midway Bike Path • Director, Dept. of Public Works Butte County • Oroville, CA, 95965 • 916-538-7681

Mill Valley-Sausalito Path • Parks, Open Space & Cultural Services Department • Marin County Civic Center • San Rafael, CA 94903 • 415-499-6387

Monterey Bay Coastal Trail • Monterey Peninsula Regional Park District • 60 Garden Ct., Suite 325 • Monterey, CA 93940 • 831-732-3196 • http://www.mprpd.org

Monterey Peninsula Recreational Trail • Director of Monterey Recreation & Community Service Dept. • 546 Dutra St. • Monterey, CA 93940 • 831-646-3866

Monterey Peninsula Recreational Trail • Director of Pacific Grove Recreation Dept. • 515 Gunipero Ave. • Pacific Grove, CA 93950 • 831-648-3130

Monterey Peninsula Recreational Trail • Program Manager, Monterey Peninsula Regional Park District • 700 W Carmel Valley Rd. • Camel Valley, CA • 93924 831-659-6068 • http://www.mprpd.org

Ohlone Greenway (Santa Fe Greenway) • Landscape Architect, Parks & Waterfront Dept., Park Design Division • City of Berkeley 2201 Dwight Way • Berkeley, CA 94704 • 510-665-3455

Ohlone Greenway • Environment Resources Coordinator, Community Development Dept. • City of Albany 1000 San Pable Ave. • Albany, CA 94706 • 510-528-5766

Ohlone Greenway • City of El Cerrito • 10890 San Pablo Ave. • El Cerrito, CA 94530 • 510-215-4382

Ojai Valley Trail • Ventura County Reservations & Information • 800 S Victoria • Ventura, CA 93009 • 805-654-3951

Pacific Electric Bicycle Trail • City of Santa Ana Parks, Recreation & Community Services

Agency • P.O. Box 1988 • Santa Ana, CA 92702 • 714-571-4200

Paradise Memorial Trailway • Community Development Director • Town of Paradise 5555 Skyway • Paradise, CA 95969 • 916-872-6291

Reedley Rail-Trail • Community Parkway City Engineer • City of Reedley Tourism • 1720 10th St. • Reedley, CA 93654 • 559-643-0770 • http://www.reedley.com

Rose Canyon Bicycle Path • Bicycle Coordinator • City of San Diego • 1010 2nd Ave., Suite 800, MS609 • San Diego, CA 92101 • 619-533-3110

Sacramento Northern Bike Trail • Bicycle Coordinator • City of Sacramento • 927 10th St. • Sacramento, CA 95814 • 916-264-8434

Sacramento River Trail • City of Redding • 777 Cypress Ave., P.O. Box 496049 • Redding, CA 96001 • 530-225-4512

San Gabriel River Bikeway • City of Seal Beach • 211 8th St. • Seal Beach, CA 90740 • 562-431-2527 • www.ci.seal-beach.ca.us

San Ramon Valley Iron Horse Regional Trail (Iron Horse Regional Trail) • East Bay Regional Park District • 2950 Peralta Oaks Ct. • P.O. Box 5381 • Oakland, CA 94605 • 510-544-2611 or 510-635-0135 • http://www.ebparks.org

Santa Ana River Bikeway • City of Seal Beach • 211 8th St. • Seal Beach, CA 90740 • 562-431-2527 • www.ci.seal-beach.ca.us

Seal Beach Regional Trail (Electric Avenue Median Park Trail) • City of Seal Beach • 211 8th St. • Seal Beach, CA 90740 • 562-431-2527 • http://www.ci.seal-beach.ca.us

Shepherd Canyon Trail • Oakland Parks & Recreation • 3590 Sanborn Dr. • Oakland, CA 94602 • 510-482-7857

Silver Strand Bikeway Bike Coordinator • City of San Diego • 1010 2nd Ave, Suite 800, MS609 • San Diego, CA 92101 • 619-533-3110

Sir Francis Drake Bikeway (Cross Marin Bike Trail) • Samuel P. Taylor State Park • P.O. Box 251 • Lagunitas, CA 94938 • 415-488-9897

Sonoma Bike Path Assistant Planner • City of Sonoma • No. 1 The Plaza • Sonoma, CA 95476 • 707-938-3794

Ten-Mile Coastal Trail (Mackerricher Haul Road Trail) • Ten-Mile Coast Trail Foundation • P.O. Box 1534 • Ft. Bragg, CA 95437 • 707-964-9340 • http://www.mcn.org/1/10milecoastaltrail

Ten-Mile Coastal Trail • Russina River-Mendocino District • California State Parks • P.O. Box 123 • Duncan Mills, CA 95430 • 707-865-3132

Ten-Mile Coastal Trail • California State Parks Dept. • Mendocino Office • P.O. Box 440 • Mendocino, CA 95460 • 707-937-5804

Tiburon Linear Park Trail • Tiburon Public Works Dept. 1505 • Tiburon Blvd. • Tiburon, CA 94920 • 415-435-7373

Tahoe City to Dollar Point Bike Trail • Resource Development Tahoe City P.U.D. • P.O. Box 33 • Tahoe City, CA 96145 • 530-583-3796 ext. 29

Tahoe City to Tahoma Bike Trail • Resource Development Tahoe City P.U.D. • P.O. Box 33 • Tahoe City, CA 96145 • 530-583-3796 ext. 29

Tahoe City Truckee River Bike Trail • Resource Development Tahoe City P.U.D. • P.O. Box 33 • Tahoe City, CA 96145 • 530-583-3796 ext. 29

Tustin Branch Trail • Trails Planner, Harbors, Beaches and Parks, EMA/County of Orange • P.O. Box 4048 • Santa Ana, CA 92702 • 714-834-3137

Tustin Branch Trail • Associate Environmental Planner • Caltrans Lake Forest, CA 92630 • 714-724-2224

Ventura River Trail • Marketing Specialist • City of Ventura • 501 Poli St., P.O. Box 99 • Ventura, CA 93002 • 805-654-7800 • http://www.ci.ventura.ca.us

Walnut Trail (Atchison Topeka & Santa Fe Trail) • Public Works Dept. • One Civic Center Plaza • P.O. Box 19575 • Irvine, CA 92623 9 • 49-724-7347 • http://www.ci.irvine.ca.us

Watts Towers Crescent Greenway • Metropolitan Transportation Authority • P.O. Box 194 • Los Angeles, CA 90053 • 213-244-6456

West County Trail & Joe Rodota Trail • Sonoma County Regional Parks • 2300 County Center Dr., Suite 120-A • Santa Rosa, CA 95403 • 707-565-2041 • http://www.sonoma-county.org/parks

Yolo Causeway / 2nd Street / Russell Blvd. Bike Paths • Solano Bike Links • 707-438-0654 • www.solanolinks.com/bikelink.htm

Colorado
General Information
Bicycle Colorado • P.O. Box 698 • Salida, CO 81201 • 719-530-0051 • http://www.bicycle-colo.org

Colorado Bicycle Program Manager • Colorado DOT • 4201 E Arkansas • DTD • Denver, CO 80222 • 303-757-9982

Colorado Division of Parks & Outdoor Recreation • Room 618, 1313 Sherman St. • Denver, CO 80203 • http://www.parks.state.co.us/

Colorado Trail • http://www.coloradotrail.org

Colorado Trail Finder • http://www.coloradoguide.com/guide4.cfm

Colorado Travel & Tourism Authority • 1672 Pennsylvania St. • Denver, CO 80203 • 800-COLORAD, 800-265-6723 or 303-832-6171

Trail Information
Animas River Trail • Durango Parks & Recreation Dept. • 949 E Second Ave. • Durango, CO 81301 • 970-385-2950 • http://www.ci.durango.co.us

Arkansas Riverwalk Trail Canon • City Metropolitan Recreation & Park District • P.O. Box 947 • Canon City, CO 81215 • 719-275-1578

Bear Creek Trail • Trails Coordinator • Denver Parks & Recreation • 945 S Huron • Denver, CO 80219 • 303-698-4903

Bear Creek Trail • Denver Bicycle Touring Club • Inc. P.O. Box 260517 • Denver, CO 80226 • 303-756-7240 • http://www.dbtc.org

Blue River Pathway • Summit County Community Development Dept. • Open Space & Trails P.O. Box 5660 • Frisco, CO 80443 • 970-668-4060

Boulder Creek Bike Path • Boulder County Alternative Transportation • P.O. Box 471 • Boulder, CO 80306 • 303-441-3900

C-470 Bikeway • Denver Bicycle Touring Club • Inc. P.O. Box 260517 • Denver, CO 80226 • 303-756-7240 • http://www.dbtc.org

Cache La Poudre Bikeway • Bicycle Colorado • P.O. Box 698 • Salida, CO 81201 • 719-530-0051 • http://www.bicyclecolo.org

Cherry Creek Trail (Denver to Cherry Creek State Recreation Area) • Trails Coordinator • Denver Parks & Recreation • 945 S Huron • Denver, CO 80219 • 303-698-4903

Cherry Creek Trail • Denver Bicycle Touring Club • Inc. P.O. Box 260517 • Denver, CO 80226 • 303-756-7240 • http://www.dbtc.org

Cherry Creek Trail (Parker) • Denver Bicycle Touring Club • Inc. P.O. Box 260517 • Denver, CO 80226 • 303-756-7240 • http://www.dbtc.org

Cherry Creek Trail • Bicycle Colorado • P.O. Box 698 • Salida, CO 81201 • 719-530-0051 • http://www.bicyclecolo.org

Clear Creek Bikeway • Denver Bicycle Touring Club • Inc. P.O. Box 260517 • Denver, CO 80226 • 303-756-7240 • http://www.dbtc.org

Corridor Trail • Parks, Recreational & Cultural Director • Town of Lyons P.O. Box 49 • Lyons, CO 80540 • 303-823-6640

Creek Trail • Denver Bicycle Touring Club • Inc. P.O. Box 260517 • Denver, CO 80226 • 303-756-7240 • http://www.dbtc.org

Dillon-Keystone Recreation Trail • Summit County Community Development Dept. • Open Space & Trails P.O. Box 5660 • Frisco, CO 80443 • 970-668-4060

Dillon Dam Trail • Summit County Community Development Dept. • Open Space & Trails P.O. Box 5660 • Frisco, CO 80443 • 970-668-4060

Fowler Trail • El Dorado Canyon State Park Box B • El Dorado Springs, CO 80025 • 303-494-3943 • http://www.coloradoparks.org

Fraser River Trail • Public Works Department • Town of Winter Park • Winter Park, CO 80482 • 970-726-8011

Frisco-Farmer's Korner Recreation Trail • Summit County Community Development Dept. • Open Space & Trails Manager • P.O. Box 5660 • Frisco, CO 80443 • 970-668-4060

Frisco Lakefront Trail • Summit County Community Development Dept. • Open Space & Trails Manager • P.O. Box 5660 • Frisco, CO 80443 • 970-668-4060

Glenwood Canyon Recreational Trail • Colorado DOT • 202 Centennial • Glenwood Springs, CO 81601 • 970-947-9361

Glenwood Canyon Recreational Trail • Bicycle Colorado • P.O. Box 698 • Salida, CO 81201 • 719-530-0051 • http://www.bicyclecolo.org

Highline Canal Trail • Trails Coordinator • Denver Parks & Recreation • 945 S Huron • Denver, CO 80219 • 303-698-4903

Interstate-70 Beaver Tunnels Alternate Bike Path • P.O. Box 698 • Salida, CO 81201 • 719-530-0051 • http://www.bicyclecolo.org

Loveland-Greeley Canal Bike Path • Bicycle Colorado • P.O. Box 698 • Salida, CO 81201 • 719-530-0051 • http://www.bicyclecolo.org

Mineral Belt Trail • Lake County Parks & Recreation Board • P.O. Box 666 • Leadville, CO 80461 • 719-486-4288

Narrow Gauge Trail • Trail Planner • Jefferson County Open Space • 700 Jeffco County Parkway, Suite 100 • Golden, CO 80401 • 303-271-5925

Platte River Greenway • Trails Coordinator • Denver Parks & Recreation • 945 S Huron • Denver, CO 80219 • 303-698-4903

Platte River Greenway • Denver Bicycle Touring Club • Inc. P.O. Box 260517 • Denver, CO 80226 • 303-756-7240 • http://www.dbtc.org

Rio Grande Trail • Pitkin County Land Management • 76 Service Center Rd. • Aspen, CO 81611 • 970-920-5214

Roaring Fork Trail • Aspen Parks Dept. • 130 S Galena • Aspen, CO 81611 • 970-920-5120

Rock Island Regional Trail • El Paso County Parks 2002 Creek Crossing • Colorado Springs, CO 80906 • 719-520-6375 • http://www.elpasoco.com/parks

Salida Trail System • Salida Trail System • 317 W 2nd P.O. Box 417 • Salida, CO 81201 • 719-539-6738

Sanderson Gulch Trail • Trails Coordinator • Denver Parks & Recreation • 945 S Huron • Denver, CO 80219 • 303-698-4903

Shooks Run Trail • City of Colorado Springs Parks • Recreation & Forestry 1421 Recreation Way • Colorado Springs, CO • 80905 719-385-6940 or 719-385-6522

Snake River Pathway (Keystone-Summit Cove Recreation Trail) • Summit County Community Development Dept. • Open Space & Trails Dept. • P.O. Box 5660 • Frisco, CO 80443 • 970-668-4060

Spring Creek Bikeway • Bicycle Colorado • P.O. Box 698 • Salida, CO 81201 • 719-530-0051 • http://www.bicyclecolo.org

Ten-Mile Canyon Recreation Trail (Vail Pass Trail) • Summit County: Summit County Community Development Dept. • Open Space & Trails Dept. • P.O. Box 5660 • Frisco, CO 80443 • 970-668-4060

Ten-Mile Canyon Recreation Trail • Eagle County: Chamber of Commerce • Vail Valley • P.O. Box 1437, 260 Beaver Creek Place • Avon, CO 81620 • 970-949-5189 • http://www.vailvalleychamber.com

Ten-Mile Canyon Recreation Trail • Bicycle Colorado • P.O. Box 698 • Salida, CO 81201 • 719-530-0051 • http://www.bicyclecolo.org

Uncompahgre River Trail • Parks Superintendent • City of Montrose • 433 S First St., P.O. Box 790 • Montrose, CO 81402 • 970-240-1411

Union Pacific Trail • Thornton Parks & Recreation Dept. • 2211 Eppinger Blvd. • Thornton, CO 80229 • 303-255-7875

Connecticut
General Information
Connecticut Bicycle Coordinator • Connecticut DOT • 2800 Berlin Turnpike, P.O. Box 317546 • Newington, CT 06131

Connecticut Dept. Of Ecnomic & Community Development • Tourism Division 505 Hudson St. • Hartford, CT 06106 • 800-CT-BOUND, 800-282-6863 or 860-270-8081 • http://www.ctbound.org

Trail Information
Captain John Bissell Greenway • Parks & Recreation Dept. • P.O. Box 191 • Manchester, CT 06045 • 860-647-3084

Charter Oak Greenway • Parks & Recreation Dept. • P.O. Box 191 • Manchester, CT 06045 • 860-647-3084

Farmington Canal Linear State Park Trail • State of Connecticut Dept. of Environmental Protection • 178 S Swamp Rd. • Farmington, CT 06032 • 860-677-1819

Milone & MacBroom Inc. • 716 S Main St. • Cheshire, CT 06410 • 203-271-1773 • http://www.viewzone.com/bikepath.html

Farmington River Trail • State of Connecticut Dept. of Environmental Protection • 178 S Swamp Rd. • Farmington, CT 06032 • 860-677-1819

Farmington River Trail • Farmington Valley Trails Council Inc. • P.O. Box 576 • Tariffville, CT 06081 • http://www.members.aol.com/fvgreenway.

Farmington Valley Greenway • Farmington Valley Trails Council • Inc. P.O. Box 576 • Tariffville, CT 06081 • http://www.members.aol.com/fvgreenway.

Farmington Valley Greenway • Parks & Recreation • Town of Avon • 60 W Main St. • Avon, CT 06001 • 860-409-4332

Middlebury Greenway • Middlebury Park & Recreation Dept. • 1212 Whittemore Rd., P.O. Box 392 • Middlebury, CT 06762 • 203-758-2520 • http://www.middlebury-ct.org

Putnam River Trail • Economic Development Commission • 112 Main St. • Putnam, CT 06260 • 860-963-6811

Stratton Brook State Park-Town Forest Trail • Simsbury Dept. of Culture • Parks & Recreation P.O. Box 495, 933 Hopemeadow St. • Simsbury, CT 06070 • 860-658-3255

Stratton Brook State Park-Town Forest Trail • Farmington Valley Trail Council Inc. • P.O. Box 576 • Tariffville, CT 06081 • http://www.fvgreenway@aol.com

Trolley Trail (Branford Ct) • Planning and Zoning Department • Town of Branford, P.O. Box 150, Town Hall Dr. • Branford, CT 06405 • 203-488-1255

Vernon Rail-Trail (Town of Vernon Rails-to-trails System) • Vernon Parks & Recreation • 120 South St. • Vernon, CT 06066 • 860-870-3520 or 860-872-6118

Delaware
General Information
Delaware Bicycle/Pedestrian Coordinator • Delaware DOT • P.O. Box 778 • Dover, DE 19903 • 302-760-2453 • http://www.state.de.us/govern/agencies/deldot/bike/welcome.htm

Delaware Tourism Office • Delaware Economic Development Center • 99 Kings Highway •

Dover, DE 19901 • 800-441-8846 or 302-739-4271 • http://www.state.de.us/tourism

Trail Information
Brandywine Park Trail • Delaware Division of Parks & Recreation • 89 Kings Highway • Dover, DE 19901 • 302-739-5285

Creek Road Trail • Delaware Division of Parks & Recreation • 89 Kings Highway • Dover, DE 19901 • 302-739-5285

District of Columbia
General Information
Bicycle Coordinator (D.C. Area) DC-DPW • 2000 14th St. N.W. • Washington, D.C. 20009 • 202-671-2308

D.C. Committee to Promote Washington • 1212 New York Ave. NW #200 • Washington, D.C. 20005 • 800-422-8644 or 202-789-7000 • http://www.washington.org

Mid-Atlantic Rail-Trails • http://www.his.com/~jmenzies/urbanatb/rtrails/index.htm

Washington Area Bicyclist Association • http://www.waba.org

Trail Information
Capital Crescent Trail • Montgomery County Dept. of Parks • 9500 Brunett Ave. • Silver Spring, MD 20901 • 301-495-2535 or 301-739-4200

Capital Crescent Trail Coalition • P.O. Box 30703 • Bethesda, MD 20824 • 202-234-4874 • http://www.cctrail.org

Chesapeake & Ohio Canal National Historic Park Trail • C&O National Historical Park Headquarters • P.O. Box 4 • Sharpsburg, MD 21782 • 301-739-4200

Metropolitan Branch Trail • Washington Area Bicyclist Association • 202-628-2500 • http://www.waba.org

Potomac River & Reflection Pool Bike Paths • Metropolitan Washington Council of Governments • 1875 Eye St. NW • Washington, D.C. 20006 • 202-223-6800

Rock Creek Park Trail • Montgomery County Dept. of Parks, Parkside Headquarters • 9500 Brunett Ave. • Silver Spring, MD 20910 • 301-495-2525

National Park Service • 5000 Glover Rd. • Washington, D.C. 20015 • 202-426-6832

Florida
General Information
Florida Bicycle Program • Florida DOT 605 Suwannee St., MS 82 • Tallahassee, FL 32399 • 850-487-1200 • http://www.dot.state.fl.us

Florida Bicycle Touring Maps • http://www.cfdc.org

Rails to Trails Conservancy, Florida Field Office • http://www.railtrails.org/FL

Visit Florida • 661 E Jefferson St. • Tallahassee, FL 32301 • 888-735-2872 or 850-488-5607 • http://www.flausa.com

Trail Information
Black Creek Trail • Northeast Florida Regional Planning Council • 9143 Phillips Highway, Suite 350 • Jacksonville, FL 32256 • 904-363-6350

Black Creek Trail • Clay County Parks & Recreation Dept. • 3557 Hwy. 17 N • Green Cove Springs, FL 32043 • 904-284-6378 or 904-269-6378

Blackwater Heritage State Trail (Military Heritage Trail) • Blackwater River State Park • 7720 Deaton Bridge Rd. • Holt, FL 32564 • 850-983-5363 or 904-983-5363 • http://www.bike-plus.com/rails

Branford Trail • Suwannee County Recreation Dept. • 1201 Silas Dr. • Like Oak, FL 32060 • 904-362-3004

Branford Trail • Suwannee River Water Management • 9225 County Route 49 • Live Oak, FL 32060 • 386-362-1001

Cady Way Trail • City of Orlando • Transportation Planning Bureau • 400 S Orange Ave. • Orlando, FL 32801 • 407-246-3395 or 407-246-2775 • http://www.cityoforlando.net/planning/transportation/cadyway.htm • http://www.ci.orlando.fl.us/departments/planning_and_development/rtc.html

Orange County Parks & Recreation • 407-836-6200

Cape Haze Pioneer Trail • Charlotte County Parks & Recreation Dept. • 4500 Harbor Blvd. • Port Charlotte, FL 33952 • 941-627-1628 • http://www.charlottecountyfl.com/parks

Cross Seminole Trail • Seminole County Parks & Recreation • 264 W North St. • Altamonte Springs, FL 32714 407-788-0405

Cross Seminole Trail • Seminole County Public Works Dept. • Engineering Division 520 W Lake Mary Blvd, Suite 200 • Sanford, FL 32773 • 407-665-2093 • http://www.co.seminole.fl.us/trails

Cross Seminole Trail • Senior Greenways & Trail Planner • Seminole County Government Comp. Planning • 1101 E First St. • Sanford, FL 32771 • 407-665-7395

Depot Avenue Rail-Trail • City of Gainesville • Public Works Dept. Station 58, P.O. Box 490 • Gainesville, FL 32602 • 352-334-5074

Depot Avenue Rail-Trail • Dickinson (Jonathan) State Park Bike Path • Jonathan Dickinson State Park • 16450 Southeast Federal Highway • Hobe Sound, FL 33455 • 561-546-2771

Fort Clinch State Park Bike Path • Ft. Clinch State Park • 2601 Atlantic Ave. • Fernandina Beach, FL 32034 • 904-277-7274

Gainesville-Hawthorne State Trail • Florida Park Service • Paynes Prairie State Preserve • Route 2, Box 41 • Micanopy, FL 32667 • 904-466-3397

Gainesville-Hawthorne State Trail • Dept. of Environmental Protection • Payne's Prairie State Preserve • 100 Savannah Blvd. • Micanopy, FL 32667 • 352-466-3397

Gandy Trail Bridge Bikeway • Hillsborough County Bicycle/Pedestrian Coordinator • 813-272-5940

Gasparilla Island Trail (Boca Grande Bike Path) • Bicycle-Pedestrian Coordinator • Lee County DOT 15 Monroe St. • Fort Myers, FL 33901 • 941-479-8900

Jacksonville-Baldwin Rail-Trail • City of Jacksonville Parks • Recreation & Entertainment Dept. 555 W 44th St. • Jacksonville, FL 32208 • 904-630-5400

Jacksonville-Baldwin Rail-Trail • Dept. of Parks & Recreation • 851 N Market St. • Jacksonville, FL 32203 • 904-630-3596

U.S.A.'s Bicycle Information Contact by State

Lake Minneola Scenic State Trail (Clermont Trail) • City of Clermont, Recreation Coordinator • P.O. Box 120-219, 400 12th St., Clermont, FL 34729 • OR • Sinclair Ave. • Clermont, FL 34711 • 352-394-6763 or 407-394-4081

Lake Minneola Scenic State Trail (Clermont Trail) • City Clerk • P.O. Box 678 • Minneola, FL 34755 • 352-394-3598

Nature Coast State Trail-Fanning Springs (Nature Coast Trail State Park or Dixie-Levy-Gilchrest Greenway) • Manatee Springs State Park • 11650 Northwest 115th St. • Chiefland, FL 32626 • 352-493-6072 or 352-493-6738 • http://www.dep.state.fl.us/parks/

Oleta River State Park Recreation Area Bike Path • Oleta River State Recreation Area 3400 Northeast 163rd St. • North Miami, FL 33160 • 305-919-1846

Overseas Heritage Trail • Dept. of Environmental Protection District 5 • Administration 3 La Croix Ct. • Key Largo, FL 33037 • 305-451-3005 • http://www.keysbeauty.org or • http://www.co.monroe.fl.us

Pinellas Trail (Fred Marquois Pinellas Trail) • Bicycle Pedestrian Planner • Pinellas County Planning Department • 14 S Ft. Harrison Ave. • Clearwater, FL 33756 • 727-464-4751 or 813-464-4751 • http://www.co.pinellas.fl.us/mpo

Pinellas Trail • 12020 Walsingham Rd. • Largo, FL 33778 • 727-549-6099 • http://www.co.pinellas.fl.us/BCC/trailgd.htm

South Dade Trail • Bicycle-Pedestrian Coordinator • Miami Dade County MPO 111 NW First St., Suite 910 • Miami, FL 33128 • 305-375-1647 • http://www.co.miami-dade.fl.us/mpo/mpo-public.htm

Stadium Drive Bike Path • Bike-Pedestrian Coordinator, Tallahassee Traffic Engineering Division • City Hall 300 S Adams St. • Tallahassee, FL • 32301 904-891-8090

State Route A1A Bike Path • Northeast Florida • Regional Planning Council 9143 Phillips Highway, Suite 350 • Jacksonville, FL 32256 • 904-363-6350

State Route A1A Bike Path • Parks & Recreation Dept. • 851 N Market St. • Jacksonville, FL 32202 • 904-630-3535

Suwannee River Greenway • Suwannee County Chamber of Commerce P.O. Drawer C • Live Oak, FL 32060 • 904-362-3071

Suwannee River Greenway • Suwannee River Water Management • 9225 County Route 49 • Live Oak, FL 32060 • 386-362-1001

Tallahassee-St. Marks Historic Railroad State Trail • Dept. of Environmental Protection, Florida Park Service • Tallahassee-St. Marks Geo Park 1022 Desoto Park Dr. • Tallahassee, FL 32301 • 850-922-6007 or 904-922-6007 • http://www.myflorida.com

Upper Tampa Bay Trail • Trail Manager • Hillsborough County Parks and Recreation Dept. 7508 Ehrlich Rd. • Tampa, FL 33625 • 813-264-8511 • http://www.homestead.com/trail-sofhillsbourgh/open.html

Van Fleet (General James A.) State Trail • Florida Park Service • 12549 State Park Dr. • Clermont, FL 34711 • 352-394-2280 • http://www.myflorida.com/communities/learn/stateparks/index.html

Waldo Road Trail • City of Gainesville • Public Works Dept. • Station 58 P.O. Box 490 • Gainesville, FL 32602 • 352-334-5074

West Orange Trail • Orange County Parks & Recreation • 501 Crown Point Crossroad • Winter Garden, FL • 34787 407-654-1108

Withlacoochee State Trail • Trail Manager • Florida Division of Recreation & Parks 12549 State Park Dr. • Clermont, FL 34711 • 352-394-2280 • http://www.nccentral.com/railstotrails

Georgia
General Information
Georgia Bicycle & Pedestrian Coordinator • Georgia DOT #2 Capitol Square, Room 347 • Atlanta, GA 30334 4 • 04-657-6692

Georgia State Parks & Historic Sites • 205 Butler St. SE, Suite 1352 • Atlanta, GA 30334 • http://www.ganet.org/dnr

Georgia Trails & Greenways • http://www.serve.com/bike/georgia/trails/

Georgia Tourism Division • P.O. Box 1776 • Atlanta, GA 30301 • 800-847-4842 or 404-656-3590 • http://www.georgia.org/itt/tourism

Trail Information
Chattahoochee River Walk Trail • Columbus Parks & Recreation Department • P.O. Box 1340 • Columbus, GA 31902 • 706-653-4175

Heritage Park Trail (Heritage Riverways Trail System) • Rome-Floyd Parks & Recreation Authority • 300 W Third St. • Rome, GA 30165 • 706-291-0766

McQueen's Island Multi-Use Historic-Scenic Trail (Old Savannah-Tybee Rail-Trail) • Chatham County Parks • Recreation & Cultural Affairs • P.O. Box 1746 • Savannah, GA 31402 • 912-652-6783

North Oconee Greenway • Bike Athens • P.O. Box 344 • Athens, GA 30603 • http://www.bikeathens.com

Silver Comet Trail • Transportation Planning Division • Cobb County DOT • 1890 County Services Parkway • Marietta, GA 30008 • 707-528-1600

Silver Comet Trail • Path Foundation • P.O. Box 14327 • Atlanta, GA 30324 • 404-875-7284 • http://www.pathfoundation.org

Stone Mountain-Atlanta Greenway Trail • Atlanta City Hall Bureau of Planning • 68 Mitchell St. SW, Suite 3350 • Atlanta, GA 30335 • 404-330-6145

Tallulah Falls Rail-Trail (Short Line Trail) • Tallulah Gorge State Park • P.O. Box 248 • Tallulah Falls, GA 30573 • 706-754-7970

Tom "Babe" White Linear Park • Moultrie-Colquitt County Parks & Recreation • P.O. Box 3368 • Moultrie, GA 31776 • 229-890-5429 • http://www.recdepartment@alltel.net

Trolley Line Greenway Trail • Atlanta City Hall Bureau of Planning • 68 Mitchell St. SW, Suite 3350 • Atlanta, GA 30335 • 404-330-6145

Westside Trail (Atlanta GA) • Atlanta City Hall Bureau of Planning • 68 Mitchell St. SW, Suite 3350 • Atlanta, GA 30335 • 404-330-6145

Hawaii
General Information
Hawaii Bicycle Coordinator, Department of Transportation Services • City & County of Honolulu • 711 Kapiolani Blvd. #1200 • Honolulu, HI 96813 • 808-527-5044

Hawaii Visitor & Convention Bureau • 2270 Kalakaua Ave., Suite 801 • Honolulu, HI 96815 • 800-853-5846 or 808-923-1811 • http://www.visit.hawaii.org

Trail Information

Kapa's Bike Path • Kauai County Parks & Recreation • 4444 Rice St., Suite 150 • Lihue, HI 96766 • 808-241-6670

Ke Ala Pupukea Bike Path • Department of Transportation Services • City & County of Honolulu • 711 Kapiolani Blvd. #1200 • Honolulu, HI 96813 • 808-527-5044

Lanikai Bike Path • Department of Transportation Services • City & County of Honolulu • 711 Kapiolani Blvd. #1200 • Honolulu, HI 96813 • 808-527-5044

Nimitz Bike Path • Department of Transportation Services • City & County of Honolulu • 711 Kapiolani Blvd. #1200 • Honolulu, HI 96813 • 808-527-5044

Pearl Harbor Bike Path • Bike-Pedestrian Coordinator, Department of Transportation • HWY-T, 601 Kamokila Blvd., Room 602 • Kapolei, HI 96707 • 808-692-7675

Pearl Harbor Bike Path • Department of Transportation Services • City & County of Honolulu 711 Kapiolani Blvd. #1200 • Honolulu, HI 96813 • 808-527-5044

Pearl Harbor Bike Path • Friends of Pearl Harbor Bike Path • P.O. Box 2893 • Aiea, HI 96701 • 808-487-9160 • http://www.aiea-community-assoc.org

West Loch Bike Path • Department of Transportation Services • City & County of Honolulu • 711 Kapiolani Blvd. #1200 • Honolulu, HI 96813 • 808-527-5044

Idaho
General Information

Idaho Bike/Pedestrian Coordinator • P.O. Box 7129 • Boise, ID 83707 • 208-334-8272 • http://www2.state.id.us/itd/planning/abouttpd/ips/ip_staff.htm

Idaho Travel Council • 700 W State St., P.O. Box 83720 • Boise, ID 83720 • 800-VISIT-ID or 800-847-4843 • http://www.visitid.org

Trail Information

Ada County Ridge to Rivers Bikeway (Greenbelt Trail) • Ada County Parks & Waterways • 4049 S Eckert Rd. • Boise, ID 83716 • 208-343-1328

Nampa to Stoddard Trail • Parks & Recreation Director • 411 Third St. South Nampa • ID 83651 • 208-465-2220

North Idaho Centennial Trail • Kootenai County Commissioner • P.O. Box 9000 • Coeur d'Alene, ID 83816 • 208-769-4450

Palouse (Bill Chipman) Trail • Whitman County Parks • 310 N Main St. • Colfax, WA 99111 • 509-397-6238

Wood River Trails • Blaine County Recreation District • 308 N Main St., P.O. Box 297 • Hailey, ID 83333 • 208-788-2177

Illinois
General Information

Illinois Bicycle Program Manager • Illinois DOT • 2300 Dirksen Pkwy. • Springfield, IL 62764 • 217-782-3194

Illinois Office of Tourism • 620 E Adams St. • Springfield, IL 62701 • 800-226-6632 or 217-

782-7500 • http://www.enjoyillinois.com or
http://www.commerce.state.il.us/tourism/newhome.htm

Trail Information

Burnham Greenway • Calumet-Memorial Park District • P.O. Box 1158, 626 Wentworth Ave. • Calumet City, IL 60409 • 708-868-2530 • http://www.cmpdslw@ameritech.net

Busse Woods Bicycle Trail • Cook County Forest Preserve District • 536 Harlem Ave. • River Forest, IL 60305 • 773-261-8400 or 708-366-9420

Chain O'Lakes State Park Trail • Illinois DNR, Chain O'Lakes State Park • 8916 Wilmot Rd. • Spring Grove, IL 60081 • 847-587-5512

Chicago Lakefront Bike Path • Chicago Park District, Administration Building • 425 E McFetridge • Chicago, IL 60505 • 312-747-PLAY or 312-747-7529

Confluence Bikeway • Madison County Transit District • 1 Transit Way • Granite City, IL 62040 • 618-874-7433

Constitution Trail, Bloomington-Normal, Parks & Recreation Department • 109 E Olive St. • Bloomington, IL 61701 • 309-823-4260

Danada • Herrick Lake & Blackwell Trails • Forest Preserve District of DuPage County • 185 Spring Ave. • Glen Ellyn, IL 60138 • 630-933-7248

Dekalb Nature Trail • Dekalb County Forest Preserve • 110 E Sycamore St. • Sycamore, IL 60178 • 815-895-7191

Dekalb-Sycamore Trail • Dekalb County Forest Preserve • 110 E Sycamore St. • Sycamore, IL 60178 • 815-895-7191

Des Plaines River Trail • Lake County Forest Preserve District • 2000 N Milwaukee Ave. • Libertyville, IL 60048 • 847-367-6640

El Paso Walking Trail • City Administrator • Town of El Paso, 475 W Front St. • El Paso, IL 61738 • 309-527-4005

Foster (Ronald J.) Heritage Trail (Glen Carbon Heritage Trail) • Village Treasurer • Village of Glen Carbon • 151 N Main St. • Glen Carbon, IL 62034 • 618-288-1200 or 314-606-3167 • http://www.glen-carbon.il.us

Fox River Trail • Cities of St. Charles, Batavia, Geneva & Elgin, Fox Valley Park District • Kane County Forest Preserve District • 719 Batavia Ave. • Geneva, IL 60134 • 630-232-5980

Fox River Trail • Fox Valley Park District • 712 S River St. • Aurora, IL 60506 • 708-897-0516

Grant Woods Forest Preserve Trail • Lake County Forest Preserve District • 2000 N Milwaukee Ave. • Libertyville, IL 60048 • 847-367-6640

Gilman (Virgil L.) Nature Trail • Landscape Architect • Fox Valley Park District • 712 S River St. • Aurora, IL 60506 • 708-897-0516

Fox Valley Park District • 712 S River St. • Aurora, IL 60506 • 630-897-0516

Great River Trail • Bikeway Coordinator, Bi-State Regional Commission • 1504 Third Ave. • Rock Island, IL 61201 • 309-793-6300

Great River Trail • Bi-State Regional Commission (Delegates Authority) • P.O. Box 3368 • Rock Island, IL 61204 • 309-793-6300

Great Western Trail (West Chicago to Villa Park) • Principal Planner • DuPage County DOT, 130 N County Farm Rd. • Wheaton, IL 60187 • 603-682-7318

Great Western Trail (West Chicago to Villa Park) • Director of Field Services, Kane County Forest Preserve • 719 Batavia Ave. • Geneva, IL 60134 • 708-232-5981

Great Western Trail (St. Charles to Sycamore) • Director of Field Services, Kane County Forest Preserve • 719 Batavia Ave. • Geneva, IL 60134 • 708-232-5981

Great Western Trail (St. Charles to Sycamore) • DuPage County Division of Transportation • 130 N County Farm Rd. • Wheaton, IL 60187 • 630-682-7318

Green Bay Trail • Winnetka Park District • 520 Glendale • Winnetka, IL 60093 • 847-501-2040

Green Bay Trail • Wilmette Park District • 3555 Lake Ave. • Wilmette, IL 60091 • 847-256-6100

Illinois & Michigan Canal Trail State Park; Cook County • Cook County Forest Preserve District • 536 Harlem Ave. • River Forest, IL 60305 • 773-261-8400 or 708-366-9420

Illinois & Michigan Canal Trail State Park; Will County (Heritage-Donnelley Trail) • Will County Forest Preserve District • P.O. Box 1069 • Joliet, IL 60434 • 815-727-8700

Illinois & Michigan Canal Trail State Park; La Salle, Grundy & Will Counties • Illinois DNR • Illinois & Michigan Canal Trail State Park; La Salle, Grundy & Will Counties • Hennepin Canal Parkway State Park • 16006-875 East St. • Sheffield, IL 61361 • 815-454-2328

Canal Corridor Association • 220 S State St., Suite 1880 • Chicago, IL 60604 • 312-427-3688

Illinois Beach State Park Trail • Illinois DNR, Illinois Beach State Park • Lakefront • Zion, IL 60099 • 847-662-4811

Illinois Prairie Path • Principal Planner • 130 N County Farm Rd. • Wheaton, IL 60187 • 630-682-7318 • http://www.ipp.org or http://www.mcs.net/~msc/IPP/

DuPage County Division of Transportation • 130 N County Farm Rd. • Wheaton, IL 60187 • 630-682-7318

Interurban Trail • Springfield Park District • 2500 S 11th St. • Springfield, IL 62703 • 217-544-1751

Interurban Trail • City of Springfield • 300 S 7th St. • Springfield, IL 62701 • 217-789-2000

Jim Edgar Panther Creek State Fish & Wildlife Area Bike Route • Illinois DNR, Jim Edgar Panther Creek State Fish & Wildlife Area • 10149 County Highway-11 • Chandlerville, IL 62627 • 217-452-7741

Kankakee River State Park Trail • Illinois DNR, Kankakee River State Park • 5314 W.R. 102 • Burbonnais, IL 60914 • 815-933-1383

Kishwaukee Kiwanis Pathway • DeKalb Park District • 1403 Sycamore Rd. • DeKalb, IL 60115 • 815-756-9939

Libertyville Trail • Director of Public Works, Town of Libertyville • 200 E Cook Ave. • Libertyville, IL 60048 • 708-362-2430

Lincoln Prairie Grass Trail • Coles County Regional Planning & Development Commission • Room 309, 651 Jackson • Charleston, IL 61920 • 217-258-0521

Lincoln Prairie Trail • Pana Office of Development • 120 E 3rd St. • Pana, IL 62557 • 217-562-3109

Long Prairie Trail • Boone County Conservation District • 7600 Appleton Rd. • Belvidere, IL 61008 • 815-547-7935

Lost Bridge Trail • Village of Rochester • 1 Community Dr. • Rochester, IL 62563 • 217-498-7192

Lowell Parkway Path • Director of Administration & Recreation, Dixon Park District • 804 Palmyra Ave. • Dixon, IL 61021 • 815-284-3306

McHenry County Prairie Trail • McHenry County Conservation District • 6512 Harts Rd. • Ringwood, IL 60072 • 815-678-4361

Madison County Transit's Nature Trail (Sam Vadalabene Nature Trail or Madison County Nature Trail) • Madison County Transit District • 1 Transit Way • Granite City, IL 62040 • 618-874-7433

Madison County Transit's Nature Trail (Sam Vadalabene Nature Trail or Madison County Nature Trail) • Madison County Trail Volunteers • 1306 St. Louis St. • Edwardsville, IL 62025 • 618-656-3994

Moraine Hills State Park Trail • Illinois DNR, Moraine Hills State Park • 914 S River Rd. • McHenry, IL 60050 • 815-385-1624

Morris (Delyte) Bikeway • Associate Director of Campus R.S.I.U. at Edwardsville Recreation Dept. • P.O. Box 1157 • Edwardsville, IL 62026 • 618-650-3235

North Branch Trail • Cook County Forest Preserve District • 536 Harlem Ave. • River Forest, IL 60305 • 773-261-8400 or 708-366-9420

North Shore Channel Trail • Village of Skokie • 5127 Oakton St. • Skokie, IL 60077 • 847-933-8447

North Shore Path (Robert Mcclorey Bike Path) • Lake County Division of Transportation • 600 W Winchester Rd. • Libertyville, IL 60048 • 847-362-3950

Old Chain of Rocks Bridge Bikeway • Trailnet Inc. • 3900 Reavis Barracks Rd. • St. Louis, MO 63125 • 314-416-9930 or 618-874-8554 • http://www.trailnet.org

Old Plank Road Trail • Will County Forest Preserve District • P.O. Box 1069 • Joliet, IL 60434 • 815-727-8700

O'Malley's Alley Trail • Director of Operations, Champaign Park District • 706 Kenwood Dr. • Champaign, IL 61821 • 217-398-2550

Palatine Trail • Landscape Architect, Palatine Park District • 250 E Wood St. • Palatine, IL 60067 • 847-991-0333 or 847-705-5140

Perryville Path • Rockford Park District • 1401 N 2nd • Rockford, IL 61107 • 815-987-8800

Pimiteoui Bike Trail • Peoria Pleasure Driveway & Park District • 2218 N Prospect Rd. • Peoria, IL 61603 • 309-682-1200

Pioneer Parkway Trail (Rock Island Trail Extension) • Peoria Park District • 2218 N Prospect Rd. • Peoria, IL 61603 • 309-682-1200

Poplar Creek Trail • Cook County Forest Preserve District • 536 Harlem Ave. • River Forest, IL 60305 • 773-261-8400 or 708-366-9420

Rend Lake Bike Trail • Illinois DNR, Wayne Fitzgerrell State Park • 10084 Ranger Rd. • Whittington, IL 62897 • 618-629-2320

River Trail of Illinois • Fon Du Lac Park District • 201 Veterans Drive • East Peoria, IL 61611 • 309-699-3923 • http://www.fondulacpark.com

Rock Island Trail State Park • Illinois DNR, Rock Island Trail State Park • 311 E Williams St. • Wyoming, IL 61491 • 309-695-2228 •

Rock Island Trail State Park • Illinois DNR • P.O. Box 64 • Wyoming, IL 61491 • 309-695-2225

Rock River Recreation Path/Bauer Memorial Path • Planning & Development Manager, Rockford Park District • 1401 N Second St. • Rockford, IL 61107 • 815-987-8865

Rock Springs-Fairview Bikeway • Macon County Conservation District • 3939 Nearing Ln. • Decatur, IL 62521 • 217-423-7708

Salt Creek Trail • Cook County Forest Preserve District • 536 Harlem Ave. • River Forest, IL 60305 • 773-261-8400 or 708-366-9420

Skokie Valley Bikeway • Lake County Division of Transportation • 600 W Winchester Rd. • Libertyville, IL 60048 • 847-362-3950

Stengel (Joe) Trail • Dixon Park District • 804 Palmyra St. • Dixon, IL 61021 • 815-284-3306

Stone Bridge Trail • Roscoe Township Offices • 5792 Elevator Rd. • Roscoe, IL 61073 • 815-623-7323

Thorn Creek Trail • Cook County Forest Preserve District • 536 Harlem Ave. • River Forest, IL 60305 • 773-261-8400 or 708-366-9420

Tinley Creek Trail • Cook County Forest Preserve District • 536 Harlem Ave. • River Forest, IL 60305 • 773-261-8400 or 708-366-9420

Tunnel Hill State Trail • Illinois DNR, Tunnel Hill State Trail • Highway 146 East, P.O. Box 671 • Vienna, IL 62995 • 618-658-2168

Southeastern Regional Planning & Development Commission • P.O. Box 606 • Harrisburg, IL 62946 • 618-252-7463

University Park Trail • Village of University Park, Dept. of Parks & Recreation • 698 Burnham Dr. • University Park, IL 60466 • 708-534-6456

Vadalabene (Sam) Great River Road Bike Trail • District Engineer, Illinois DOT • 1102 Eastport Plaza Dr., P.O. Box 988 • Collinsville, IL 62234 • 618-346-3100

Village Bike Path, Village Engineer • Village of Northbrook • 1225 Cedar Lane • Northbrook, IL 60062 • 847-272-5055

Waterfall Glen Multipurpose Trail • Forest Preserve District of DuPage County • 185 Spring Ave. • Glen Ellyn, IL 60138 • 630-933-7248

West Alton Trail • Trailnet Inc. • 3900 Reavis Barracks Rd. • St. Louis, MO 63125 • 314-416-9930 or 618-874-8554 • http://www.trailnet.org

Willow Creek-Rock Cut State Park Trail • Village of Machesney Park • 300 Machesney Rd. • Machesney Park, IL 61115 • 815-877-5432

Zion Bike Trail • Zion Park District • 2400 Dowie Memorial Dr. • Zion, IL 60099 • 847-746-5500

Indiana

General Information

Indiana Bicycle/Pedestrian Coordinator, Indiana DOT • 100 N Senate Ave., Room N901 • Indianapolis, IN 46204 • 317-232-5653

Indiana DNR, Map Sales • 402 W Washington St., Rm. 160 • Indianapolis, IN 46204 • 317-232-4180 • http://www.state.in.us/dnr/outdoor/trails.html

Indiana Division of Tourism, Dept. of Commerce, One North Capitol • Suite 700 • Indianapolis, IN 46204 • 800-289-6646 or 317-232-8860 • http://www.ai.org/tourism

Rail Trails in Indiana • http://www.state.in.us:80/dnr/outdoor/railtrai.htm

Streams & Trails Section: Indiana DNR • http://www.state.in.us/dnr/outdoor/trails/index.htm • http://www.state.in.us/dnr/outdoor/bikeinfo/htm

Trail Information

Auburn to Waterloo Bike Trail• Auburn Parks Dept. • P.O. Box 506, 1500 S Cedar • Auburn, IN 46706 • 219-925-8245 • http://www.ci.auburn.in.us

Calumet Trail • Indiana DNR Map Sales • 402 W Washington St., Room 160 • Indianapolis, IN 46204 • 317-232-4180 • www.state.in.us/dnr/outdoor/trails.htm

Cardinal Greenway • Cardinal Greenways Inc • 614 E Wysor St. • Muncie, IN 47305 • 765-287-0399 • http://www.cardinalgreenway.org

Central Canal Towpath Trail • Indianapolis Greenways • 151 S East St. • Indianapolis, IN 46202 • 317-327-7431 • http://www.indygov.org/parks/greenways

Cross-Town Trail • Highland Parks & Recreation Department • 2450 Lincoln St. • Highland, IN 46322 • 219-838-0114

East Bank Trail • South Bend Parks Department • 301 S St. Louis Blvd. • South Bend, IN 46617 • 219-235-9401

Fall Creek Trail • Indianapolis Greenways, The Depot • 900 E 64th St. • Indianapolis, IN 46208 • 317-327-7431 • http://www.indygov.org/parks/greenways or http://www.indygreen-ways.org

Hammond-Erie-Lackawanna Bike Trail (Erie Trail Linear Park) • Schereville Parks & Recreation • 833 W Lincoln Highway, Suite B-30-W • Schereville, IN 46375 • 219-853-6378

Hammond-Erie-Lackawanna Bike Trail (Erie Trail Linear Park) • Hammond Parks Dept. • 5825 Sohl Ave. • Hammond, IN 46320 • 219-853-6378

Lake Michigan Heritage Greenway (Prairie-Duneland Trail or Oak Savannah Trail) • City of Portage Parks & Recreation • 2100 Willowcreek Rd. • Portage, IN 46368 • 219-762-1675 • http://www.woodland@netnitco.net

Mill Race Trail (Maple City Greenway) • Goshen Park & Recreation Department • 607 W Plymouth Ave. • Goshen, IN 46526 • 219-534-2901

Monon Rail-Trail • Indianapolis Greenways, The Depot • 900 E 64th St. • Indianapolis, IN 46208 • 317-327-7431 • http://www.indygov.org/parks/greenways or http://www.indygreen-ways.org

Pleasant Run Trail • Indianapolis Greenways, The Depot • 900 E 64th St. • Indianapolis, IN 46208 • 317-327-7431 • http://www.indygov.org/parks/greenways or http://www.indygreen-ways.org

Pumpkinvine Nature Trail • Friends of the Pumpkinvine Nature Trail Inc. • 200 Westwood Rd. • Goshen, IN 46526 • 219-534-0779

White River Wapahani Trail • Indianapolis Greenways, The Depot • 900 E 64th St. • Indianapolis, IN 46208 • 317-327-7431 • http://www.indygov.org/parks/greenways or http://www.indygreenways.org

Iowa
General Information
Iowa Bicycle Coordinator • Iowa DOT, 800 Lincoln Way • Ames, IA 50010 • 515-239-1621 • http://www.state.ia.us/government/dot/sitemap.htm#travel

Iowa Tourism Division, Iowa Dept. of Economic Development • 200 E Grand • Des Moines, IA 50309 • 800-345-IOWA, 800-345-4692 or 515-242-4705 • http://www.traveliowa.com

Iowa Trails Council • P.O. Box 131 • Center Point, IA 52213 • 319-849-1844 • http://www.state.ia.us/parks/trails.htm

Trails of Iowa • http://www.nishna.net/trails/

Trail Information
Butler County Nature Trail (Shell Rock River Trail) • Butler County Conservation Board • 28727 Timber Rd. • Clarksville, IA 50619 • 319-278-4237

Carlisle-Indianola-WCCB Trail (Summerset Trail) • Warren County Conservation • 155 118th Ave. • Indianola, IA 50125 • 515-961-6169

Cedar Valley Nature Trail • Black Hawk County Conservation Board • 2410 W Lone Tree Rd. • Cedar Falls, IA 50613 • 319-266-0328 or 319-277-1536 • http://www.co.linn.ia.us/conservation/activities/trails.html or http://www.co.black-hawk.ia.us

Cedar Valley Trail Network; Cedar Prairie Trail, Cedar Falls Parks Division • 606 Union Rd. • Cedar Falls, IA 50613 • 319-273-8625

Cedar Valley Nature Trail • Black Hawk County Conservation Board • 2410 W Lone Tree Rd. • Cedar Falls, IA 50613 • 319-266-0328

Cedar Valley Trail Network; Cedar Valley Lakes Trail • Cedar Falls Parks Division • 606 Union Rd. • Cedar Falls, IA 50613 • 319-273-8625

Cedar Valley Trail Network; Cedar Valley Lakes Trail • Black Hawk County Conservation Board • 2410 W Lone Tree Rd. • Cedar Falls, IA 50613 • 319-266-0328

Cedar Valley Trail Network; Dr. Martin Luther King Jr. Trail • Cedar Falls Parks Division • 606 Union Rd. • Cedar Falls, IA 50613 • 319-273-8625

Cedar Valley Trail Network; Dr. Martin Luther King Jr. Trail • Black Hawk County Conservation Board • 2410 W Lone Tree Rd. • Cedar Falls, IA 50613 • 319-266-0328

Cedar Valley Trail Network; Evansdale Trail • Cedar Falls Parks Division • 606 Union Rd. • Cedar Falls, IA 50613 • 319-273-8625

Cedar Valley Trail Network; Evansdale Trail • Black Hawk County Conservation Board • 2410 W Lone Tree Rd. • Cedar Falls, IA 50613 • 319-266-0328

Cedar Valley Trail Network; Sergeant Road Trail • Cedar Falls Parks Division • 606 Union Rd. • Cedar Falls, IA 50613 • 319-273-8625

Cedar Valley Trail Network; Sergeant Road Trail • Black Hawk County Conservation Board • 2410 W Lone Tree Rd. • Cedar Falls, IA 50613 • 319-266-0328

Cedar Valley Trail Network; South Riverside Trail • Cedar Falls Parks Division • 606 Union Rd. • Cedar Falls, IA 50613 • 319-273-8625

Cedar Valley Trail Network; South Riverside Trail • Black Hawk County Conservation Board • 2410 W Lone Tree Rd. • Cedar Falls, IA 50613 • 319-266-0328

Cedar Valley Trail Network; South Riverside Trail • Director of Transportation • 501 Sycamore St., Suite 333 • Waterloo, IA 50703 • 319-235-0311

Cedar Valley Trail Network; Trolley Trail • Cedar Falls Parks Division • 606 Union Rd. • Cedar Falls, IA 50613 • 319-273-8625

Cedar Valley Trail Network; Trolley Trail • Black Hawk County Conservation Board • 2410 W Lone Tree Rd. • Cedar Falls, IA 50613 • 319-266-0328

Cedar View Trail (Jefferson County Park Bike Trail) • Jefferson County Parks, Conservation Board • 2003 Libertyville Rd. • Fairfield, IA 52556 • 641-472-4421

Chichaqua Valley Trail • Jasper County Conservation Board • 115 N Second Ave. • Newton, IA 50208 • 515-792-9780 or 515-323-5300

Chichaqua Valley Trail • Polk County Conservation Board • Jester Park • Granger, IA 50109 • 515-999-2557

Cinder Path • Lucas County Conservation • P.O. Box 78 • Chariton, IA 50049 • 641-774-5557 or 515-774-2314

Clive Greenbelt Trail • Clive Park & Recreation Dept. • 9289 Swanson Blvd. • Clive, IA 50325 • 515-223-6230

Comet Trail • Grundy County Conservation Board • 204 4th St., P.O. Box 36 • Morrison, IA 50657 • 319-345-2688 • http://www.grundycenter.com/grundycountyconservation

Cook (Harry) Nature Trail • Parks & Recreation Dept. • 114 S 7th St., P.O. Box 29, City Hall • Osage, IA 50461 • 515-732-3709

Davenport Riverfront Trail • City of Davenport Park Office • 2816 Eastern Ave. • Davenport, IA 52803 • 319-326-7812 • http://www.riveraction.org

Dickinson County Trail (Great Lakes Spine Trail) • Dickinson County Conservation Board • 1924 240th St. • Milford, IA 51351 • 712-338-4786

Dorrian (John Pat) Trail (Saylorville Trail) • City of Des Moines Parks & Recreation Dept. • 3226 University • Des Moines, IA 50311 • 515-237-1386

Duck Creek Parkway Bike Path • City of Davenport Park Office • 2816 Eastern Ave. • Davenport, IA 52803 • 319-326-7812

Fort Dodge Nature Trail • Parks & Recreation Supervisor • 813 First Ave. South • Ft. Dodge, IA 50501 • 515-573-5791

Four-Mile Creek Greenway Trail • Polk County Conservation Board • 11407 NW Jester Park Dr. • Granger, IA 50109 • 515-323-5300 • http://www.conservationboard.org

Franklin Grove Heritage Trail • City of Belmond 112 Second Ave. NE, P.O. Box 192 • Belmond, IA 50421 • 515-444-3386 or 641-444-3386 • http://www.kalnet.com/~bacoc

Great Western Trail • Polk County Conservation Board • Jester Park • Granger, IA 50109 • 515-323-5300 • http://www.conservationboard.org or http://www.co.polk.ia.us

Great Western Trail • Warren County Conservation Board • 1565 118th Ave. • Indianola, IA 50125 • 515-961-6169

Heart of Iowa Nature Trail • Deputy Director, McFarland Park • 56269 180th St. • Ames, IA 50010 • 515-232-2516

Heart of Iowa Nature Trail • Story County Conservation • 56461 180th St. • Ames, IA 50010 • 515-232-2516 • http://www.storycounty.com

Heart of Iowa Nature Trail • Marshall County Conservation Board • 1302 E Olive St. • Marshalltown, IA 50158 • 515-754-6303

Heritage Trail • Dubuque County Conservation Board • 13768 Swiss Valley Rd. • Peosta, IA 52068 • 319-556-6745 or 563-556-6745 • http://www.dubuquecounty.com

Hoover Nature Trail • Hoover Nature Trail • P.O. Box 531 • Muscatine, IA 52761 • 319-263-4043 or 319-627-2626

Iowa River Corridor Trail • Planning & Community Development • 410 E Washington St • Iowa City, IA 52240 • 319-356-5230

Iowa River Corridor Trail • Coralville Parks & Recreation Center • 1506 8th St. • Coralville, IA 52241 • 319-351-1266 or 319-354-3006 • http://www.coralville.org

Jackson County Recreational Trail • Jackson County Conservation • 201 W Platt • Maquoketa, IA 52060 • 319-652-3783 or 319-652-4782

Jordan Creek Trail • West Des Moines Parks & Recreation • P.O. Box 65320 • West Des Moines, IA 50265 • 515-222-3444

Kewash Nature Trail • Washington County Conservation Board, Courthouse • P.O. Box 889 • Washington, IA 52353 • 319-653-7765 • http://www.co.washington.ia.us/departments/conservation

Laurens Trail • Iowa Trails Council • P.O. Box 131, 1201 Central Ave. • Center Point, IA 52213 • 319-849-1844

Laurens Trail • Town of Laurens • Laurens, IA 50554 • 712-841-4526

Linn Creek Greenbelt Parkway Bike Trail • Marshalltown Parks & Recreation Dept. • 803 N 3rd Ave. • Marshalltown, IA 50158 • 515-754-5715

Little River Nature Trail (Little River Scenic Pathway) • City Clerk • City Hall 104 First St. • Leon, IA 50144 • 515-446-1446

Little River Nature Trail • City of Leon • P.O. Box 210 • Leon, IA 50144 • 641-446-6221

Maple Leaf Pathway • Ringgold County Conservation Board • Box 83A, RR 1 • Mount Ayr, IA 50854 • 515-464-2787

McVay Trail • Indianola Parks & Recreation Department • 2204 W 2nd Ave. • Indianola, IA 50125 • 515-961-9420

North Ridge-North Liberty Trail • Coralville Parks & Recreation Center • 1506 8th St. • Coralville, IA 52241 • 319-351-1266 or 319-354-3006 • http://www.coralville.org

Pioneer Trail • Grundy County Conservation Board • 204 4th St., P.O. Box 36 • Morrison, IA

50657 • 319-345-2688 • http://www.grundycenter.com/grundycountyconservation

"Praeri" Rail-Trail • Deputy Director, McFarland Park • 56269 180th St. • Ames, IA 50010 • 515-232-2516

"Praeri" Rail-Trail • Story County Conservation • 56461 180th St. • Ames, IA 50010 • 515-232-2516 • http://www.storycounty.com

Prairie Farmer Recreational Trail (Winneshiek County Trail) • Winneshiek County Conservation Board • 2546 Lake Meyer Rd. • Fort Atkinson, IA 52144 • 319-534-7145

Puddle Jumper Trail • Orange City Parks & Recreation Department • City Hall • Orange City, IA 51041 • 712-737-4885

Raccoon River Valley Trail • Iowa Trails Council • 1201 Central Ave. • Center Point, IA 52213 • 319-849-1844

Raccoon River Valley Trail • Dallas County Conservation Board • 1477 K Ave. • Perry, IA 50220 • 515-465-3577 • http://www.dallascountyconservation.org

Raccoon River Valley Trail • Guthrie County Conservation Board • RR 2 Box 4A17 • Panora, IA 50216 • 641-755-3061

Raccoon River Valley Trail • Greene County Conservation Board, Greene County Courthouse • 114 N Chestnut • Jefferson, IA 50129 •

River City Greenbelt & Winnebago Trails • Cerro Gordo Conservation Board • 3501 Lime Creek Rd. • Mason City, IA 50401 • 641-423-5309

Rock Island-Old Stone Arch Nature Trail • City of Shelby • 419 East St. • Shelby, IA 51570 • 712-544-2638

Sac & Fox Trail • Cedar Rapids Parks Dept. • City Hall • Cedar Rapids, IA 52401 • 319-398-5080

Sauk Rail-Trail • Sac County Conservation Board • 2970 280th St. • Sac City, IA 50583 • 712-662-4530 or 712-792-4614

Saylorville-Des Moines River Trail • City of Des Moines Parks & Recreation Dept. • 3226 University • Des Moines, IA 50311 • 515-237-1386

Storm Lake's Lake Trail • City of Storm Lake • P.O. Box 1086, 620 Erie St. • Storm Lake, IA 50588 • 712-732-8027

Storm Lake's Lake Trail • Storm Lake Chamber of Commerce • P.O. Box 584 • Storm Lake, IA 50588 • 712-732-3780 • http://www.stormlake.org

Three Rivers Trail • Humboldt County Conservation Board • Court House • Dakota City, IA 50529 • 515-332-4087

Trolley Trail (Clear Lake-Mason City) • Cerro Gordo Conservation Board • 3501 Lime Creek Rd. • Mason City, IA 50401 • 641-423-5309

Volksweg Trail • Marion County Conservation Board • Courthouse-4th Floor • Knoxville, IA 50138 • 515-828-2213 or 515-423-5309

Wabash Trace Nature Trail • Trails & Greenways Coordinator, Iowa Natural Heritage Foundation • 505 Fifth Ave, Suite 444 • Des Moines, IA 50309 • 515-288-1846 or 712-542-3864 • http://www.forum.heartland.net/community/wabash-trace/

Wabash Trace Nature Trail • P.O. Box 581 • Shenandoah, IA 51601 • 712-246-4444

Wabash Trace Nature Trail • P.O. Box 524 • Council Bluffs, IA 51502 • 712-328-6836

Wapsi-Great Western Trail • Wapsi-Great Western Line Committee • P.O. Box 116 • Riceville, IA 50466 • 515-985-4030

Waverly Rail-Trail • Waverly Parks & Recreation Dept. • P.O. Box 616 • Waverly, IA 50677 • 319-352-6263 • http://www.waverlyia.com

Waverly Rail-Trail • Waverly Area Development Group • 112 W Bremer Ave. • Waterly, IA 50677 • 319-352-4526

Waverly Rail-Trail • Iowa Trails Council • 1201 Central Ave. • Center Point, IA 52213 • 319-849-1844

Western Historic Trail Center Trail • Council Bluffs Parks & Recreation & Public Property • 209 Pearl St. • Council Bluffs, IA 51503 • 712-328-4650

Kansas
General Information
Kansas Bicycle & Pedestrian Coordinator • Kansas DOT, 2nd Floor, Thacher Bldg. 217 SE 4th St. • Topeka, KS 66603 • 913-296-7448

Kansas Rails-to-Trails • http://www.ukans.edu/~hisite/franklin/railtrail/trailmap.htm

Kansas Travel & Tourism • 700 SW Harrison St., Suite 1300 • Topeka, KS 66603 • 800-2-KANSAS or 800-252-6727 • http://www.kansascommerce.com

Trail Information
Arkansas River Bike Trail • Wichita Bicycle Committee, City Treasurer's Office • 455 N Main, 10th Floor • Wichita, KS 67202 • 316-268-4391

Clinton Parkway Bike Path • Lawrence Parks & Recreation Department • Box 708 • Lawrence, KS 66044 • 785-832-3450 • http://www.ci.lawrence.ks.us

Gypsum Creek Bike Path • Wichita Bicycle Committee • City Treasurer's Office • 455 N Main 10th Floor • Wichita, KS 67202 • 316-268-4391

Haskell Rail-Trail (Lawrence Rail-Trail) • Lawrence Parks & Recreation Department • Box 708 • Lawrence, KS 66044 • 785-832-3450 • http://www.ci.lawrence.ks.us

Interstate-135 Bike Trail • Wichita Bicycle Committee • City Treasurer's Office • 455 N Main 10th Floor • Wichita, KS 67202 • 316-268-4391

K-96 Bike Path • Wichita Bicycle Committee • City Treasurer's Office • 455 N Main 10th Floor • Wichita, KS 67202 • 316-268-4391

Prairie Spirit Rail-Trail • Friends of the Prairie Spirit Trail • P.O. Box 71 • Garnett, KS 66032 • 785-448-6767 • http://www.kanza.net/~prairiespirit or http://www.ukans.edu/~hisite/franklin/railtrail/

Prairie Spirit Rail-Trail • Kansas Dept. of Wildlife & Parks • 419 S Oak • Garnett, KS 66032 • 785-448-6767

Prairie Spirit Rail-Trail • South Lawrence Trafficway Bike Path, Lawrence Parks & Recreation Department • Box 708 • Lawrence, KS 66044 • 785-832-3450 • http://www.ci.lawrence.ks.us

Whistle Stop Park Trail • Whistle Stop Park Committee • P.O. Box 70 • Elkhart, KS 67950 • 316-697-2340 or 316-697-2402

Kentucky
General Information
Kentucky Bicycle/Pedestrian Coordinator Kentucky Transportation Cabinet, Division of Multi-Modal Programs • 125 Holmes St., 3rd Floor • Frankfort, KY 40622 • 503-564-7686 • http://www.kytc.state.ky.us/

Kentucky Dept. Of Travel, Capital Plaza Tower • 500 Mero St., Suite 22 • Frankfort, KY 40601 • 800-225-8747 or 502-564-4930 • http://www.kentuckytourism.com

Kentucky Rails to Trails Council, Inc. • http://www.kyrailtrail.org

Trail Information
Cadiz Railroad Walking Trail • City Clerk, City of Cadiz • P.O. Box 1465 • Cadiz, KY 42211 • 270-522-3892

Louisville Beargrass Creek Trail • Kentucky-Indiana Regional Planning Agency • 11520 Commonwealth Dr. • Louisville, KY 40299 • 502-266-6084

Louisville Riverwalk Trail • Kentucky-Indiana Regional Planning Agency • 11520 Commonwealth Dr. • Louisville, KY 40299 • 502-266-6084

Louisville Riverwalk Trail • Manager of Planning, City of Louisville Dept. of Public Works • City Hall 601 W Jefferson • Louisville, KY 40202 • 502-574-3102

Paradise Trail • Mulenburg County Rails-to-Trails • P.O. Box 137 • Greenville, KY 42345 • 270-338-2520

Louisiana
General Information
Louisiana Bicycle Coordinator • Louisiana DOT • P.O. Box 15337 • Baton Rouge, LA 70895 • 225-935-0128

Louisiana Office of Tourism • P.O. Box 94291 • Baton Rouge, LA 70804 • 800-33-GUMBO, 800-334-8626 or 504-342-8100 • http://www.louisianatravel.com

Trail Information
Jefferson Lakefront Linear Park Path • The Board of Levee Commissioners of the East Jefferson Levee District • 203 Plauche Ct. • Harahan, LA 70123 • 504-733-0087

Jefferson Parish Bicycle & Pedestrian Path • The Board of Levee Commissioners of the East Jefferson Levee District • 203 Plauche Ct. • Harahan, LA 70123 • 504-733-0087

Tammany Trace Trail • Transportation Planner, St. Tammany Parish Police Jury • 428 E Boston St., P.O. Box 628 • Covington, LA 70434 • 800-43-TRACE or 800-438-7223, ext. 202, 504-898-2529 or 504-867-9490 • http://www.stp.pa.st-tammany.la.us/departments/trace/trace.html

Maine
General Information
Maine Bicycle & Pedestrian Coordinator • Maine DOT, 16 State House Station • Augusta, ME 04333 • 207-287-6600 or TTD: 207-287-3392 • http://www.janus.state.me.us/mdot/opt/bike/homepage.htm

Maine Office of Tourism • 59 State House Station • Augusta, ME 04333 • 888-MAINE-45 or 888-624-6345 • http://www.visitmaine.com

Maine Publicity Bureau • P.O. Box 2300 • Hallowell, ME 04347 • 800-533-9595 or 207-623-0363 • http://www.mainetourism.com

New England Rail-Trails • http://www.new-england-rail-trails.org

Trail Information
Androscoggin River Bike Path • Maine DOT • #16 House Station, Child St. • Augusta, ME 04333 • 207-287-6600

Back Cove Trail • Great Portland Council of Governments • 207-774-9891

Calais Waterfront Walkway Trail • Community Development Director • City of Calais • P.O. Box 413 • Calais, ME 04619 • 207-454-2521

Eastern Promenade Trail • Great Portland Council of Governments • 207-774-9891

St. John Valley Heritage Trail • Town of Fort Kent • 416 W Main St. • Fort Kent, ME 04743 • 207-834-3507

South Portland Greenbelt Walkway • Planning Dept. • City of South Portland • P.O. Box 9422, 6 Cottage Rd. • South Portland, ME 04116 • 207-767-7602 • http://landesk.spsd.org/

South Portland Greenbelt Walkway • Great Portland Council of Governments • 207-774-9891

Spring Point Shoreway • Planning Dept. • City of South Portland • P.O. Box 9422, 6 Cottage Rd. • South Portland, ME 04116 • 207-767-7602 • http://landesk.spsd.org/

Spring Point Shoreway • Great Portland Council of Governments • 207-774-9891

Maryland
General Information
Maryland Bicycle/Pedestrian Coordinator, Maryland State Highway Administration • 707 Calvert St., Mailstop C-502 • Baltimore, MD 21202 • 800-252-8776

Maryland DNR, State Forest & Park Service, Tawes State Office • Building E-3 • Annapolis, MD 21401 • 800-830-3974 or 410-260-8186 • http://www.dnr.state.md.us

Maryland Tourism • 800-MD-IS-FUN, 800-634-7386 or 410-767-3400 • http://www.mdis-fun.org

Mid-Atlantic Rail-Trails • http://www.his.com/~jmenzies/urbanatb/rtrails/index.htm

Trail Information
Anacostia Tributary Trail System • Dept. of Park & Planning, Montgomery County • 9500 Brunett Ave. • Silver Spring, MD 20901 • 301-495-2503

Baltimore & Annapolis Trail Park • Baltimore & Annapolis Trail Park • P.O. Box 1007, 51 W Earleigh Heights Rd. • Severna Park, MD 21146 • 410-222-6244 or 410-222-8820 • http://www.his.com/~jmenzies/urbanatb/rtrails/ba/ba.htm or http://www.web.aacpl-net/rp.

Bethesda Trolley Trail • Montgomery County DOT • 101 Monroe St., 10th Floor • Rockville, MD 20850 • 301-217-2145

B.W.I. Trail, Baltimore & Annapolis Trail Park • P.O. Box 1007, 51 W Earleigh Heights Rd. • Severna Park, MD 21146 • 410-222-6244 or 410-222-8820 • http://www.his.com/~jmen-zies/urbanatb/rtrails/ba/ba.htm or http://www.web.aacpl-net/rp.

Capital Crescent Trail • Capital Crescent Trail Coalition • P.O. Box 30703 • Bethesda, MD 20824 • 202-234-4874 • http://www.cctrail.org

Capital Crescent Trail • Montgomery County Department of Parks • 9500 Brunett Ave. • Silver Spring, MD 20901 • 301-495-2535 or 301-739-4200

Chesapeake Beach Railroad Trail • P.G. County Planning Dept. • 14741 Governor Oden Bowie Dr. • Upper Marlboro, MD 20772 • 301-952-3522

Chesapeake & Delaware Canal Trail • Civil Engineer, U.S. Army Corps of Engineers • P.O. Box 77 • Chesapeake City, MD 21915 • 410-885-5621

Chesapeake & Ohio Canal National Historic Park Trail • C & O National Historical Park Headquarters • P.O. Box 4 • Sharpsburg, MD 21782 • 301-739-4200 • http://www.nps.gov/choh

Cross Island Trail • Queen Anne's County, Dept. of Parks & Recreation • P.O. Box 37, 1945 4-H Park Rd. • Centerville, MD 21617 • 410-758-0835

Henson Creek Bike Trail • W. B. & A. Recreational / Commuter Trail Association • 9430 Lanham-Severn Rd • Seabrook, MD 20706 • 301-459-7090

Little Falls Branch Hiker-Biker Trail • Dept. of Park & Planning, Montgomery County • 9500 Brunett Ave. • Silver Spring, MD 20910 • 301-495-2503

Magruder Branch Hiker-Biker Trail • Dept. of Park & Planning, Montgomery County • 9500 Brunett Ave. • Silver Spring, MD 20910 • 301-495-2503

Metropolitan Branch Trail • Washington Area Bicyclist Association • 202-628-2500 • http://www.waba.org

Mill Trail • Howard County Recreation & Parks • 7120 Oakland Mills Rd. • Columbia, MD 21046 • 410-313-4687

Northern Central Railroad Trail • Gunpowder Falls State Park • P.O. Box 480, 2813 Jerusalem Rd. • Kingsville, MD 21087 • 410-592-2897 • http://www.his.com/~jmenzies/urbanatb/rtrails/ncr/ncr.htm

Number 9 Trolley Line Trail • Howard County Tourism Council • 8267 Main St. • Ellicott City, MD 21041 • 800-288-8747

Number 9 Trolley Line Trail • Baltimore County Dept. of Recreation & Parks, Banneker Center • Main & Wesley Avenues • Catonsville, MD 21228 • 410-887-0956

Paint Branch Hiker-Biker Trail • Dept. of Park & Planning • Montgomery County • 9500 Brunett Ave. • Silver Spring, MD 20910 • 301-495-2503

Poplar Trail • Pathways Coordinator, City of Annapolis • 2009 Homewood Rd. • Annapolis, MD 21402 • 410-757-5916

Poplar Trail • 160 Duke of Glousester St. • Annapolis, MD 21402 • 410-263-7959 • http://www.ci.annapolis.md.us

Rock Creek Stream Valley Park Trail • Montgomery County Dept. of Parks, Parkside Headquarters • 9500 Brunett Ave. • Silver Spring, MD 20910 • 301-495-2525

Rock Creek Stream Valley Park Trail • National Park Service • 5000 Glover Rd. • Washington, D.C. 20015 • 202-426-6832

Sligo Creek Hiker-Biker Trail • Dept. of Parks & Planning, Montgomery County • 9500 Brunett

Ave. • Silver Spring, MD 20910 • 301-495-2503

Washington, Baltimore & Annapolis Recreational Trail • W. B. & A. Recreational/Commuter Trail Association • 9430 Lanham-Severn Rd. • Seabrook, MD 20706 • 301-459-7090

Washington, Baltimore & Annapolis Recreational Trail • Maryland-National Capital Park & Planning Commission • 301-699-2407

Western Maryland Rail-Trail • Fort Frederick State Park, Maryland Department of Natural Resources • 11100 Fort Frederick Rd. • Big Pool, MD 21711 • 800-825-PARK, 800-825-7275 or 301-842-2155 • http://www.hancockmd.com/visit/

Winterplace Park Trail • Greenways Coordinator, Wicomico County Parks, Recreation & Tourism • 500 Glen Ave. • Salisbury, MD 21804 • 410-548-4900 Ex 112

Massachusetts
General Information
Massachusetts Bicycle/Pedestrian Coordinator, Mass Highway Planning • 10 Park Plaza, Room 4150 • Boston, MA 02116 • 617-973-7329

Massbike Online, Bicycle Coalition of Massachusetts World Wide Web Site, Bikeways & Trails • http://www.massbike.org/bikeways/

New England Rail-Trails • http://www.new-england-rail-trails.org

Rubel Bike Maps • P.O. Box 401035 • Cambridge, MA 02140 • 617-776-6567 • http://www.bikemaps.com

Trail Information
Bedford Narrow Gauge Rail-Trail • Friends of Bedford Depot Park Inc. • 120 South Rd. • Bedford, MA 01730 • 781-687-6180 • http://www.bedforddepot.org

Cape Cod Rail-Trail • Bikeway & Rail-Trail Planner, Dept. of Environmental Management, Division of Resource Conservation • 100 Cambridge St., Room 1404 • Boston, MA 02202 • 800-831-0569 or 617-727-3180 • http://www.magnet.state.ma.us/dem.htm

Cape Cod Canal Bicycle Trail • U.S. Army Corp of Engineers, Cape Cod Canal Field Office • P.O. Box J • Buzzards Bay, MA 02532 • 508-759-4431 or 508-759-5991

Charles River Reservation Bikeway • Metropolitan District Commission • 20 Somerset St. • Boston, MA 02108 • 617-727-5114

Chicopee Memorial State Park Bike Path • Chicopee Memorial State Park • 570 Burnett Rd. • Chicopee, MA 01020 • 413-594-9416

Falmouth Shining Sea Trail (Shining Sea Bikeway) • Falmouth Bikeways Committee • 52 Town Hall Square • Falmouth, MA 02540 • 508-968-5293 or 508-548-7611 • http://www.members.aol.com/fal-bike/bike/bike/index.html

Lowell Canalway System Trails • Lowell National Historical Park • 67 Kirk St. • Lowell, MA 01852 • 978-275-1725 or 508-458-7653 • http://www.nps.gov/lowe

Lynn-Nahant Beach Reservation Bike Path • Metropolitan District Commission, Public Information Office • 20 Somerset St. • Boston, MA 02108 • 617-727-5114

Minuteman Commuter Bikeway • Dept. of Environmental Management, Division of Resource Conservation • 100 Cambridge St., Room 1404 • Boston, MA 02202 • 617-727-1388

Minuteman Commuter Bikeway • Planning & Community Development • Town of Arlington

730 Massachusetts Ave. • Arlington, MA 02174 • 781-316-3090 or 781-316-3091

Myles Standish State Forest Bike Paths • Myles Standish State Forest • P.O. Box 66, Cranberry Rd. • South Carver, MA 02366 • 508-866-2526

Nickerson State Park Bike Paths • Nickerson State Park • 3488 Main St. • Brewster, MA 02631 • 508-896-3491

North Central Pathway • North Central Pathway Inc. • 135 Gardner Rd. • Winchendon, MA 01475 • 978-297-2167

Northampton Bike Path • Northampton Office of Planning & Development • 210 Main St., Room 11 City Hall • Northampton, MA 01060 • 413-586-6950 • http://www.northampton-planning.org or http://www.state.ma.us/dem

Norwottuck Rail-Trail (Five Colleges Bikeway) • Department of Environmental Management, Division of Resource Conservation • 100 Cambridge St., Room 1404 • Boston, MA 02202 • 800-831-0569 or 617-727-3180 • http://www.magnet.state.ma.us/dem.htm

Norwottuck Rail-Trail • 136 Damon Rd. • Northampton, MA 01060 • 413-586-8706 •

Olmstead Park & The Riverway • Boston Dept. of Parks & Recreation • 1010 Massachusetts Ave. • Boston, MA 02118 • 617-727-5114

Province Lands Bicycle Trail • Cape Cod National Seashore • 99 Marconi Site Rd. • Wellfleet, MA 02667 • 508-349-3785

Province Lands Bicycle Trail • Province Lands Visitor Center • 508-487-1256

Roadside Bike Paths (Martha's Vineyard) • Martha's Vineyard Chamber of Commerce • P.O. Box 1698 • Vineyard Haven, MA 02568 • 508-693-0085

Roadside Bike Paths (Nantucket) • Nantucket Visitor Services & Information Bureau • 25 Federal St. • Nantucket, MA 02554 • 508-228-0925 Or 508-228-7207

Southwest Corridor Park Trail • Southwest Corridor Park • 38 New Heath St. • Jamaica Plain, MA 02130 • 617-727-0057

Wompatuck State Park Bike Trails • Wompatuck State Park • Union St. • Hingham, MA 02043 • 617-749-7160 • http://www.state.ma.us/wompatuck

Michigan
General Information
Lake Michigan Car Ferry • 701 Maritime Dr. • Ludington, MI 49431 • AND • 900 S Lakeview Dr. • Manitowoc, WI 54220 • 800-841-4243 • http://www.ssbadger.com

Michigan Non-Motorized Coordinator, Inter-Modal Section, Michigan DOT • P.O. Box 30050 • Lansing, MI 48909 • 517-335-2823, 517-373-9049 or 517-373-9815 • http://www.mdot.state.mi.us/planning/mibike

Parks & Recreation Division, Michigan DNR • Box 30257 • Lansing, MI 48909 • 517-335-3147 • http://www.dnr.state.mi.us

Rails to Trails Conservancy, Michigan Field Office • http://www.railtrails.org/MI

Travel Michigan • 4225 Miller Rd., Suite 4 • Flint, MI 48507 • 888-78-GREAT or 888-784-7328 • http://www.michigan.org

Trail Information

Anderson (Frank N.) Nature Trail • Bay City State Recreation Area • 3582 State Park Dr. • Bay City, MI 48706 • 989-684-3020 or 989-667-0717 • http://www.dnr.state.mi.us

Ann Arbor's Huron River Trail (Gallup Park Trail) • Ann Arbor Dept. of Parks & Recreation • P.O. Box 8647, 100 N 5th Ave. • Ann Arbor, MI 48107 • 734-994-2423

Battle Creek Linear Park Trail • City of Battle Creek, Office of the Recreation Director • 35 Hambin Ave. • Battle Creek, MI 49017 • 616-966-3431 • http://www.bcparks.org

Baw Beese Trail • Hillsdale Recreation Department • 43 McCollum St. • Hillsdale, MI 49242 • 517-437-3579

Hillsdale Chamber of Commerce • 517-437-5619

Bay Hampton Rail-Trail (Bay City Loop Rail-Trail) • Community Development Planner • 301 Washington St. • Bay City, MI 48708 • 517-894-8154

Bay Hampton Rail-Trail (Bay City Loop Rail-Trail) • Bay Area Community Foundation • 517-893-4438

Betsie Valley Trail • Betsie Valley Trail Management Council • P.O. Box 349 • Beulah, MI 49617 • 231-882-0025

Bridge to Bay Trail • St. Clair City Parks & Recreation • 411 Trumbull St. • St. Clair, MI 48079 • 810-329-7121 or 810-329-6691

Flint River Trail • Friends of Flint River Trail • 2602 Hill Crest Ave. • Flint, MI 48507 • 810-742-0071

Friends of Flint River Trail • Mott Community College • 1401 E Court St. • Flint, MI 48503 • 810-232-3161 • http://www.edtech.mcc.edu/ffrt

Freedom Trail (Kensington Hike-Bike Trail) • Huron-Clinton Metropark Authority • P.O. Box 46905, 31300 Metro Parkway • Mt. Clemens, MI 48386 • 810-463-4581

Grand Haven Boardwalk Trail • Grand Haven Visitors Bureau • 1 S Harbor Dr. • Grand Haven, MI 49417 • 800-303-4096 or 616-842-4499 • http://www.grandhavenchamber.org

Grand River Edges Trail • Landscape Architect, Grand Rapids Planning Dept. • 300 Monroe Ave. NW • Grand Rapids, MI 49503 • 616-456-3031

Grosse Ile Trail System (John Neidhart Memorial Bike Path) • Grosse Ile Township • P.O. Box 300, 9601 Groh Rd. • Grosse Ile, MI 48318 • 734-676-4422

Grosse Ile Recreation Dept. • 25797 Third St., P.O. 185 • Grosse Ile, MI 48138 • 734-675-2364 • http://www.grosseile.com

Hancock-Calumet Trail • Michigan Department of Natural Resources • 427 U.S. Highway 41 N • Baraga, MI 49908 • 906-353-6651

Harbor Beach Pedestrian-Bike Path • City Administrator, City of Harbor Beach • 766 State St. • Harbor Beach, MI 98441 • 517-479-3363

Harrison Township Bike Trail • 3815 L'Anse Creuse • Harrison Township, MI 48045 • 810-466-1463

Hart-Montague Bicycle Trail State Park • Michigan DNR, Parks & Recreation Division, Hart-Montague Trail • 9679 West State Park Rd. • Mears, MI 49436 • 231-873-3083

Henry (Paul) Thornapple Trail (Kentwood Section) • Kentwood Parks & Recreation Dept. •

355 48th St. • Kentwood, MI 49548 • 616-261-1044 or 616-531-3398

Henry (Paul) Thornapple Trail (Middleville Section) • Kentwood Parks & Recreation Dept. • 355 48th St. • Kentwood, MI 49548 • 616-261-1044 or 616-531-3398

Houghton Waterfront Trail • Assistant City Manager • City of Houghton, P.O. Box 406 • Houghton, MI 49931 • 906-482-1700

Huron Valley Trail (South Lyon Rail-Trail) • Western Oakland County Railway Management Council • 58000 Grand River Ave. • New Hudson, MI 48165 • 248-437-2240 • http://www.southlyonmi.org

Huron Valley Trail (South Lyon Rail-Trail) • City Manager, City of South Lyon • 335 S Warren • South Lyon, MI 48178 • 248-437-1735

Interstate-275 Bike Path • Michigan DOT, Bike Maps • P.O. Box 30050 • Lansing, MI 48909 • 517-313-9815 • http://www.mdot.state.us/planning/mibike/onroad.htm

Iona River Trail • City of Iona, Parks & Recreation Dept. • 439 W Main St. • Iona, MI 48846 • 616-523-1800

Kal-Haven Trail State Park • Van Buren State Park • 23960 Ruggles Rd. • South Haven, MI 49090 • 616-637-2788 or 616-637-4984

Kent Trails • Kent County Parks Dept. • 1500 Scribner NW • Grand Rapids, MI 49504 • 616-336-3697 • http://www.kentcounty.org/parks

Kiwanis Trail • Community Services Director, Adrian City Hall • 100 E Church St. • Adrian, MI 49221 • 517-263-2161

Lake Huron, Willow & Oakwoods Metroparks Bike Paths • Huron-Clinton Metropark Authority • P.O. Box 46905, 31300 Metro Parkway • Mt. Clemens, MI 48386 • 810-463-4581

Lakelands Trail State Park • Michigan DNR, Pickney Recreation Area • 8555 Silver Hill • Pinckney, MI 48169 • 734-426-4913

Lakeshore Trail • Grand Haven Visitors Bureau • 1 S Harbor Dr. • Grand Haven, MI 49417 • 800-303-4096 or 616-842-4499 • http://www.grandhavenchamber.org

Lakeside Trail Linear Park • Village of Spring Lake • 102 W Savidge St. • Spring Lake, MI 49456 • 616-842-1393 • http://www.springlakevillage.org

Lansing River Trail • City of Lansing, Parks & Recreation Dept. • 318 N Capital Ave. • Lansing, MI 48933 • 517-483-4277

Leelanau Trail • T.A.R.T. Trails Inc. • P.O. Box 252 • Traverse City, MI 49685 • 231-883-TART or 231-883-8278

Little Traverse Wheel Way • Top of Michigan Trails Council • 445 E Mitchell St. • Petoskey, MI 49770 • 231-348-8280

Mackinac Island Bikeways • Michigan DNR, Parks & Recreation Division • P.O. Box 370 • Mackinac Island, MI 49757 • 906-847-3328 • http://www.mackinac.com/historicparks

Mattson Lower Harbor Park Trail • City of Marquette Parks & Recreation Dept. • 410 E Fair Ave. • Marquette, MI 49855 • 906-228-0460

Meijer (Fred) Heartland Trail • Friends of Fred Meijer Heartland Trail • P.O. Box 455 • Edmore, MI 48829 • 517-427-5555 • http://www.montcalm.org./trail/

Middle Route Bike Path (Hines Drive Bike Trail) • Wayne County Parks & Recreation • 33175 Ann Arbor Trail • Westland, MI 48185 • 734-261-1990 • http://www.waynecountyparks.com

Musketawa Trail • Friends of the Musketawa Trail • 3734 Center St. • Ravenna, MI 49451 • 231-853-5476 • http://www.busytrail@aol.com

Musketawa Trail • Village of Ravenna • 12090 Crockery Creek Dr. • Ravenna, MI 49451 • 616-853-2360

Musketawa Trail • Ottawa County Parks & Recreation • 1211 Fillmore Rd. • West Olive, MI 49460 • 616-738-4810

Paint Creek Trail • Paint Creek Trailways Commission • 4393 Collins Rd. • Rochester, MI 48306 • 248-651-9260 • http://www.paintcreektrail.bizland.com

Pere Marquette Rail-Trail of Mid-Michigan • Michigan DNR, Trailways Program • P.O. Box 30452 • Lansing, MI 48909 • 517-373-4175

Pere Marquette Rail-Trail of Mid-Michigan • Midland County Parks & Recreation Dept. • 220 W Ellsworth St. • Midland, MI 48640 • 517-832-6870 • http://www.multimag.com/city/mi/readcity/pere.html • http://www.users.mdn.net/fopmrt/friends.html

Portland River Trail (River Trail Park) • Portland Recreation Dept. • 259 Kent St. • Portland, MI 48875 • 517-647-7985

Portland River Trail (River Trail Park) • Parks & Recreation Dept., City of Portland • 259 Kent St. • Portland, MI 48875 • 517-647-7985

Rogers City Trail • City of Rogers City, City Hall • 193 E Michigan Ave. • Rogers City, MI 49779 • 517-734-2191

St. Ignace to Trout Lake Trail • Hiawatha National Forest • 1498 W U.S. 2 • St. Ignace, MI 49781 • 906-643-7900

Six-Mile Bike Path (Northville Twp-Wayne County, MI) • Northville Township • 41600 Six-Mile Rd. • Northville, MI 48167 • 248-348-5800

Traverse Area Recreation Trail (T.A.R.T.) • Grand Traverse County Road Commission • 3949 Silver Lake Rd. • Traverse City, MI 49684 • 616-922-4848

Traverse Area Recreation Trail (T.A.R.T.) • T.A.R.T. Trails Inc. • P.O. Box 252 • Traverse City, MI 49685 • 231-883-TART or 231-883-8278

Trolley Line Trail (Clio Area Bike Path) • Clio Chamber of Commerce • P.O. Box 543, 130 Griffes • Clio, MI 48420 • 810-686-4480 • http://www.trolleylinetrail.org

Vicksburg Recreation Area Trailway • Village of Vicksburg • 126 N Kalamazoo Ave. • Vicksburg, MI 49097 • 646-649-1919

West Bloomfield Trail Network • West Bloomfield Parks & Recreation Commission • 4640 Walnut Lake Rd. • West Bloomfield, MI 48323 • 248-738-2500 • http://www.westbloomfield-parks.org

West Campus Bicycle Path • Project Manager, Eastern Michigan University Physical Plant • Ypsilanti, MI 48197 • 734-487-1337

White Pine Trail State Park (includes Crossroads Trail) • Michigan DNR, Parks & Recreation Division • P.O. Box 30257 • Lansing, MI 48909 • 517-335-4824 •

http://www.multimag.com/city/mi/reedcity/white.html

White Pine Trail State Park (includes Crossroads Trail) • Parks & Recreation Bureau • P.O. Box 30028 • Lansing, MI 48910 • 231-832-0795 • sheepdog@msn.com

Minnesota

General Information

Division of Parks & Recreation, Minnesota DNR • 500 Lafayette Rd. • St. Paul, MN 55155 • 888-646-6367 or 651-296-6157 • http://www.dnr.state.mn.us/trails_and_waterways/state_trails/maps/index.html

Explore Minnesota Bikeways; Bookstore, Minnesota Bookstore • 117 University Ave. • St. Paul, MN 55155 • 800-657-3757 or 612-297-3000

Minnesota Bicycle Coordinator, Minnesota DOT • 395 Transportation Building, M.S. 315 • St. Paul, MN 55155 • 612-296-9966

Minnesota Office of Tourism • 500 Metro Square, 121 7th Place E • St. Paul, MN 55101 • 800-657-3700 or 651-296-5029 • http://www.exploreminnesota.com

Trail Information

Afton State Park Bike Path • Afton State Park • 6959 Peller Ave. S • Hastings, MN 55033 • 651-436-5391

Alex Laveau Memorial Trail • Minnesota DNR, Trails & Waterways Unit • 701 S Kenwood • Moose Lake, MN 55767 • 218-485-5410

Beaver Island Trail (Tileston Mill Spur) • St. Cloud Parks Dept. • 400 2nd. St. S • St. Cloud, MN 56301 • 612-255-7216

Big Rivers Regional Trail • Dakota County Office of Planning, Spring Lake Park • Hastings, MN 55033 • 651-438-4660

Burlington Northern Regional Trail • Ramsey County Parks & Recreation Dept. • 2015 N Van Dyke St. • Maplewood, MN 55109 • 651-748-2500 • http://www.co.ramsey.mn.us

Burlington Northern Regional Trail • City of St. Paul, Division of Parks & Recreation • 300 City Hall Annex, 25 W 4th St. • St. Paul, MN 55102 • 651-266-6425

Cannon Valley Trail • Superintendent, Cannon Valley Trail • City Hall 306 W Mill St. • Cannon Falls, MN 55009 • 507-263-0508 • http://www.cannonvalleytrail.com or http://www.cannon-falls.org

Cedar Lake Trail • Minneapolis Transportation Department • City Hall 350 S 5th St. Room 233 • Minneapolis, MN 55415 • 612-673-2411

Central Lake Trail • Park Superintendent, Douglas County Public Works Dept. • P.O. Box 398 • Alexandria, MN 56308 • 320-763-6001

Currie-Lake Shetek State Park Bike Trail • Lake Shetek State Park • 163 State Park Rd. • Currie, MN 56123 • 507-763-3256

Douglas State Trail • Minnesota Department of Natural Resources, Trails & Waterways Unit • 2300 Silver Creek Rd. NE • Rochester, MN 55906 • 507-285-7176 • http://www.dnr.state.mn.us

Fort Snelling State Park Bike Path • Ft. Snelling State Park • Highway 5 & Post Rd. • St. Paul, MN 55111 • 651-725-2390

Gateway State Trail • Minnesota Department of Natural Resources • 1200 Warner Rd. • St. Paul, MN 55106 • 651-772-7935 • http://www.dnr.state.mn.us

Glacial Lakes State Trail • Trail Manager, Minnesota DNR • P.O. Box 508 • New London, MN 56273 • 320-354-4940 • http://www.dnr.state.mn.us/trails_and_waterways

Grand Forks-East Grand Forks Bikeway • Grand Forks-East Grand Forks Metropolitan Planning Organization • 255 N 4th St., P.O. Box 5200 • Grand Forks, ND 58206 • 701-746-2656

Grand Rounds Parkway System Trail • Minneapolis Park & Recreation Board • 400 S 4th St., Suite 200 • Minneapolis, MN 55415 • 612-661-4800

Hardwood Creek Regional Trail • Washington County Parks • 1515 Keats Ave. N • Lake Elmo, MN 55042 • 651-430-8370 • http://www.co.washington.mn.us

Hardwood Creek Regional Trail • Washington County Parks • 11660 Myeron Rd. North • Stillwater, MN 55082 • 651-460-4303

Harmony-Preston Valley State Trail (Root River State Trail) • Trail Office • P.O. Box 376 • Lanesboro, MN 55949 • 507-467-2552

Harmony-Preston Valley State Trail (Root River State Trail) • Minnesota Department of Natural Resources • Trails & Waterways Unit • 2300 Silver Creek Rd. NE • Rochester, MN 55906 • 507-285-7176 or 507-280-5061 • http://www.dnr.state.mn.us

Heartland State Trail • Trails & Waterways Technician, Heartland State Trail • P.O. Box 112 • Nevis, MN 56467 • 218-652-4054

Itasca State Park Bike Trail (Wilderness Drive) • Itasca State Park • HC 05, Box 4 • Park Rapids, MN 56470 • 218-266-2100 or 218-266-2110

Lake Wobegon Trail • Stearns County Parks Dept. • 1802 County Rd. 137 • Waite Park, MN 56387 • 320-255-6172 • http://www.lakewobegontrails.com or http://www.co.stearns.mn.us

Lakewalk Trail-Duluth • City Trail Coordinator, Forestry Division • 2nd Floor City Hall • Duluth, MN 55802 • 218-723-3586 • http://www.ci.duluth.mn.us

Lakewalk Trail-Duluth • Duluth Parks & Recreation Dept., City Hall • Room 330, 411 W 1st St. • Duluth, MN 55802 • 218-723-3337

Luce Line State Trail • Minnesota DNR, Trails & Waterways Unit • 9925 Valley View Rd. • Eden Prairie, MN 55344 • 952-826-6769

Mesabi Trail • St. Louis & Lake Countries Regional RR Authority • Suite 6B, U.S. Bank Place, 230 1st St. South • Virginia, MN 55792 • 877-637-2241 or 218-749-0697 • http://www.mesabitrail.com

Minnehaha Trail • Fort Snelling State Park • 1 Post Rd. • St. Paul, MN 55111 • 612-725-2389 • http://www.dnr.state.mn.us

Minnesota Valley State Park Bike Path • Minnesota Valley State Recreation Area • 19825 Park Blvd. • Jordan, MN 55352 • 612-492-6400

Minnesota Valley State Trail • Trails Coordinator, Minnesota DNR • 1200 Warner Rd. • St. Paul, MN 55106 • 612-722-7994

Minnetonka Loop Trail System • Loop Trail Coordinator, City of Minnetonka • 14600 Minnetonka Blvd. • Minnetonka, MN 55345 • 952-93-TRAIL or 952-938-7245 •

http://www.ci.minnetonka.mn.us/html/recreation2.htm#trails

Mississippi River Regional Trail • Anoka County Parks & Recreation Dept. • 550 Bunker Lake Blvd. NW • Andover, MN 55304 • 763-757-3920 • http://www.co.anoka • mn.us/departments/park_rec/

Owatonna Bike Path • Parks & Recreation Dept. • 540 West Hill Circle • Owatonna, MN 55060 • 507-444-4321

Paul Bunyan State Trail • Volunteer Coordinator, Paul Bunyan Trail • P.O. Box 356, 124 N 6th St. • Brainerd, MN 56401 • 218-829-2838 • http://www.brainerd.com/pbtrail/pbtrail.html

Paul Bunyan State Trail • Trails & Waterways Technician, Heartland State Trail • P.O. Box 112 • Nevis, MN 56467 • 218-652-4054

Red Jacket Trail • Park Superintendent, Parks Dept. • P.O. Box 3083 • Mankato, MN 56002 • 507-625-3281

Rochester Bike Paths • Rochester Parks • 201 4th St. S.E. • Rochester, MN 55904 • 507-281-6160

Root River State Trail • Trail Office • P.O. Box 376 • Lanesboro, MN 55949 • 507-467-2552

Root River State Trail • Minnesota Department of Natural Resources, Trails & Waterways Unit • 2300 Silver Creek Rd. NE • Rochester, MN 55906 • 507-285-7176 or 507-280-5061 • http://www.dnr.state.mn.us

St. Anthony Falls Heritage Trail (Stone Arch Bridge) • Minnesota Historical Society • 125 Main St. SE • Minneapolis, MN 55414 • 612-627-5433 • http://www.mnhs.org

St. Croix State Park Bike Path • St Croix State Park • Route 3, Box 450 • Hinckley, MN 55037 • 320-384-6591

Sakatah Singing Hills State Trail • Minnesota DNR, Sakatah State Park • P.O. Box 11 • Elysian, MN 56028 • 507-267-4774 • http://www.dnr.mn.state.us

Sibley State Park Bike Path • Sibley State Park • 800 Sibley Park Road NE • New London, MN 56273 • 320-354-2055 • http://www.dnr.state.mn.us

Silver Creek Bike Trail • Transportation Engineer, Rochester Public Works Dept. • 201 4th St. SE, Rm 108 • Rochester, MN 55904 • 507-281-6194

Soo Line Trail • Chippewa National Forest • Route 3, P.O. Box 244 • Cass Lake, MN 56633 • 218-335-2283

Soo Line Trail • Minnesota DNR Information Center • 500 LaFayette Rd. • St. Paul, MN 55155

Southwest Regional L.R.T. Trail; Hopkins to Victoria • Trails Coordinator, Hennepin County Parks • 12615 County Rd. 9 • Plymouth, MN 55441 • 612-559-9000 or 612-559-6778 • http://www.hennepinparks.org/

Southwest Regional L.R.T. Trail; Hopkins to Chaska • Trails Coordinator, Hennepin County Parks • 12615 County Rd. 9 • Plymouth, MN 55441 • 612-559-9000 or 612-559-6778 • http://www.hennepinparks.org/

Sunrise Prairie Trail • Chisago County Parks & Recreation • P.O. Box 428 • Center City, MN 55012 • 651-674-2345 • http://www.co.chisago.mn.us

U.S. Route 2 Duluth-Superior Bike Trail • City Trail Coordinator, Forestry Division • 2nd Floor,

City Hall • Duluth, MN 55802 • 218-723-3586 • www.ci.duluth.mn.us

Virginia Trails • City of Virginia Park & Recreation Dept. • Virginia, MN 55792 • 218-741-3583

West Mankato Trail • City of Mankato Parks & Forestry • P.O. Box 3368 • Mankato, MN 56002 • 507-387-8650

West River Parkway Trail • Minneapolis Park & Recreation Board • 200 Grain Exchange, 400 S 4th St • Minneapolis, MN 55415 • 612-661-4800

Willard Munger State Trail (Hinckley Fire State Trail) • Minnesota DNR, Trails & Waterways Unit • 701 S Kenwood • Moose Lake, MN 55767 • 218-485-5410

Mississippi
General Information
Bicycle & Pedestrian Coordinator, Mississippi DOT • 85-01, P.O. Box 1850 • Jackson, MS 39215 • 601-359-7685

Mississippi Tourism Development • P.O. Box 849 • Jackson, MS 39205 • 800-WARMEST, 800-927-6378 or 601-359-3297h • http://www.visitmississippi.org

Trail Information
Longleaf Trace Trail • Hattiesburg Convention & Visitor's Bureau • One Convention Center Plaza • Hattiesburg, MS 39401 • 800-638-6877

Longleaf Trace Trail • 707 Hutchinson Ave. • Hattiesburg, MS 39401 • 601-544-1978

Longleaf Trace Trail • Manager • P.O. Box 15187 • Hattiesburg, MS 39404 • 601-550-3518 • http://www.longleaftrace.org or http://www.mylongleaftrace.com

Missouri
General Information
Biking Missouri's Rail-Trails (Rail-Trail & Bike Trail Maps), Adventure Publications Inc. • 820 Cleveland St. S • Cambridge, MN 55008 • 800-678-7006 • http://www.BikingUSARailTrails.com

Missouri Bicycle/Pedestrian Coordinator, Missouri DOT • P.O. Box 270 • Jefferson City, MO 65102

Missouri Trails Coordinator & Division of State Parks, Missouri DNR • P.O. Box 176 • Jefferson City, MO 65102 • 800-334-6946 or 573-751-2479 • http://www.dnr.state.mo.us

Missouri Division of Tourism • P.O. Box 1055, Truman State Office Building • Jefferson City, MO 65102 • 800-877-1234 or 573-751-4133 • http://www.missouritourism.com

Trail Information
Babler (Dr. Edmund A.) Memorial State Park Bike Path • Missouri DNR • P.O. Box 176 • Jefferson City, MO 65102 • 800-334-6946

Bear Creek Trail • City of Columbia Parks & Recreation Dept. • P.O. Box 6015 • Columbia, MO 65205 • 573-874-7460 • http://www.ci.columbia.mo.us/dept/park/trails

Forest Park Bike Paths • St. Louis Dept. of Parks, Recreation & Forestry • 5600 Clayton Ave. • St. Louis, MO 63110 • 314-289-5310

Forest Park Bike Paths • Forest Park Forever, Lindell Pavilion • 5595 Grand Dr. • St. Louis, MO 63112 • 314-367-7275

Frisco Greenway Trail • Joplin Trails Coalition • P.O. Box 2102 • Joplin, MO 64803 • 417-625-3114

Frisco Highline Trail • Ozark Greenways • P.O. Box 50733 • Springfield, MO 68505 • 417-864-2014 • http://www.ozarkgreenways.org

Galloway Creek Greenway • Ozark Greenways • P.O. Box 50733 • Springfield, MO 68505 • 417-864-2014 • http://www.ozarkgreenways.org

Grant's Trail • Trailnet Inc. • 3900 Reavis Barracks Rd. • St. Louis, MO 63125 • 314-416-9930 or 618-874-8554 • http://www.trailnet.org

Hinkson Creek Trail • City of Columbia Parks & Recreation Dept. • P.O. Box 6015 • Columbia, MO 65205 • 573-874-7460 • http://www.ci.columbia.mo.us/dept/park/trails

Jefferson City Greenway • City of Jefferson, Dept. of Parks & Recreation • 320 E McCarty • Jefferson City, MO 65101 • 573-634-6482

Jones (Ted & Pat) Trail (St. Louis, MO) • Trailnet Inc. • 3900 Reavis Barracks Rd. • St. Louis, MO 63125 • 314-416-9930 or 618-874-8554 • http://www.trailnet.org

Katy Trail State Park • Missouri DNR • P.O. Box 176 • Jefferson City, MO 65102 • 800-334-6946 800-379-2419 (TDD) • http://www.katytrail.showmestate.com or http://www.global-image.com/katytrail/intro.html

Katy Trail State Park • Missouri River District • P.O. Box 166 • Boonville, MO 65233 • 660-882-8196 • http://katytrailstatepark.com

M.K.T. Nature/Fitness Trail • City of Columbia Parks & Recreation Dept. • P.O. Box 6015 • Columbia, MO 65205 • 573-874-7460 • http://www.ci.columbia.mo.us/dept/park/trails

Old Chain of Rocks Bridge Bikeway • Trailnet Inc. • 3900 Reavis Barracks Rd. • St. Louis, MO 63125 • 314-416-9930 or 618-874-8554 • http://www.trailnet.org

St. Joe State Park Bike Path • Missouri DNR • P.O. Box 176 • Jefferson City, MO 65102 • 800-334-6946 and 573-431-1069

St. Joe State Park Bike Path • St. Joe State Park • 2800 Pimville Rd. • Park Hills, MO 63601 • 573-431-1069 • http://www.MOBOT.org/stateparks/stjoe-html

St. Joseph Urban Trail • Dept. of Public Works and Transportation • 1100 Frederick Ave., Room 204 • St. Joseph, MO 64501 • 816-271-4653 • http://www.ci.st-joseph.mo.us/mpo.html

St. Louis Riverfront Trail • Trailnet Inc. • 3900 Reavis Barracks Rd. • St. Louis, MO 63125 • 314-416-9930 or 618-874-8554 • http://www.trailnet.org

South Creek/Wilson Creek Greenway • Ozark Greenways • P.O. Box 50733 • Springfield, MO 68505 • 417-864-2014 • http://www.ozarkgreenways.org

Watkins Mill State Park Bike Path • Missouri DNR, Division of Parks & Historic Preservation, • P.O. Box 176 • Jefferson City, MO 65102 • 800-334-6946, 816-296-3357 and 816-296-3387

West Alton Trail • Trailnet Inc. • 3900 Reavis Barracks Rd. • St. Louis, MO 63125 • 314-416-9930 or 618-874-8554 • http://www.trailnet.org

Weston Bend State Park Bike Path • Missouri DNR, Weston Bend State Park • 16600 Hwy. 45 N, P.O. Box 115 • Weston, MO 64098 • 800-334-6946 or 816-640-5443

Montana

General Information

Montana Bicycle & Pedestrian Coordinator, Transportation Planning Division • Montana DOT • P.O. Box 201001, 2701 Prospect Ave. • Helena MT 59620 • 406-444-9273 • http://www.mdt.state.mt.us

Montana DOT, Transportation Planning Division • 2701 Prospect Ave. • Helena, MT 59620 • 800-714-7296 • http://www.mdt.state.mt.us

Travel Montana • 1424 9th Ave., P.O. Box 200533 • Helena, MT 59620 • 800-VISIT-MT or 800-847-4868 • http://www.visitmt.com

Trail Information

Bitterroot Branch Trail (Southside Trail) • Missoula Parks & Recreation Department • 100 Hickory St. • Missoula, MT 59801 • 406-721-7275

Centennial Park Trail (Spring Meadows Lake & Centennial Park Trail) • Helena Area Resource Office of Fish, Wildlife & Parks • 930 Custer West • Helena, MT 59620 • 405-447-8463

Gallagator Linear Trail • Bozeman Recreation Dept. • P.O. Box 1230, 1211 W Main St. • Bozeman, MT 59771 • 406-587-4724 • http://www.bozeman.com

Great Northern Historical Trail • Rails-to-Trails of Northwest Montana • P.O. Box 1103 • Kalispell, MT 59903 • 406-755-0628 or 406-756-9434

Kiwanis Bike Trail (Heights Bike Trail) • Department of Parks, Recreation and Public Lands • 510 N Broadway, 4th Floor Library • Billings, MT 59101 • 406-657-8369

River's Edge Trail • Recreational Trails Inc. • P.O. Box 553 • Great Falls, MT 59403 • 406-761-4966

Nebraska

General Information

Nebraska Bicycle Coordinator, Nebraska Dept. of Roads • P.O. Box 94759 • Lincoln, NE 68509 • 402-479-4338

Nebraska Biking & Hiking Trails, Nebraska Game & Parks Commission • 2200 N 33rd St., P.O. Box 30370 • Lincoln, NE 68503 • 402-471-5424 • http://www.ngpc.state.ne.us/infoeduc/trails.html

Nebraska Cycling Info • http://www.joyner.com/sports/biking/biking/htm

Nebraska Division of Travel & Tourism • P.O. Box 98907 • Lincoln, NE 68509 • 800-228-4307 • http://www.visitnebraska.org

Nebraska State Parks & Recreation Areas • http://www.tconl.com/~wjoyner/html/state_parks.htm

Rails to Trails, Recreation Trail Development in Nebraska • http://ngp/ngpc.state.ne.us/infoeduc/rails.html

Trail Information

Back to the River Trail • City of Omaha Parks, Recreation & Public Property Dept., Omaha-Douglas Civic Center • 1819 Farnam St., Room 701 • Omaha, NE 68183 • 402-444-5900 • http://www.ci.omaha.ne.us/parks

Bellevue Loop Trail • City of Omaha Parks, Recreation & Public Property Dept., Omaha-

Douglas Civic Center • 1819 Farnam St., Room 701 • Omaha, NE 68183 • 402-444-5900 • http://www.ci.omaha.ne.us/parks

Big Papio Trail • City of Omaha Parks, Recreation & Public Property Dept., Omaha-Douglas Civic Center • 1819 Farnam St., Room 701 • Omaha, NE 68183 • 402-444-5900 • http://www.ci.omaha.ne.us/parks

Blackbird Trail • Omaha Tribe of Nebraska • P.O. Box 400 • Macy, NE 68039 • 402-837-5391

Cottonmill Hike-Bike Trail • Kearney Parks & Recreation Dept. • P.O. Box 1180 • Kearney, NE 68848 • 308-233-3230

Cottonmill Hike-Bike Trail • Cottonmill Park • 2795 Cottonmill Ave. • Kearney, NE 68845 • 308-237-7251

Cowboy Recreation & Nature Trail • State Trail Coordinator, Nebraska Games & Parks Commission • 2201 N 13th St. • Norfolk, NE 68701 • 402-370-3374 • http://www.ngp.ngpc.state.ne.us/infoeduc/cowboy.html

Dannebrog Rail-Trail • Treasurer & Public Relations, Dannenbrog Trail Association • P.O. Box 216, 522 E Roger Welsch Ave. • Dannenbrog, NE 68831 • 308-226-2237

Dannebrog Rail-Trail • 403 N Maple • Dannebrog, NE 68831 • 308-226-2268 • http://www.dannebrog.org

Desoto Bend Trail • Nebraska Bicycle Coordinator, Nebraska Dept. of Roads • P.O. Box 94759 • Lincoln, NE 68509 • 402-479-4338

Field Club Trail • Douglas County Environmental Services • 3015 Menke Circle • Omaha, NE 68134 • 402-444-6362 • http://www.co.douglas.ne.us

Ft. Kearney Hike-Bike Trail • Fort Kearney State Historical Park • 1020 U Rd. • Kearney, NE 68847 • 308-865-5305 • http://www.ngpc.state.ne.us

Hickman Linear Path • Mayor, City of Hickman • 115 Locust, P.O. Box 127 • Hickman, NE 68372 • 402-792-2212

Keystone Trail • City of Omaha Parks, Recreation & Public Property Dept., Omaha-Douglas Civic Center • 1819 Farnam St., Room 701 • Omaha, NE 68183 • 402-444-5900 • http://www.ci.omaha.ne.us/parks

Mopac East Trail • Lower Platte South Natural Resource District • 3125 Portia St., P.O. Box 83581 • Lincoln, NE 68501 • 402-476-2729 • http://www.lpsnrd.org

Mopac Trail • City of Lincoln Parks & Recreation Department • 2740 A St. • Lincoln, NE 68502 • 402-441-7847 • http://www.ci.lincoln.ne.us/city/parks/index.htm

Niobrara Trail • Niobrara State Park • P.O. Box 226 • Niobrara, NE 68760 • 402-857-3373

North Platte Trails • Nebraska Bicycle Coordinator, Nebraska Dept. of Roads • P.O. Box 94759 • Lincoln, NE 68509 • 402-479-4338 •

Oak Creek Trail • Lower Platte South Natural Resource District • 3125 Portia St., P.O. Box 83581 • Lincoln, NE 68501 • 402-476-2729 • http://www.lpsnrd.org

Rock Island Trail • City of Lincoln Parks & Recreation Department • 2740 A St. • Lincoln, NE 68502 • 402-441-7847 • http://www.ci.lincoln.ne.us/city/parks/index.htm

Steamboat-Trace Trail • Nemaha Natural Resources District • 125 Jackson St. • Tecumseh,

NE 68450 • 402-335-3325

Steamboat-Trace Trail • Steamboat Trace Association • P.O. Box 2 • Auburn, NE 68305 • 402-335-3325 • http://www.ci.brownville.ne.us/trace

West Papio Trail • City of Omaha Parks, Recreation & Public Property Dept., Omaha-Douglas Civic Center • 1819 Farnam St., Room 701 • Omaha, NE 68183 • 402-444-5900 • http://www.ci.omaha.ne.us/parks

Nevada
General Information
Nevada Bicycle/Pedestrian Coordinator, Nevada DOT • 1263 S Stewart St. • Carson City, NV 89712 • 775-0888-7433

Nevada Commission on Tourism • 401 N Carson City, NV 89701 • 800-NEVADA-8 800-638-2328 or 775-687-4322 • http://www.travelnevada.com

Trail Information
Historic Railroad Hiking Trail • Lake Mead National Recreation Area • 601 Nevada Highway, Boulder City, NV, 89005 • 702-293-8907

New Hampshire
General Information
Bureau of Trails, New Hampshire Division of Parks & Recreation • 172 Pembroke Rd., P.O. Box 1856 • Concord, NH 03302 • 603-271-3556 • http://www.nhparks.state.nh.us/trbureau.html

New England Rail-Trails • http://www.new-england-rail-trails.org

New Hampshire Bicycle/Pedestrian Coordinator, New Hampshire DOT, Bureau of Transportation Planning • P.O. Box 483 • Concord, NH 03302 • 603-271-3344

New Hampshire Office of Travel & Tourism Development • P.O. Box 1856 • Concord, NH 03302 • 800-386-4664 (ext. 200) or 603-271-2343 • http://www.visitnh.gov

Trail Information
Cotton Valley Trail (Wolfeboro-Sanbornville Recreational Trail) • New Hampshire Division of Parks & Recreation, Trails Bureau • P.O. Box 495 • Concord, NH 03302 • 603-271-2629

Franconia Notch State Park Recreation Trail • Franconia Notch State Park • Franconia Pkwy. • Franconia, NH 03580 • 603-823-5563 • www.flumegorce.com or www.nhparks.state.nh.us

Nashua-Worcester Rail-Trail • Community Development, Division of the City of Nashua • 229 Main St. • Nashua, NH 03060 • 603-594-3360

New Jersey
General Information
New Jersey Bicycle/Pedestrian Advocate, New Jersey DOT • 1035 Parkway Ave., P.O. Box 609 • Trenton, NJ 08625 • 609-530-8062 • http://www.state.nj.us/transportation and http://www.state.nj.us/njcommuter/html/bikewalk.htm

New Jersey Office of Travel & Tourism • P.O. Box 820 • Trenton, NJ 08625 • 800-VISIT-NJ, 800-847-4865 or 609-777-0885 • http://www.state.nj.us/travel

New Jersey Rail-Trails • P.O. Box 23 • Pluckemin, NJ 07978 • 215-340-9974

Trail Information

Columbia Trail • Hunderdon County Parks System • 1020 Highway 13 • Lebanon, NJ 08833 • 908-782-1158

Delaware & Raritan Canal State Park Trail • Delaware & Raritan Canal State Park Trail • 625 Canal Rd. • Somerset, NJ 08873 • 732-873-3050 • http://www.dandrcanal.com

Edison Branch Rail-Trail • Morris County Park Commission, Division of Visitor Services • P.O. Box 1295 • Morristown, NJ 07962 • 973-326-7600 • http://www.parks.morris.nj.us

Felix (Edgar) Bike Path • Wall Township Parks & Recreation • 2700 Allaire Rd. • Wall, NJ 07719 • 908-449-8444

Edgar Felix Bike Path • P.O. Box 23 • Pluckemin, NJ 07978 • 908-787-4447

Edgar Felix Bike Path • Allaire State Park • 732-938-2372

Hudson (Henry) Trail; Atlantic Highlands to Matawan • Monmouth County Park System • 850 Newman Springs Rd. • Lincroft, NJ 07738 • 732-842-4000

Hudson (Henry) Trail (Formerly Monmouth Heritage Trail); Matawan to Freehold • Monmouth County Park System • 850 Newman Springs Rd. • Lincroft, NJ 07738 • 732-842-4000

Monmouth Heritage Trail • c/o Bicycle Hub • 455 Route 520 • Marlboro, NJ 07746 • 732-972-8822

Johnson Trolley Line Trail • New Jersey Dept. of Environmental Protection, Division of Parks & Forestry • P.O. Box 404, 22 S Clinton St. • Trenton, NJ 08625 • 609-984-1173

Lebanon State Forest Bike Path • Lebanon State Forest • P.O. Box 215 • New Lisbon, NJ 08064 • 609-726-1191

Lenape Trail • South Mountain Reservation • 115 Clifton Ave. • Newark, NJ 07104 • 973-268-3500

Linwood Bike Path (George K. Francis Bike Path) • City Clerk, Linwood City Hall • 400 Poplar Ave. • Linwood, NJ 08221 • 609-927-4108

Monroe Township Bike Path • Monroe Township Parks & Recreation • 301 Blue Bell Rd. • Williamstown, NJ 08094 • 856-728-9840 • http://www.monroetownshipnj.org

Ocean City Trail • Ocean City Public Works Dept. • 1040 Haven Ave. • Ocean City, NJ 08226 • 609-525-9261

Patriots' Path • Trail Coordinator, Morris County Park Commission • P.O. Box 1295 • Morristown, NJ 07962 • 973-326-7600 or 973-326-7604

Pemberton Rail-Trail • Pemberton Rotary Club • 128 Hanover St. • Pemberton, NJ 08068 • 609-894-2930

Ringwood State Park Bike Path • Ringwood State Park • 1304 Sloatsburg Rd. • Ringwood, NJ 07456 • 973-962-7031

Somers Point Bike Path • New Jersey Dept. of Environmental Protection, Division of Parks & Forestry • P.O. Box 404, 22 S Clinton St. • Trenton, NJ 08625 • 609-984-1173

Somers Point Bike Path • City Hall • 1 W New Jersey Ave. • Somers Point, NJ 08244 • 609-927-9088 ex122h • ttp://www.somerspoint-nj.com

Traction Line Recreation Trail • Trail Coordinator, Morris County Park Commission • P.O. Box 1295 • Morristown, NJ 07962 • 973-326-7600 or 973-326-7604

Washington (George) Bridge Bikeway • New York City DOT, Bicycle Projects Group • 40 Worth St., Room 1035 • New York, NY 100 • 13212-442-7816 • http://www.nyc.gov/calldot

West Essex Trail • Essex County Dept. of Parks • 115 Clifton Ave. • Newark, NJ 07104 • 973-268-3500

New Mexico
General Information
New Mexico Bicycle/Pedestrian/Equestrian Coordinator, New Mexico Highway & Transportation Dept., Strategic Planning Bureau, Long Range Planning Section • P.O. Box 1149, SB-1 • Santa Fe, NM 87504 • 800-827-5514 or 505-827-5248

New Mexico Dept. Of Tourism • P.O. Box 20002 • Santa Fe, NM 87501 • 800-733-6396 or 505-827-7400 • http://www.newmexico.org

Trail Information
Gillinas Hiking Trail • Las Vegas Recreation Dept. • P.O. Box 179 • Las Vegas, NM 87701 • 505-454-1158

Mariposa-Riverview Bike Trail • City of Albuquerque Parks & Recreation Dept., Bicycle/Pedestrian Safety Education Program • P.O. Box 1293 • Albuquerque, NM 87103 • 505-768-5300

Paseo Del Bosque-Atvisco Riverside Drain Bike Trail • City of Albuquerque Parks & Recreation Dept., Bicycle/Pedestrian Safety Education Program • P.O. Box 1293 • Albuquerque, NM 87103 • 505-768-5300

Paseo Del Nordeste Bike Trail • City of Albuquerque Parks & Recreation Dept., Bicycle/Pedestrian Safety Education Program • P.O. Box 1293 • Albuquerque, NM 87103 • 505-768-5300

Paseo Del Norte Bike Trail • City of Albuquerque Parks & Recreation Dept.,. Bicycle/Pedestrian Safety Education Program • P.O. Box 1293 • Albuquerque, NM 87103 • 505-768-5300

Tramway Boulevard Bike Trail • City of Albuquerque Parks & Recreation Dept., Bicycle/Pedestrian Safety Education Program • P.O. Box 1293 • Albuquerque, NM 87103 • 505-768-5300

New York
General Information
Canalway Trail Partnership, New York Parks & Conservation Association • 29 Elk St. • Albany, NY 12207 • 518-434-1583 • http://www.nypca.org

New England Rail-Trails • http://www.new-england-rail-trails.org

New York State Bicycle/Pedestrian Program Manager, New York State DOT • Building 4, Room 115, 1220 Washington Ave. • Albany, NY 12232 • 888-BIKENYS, 888-245-3697 or 518-457-8307 • http://www.gw.dot.state.ny.us

New York State Division of Tourism • 800-CALL-NYS or 800-225-5697 • http://www.ilove-ny.state.ny.us

Trail Information

Allegheny River Valley Trail • Greater Olean Area Chamber of Commerce • 120 N Union St. • Olean, NY 14760 • 716-372-4433http://www.oleanny.com

Bronx River Parkway Bikeway • New York City DOT, Bicycle Projects Group • 40 Worth St., Room 1035 • New York, NY 10013 • 212-442-7816 • http://www.nyc.gov/calldot

Bronx River Pathway • Westchester County Parks & Recreation • 25 Moore Ave. • Mount Kisco, NY 10549 • 914-864-7000, 914-242-PARK or 914-242-7275 • http://www.westch-estergov.com/parks

Brooklyn Bridge Bikeway • New York City DOT, Bicycle Projects Group • 40 Worth St., Room 1035 • New York, NY 10013 • 212-442-7816 • http://www.nyc.gov/calldot

Canalway Trail (Montgomery County) • New York State Canal Corporation • P.O. Box 189 • Albany, NY 12201 • 800-4-CANAL-4 or 800-422-6254

Canalway Trail (Montgomery County) • Montgomery County Dept. of Planning & Development, County Annex Building • P.O. Box 1500 • Fonda, NY 12068 • 518-853-8155 • http://www.montgomeryny.com

Catskill Scenic Trail • Catskill Revitalization • P.O. Box 310 • Stamford, NY 12167 • 607-652-2821

Caumsett State Park Bike Paths • New York State DOT, New York State Office Bldg., Planning Dept. • 250 Veterans Memorial Hwy. • Hauppauge, NY 11788 • 888-BIKE-NYS or 888-245-3697 • http://www.dot.state.ny.us

Caumsett State Park Bike Paths • Caumsett State Park • 25 Lloyd Harbor Rd. • Huntington, NY 11743 • 631-423-1770

Chautauqua Rails to Trails • Chautauqua Rails to Trails • P.O. Box 151 • Mayville, NY 14757 • 716-269-3666 • http://www2.cecomet.net/railtrails

Clarke (Joseph B.) Rail-Trail • Town of Orangetown • 81 Hunt Rd. • Orangeburg, NY 10962 • 845-359-6503 • http://www.orangetown.com/parks/index-html

Clemente (Roberto) State Park Bikeway • New York City DOT, Bicycle Projects Group • 40 Worth St., Room 1035 • New York, NY 10013 • 212-442-7816 • http://www.nyc.gov/calldot

Clemente (Roberto) State Park Bikeway • Roberto Clemente State Park • W Tremont & Mattewson Rd. • Bronx, NY 10453 • 718-299-8750

Coney Island Boardwalk • New York City DOT, Bicycle Projects Group • 40 Worth St., Room 1035 • New York, NY 10013 • 212-442-7816 • http://www.nyc.gov/calldot

Cross Island Parkway Bikeway • New York City DOT, Bicycle Projects Group • 40 Worth St., Room 1035 • New York, NY 10013 • 212-442-7816 • http://www.nyc.gov/calldot

East Ithaca Recreation Way • Assistant Town Planner, Town of Ithaca • 126 E Seneca St. • Ithaca, NY 14850 • 607-273-1747

East River Greenway • New York City DOT, Bicycle Projects Group • 40 Worth St., Room 1035 • New York, NY 10013 • 212-442-7816 • http://www.nyc.gov/calldot

Erie Canal Heritage Trail • New York State Canal Corporation • P.O. Box 189 • Albany, NY 12201 • 800-4-CANAL-4 or 800-422-6254

Esposito (Raymond G.) Memorial Trail • Village of South Nyack • 282 S Broadway • South Nyack, NY 10960 • 845-358–0287

Feeder Canal Park Heritage Trail (Glen Falls to Hudson Falls) • Adirondack/Glens Falls Transportation Council, Washington County Municipal Center • 383 Upper Broadway • Ft. Edward, NY 12828 • 518-746-2199

Flat Bush & Marine Parkway Bridge Bikeway • New York City DOT, Bicycle Projects Group • 40 Worth St., Room 1035 • New York, NY 10013 • 212-442-7816 • http://www.nyc.gov/call-dot

Flushing Bay Promenade Bikeway • New York City DOT, Bicycle Projects Group • 40 Worth St., Room 1035 • New York, NY 10013 • 212-442-7816 • http://www.nyc.gov/calldot

Genesee Valley Greenway • Friends of the Genesee Valley Greenway Inc. • P.O. Box 42 • Mt. Morris, NY 14510 • 716-658-2569 • http://www.fogvg.org or http://www.netacc.net/~fogvg/index.htm

Genesee Valley Greenway • Genesee Transportation Council, Bicycle & Pedestrian Planning Program • 65 W Broad St., Suite 101 • Rochester, NY 14614 • 716-232-6240 • http://www.frontiernet.net/~gtcmpo

Gorge Trail • Cazenovia Preservation Foundation • P.O. Box 627 • Cazenovia, NY 13035 • 315-655-2224

Harlem Valley Rail-Trail • Harlem Valley Rail-Trail Association Inc. • 51 S Center St., P.O. Box 356 • Millerton, NY 12546 • 518-789-9591 • http://www.hvrt.org

Harlem Valley Rail-Trail • Dutchess County Dept. of Parks, Recreation & Conservation • 85 Sheafe Rd. • Wappingers Falls, NY 12590 • 914-297-1224 • http://www.bmtsinc.com/clc/hvrail.htm

Heckscher State Park Bike Path • New York State DOT, New York State Office Bldg., Planning Dept. • 250 Veterans Memorial Hwy. • Hauppauge, NY 11788 • 888-BIKE-NYS or 888-245-3697 • http://www.dot.state.ny.us

Heckscher State Park Bike Path • Heckscher State Park • P.O. Box 160 • East Islip, NY 11730 • 631-581-2100

Hempstead Lake State Park Bike Path • New York State DOT, New York State Office Bldg., Planning Dept. • 250 Veterans Memorial Hwy. • Hauppauge, NY 11788 • 888-BIKE-NYS or 888-245-3697 • http://www.dot.state.ny.us

Hempstead Lake State Park Bike Path • Hempstead Lake State Park • West Hempstead, NY 11552 • 516-766-1029

Heritage Trail (Orange Heritage Trail) • Orange County Dept. of Parks, Recreation & Conservation • 211 Route 416 • Montgomery, NY 12549 • 845-457-4900 • http://www.ocgovernment1home.html

Hook Mount/Nyack Beach Bikeway • Rockland County Tourism • 1 Main St. • Nyack, NY 19060 • 800-295-5723 or 914-353-5533

Hudson River Greenway • New York City DOT, Bicycle Projects Group • 40 Worth St., Room 1035 • New York, NY 10013 • 212-442-7816 • http://www.nyc.gov/calldot

Hudson Valley Trailway • Town of Lloyd • 12 Church St. • Highland, NY 12528 • 845-691-2144 or 845-483-0428

Jones Beach State Park Bike Path • New York State DOT, New York State Office Bldg., Planning Dept. • 250 Veterans Memorial Hwy. • Hauppauge, NY 11788 • 888-BIKE-NYS or

888-245-3697 • http://www.dot.state.ny.us

Jones Beach State Park to Cedar Creek County Park Bike Path • New York State DOT, New York State Office Bldg., Planning Dept. • 250 Veterans Memorial Hwy. • Hauppauge, NY 11788 • 888-BIKE-NYS or 888-245-3697 • http://www.dot.state.ny.us

Jones Point Path • Rockland County Tourism • 1 Main St. • Nyack, NY 19060 • 800-295-5723 or 914-353-5533 •

Lawrence to Atlantic Beach Bike Path • New York State DOT, New York State Office Bldg., Planning Dept. • 250 Veterans Memorial Hwy. • Hauppauge, NY 11788 • 888-BIKE-NYS or 888-245-3697 • http://www.dot.state.ny.us

Lehigh Memory Trail • Trustee, Municipality of Village of Williamsville • 5565 Main St. • Williamsville, NY • 716-632-4120 • http://www.williamsville.org

Long Beach Park Bike Path • New York State DOT, New York State Office Bldg., Planning Dept. • 250 Veterans Memorial Hwy. • Hauppauge, NY 11788 • 888-BIKE-NYS or 888-245-3697 • http://www.dot.state.ny.us

Manhattan Bridge Bikeway • New York City DOT, Bicycle Projects Group • 40 Worth St., Room 1035 • New York, NY 10013 • 212-442-7816 • http://www.nyc.gov/calldot

Maple City Trail • Ogdenburg Planning Dept. • 330 Ford St. • Ogdensburg, NY 13669 • 315-393-7150

Massapequa County Preserve to Bethpage State Park Bike Path • New York State DOT, New York State Office Bldg., Planning Dept. • 250 Veterans Memorial Hwy. • Hauppauge, NY 11788 • 888-BIKE-NYS or 888-245-3697 • http://www.dot.state.ny.us

Massapequa County Preserve to Bethpage State Park Bike Path • Bethpage State Park, Bethpage Pkwy. • Farmingdale, NY 11735 • 515-249-0701

Mohawk-Hudson Bikeway Hike-Bike Trail • New York State Canal Corporation • P.O. Box 189 • Albany, NY 12201 • 800-4-CANAL-4 or 800-422-6254

Mohawk-Hudson Bikeway Hike-Bike Trail • Town of Niskayuna, One Niskayuna Circle • Niskayuna, NY 12309 • 518-386-4500 • http://www.canals.state.ny.us

Mosholu Parkway Bikeway • New York City DOT, Bicycle Projects Group • 40 Worth St., Room 1035 • New York, NY 10013 • 212-442-7816 • http://www.nyc.gov/calldot

New York State Canalway Trail System • New York State Canal Corporation • P.O. Box 189 • Albany, NY 12201 • 800-4-CANAL-4 or 800-422-6254 •

North County Trailway • Westchester County Parks & Recreation • 25 Moore Ave. • Mount Kisco, NY 10549 • 914-864-7000 • http://www.westchestergov.com/parks

Ocean Parkway Bikeway • New York City DOT, Bicycle Projects Group • 40 Worth St., Room 1035 • New York, NY 10013 • 212-442-7816 • http://www.nyc.gov/calldot

Old Champlain Canal Towpath (Fort Edward) • Adirondack/Glens Falls Transportation Council, Washington County Municipal Center • 383 Upper Broadway • Ft. Edward, NY 12828 • 518-746-2199

Old Erie Canal Trail (East Syracuse to Rome) • New York State Canal Corporation • P.O. Box 189 • Albany, NY 12201 • 800-4-CANAL-4 or 800-422-6254

Old Erie Canal Trail (Port Byron to Solvay) • New York State Canal Corporation • P.O. Box

189 • Albany, NY 12201 • 800-4-CANAL-4 or 800-422-6254

Orient Beach State Park Bike Path • New York State DOT, New York State Office Bldg., Planning Dept. • 250 Veterans Memorial Hwy. • Hauppauge, NY 11788 • 888-BIKE-NYS or 888-245-3697 • http://www.dot.state.ny.us

Orient Beach State Park Bike Path • Orient Beach State Park • P.O. Box 117 • Orient, NY 11957 • 631-323-2440

Outlet Trail • Friends of the Outlet Trail Inc. • 1939 Perry Point Rd., P.O. Box 231 • Dresden, NY 14441 • 315-536-2701

Pelham Parkway Bikeway • New York City DOT, Bicycle Projects Group • 40 Worth St., Room 1035 • New York, NY 10013 • 212-442-7816 • http://www.nyc.gov/calldot

Queensboro Bridge Bikeway • New York City DOT, Bicycle Projects Group • 40 Worth St., Room 1035 • New York, NY 10013 • 212-442-7816 • http://www.nyc.gov/calldot

Rochester, Syracuse & Eastern Trail • Director of Parks, Town of Perinton • 1350 Turk Hill Rd. • Fairport, NY 14450 • 716-223-5050

Rockaway Boardwalk • New York City DOT, Bicycle Projects Group • 40 Worth St., Room 1035 • New York, NY 10013 • 212-442-7816H • ttp://www.nyc.gov/calldot

Roosevelt Island Bikeway • New York City DOT, Bicycle Projects Group • 40 Worth St., Room 1035 • New York, NY 10013 • 212-442-7816 • http://www.nyc.gov/calldot

Saratoga Springs Bicycle System & Pedestrian Path • Saratoga Springs Open Space Project • 110 Spring St. • Saratoga Springs, NY 12866 • 518-587-5554

Shore Parkway Path (West) • New York City DOT, Bicycle Projects Group • 40 Worth St., Room 1035 • New York, NY 10013 • 212-442-7816 • http://www.nyc.gov/calldot

Shore Parkway Path (East) • New York City DOT, Bicycle Projects Group • 40 Worth St., Room 1035 • New York, NY 10013 • 212-442-7816 • http://www.nyc.gov/calldot

South County Trailway • Westchester County Parks & Recreation • 25 Moore Ave. • Mount Kisco, NY 10549 • 914-864-7000 • http://www.westchestergov.com/parks

State Canal Park Trail; Lock 20 • New York State Canal Corporation • P.O. Box 189 • Albany, NY 12201 • 800-4-CANAL-4 or 800-422-6254

State Route 104 Bike Path • Genesee Transportation Council, Bicycle & Pedestrian Planning Program • 65 W Broad St., Suite 101 • Rochester, NY 14614 • 716-232-6240 • http://www.frontiernet.net/~gtcmpo

State Route 390 Bike Path • Genesee Transportation Council, Bicycle & Pedestrian Planning Program • 65 W Broad St., Suite 101 • Rochester, NY 14614 • 716-232-6240 • http://www.frontiernet.net/~gtcmpo

Sunken Meadow State Park Bike Path • New York State DOT, New York State Office Bldg., Planning Dept. • 250 Veterans Memorial Hwy. • Hauppauge, NY 11788 • 888-BIKE-NYS or 888-245-3697 • http://www.dot.state.ny.us

Tallman Mountain State Park Bike Path • Palisades Interstate Park Commission • Bear Mountain, NY 10911 • 845-359-0544

Rockland County Tourism • 1 Main St. • Nyack, NY 19060 • 800-295-5723 or 914-353-5533

Tri-Boro Bridge Bikeway • New York City DOT, Bicycle Projects Group • 40 Worth St., Room 1035 • New York, NY 10013 • 212-442-7816 • http://www.nyc.gov/calldot

Uncle Sam Bikeway • New York State Canal Corporation • P.O. Box 189 • Albany, NY 12201 • 800-4-CANAL-4 or 800-422-6254

Uncle Sam Bikeway • Town of Niskayuna, One Nuskayuna Circle • Nuskayuna, NY 12309 • 518-386-4500 • www.canals.state.ny.us

Uncle Sam Bikeway • City of Troy Bureau of Parks & Recreation • 1 Movement Square • Troy, NY 12180 • 518-270-4553

Valley Stream State Park Bike Path • New York State DOT, New York State Office Bldg., Planning Dept. • 250 Veterans Memorial Hwy. • Hauppauge, NY 11788 • 888-BIKE-NYS or 888-245-3697 • http://www.dot.state.ny.us

Valley Stream State Park Bike Path • Valley Stream State Park • P.O. Box 670 • Valley Stream, NY 11580 • 516-825-4128

Verona Beach Trail System • Verona Beach State Park • P.O. Box 245 • Verona Beach, NY 13162 • 315-762-4463

Wagner (Bobby) Walkway • New York City DOT, Bicycle Projects Group • 40 Worth St., Room 1035 • New York, NY 10013 • 212-442-7816 • http://www.nyc.gov/calldot

Warren County Bikeway • Warren County Dept. of Public Works • 4028 Main St. • Warrensburg, NY 12885 • 518-623-5576

Warren County Bikeway • Warren County Parks & Recreation Dept. • 261 Main St., Box 10 • Warrensburg, NY 12885 • 518-623-5576

Warren County Bikeway • Adirondack/Glens Falls Transportation Council, Washington County Municipal Center • 383 Upper Broadway • Ft. Edward, NY 12828 • 518-746-2199

Washington (George) Bridge Bikeway • New York City DOT, Bicycle Projects Group • 40 Worth St., Room 1035 • New York, NY 10013 • 212-442-7816 • http://www.nyc.gov/calldot

Wells (Alison) Ney Nature Trail • Hollyloft Ski & Bike • 600 Fairmount Ave. • Jamestown, NY 14701 • 716-483-2330 • http://www.cecomet.net/railtrails/

Williamsburg Bridge Bikeway • New York City DOT, Bicycle Projects Group • 40 Worth St., Room 1035 • New York, NY 10013 • 212-442-7816 • http://www.nyc.gov/calldot

North Carolina
General Information
North Carolina Division of Bicycle & Pedestrian Transportation, North Carolina DOT • P.O. Box 25201 • Raleigh, NC 27611 • 919-733-2804 • http://www.dot.state.nc.us/transit/bicycle/

North Carolina Division of Travel & Tourism • 301 N Wilmington St., 1st Floor Education Building • Raleigh, NC 27601 • 800-VISIT-NC or 800-847-4862 • http://www.visitnc.com

North Carolina Rail-Trails • P.O. Box 61348 • Durham, NC 27715 • 919-542-0022 • http://www.ncrail-trails.org • http://www.NCRail-Trails.org/DEPOT.HTM

Trail Information
American Tobacco Trail • Durham City Parks & Recreation Department • 101 City Hall Plaza • Durham, NC 27701 • 919-560-4355 • http://www.ci.durham.nc.us/dpr

American Tobacco Trail • Triangle Rails-to-Trails Conservancy • http://www.ncrailtrail.org/TRTC

Bicentennial Greenway • Greensboro Parks & Recreation Dept., Trails Division • 5834 Owls Roost Rd. • Greensboro, NC 27410 • 336-545-5961

Lake Brandt Greenway • Greensboro Parks & Recreation Dept., Trails Division • 5834 Owls Roost Rd. • Greensboro, NC 27410 • 336-545-5961

Libba Cotton Trail • Transportation Planner, Town of Carrboro • 3071 W Main St. • Carrboro, NC 27510 • 919-918-7324 or 919-968-7713

North Buffalo Creek Greenway • Greensboro Parks & Recreation Dept., Trails Division • 5834 Owls Roost Rd. • Greensboro, NC 27410 • 336-545-5961

River to the Sea Bikeway (Bike Route 1) • Senior Transportation Planner, City of Wilmington • P.O. Box 1810 • Wilmington, NC 28402 • 910-341-3258 • http://www.co.newhanover.nc.us/plan/menu.html

Salem Creek Trail • Winston-Salem Recreation & Parks Dept., City of Winston-Salem • P.O. Box 2511 • Winston-Salem, NC 27102 • 336-727-2087

Stroll Way • Winston-Salem Recreation & Parks Dept., City of Winston-Salem • P.O. Box 2511 • Winston-Salem, NC 27102 • 336-727-2087 • http://www.ci.winston-salem.nc.us

North Dakota
General Information
North Dakota Bicycle Coordinator • North Dakota DOT • 608 E Boulevard Ave. • Bismarck, ND 58505 • 701-328-3555 • http://www.state.nd.us/dot/

North Dakota Tourism, Liberty Memorial Building • 604 E Boulevard • Bismarck, ND 58505 • 800-HELLO-ND or 800-435-5663 • http://www.ndtourism.com

Trail Information
Grand Forks-East Grand Forks Bikeway • Grand Forks-East Grand Forks Metropolitan Planning Organization • 255 N 4th St., P.O. Box 5200 • Grand Forks, ND 58206 • 701-746-2660 • http://www.grandforksgov.com

Ohio
General Information
Biking Ohio's Rail-Trails (Rail-Trail & Bike Trail Maps), Adventure Publications Inc. • 820 Cleveland St. S • Cambridge, MN 55008 • 800-678-7006 • http://www.BikingUSARailTrails.com

Cycling Ohio Trails & Bikeways • http://www.richnet.net/~bikeohio/

Ohio Bicycle Coordinator's Office, Ohio DOT • P.O. Box 889 • Columbus, OH 43216 • 614-644-7095 • http://www.dot.state.oh.us/bike

Ohio Bicycle Maps & Information, Columbus Outdoor Pursuits • P.O. Box 14384 • Columbus, OH 43214 • 614-447-1006 • http://www.columbus_outdoor_pursuits.org

Ohio Bicycle Trails: A Bike Trails Directory • http://www.bright.net/~dietsch/biketrails/index.htm

Ohio Division of Travel & Tourism • P.O. Box 1001 • Columbus, OH 43216 • 800-BUCKEYE or 800-282-5393 • http://www.ohiotourism.com

Rails to Trails Conservancy, Ohio Field Office • http://www.railtrails.org/OH

Trail Information

Bike & Hike Trail • Akron Metroparks District • 975 Treaty Line Rd. • Akron, OH 44313 • 330-867-5511 • http://www.neo.Irun.com/metroparks

Bidwell to Kerr Bike Path • Gallia County Rails-to-Trail, O.O. McIntyre Park District • 18 Locust St., Room 1262 • Gallipolis, OH 45631 • 740-446-4612 • http://www.eurekanet.com/~ovvc/biketrail.html

Bike Route 2; Creekside Trail • Greene County Park • 651 Dayton-Xenia Rd. • Xenia, OH 45385 • 937-376-7440 •

Bike Route 2; Creekside Trail • Five Rivers Metroparks • 1375 E Siebenthaler Ave. • Dayton, OH 45414 • 937-278-8231 or 937-667-7878 • http://www.metroparks.org

Bike Route 3 • Greene County Park • 651 Dayton-Xenia Rd. • Xenia, OH 45385 • 937-376-7440

Bike Route 4 (Prairie Trail) • Greene County Park • 651 Dayton-Xenia Rd. • Xenia, OH 45385 • 937-376-7440

Black River Bridgeway Trail • Lorain County Metroparks • 12882 Diagonal Rd. • La Grange, OH 44050 • 440-458-5121 • http://www.loraincountymetroparks.com

Blackhand Gorge Trail • Ohio DNR • 1889 Fountain Square F-1 • Columbus, OH 43224 • 614-265-6464

Blackhand Gorge Trail • Ohio DNR • 5213 Rock Haven Rd.SE • Newark, OH 43055 • 740-763-4411

Blanchard River Rail-Trail • Hancock Park District • 819 Park St. • Findlay, OH 45840 • 419-425-7275 • http://www.hancockparks.com

Buck Creek Bike Path (Bike Route 1) • Springfield Parks & Recreation, City Hall • 76 E High St. • Springfield, OH 45502 • 937-324-7348

Celina-Coldwater Bikeway • Celina Engineering Dept. • 426 W Market St. • Celina, OH 45822 • 419-586-1144 • http://www.bright.net/~dietsch/grandlake/biketrail.htm

Cincinnati Riverfront Bike Path • Dept. of Public Works, Division of Engineering • Room 430 City Hall • 801 Plum St. • Cincinnati, OH 45202 • 513-352-5303

Clinton Rail-Trail • Clinton Rails-to-Trails Coalition • 520 Dana Ave. • Wilmington, OH 45177 • 937-382-3200

Clinton Rail-Trail • City of Wilmington • 69 N South St. • Wilmington, OH 45177 • 937-382-4781

Coshocton to Lake Park Bike Path • Coshocton City & County Recreation Team • 45618 County Rd. 58 • Coshocton, OH 43812 • 740-622-3791

Coshocton to Lake Park Bike Path • Friends of the Parks • 23253 State Route 83 • Coshocton, OH 43812

Emerald Necklace Trail • Cleveland Metroparks • 4101 Fulton Parkway • Cleveland, OH 44144 • 216-351-6300 • http://www.clemetparks.com

Evans (Thomas J.) Bike Trail (Johnstown to Newark) • Thomas J. Evans Foundation • P.O. Box 4217 • Newark, OH 43058 • 740-349-8276

Evans (Thomas J.) Bike Trail (Johnstown to Newark) • Licking County Parks • 4309 Lancaster Rd. • SE • Granville, OH 43023 • 740-587-2535

Evans (Thomas J.) Bike Trail (Newark to Hanover or Panhandle Trail) • Thomas J. Evans Foundation • P.O. Box 4217 • Newark, OH 43058 • 740-349-8276

Evans (Thomas J.) Bike Trail (Newark to Hanover or Panhandle Trail) • Licking County Parks • 4309 Lancaster Rd. SE • Granville, OH 43023 • 740-587-2535

Gallipolis Bike Path • Gallia County Rails-to-Trails, O.O. McIntyre Park District • 18 Locust St., Room 1262 • Gallipolis, OH 45631 • 740-446-4612 • http://www.eurekanet.com/~ovvc/biketrail.html

Great Miami River Trail (River Corridor Bikeway; Bike Route 25) • Miami Valley Regional Bicycle Council, Inc. • 333 W First St., Suite 150 • Dayton, OH 45402 • 937-463-2707

Great Miami River Trail (River Corridor Bikeway; Bike Route 25) • Five Rivers Metroparks • 1375 E Siebenthaler Ave. • Dayton, OH 45414 • 937-278-8231 or 937-667-7878 • http://www.metroparks.org

Great Miami River Trail (Taylorsville Metropark; Bike Route 25) • Five Rivers Metroparks • 1375 E Siebenthaler Ave. • Dayton, OH 45414 • 937-278-8231 or 937-667-7878 • http://www.metroparks.org

Great Ohio Lake to River Greenway; Western Reserve Greenway • Western Reserve Greenway • 134 W 46th St. • Ashtabula, OH 44044 • 440-992-8132

Great Ohio Lake to River Greenway; Western Reserve Greenway • Ashtabula County Parks • 25 W Jefferson St. • Jefferson, OH 44047 • 440-576-0717 • http://www.ashtabulacounty-parks.org

Great Ohio Lake to River Greenway; Western Reserve Greenway • Trumbull County Metroparks • 347 N Park Ave. • Warren, OH 44481 • 330-675-2480

Great Ohio Lake to River Greenway; Mahoning Bikeway • Mahoning County; Canfield • P.O. Box 596 • Canfield, OH 44406 • 330-702-3000

Great Ohio Lake to River Greenway; Little Beaver Creek Greenway Trail • Columbiana County Park District • 130 W Maple St. • Lisbon, OH 44432 • 330-424-9078

Hamilton Bikeway • Great Miami Path • 565 N 5th St. • Hamilton, OH 45011 • 513-868-8476

Harrison County Conotton Creek Trail • Crossroads Resource Conservation & Development Council, Inc. • 277 Canal Ave SE, Suite C • New Philadelphia, OH 44663 • 330-339-9317 • http://www.crossroadsrcd.org/hctrail

Headwaters Trail • Portage County Park District • 449 Meridian St. • Ravenna, OH 44266 • 330-673-9404

Heritage Rail-Trail • Heritage Rail-Trail Coalition c/o Homestead Park • 4675 Gosgray Rd. • Amlin, OH 43002 • 614-876-9554 or 614-876-2020

Hockhocking-Adena Bikeway/Riverside Bikeway • Athens County Convention & Visitors Bureau • 607 E State St. • Athens, OH 45701 • 800-878-9797 • http://www.seorf.ohiou.edu/~xx088/

Holmes County Rail-Trail • Holmes County Rails-to-Trails Coalition • P.O. Box 95 • Millersburg, OH 44654 • 330-674-1643 • http://www.holmesrailstotrails.org

Holmes County Rail-Trail • Chamber of Commerce & Tourist Bureau • 35 N Monroe St. • Millersburg, OH 44654 • 330-674-3975

Huron River Greenway • Erie Metroparks • 3910 E Perkins Ave. • Huron, OH 44839 • 419-625-7783

Huron River Greenway • Huron River Greenway Coalition • 632 River Rd. • Huron, OH 44839 • 419-443-6180

Interstate-480 Bikeway • City of North Olmsted • 5200 Dover Center Rd. • North Olmsted, OH 44070 • 440-777-8000

Interstate-670 Bikeway • City of Columbus, Division of Traffic Engineering • 109 N Front St. • Columbus, OH 43215 • 614-645-7790

Kauffman Avenue Bike Path • Greene County Parks • 651 Dayton-Xenia Rd. • Xenia, OH 45385 • 937-376-7440

Kokosing Gap Trail • Kokosing Gap Trail • P.O. Box 129 • Gambier, OH 43022 • 740-427-4509 or 740-587-6267

Lake Metroparks Greenway Trail • Lake Metroparks • 11211 Spear Rd. • Concord Township, OH 44077 • 440-639-7275

Lester Rail-Trail • Medina County Park District • 6364 Deerview Lane • Medina, OH 44256 • 330-722-9364

Little Miami Scenic Trail/Bike Route 1 • State Park Section (Southern), Little Miami State Park • 8570 E State Route 73 • Waynesville, OH 45068 • 513-897-3055 • http://www.dnr.state.oh.us/odnr/parks/directory/lilmiami.htm or http://www.greenlink.org/miami/lmtrail.html

Little Miami Scenic Trail/Bike Route 1 • Clark County Section (Northern), Springfield Parks & Recreation, City Hall • 76 E High St. • Springfield, OH 45502 • 937-324-7348

Little Miami Scenic Trail/Bike Route 1 • Greene County Section (Central), Greene County Park • 651 Dayton-Xenia Rd. • Xenia, OH 45385 • 937-376-7440 • http://www.yellowsprings.com/bikepath.html

Lunken Airport Bike Path • Lunken County Airport • 621 E Mehring Way • Suite 301 • Cincinnati, OH 45202

Mad River Bikeway/Bike Route 8 • Miami Valley Regional Bicycle Council, Inc. • 333 W First St., Suite 150 • Dayton, OH 45402 • 937-463-2707

Miami & Erie Canal Towpath Trail • Toledo Area Metroparks • 5100 W Central • Toledo, OH 43615 • 419-535-3050

Mohican Valley Trail • Mohican Valley Trail Board • P.O. Box 90 • Danville, OH 43014 • 740-599-7900

Muskingum Recreational Trail • Muskingum Recreational Trail • P.O. Box 3042 • Zanesville, OH 43702 • 740-455-8531

National Road Bikeway • City Recreation Dept. • 100 Fair St. • St. Clairsville, OH 43950 • 740-695-2037

Nickelplate Trail • Stark County Park District • 5300 Tyner St. • NW • Canton, OH 44708 • 330-477-3552

North Coast Inland Bike Path • Lorain County: Lorain County Metroparks • 12882 Diagonal Rd. • La Grange, OH 44050 • 440-458-5121 • http://www.loraincountymetroparks.com

North Coast Inland Bike Path • Sandusky County: Sandusky County Park District • 1970 Countryside Place • Fremont, OH 43420 • 419-334-4495 • http://www.clydeohio.org/trail.htm or http://www.scpd-parks.org/ncit.html

Ohio to Erie Trail • Ohio to Erie Trail Fund • P.O. Box 21246 • Columbus, OH 43221 • 614-451-8776 • http://www.ohio-to-erie-trail.org

Olentangy/Lower Scioto Bikeways (Bike Route 47) • Columbus Recreation & Parks Dept. • 200 Greenlawn Ave. • Columbus, OH 43223 • 614-645-3308

Piqua Activity Trail for Health (P.A.T.H.) • City of Piqua, Parks & Recreation • 635 Gordon St. • Piqua, OH 45356 • 937-778-2085

Richland B & O Trail • Mansfield-Richland Visitors Bureau • 52 Park Ave. West • Mansfield, OH 44902 • 419-525-1300 • http://www.virtualmansfield.com/bno-bike-trail.htm

Richland B & O Trail • Richland County Park District • 2295 Lexington Ave. • Mansfield, OH 44907 • 419-884-3764

Simon-Kenton Trail • Simon-Kenton Pathfinders • 3420 Urbana-Moorefield Pike • Urbana, OH 43078 • 937-484-3335 • http://www.simonkentontrail.org

Sippo Valley Trail • Rails-to-Trails of Wayne County • P.O. Box 1566 • Wooster, OH 44691 • 330-682-7188

Sippo Valley Trail • 2786 Chippewa Rd. • Orrville, OH 44667 • 330-682-7188

Sippo Valley Trail • Village of Dalton • 1 W Main St. • Dalton, OH 44618 • 330-828-2221

Slippery Elm Trail • Wood County Park District • 18729 Mercer Rd. • Bowling Green, OH 43402 • 419-353-1897

Stavich Bicycle Trail • Falcon Foundry • 6th & Water Streets • P.O. Box 301 • Lowellville, OH 44436 • 216-536-6221

Stillwater River Trail/Bike Route 7 (River Corridor Bikeway) • Miami Valley Regional Bicycle Council, Inc. • 333 W First St. • Suite 150 • Dayton, OH 45402 • 937-463-2707

Stillwater River Trail/Bike Route 7 • Five Rivers Metroparks • 1375 E Siebenthaler Ave. • Dayton, OH 45414 • 937-278-8231 or 937-667-7878 • http://www.metroparks.org

Towners Woods Rail-Trail • Portage County Park District • 499 Meridan St. • Ravenna, OH 44266 • 330-673-9404

Towpath Trail (Ohio & Erie Canal) • Ohio & Erie Canal Corridor Coalition • 520 S Main St. • Suite 2541-F • Akron, OH 44311 • 330-434-5657

Towpath Trail (Ohio & Erie Canal) • Cuyahoga Valley National Park, Cuyahoga Valley National Park • 15610 Vaughn Rd. • Brecksville, OH 44141 • 216-526-5256 • http://www.nps.gov/cuva/ohioerie.htm

Towpath Trail (Ohio & Erie Canal) • Cuyahoga County: Cleveland Metroparks • 4101 Fulton Parkway • Cleveland, OH 44144 • 216-351-6300 • http://www.clemetparks.com

Towpath Trail (Ohio & Erie Canal) • Stark County: Stark County Park District • 5300 Tyner St. NW • Canton, OH 44708 • 330-477-3552 • http://www.starkparks.com/Default.htm

Towpath Trail (Ohio & Erie Canal) • Summit County: Summit County Metroparks • 975 Treaty Line Rd. • Akron, OH 44313 • 330-867-5511 • http://www.neo.Irun.com/metroparks

Tri-County Triangle Trail • Tri-County Triangle Trail • 428 Jefferson St. • Greenfield, OH 45123 • http://www.members.tripod.com/tricotrail/

Tri-County Triangle Trail • Ross County Park District • 16 N Paint St. • Chillicothe, OH 45601 • 740-773-8794

University-Parks Hike-Bike Trail • Toledo Area Metroparks • 5100 W Central • Toledo, OH 43615 • 419-535-3050

Wabash Cannonball Trail • Northwestern Ohio Rails-to-Trails Association, Inc. (NORTA, Inc.) • P.O. Box 234 • Delta, OH 43515 • 800-951-4788 or 419-822-4788 • http://www.toltbbs.com/~norta/

Westerville Bikeway • Westerville Dept. of Parks & Recreation, • 350 N Cleveland Ave. • Westerville, OH 43082 • 614-901-6504 or 888-368-8289 • http://www.westerville.org

Wilberforce Spur Trail • Greene County Park • 651 Dayton-Xenia Rd. • Xenia, OH 45385 • 937-376-7440

Wolf Creek Rail-Trail • Five Rivers Metroparks • 1375 E Siebenthaler Ave. • Dayton, OH 45414 • 937-278-8231 or 937-667-7878 • http://www.whizlinc.com/2000/wolfcreektrail/trail-welcome.htm or http://www.metroparks.org

Zanes Landing Trail • City of Zanesville • 401 Market St. • Zanesville, OH 43701 • 740-455-0609

Oklahoma
General Information
Oklahoma Bicycle/Pedestrian Coordinator, Special Projects Branch, Oklahoma DOT, • 200 NE 21st St. • Oklahoma City, OK 73105 • 405-522-3797 • http://www.odot.org

Oklahoma Tourism & Recreation Department • 15 N Robinson, Suite 100 • Oklahoma City, OK 73102 • 800-652-OKLA 800-652-6552 or 405-521-2406 • http://www.otrd.state.ok.us

Trail Information
Cleveland Trail • City of Cleveland • 201 N Broadway St. • Cleveland, OK 74020 • 918-358-3506

Creek Turnpike Trail • River Parks Authority • 707 S Houston, Suite 202 • Tulsa, OK 74127 • 918-596-2006

Indian Nations Recreation Trail • Indian Nations Recreation Trail, Inc. • P.O. Box 53 • Warner, OK 74469 • 918-463-2931

Katy Trail • River Parks Authority • 707 S Houston, Suite 202 • Tulsa, OK 74127 • 918-596-2006

Midland Valley Trail & River Parks Pedestrian Bridge • River Parks Authority • 707 S Houston • Suite 202 • Tulsa, OK 74127 • 918-596-2006

Old Frisco Trail • Old Frisco Trail Lake Wister Association • P.O. Box 890 • Wister, OK 74966

River Park Trail (Arkansas River) • River Parks Authority • 707 S Houston, Suite 202 • Tulsa, OK 74127 • 918-596-2006

Oregon

General Information

Oregon Bicycle & Pedestrian Program Manager • Oregon DOT Building, Room 210 • Salem, OR 97310 • 503-986-3555 • http://www.odot.state.or.us/techserv/bikewalk

Oregon Tourism Commission, Oregon Economic Development Dept. • 775 Summer St. NE • Salem, OR 97310 • 800-547-7842 (Outside OR) or 800-543-8838 (OR) or 503-986-3154 • http://www.traveloregon.com

Trail Information

Astoria River Trail • Community Development Director, City of Astoria, City Hall • 1095 Duane St. • Astoria, OR 97103 • 503-338-5183

Banks-Vernonia State Trail • Banks-Vernonia State Trail • 24600 NW. Bacona Rd. • Buxton, OR 97109 • 503-324-0606 or 800-551-6949 • http://www.oregonstateparks.org

Bascom (Ruth) Riverbank Trail; North & East Bank (Willamette River Recreational Corridor Trail) • City of Eugene Dept. of Public Works, Bicycle Coordinator • 858 Pearl St., 3rd Floor • Eugene, OR 97401 • 541-682-5471 • http://www.ci.eugene.or.us/pw/bike/bikesite/trailmix.pdf

Bascom (Ruth) Riverbank Trail; West & South Bank (Willamette River Recreation Corridor) • City of Eugene Dept. of Public Works, Bicycle Coordinator, • 858 Pearl St., 3rd Floor • Eugene, OR 97401 • 541-682-5471 • http://www.ci.eugene.or.us/pw/bike/bikesite/trailmix.pdf

Columbia River Gorge Bikeway (Old U.S. Route 30) • Oregon DOT, • Transportation Building • Salem, OR 97310 • 503-986-3556 • http://www.odot.state.or.us/techserv/bikewalk

Fanno Creek Trail (Oregon Electric R.O.W. Trail & Linear Park) • Planning & Natural Resources, Tualatin Hills Parks & Recreation District • 15707 SW Walker Rd. • Beaverton, OR 97006 • 503-645-6433

Fort Stevens State Park Bike Paths • Fort Stevens State Park • 100 Peter Iredale Rd. • Hammond, OR 97121 • 503-861-1671 or 503-861-2000

Interstate-84 Bikeway • Metropolitan Service District • 2000 SW First Ave. • Portland, OR 97201 • 971-221-1646

Interstate-205 Bikeway • Metropolitan Service District • 2000 SW First Ave. • Portland, OR 97201 • 971-221-1646

Marine Drive Bikeway • Metropolitan Service District • 2000 SW First Ave. • Portland, OR 97201 • 971-221-1646

Mill City Trail • City Administrator, City of Mill City • 252 SW. Cedar St. • P.O. Box 256 • Mill City, OR 97360503-897-2302

O.C. & E. Woods Line State Trail • Oregon State Parks & Recreation Dept. Collier State Park, • 46000 Highway 97 North • Chiloquin, OR 97624 • 541-783-2471

Row River Trail • Eugene District Bureau of Land Management • P.O. Box 10226 • Eugene, OR 97440 • 541-683-6600 • http://www.158.68.104.192/

Springwater Corridor Trail • City of Portland, Parks & Recreation Department • 1120 SW Fifth Ave. • #1302 • Portland, OR 97204 • 503-823-6183

Pennsylvania
General Information
Mid-Atlantic Rail-Trails • http://www.his.com/~jmenzies/urbanatb/rtrails/index.htm

Pennsylvania Pedestrian & Bicycling Program Manager, Pennsylvania DOT, Bureau for Highway Safety & Traffic Engineering • P.O. Box 2047 • Harrisburg, PA 17105 • 717-783-8444 • http://www.dot.state.pa.us

Pennsylvania Center for Travel, Tourism & Film • Room 404 Forum Building • Harrisburg, PA 17120 • 800-VISIT-PA or 800-847-4872 or 717-787-5453 • http://www.state.pa.us

Pennsylvania Rails to Trails • http://www.dcnr.state.pa.us/rails/index.html

Pennsylvania Trails (Bureau of State Parks) • P.O. Box 8551 • Harrisburg, PA 17105 • 888-PA-PARKS or 888-727-2757 • http://www.dcnr.state.pa.us

Rails to Trails Conservancy, Pennsylvania Field Office • http://www.railtrails.org/PA

Trail Information
Allegheny Highlands Trail • Somerset County Rails-to-Trails • P.O. Box 413, 829 N Center Ave. • Somerset, PA 15501 • 814-445-6431 • http://www.atatrail.org

Allegheny River Trail • Allegheny Valley Trails Assocation • 1256 Liberty St. • Franklin, PA 16323 • 814-437-5621 • http://eagle.clarion.edu/~grads/avta

Armstrong Trail • Allegheny Valley Land Trust • P.O. Box 777 • Kittanning, PA 16201 • 724-543-4478

Arrowhead Trail • Arrowhead Trail • 200 Municipal Dr. • McMurray, PA 15317 • 724-942-5000

Arrowhead Trail • Peters Township, Department of Parks & Recreation • 610 E McMurray Rd. • McMurray, PA 15317 • 724-942-5000 • http://www.atatrail.org

Back Mountain Trail • Anthracite Scenic Trails Association • P.O. Box 212 • Dallas, PA 18612 • 570-675-9016 • http://www.bmt.editthispage.com

Betzwood Rail-Trail • Valley Forge National Historic Park • P.O. Box 953 • Valley Forge, PA 19482 • 610-783-1046

Bristol Spurline Park Trail • Borough of Bristol • 250 Pond St. • Bristol, PA 19007 • 215-788-3828

Butler-Freeport Community Trail • Butler-Freeport Community Trail Council, Inc. • P.O. Box 533 • Saxonburg, PA 16056 • 724-352-4783

Canoe Creek State Park Bike Paths • Canoe Creek State Park • RR 2, P.O. Box 560 • Hollidaysburg, PA 16648 • 814-695-6807 or 800-63-PARKS or 800-637-2757

Capital Area Greenbelt Trail • Capital Area Greenbelt Association • P.O. Box 15405 • Harrisburg, PA 17105 • 717-652-4079 • http://www.caga.org

Chester Valley Trail • Chester County Parks & Recreation • 601 Westtown Rd., Suite 160, P.O. Box 2747 • West Chester, PA 19380 • 610-344-6415 • http://www.chesco.org/ccparks

Clarion River-Little Toby Creek Trail • Tri-County Rails-to-Trails Association c/o Love's Canoe • 3 Main St. • Ridgeway, PA 15853 • 814-776-6285

Clarion River-Little Toby Creek Trail • P.O. Box 115 • Ridgeway, PA 15853

Clearfield to Grampian Rail-Trail • Clearfield County Rails-to-Trails Association • 310 E Cherry St. • Clearfield, PA 16830 • 814-765-1701 • http://www.dcnr.state.pa.us/rails/curwensvillet-gt.html

Conewago Trail • Lancaster County Parks & Recreation • 1050 Rockford Rd. • Lancaster, PA 17602 • 717-299-8217 • http://www.co.lancaster.pa.us/parks.htm

Cumberland County Biker-Hiker Trail • Pine Grove Furnace State Park • 1100 Pine Grove Rd. • Gardeners, PA 17324 • 717-486-7174 • http://www.pinegrove@dcnr.state.pa.us

Duncan Trail • Bald Eagle State Forest • P.O. Box 147 • Laurelton, PA 17835 • 570-922-3344

Eliza Furnace Trail • Office of the Mayor • 414 Grant St., 5th Floor, City-County Building • Pittsburgh, PA 15219 • 412-255-2626 • http://www.city.pittsburgh.pa.us

Five Star Trail • Five Star Trail Chapter • R.R. #12, P.O. Box 203 • Greensburg, PA 15601 • 724-830-3962

Regional Trail Council • 101 N Water St., P.O. Box 95 • West Newton, PA 15089 • 412-872-5586

Forks Township Recreation Trail • Forks Township Recreation Board • 1606 Sullivan Trail • Easton, PA 18040 • 610-252-0785

French Creek Recreational Trail (Ernst Bike Trail) • Crawford County Visitors Bureau • 211 Chestnut St. • Meadville, PA 16335 • 800-332-2338

French Creek Recreational Trail (Ernst Bike Trail) • French Creek Recreational Trails. Inc. c/o Community Health Services • 747 Terrace St. • Meadville, PA 16335

Ghost Town Trail • Indiana County Parks • 1128 Blue Spruce Rd. • Indiana, PA 15701 • 724-463-8636 • http://www.indiana-co-pa-tourism.org

Heritage Rail-Trail County Park (York County Heritage Rail-Trail) • Project Coordinator, York County Trail Authority • 5922 Nixon Dr. • York, PA 17403 • http://www.southernyorkcounty.com/org/railtrail/

Heritage Rail-Trail County Park (York County Heritage Rail-Trail) • York County Parks • 400 Mundis Race Rd. • York, PA 17402 • 717-840-7440 • http://www.york-county.org

Hoodlebog Trail • Indiana County Parks • 1128 Blue Spruce Rd • Indiana, PA 15701 • 724-463-8036 • http://www.indiana-co-pa-tourism.org

Houtzdale Line Trail • Houtzdale Line Trail • 501 David St. • Houtzdale, PA 16651 • 814-378-7817

Indian Creek Valley Hiking & Biking Trail • Secretary/Treasurer, Salt Lick Township • 147 Municipal Building Rd., P.O. Box 403 • Melcroft, PA 15462 • 724-455-2866

Ironton Rail-Trail • Bureau Chief of Recreation, Whitehall Township • 3219 MacArthur Rd. • Whitehall, PA 18052 • 610-437-5524, ext 160. • http://www.irontonrailtrail.org

Justus (Samuel) Recreation Trail • Secretary, Cranberry Township • P.O. Box 378 • Seneca, PA 16346 • 814-676-8812

Kennedy (John F.) Walking Trail • Schuylkill Conservation District • 1206 Ag Center Dr. • Pottsville, PA 17901 • Whitehall, PA 18052 570-622-4124, ext. 113 or 570-622-4009

Lackawanna River Heritage Trail • Lackawanna River Heritage Trail • P.O. Box 368 •

Scranton, PA 15501 • 570-347-6311

Lambs Creek Hike & Bike Trail • Tioga-Hammond Lakes • RR #1 Box 65 • Tioga, PA 16946 • 570-835-5281

Lancaster Junction Trail • Lancaster County Parks & Recreation • 1050 Rockford Rd. • Lancaster, PA 17602 • 717-299-8217 • http://www.co.lancaster.pa.us/parks.htm

Lehigh Gorge State Park Trail • Lehigh Gorge State Park • RR 1, P.O. Box 81 • White Haven, PA 18661 • 570-443-0400 • http://www.dcnr.state.pa.us/rails/index.html

Lititz-Warwick Trailway • Warwick Township • P.O. Box 308 • Lititz, PA 17543 • 717-626-8900 • http://www.warwicktownship.org

Lower Trail (Pennsylvania Mainline Canal Trail) • Central Pennsylvania Rail-to-Trails • P.O. Box 592 • Hollidaysburg, PA 16648 • http://www.woodstock.uplink.net/~cmiller2/lowertrail

Luzerne County Rail-Trail • Luzerne County Parks Dept. • 2000 Wyoming Ave. • Forty Fort, PA 18704 • 570-331-7046

Lycoming Creek Bikeway • Lycoming County Planning Commission • 48 W 3rd St. • Williamsport, PA 17701 • 570-320-2130

Mayer (Jim) Rivers Walk • Cambria County Transit Authority • 726 Central Ave. • Johnstown, PA 15902 • 814-535-5526

Montour Trail; Coraopolis-Thompsonville • Montour Trail Council • P.O. Box 11866 • Pittsburgh, PA 15228 • 412-831-2030 • http://www.atatrail.org or http://www.montourtrail.org

Montour Trail; Bethel Branch, Montour Trail Council • P.O. Box 11866 • Pittsburgh, PA 15228 • 412-831-2030 • http://www.atatrail.org

Nor-Bath Trail (Bath-Allen Trail) • County of Northampton, Parks & Recreation • Greystone Building • Nazareth, PA 18064 • 610-746-1975

Oil Creek State Park Trail • Oil Creek State Park • RR 1, P.O. Box 207 • Oil City, PA 16301 • 814-676-5915 • http://www.dcnr.state.pa.us

Palmer Township Bike Path (National Trails Towpath Bike Trail) • Palmer Township Board of Supervisors • 3 Weller Place, P.O. Box 3039 • Palmer, PA 18043 • 610-253-7191

Pine Creek Trail • Bureau of Forestry, Tioga State Forest • Wellsboro, PA 16901 • 570-724-2868

Plainfield Township Recreation Trail • Treasurer, Plainfield Township • 6292 Sullivan Trail • Nazareth, PA 18064 • 610-759-6944

Roaring Run Trail • Roaring Run Watershed Association • P.O. Box 333 • Apollo, PA 15613 • 724-478-3366 • http://www.nk.psu.edu/roaringrun or http://www.roaring.run.org

Schuylkill River Trail (Philadelphia to Valley Forge Bikeway) • Montgomery County Courthouse, Planning Commission • P.O. Box 311, Courthouse • Norristown, PA 19404 • 610-278-3557 • http://www.montcopa.org/parks

Stavich Bicycle Trail • Falcon Foundry • 6th & Water Streets, P.O. Box 301 • Lowellville, OH 44436 • 216-536-6221

Steel Valley Trail • Montour Trail Council • P.O. Box 11866 • Pittsburgh, PA 15228 • 412-831-2030 • www.atatrail.org or www.montourtrail.org

Steel Valley Trail • Friends of the Riverfront • P.O. Box 42434 • Pittsburgh, PA 15203 • 412-488-0212 • www.atatrail.org

Stony Valley Railroad Grade Trail • Federal-State Coordination Division, Pennsylvania Game Commission • 2001 Elmerton Ave. • Harrisburg, PA 17110 • 717-787-9612

Struble Trail • Chester County Parks & Recreation Dept. • 601 Westtown Rd., Suite 160, P.O. Box 2747 • West Chester, PA 19380 • 610-344-6415 • http://www.chesco.org/ccparks.html

Switchback Railroad Trail • Carbon County Park & Recreation Dept. • 625 Lentz Trail Rd. • Jim Thorpe, PA 18229 • 570-325-3669 • http://www.dcnr.state.pa.us

Three Rivers Heritage Trail • Friends of the Riverfront • P.O. Box 42434 • Pittsburgh, PA 15203 • 412-488-0212 • http://www.atatrail.org

Tyler State Park Bike Paths • Tyler State Park • 101 Swamp Rd. • Newtown, PA 18940 • 215-968-2021 • http://www.dcnr.state.pa.us

Valley Forge National Historic Park Bike Paths • Valley Forge National Historical Park • P.O. Box 953 • Valley Forge, PA 19482 • 610-783-1046

Warren-North Warren Bike-Hike Trail • Warren County Planning Commission • 207 W Fifth Ave. • Warren, PA 16365 • 814-726-3861

Youghiogheny River Trail • Regional Trail Council • 101 N Water St., P.O. Box 95 • West Newton, PA 15089 • 412-872-5586 • http://www.youghrivertrail.com

Ohiopyle State Park • P.O. Box 105 • Ohiopyle, PA 15470 • 724-329-8591 • http://www.atarail.org or http://www.dcnr.state.pa.us

Rhode Island
General Information
Rhode Island Bicycle Coordinator • Rhode Island DOT

Inter-Modal Transportation Planning • 2 Capitol Hill • Providence, RI 02903 • 401-222-4203 (ext. 4034) • http://www.dot.state.ri.us

Rhode Island Division of Parks & Recreation, Rhode Island Dept. of Environmental Management • 2321 Hartford Ave. • Johnston, RI 02919 • 401-222-2632, 401-222-2633 or 401-222-2634 • http://www.riparks.com

Rhode Island Tourism • 800-556-2484 or 401-222-2601 • http://www.visitrhodeisland.com

Trail Information
Blackstone River Bike Path • Lincoln Woods State Park • 2 Manchester Print Works Rd. • Lincoln, RI 02865 • 401-723-7892 • http://www.riparks.com

Blackstone River Bike Path • Rhode Island Dept. of Environmental Management • 83 Park St. • Providence, RI 02903 • 401-222-6800

Coventry Greenway • Parks & Recreation Dept. • 1670 Flat River Rd. • Coventry, RI 02816 • 401-822-9107

East Bay Bike Path • Regional Manager, Colt State Park • Bristol, RI 02809 • 401-253-7482 • http://www.riparks.com

South County Bike Path • Rhode Island DOT • 2 Capitol Hill • Providence, RI 02903 • 401-222-2023

Washington Secondary Bicycle Path • Supervising Planner • State of Rhode Island • 401-222-2023 Ext. 4063

South Carolina
General Information
Palmetto Trails • http://www.palmettoconservation.org/trails.html

South Carolina Bicycle/Pedestrian Coordinator, Traffic Engineering, South Carolina DOT • 955 Park St., P.O. Box 191 • Columbia, SC 29202 • 803-737-1052 • http://www.dot.state.sc.us/

South Carolina Trails Program, State Trails Coordinator, South Carolina Dept. of Parks, Recreation & Tourism • 1205 Pendleton St., Suite 235 • Columbia, SC 29201 • 803-734-0130 • http://www.sctrails.net

Trail Information
Hilton Head Island Bike Paths • Hilton Head Island Chamber of Commerce Visitor & Convention Bureau • P.O. Box 5647 • Hilton Head Island, SC 20038 • 800-523-3373 or 843-785-3673 • http://www.hiltonhead-usa.com/bike.html

Marion Hike & Bike Trail • City of Marion Parks & Recreation Dept. • P.O. Box 1190 • Marion, SC 29571 • 843-423-5410

North Augusta "Greeneway" • North Augusta Parks & Recreation • P.O. Box 6400 • North Augusta, SC 29841 • 803-441-4300 • http://www.nirthaugusta.net

West Ashley Bikeway • Charleston Dept. of Parks • 823 Meeting St. • Charleston, SC 29403 • 843-724-7324

South Dakota
General Information
South Dakota Bicycle/Pedestrian Coordinator, South Dakota DOT • 700 Broadway Ave. East • Pierre, SD 57501 • 605-773-4912

South Dakota Dept. Of Tourism, Capitol Lake Plaza • 711 E Wells Ave., c/o 500 E Capitol Ave. • Pierre, SD 57501 • 800-S-DAKOTA, 800-732-5682 or 605-773-3301 • http://www.travelsd.com

Trail Information
Mickelson (George S.) Trail • Trails Program Specialist, South Dakota Dept. of Game, Fish & Parks • 523 E Capitol Ave. • Pierre, SD 57501 • 605-773-3930 • http://www.state.sd.us/state/executive/gfp/index.htm

Rapid City Recreational Path • Rapid City Area Transportation Planning • 300 6th St. • Rapid City, SD 57701 • 605-394-4120

Rapid City Recreational Path • Rapid City Parks & Recreation Dept. • 2915 Canyon Lake Dr. • Rapid City, SD 57702 • 605-394-4175

Spearfish Recreation Trail • City of Spearfish • 625 Fifth St. • Spearfish, SD 57783 • 605-642-1333 • http://www.city.spearfish.sd.us

Yankton Trail, City of Sioux Falls • City Clerk • 224 W 9th St. • Sioux Falls, SD 57104 • 605-367-8696

Tennessee
General Information

Tennessee Bicycle Coordinator, Tennessee DOT • 505 Deaderick St., Suite 900, James K. Polk Building • Nashville, TN 37243 • 615-741-5310

Tennessee Department of Tourism • 320 6th Ave., North, Rachel Jackson Building, 5th Floor • Nashville, TN 37243 • 800-GO-2-TENN, 800-462-8366 or 615-741-2159 • http://www.tourism.state.tn.us

TRAC, Tennessee Rail-Trail Advisory Council • http://www.members.aol.com/trac2trail/main.htm

Trail Information
Cumberland River Bicentennial Trail • Ashland City Parks & Recreation • P.O. Box 36 • Ashland City, TN 37015 • 615-792-2655

Ligon (Betsy) Park & Walking Trail • Recorder Erin City Hall • P.O. Box 270 • Erin, TN 37061 • 931-289-4108

Tellico Plains Rail-Trail • Mayor, City Hall • 201 Southard St. • Tellico Plains, TN 37385 • 423-253-2333

Texas
General Information
Texas Bicycle/Pedestrian Coordinator, Texas DOT • P.O. Box 149217 • Austin, TX 78714 • 512-416-2342 • http://www.dot.state.tx.us

Texas Parks & Wildlife Department • 4200 Smith School Rd. • Austin, TX 78744 • 800-792-1112 or 512-389-8950 • http://www.tpwd.state.tx.us/park/

Texas Tourism Information • 800-8888-TEX or 800-888-8839 • http://www.traveltex.com

Trail Information
Bachman Lake Park Trail • Dallas Parks & Recreation, Dallas City Hall • 1500 Marilla St., Room 6-F South • Dallas, TX 75201 • 214-670-4282 or 214-670-4100

Brazos Bend State Park Bike Path • Brazos Bend State Park • 21901, FM 762 • Needville, TX 77461 • 979-553-5101

Cargill Long Park Trail • City of Longview, Longview Parks & Recreation • P.O. Box 1952 • Longview, TX 75606 • 903-237-1270 • http://www.ci.longview.tx.us

Crawford Park Trail • Dallas Parks & Recreation, Dallas City Hall • 1500 Marilla St., Room 6-F South • Dallas, TX 75201 • 214-670-4282 or 214-670-4100

Fireside Park Trail • Dallas Parks & Recreation, Dallas City Hall • 1500 Marilla St., Room 6-F South • Dallas, TX 75201 • 214-670-4282 or 214-670-4100

Glendale Park Trail • Dallas Parks & Recreation, Dallas City Hall • 1500 Marilla St., Room 6-F South • Dallas, TX 75201 • 214-670-4282 or 214-670-4100

Harrisburg-Sunset Rail-Trail (Houston, TX) • Public Works & Engineering • 611 Walker • Houston, TX 77002 • 713-837-0003 • http://www.houstonbikeways.org

Katy Trail • Dallas Parks & Recreation, Dallas City Hall • 1500 Marilla St., Room 6-F South • Dallas, TX 75201 • 214-670-4282 or 214-670-4100

Kiest Park Trail • Dallas Parks & Recreation, Dallas City Hall • 1500 Marilla St., Room 6-F South • Dallas, TX 75201 • 214-670-4282 or 214-670-4100

Lake Mineral Wells State Trailway • Lake Mineral Wells State Park • Park Rd. 71 • Mineral

Wells, TX 76067

Lake Mineral Wells State Trailway • Texas Parks & Wildlife, RR4 • Box 39-C • Mineral Wells, TX 76967 • 940-328-1171 • http://www.tpwd.state.tx.us

McKinney Falls State Park Bike Path • McKinney Falls State Park • 5080 McKinney Falls Parkway • Austin, TX 78744 • 512-243-1643 • http://www.tpwd.state.tx.us

Phelps (John C.) Trail • Dallas Parks & Recreation, Dallas City Hall • 1500 Marilla St., Room 6-F South • Dallas, TX 75201 • 214-670-4282 or 214-670-4100

Ray Roberts Lake State Park Bike Path • Ray Roberts Lake State Park • Isle Du Bois Unit #100 PW 4137 • Pilot Point, TX 76258 • 940-686-2148

Ray Roberts Lake State Park Bike Path • Ray Roberts Lake State Park • Johnson Branch Unit #100 PW 4153 • Valley View, TX 76272 • 940-637-2294

Rochester Park Trail • Dallas Parks & Recreation, Dallas City Hall • 1500 Marilla St., Room 6-F South • Dallas, TX 75201 • 214-670-4282 or 214-670-4100

White Rock Creek Trail • Dallas Parks & Recreation, Dallas City Hall • 1500 Marilla St., Room 6-F South • Dallas, TX 75201 • 214-670-4282 or 214-670-4100

White Rock Lake Hike & Bike Trail • Dallas Parks & Recreation, Dallas City Hall • 1500 Marilla St., Room 6-F South • Dallas, TX 75201 • 214-670-4282 or 214-670-4100

White Rock Lake Hike & Bike Trail •Williams (Raymond W.) Hike & Bike Trail, Dallas Parks & Recreation, Dallas City Hall • 1500 Marilla St., Room 6-F South • Dallas, TX 75201 • 214-670-4282 or 214-670-4100

Utah
General Information
Bicycle Utah • 2273 East, 6200 South • Salt Lake City, UT 84121 • 801-278-6294 • http://www.bicycleutah.com

Utah Bicycle/Pedestrian Planner, Utah DOT-Program Development • 4501 South, 2700 West, Box 143600 • Salt Lake City, UT 84114 • 801-965-3897 • http://www.dot.state.ut.us/progdev

Utah Cycling Network • http://www.redrocks.com

Utah Travel Council • Capitol Hill • Salt Lake City, UT 84114 • 800-200-1160 OR 801-538-1030

Trail Information
Historic Union Pacific Rail-Trail State Park • Mountain Trails Foundation • P.O. Box 754 • Park City, UT 84060 • 435-649-6839

Provo Jordan River Parkway Trail • Engineer, Utah County • 2855 S State • Provo, UT 84606 • 801-370-8624

Provo River Bike Path (Salt Lake City) • Salt Lake City Transportation • 333 S 200 East • Salt Lake City, UT 84111 • 801-535-7704 • www.ci.slc.ut.us

Vermont
General Information
New England Rail-Trails • http://www.new-england-rail-trails.org

Regional Recreation Maps & Guides for Vermont, Huntington Graphics • P.O. Box 373 • Burlington, VT 05402 • 802-660-3605

Vermont Bicycle/Pedestrian Coordinator • 133 State St. • Montpelier, VT 05633 • 802-828-5799 • http://www.travel-vermont.vermont.com/repage/bicycle.htm

Vermont Department of Tourism & Marketing • 6 Baldwin St., Drawer 33 • Montpelier, VT 05633 • 800-VERMONT, 800-937-6668 or 802-828-3237 • http://www.travel-vermont.com

Trail Information
Beebe Spur Recreation Trail • Bicycle & Pedestrian Coordinator, Local Transportation Facilities, State of Vermont Agency of Transportation • 133 State St. • Montpelier, VT 05633 • 802-828-5799 • http://railtrails.megalow.com/vt/index.htm

Burlington Bike Path • Burlington Dept. of Parks & Recreation • 645 Pine St., Suite B • Burlington, VT 05401 • 802-864-0123 or 802-652-2453 (Trail Ferry)

Causeway Park Rail-Trail • Colchester Parks & Recreation Dept. • P.O. Box 55 • Colchester, VT 05446 • 802-655-0811 or 802-652-2453 (Trail Ferry)

Graniteville Trails • Town Manager, Town of Berrytow • Municipal Building • Websterville, VT 05678 • 802-479-9931

Missisquoi Valley Rail-Trail • Northwest Regional Planning Commission • 7 Lake St., #201 • St. Albans, VT 05478 • 802-524-5958 • http://www.new-england-rail-trails.org

Toonerville Trail (Springfield Trail) • Springfield Trails & Greenways Committee • 108 Summer St. • Springfield, VT 05156 • 802-885-9687

Toonerville Trail (Springfield Trail) • Springfield Parks & Recreation • 96 Main St. • Springfield, VT 05156 • 802-885-2727 • http://www.springfieldchamber.com

Valley Trail • Town of Dover-The Valley Trail • 102 Route 100, P.O. Box 428 • West Dover, VT 05356 • 802-464-8000

Virginia
General Information
Mid-Atlantic Rail-Trails • http://www.his.com/~jmenzies/urbanatb/rtrails/index.htm

Virginia Bicycle Coordinator, Virginia DOT • 1401 E Broad St. • Richmond, VA 23219 • 800-835-1203 • http://www.vdot.state.va.us

Virginia Division of Tourism • 901 E Byrd St. • Richmond, VA 23219 • 800-VISIT-VA, 800-847-4882 or 804-786-4484 • http://www.virginia.org

Trail Information
Blackwater Creek Trail • City of Lynchburg Parks & Recreation Division • 301 Grove St. • Lynchburg, VA 24501 • 804-847-1640

Bluemont Junction Trail • Arlington County, Virginia, Dept. of Public Works • 1 Courthouse Plaza, 2100 Clarendon Blvd, Suite 717 • Arlington, VA 33301 • 703-228-3699 • http://www.co.arlington.va.us/dpw

Chester Linear Park Trail • Chesterfield County Dept. of Parks & Recreation • P.O. Box 40 • Chesterfield, VA 23832 • 804-748-1624

Custis Trail (Includes Interstate-66 Bikeway) • Arlington County, Virginia, Dept. of Public Works • 1 Courthouse Plaza, 2100 Clarendon Blvd, Suite 717 • Arlington, VA 33301 • 703-

228-3699 • http://www.co.arlington.va.us/dpw

Four-Mile Run Trail (Includes Wayne F. Anderson Bikeway) • Arlington County, Virginia, Dept. of Public Works • 1 Courthouse Plaza, 2100 Clarendon Blvd, Suite 717 • Arlington, VA 33301 • 703-228-3699 • http://www.co.arlington.va.us/dpw

Guest River Gorge Trail • Clinch Ranger District of Jefferson National Forest • 9416 Darden Dr. • Wise, VA 24293 • 540-328-2931

Hanging Rock Battlefield Trail • Hanging Rock Battlefield & Railway Preservation • 620 High St. • Salem, VA 24153

Huckleberry Trail • Montgomey County Planning, Annex Building • 4 S Franklin St., P.O. Box 6126 • Christainsburg, VA 24068 • 540-382-5750

Huckleberry Trail • Town of Blacksburg, Planning & Engineering Dept. • 300 S Main St. • Blacksburg, VA 24062 • 540-961-1126 • http://www.blacksburg.va.us

Mt. Vernon Trail • George Washington Memorial Parkway • Turkey Run Park • McLean, VA 22101 • 703-289-2550 • http://www.nps.gov/gwmp/mut.html

Orange & Alexandria Historical Trail • Arlington County, Virginia, Dept. of Public Works • 1 Courthouse Plaza, 2100 Clarendon Blvd, Suite 717 • Arlington, VA 33301 • 703-228-3699 • http://www.co.arlington.va.us/dpw

Park Connector Bikeway • Dept. of Planning • Room 115, Operations Building, 2405 Courthouse Rd. • Virginia Beach, VA 23456 • 757-427-4621

Virginia Central Railway Trail • Planning Dept. • Spotsylvania Parks & Recreation Dept.,P.O. Box 28 • Spotsylvania, VA 22553 • 540-5898-7529 • www.parks&rec@spotsylvania.va.us

Warrenton Branch Greenway • Fauquier County Parks & Recreation • 62 Culpeper St. • Warrenton, VA 20186 • 540-347-6896 • http://www.co.fauquier.va.us/services/parks

Washington & Old Dominion (W. & O. D.) Railroad Regional Park Trail • Northern Virginia Regional Park Authority • 5400 Ox Rd. • Fairfax Station, VA 22039 • 703-352-5900

Washington & Old Dominion (W. & O. D.) Railroad Regional Park Trail • Friends of the W. & O. D., Washington & Old Dominion Railroad Regional Park Trail • 21293 Smiths Switch Rd. • Ashburn, VA 20147 • 703-729-0596 • http://www.wodfriends.org

Washington State
General Information
Alaska Marine Highway System (From Bellingham, WA to Alaska) • Alaska DOT • 907-465-3900 for reservations • http://www.dot.state.ak.us/external/amhs/home.html

Washington State Bicycle & Pedestrian Program, Washington State DOT, Bicycle & Pedestrian Program • P.O. Box 47393 • Olympia, WA 98504 • 360-705-7277 • http://www.wsdot.wa.gov

Washington State Ferry Schedules, Washington State DOT, Bicycle & Pedestrian Program • P.O. Box 47393 • Olympia, WA 98504 • 360-705-7277 • http://www.wsdot.wa.gov

Washington State Tourism • P.O. Box 42500 • Olympia, WA 98504 • 800-544-1800 • http://www.tourism.wa.gov

Trail Information
Alki Trail (Seattle Waterfront Trail) • Seattle Transportation, Bicycle & Pedestrian Program •

600 4th Ave., Room 708 • Seattle, WA 98104 • 206-684-7583 • http://www.ci.seattle.wa.us/td/bicycle.asp

B. P. A. Trail • King County Park System Headquarters, Luther Burbank Park • 2040 84th Ave. SE • Mercer Island, WA 98040 • 206-296-4232 • http://www.metrokc.gov/parks

Burke-Gilman Trail • Seattle Transportation, Bicycle & Pedestrian Program • 600 4th Ave., Room 708 • Seattle, WA 98104 • 206-684-7583 • http://www.ci.seattle.wa.us/td/bicycle.asp

Burlington Rail-Trail • Skagit County Parks and Recreation • 219 S. Skaqit St. • Burlington, WA 98233 • 360-755-9649 • http://www.skagitcounty.net

King County Park System Headquarters • Luther Burbank Park • 2040 84th Ave. SE • Mercer Island, WA 98040 • 206-296-4232 • http://www.metrokc.gov/parks

Cascade Trail • Skagit County Parks • 315 S. 3rd. • Mt. Vernon, WA 98273 • 360-336-9414

Cedar River Trail • King County Park System Headquarters, Luther Burbank Park • 2040 84th Ave. SE • Mercer Island, WA 98040 • 206-296-4232 • http://www.metrokc.gov/parks

Chehalis Western Trail • Thurston County Parks & Recreation • 2617-A 12th Court SW • Olympia, WA 98502 • 360-7865595 • http://www.thurston-parks.org

Columbia Plateau Trail • Washingotn State Parks & Recreation Commission • P.O. Box 157 • Starbuck, WA • 509-646-9218 • http://www.parks.wa.gov

Commencement Bay Bike Path • Pierce County Public Works & Utilities, Program Development Division • 2401 S 35th St. • Tacoma, WA 98409 • 253-798-7250

Corridor Trail • City of Snoqualmie Park Board • P.O. Box 987 • Snoqualmie, WA 98065 • 206-888-1555

Dungeness River Bridge Trail • Jefferson County Parks & Recreation • P.O. Box 2070 • Port Townsend, WA 98368 • 360-385-9160 • http://www.co.jefferson.wa.us/publicworks/park-srec/default.htm

Duwamish Trail • Seattle Transportation, Bicycle & Pedestrian Program • 600 4th Ave., Room 708 • Seattle, WA 98104 • 206-684-7583 • http://www.ci.seattle.wa.us/td/bicycle.asp

Duwamish Trail • King County Park System Headquarters, Luther Burbank Park • 2040 84th Ave. SE • Mercer Island, WA 98040 • 206-296-4232 • http://www.metrokc.gov/parks

Elliot Bay Trail (Myrtle Edwards Park Trail & Terminal-91) • Seattle Transportation, Bicycle & Pedestrian Program • 600 4th Ave., Room 708 • Seattle, WA 98104 • 206-684-7583 • http://www.ci.seattle.wa.us/td/bicycle.asp

Elliot Bay Trail (Myrtle Edwards Park Trail & Terminal-91) • King County Park System Headquarters, Luther Burbank Park • 2040 84th Ave. SE • Mercer Island, WA 98040 • 206-296-4232 • http://www.metrokc.gov/parks

Everett-Shoreline Interurban Trail • Snohomish County Parks & Recreation Dept. • 3000 Rockefeller Ave., MS 303 • Everett, WA 98201 • 425-388-6621 or 425-388-6600 • http://www.co.snohomish.wa.us/parks

Fish Lake Trail • City of Parks & Recreation • 520 4th St. • Cheney, WA 99004 • 509-235-7295

Foothills Trail • Foothills Rails-to-Trails Coalition • P.O. Box 192 • Puyallup, WA 98371 • 253-841-2570 • http://www.piercecountytrails.org

Green River Trail • King County Park System Headquarters, Luther Burbank Park • 2040 84th Ave. SE • Mercer Island, WA 98040 • 206-296-4232 • http://www.metrokc.gov/parks

Interstate-90 Bikeway • King County Park System Headquarters, Luther Burbank Park • 2040 84th Ave. SE • Mercer Island, WA 98040 • 206-296-4232 • http://www.metrokc.gov/parks

Interstate-205 Bikeway • Metropolitan Service District • 2000 SW First Ave. • Portland, OR 97201 • 971-221-1646

Interurban Trail (Snohomish County) • Everett Parks & Recreation • 802 E Mukilteo Ave. • Everett, WA 98203 • 425-257-8300 • http://www.ci.everett.wa.us/EVERETT/parks

King County Interurban Trail • King County Park System Headquarters, Luther Burbank Park • 2040 84th Ave. SE • Mercer Island, WA 98040 • 206-296-4232 • http://www.metrokc.gov/parks

King County Interurban Trail • Trails Coordinator, King County Office of Open Spaces • 2040 84th Ave. SE • Mercer Island, WA 98040 • 206-296-7808

Lake Washington Trail • King County Park System Headquarters, Luther Burbank Park • 2040 84th Ave. SE • Mercer Island, WA 98040 • 206-296-4232 • http://www.metrokc.gov/parks

Lower Padden Creek Trail (Lanabee Trail) • Bellingham Parks & Recreation Dept. • 3424 Meridian • Bellingham, WA 98225 • 360-676-6985

Lower Yakima Valley Pathway • Yakima County Parks • 1000 Ahtanum Rd. • Union Gap, WA 98903 • 509-574-2430

Neppel Landing Trail • City of Moses Lake Parks & Recreation • 401 S Balsam, P.O. Box 1579 • Moses Lake, WA 98837 • 509-766-9240

North Bend-Tanner Trail (Northwest Timber Trail) • Washington State DNR • P.O. Box 68 • Enumclaw, WA 98022 • 360-825-1631

North Bend-Tanner Trail (Northwest Timber Trail) • Public Works Director • P.O. Box 896 • North Bend, WA 98045 • 206-888-1211

Palouse (Bill Chipman) Trail • Whitman County Parks • 310 N Main St. • Colfax, WA 99111 • 509-397-6238

Preston-Snoqualmie Trail • Trails Coordinator, King County Office of Open Spaces • 2040 84th Ave. SE • Mercer Island, WA 98040 • 206-296-7808

Preston-Snoqualmie Trail • King County Park System Headquarters, Luther Burbank Park • 2040 84th Ave. SE • Mercer Island, WA 98040 • 206-296-4232 • http://www.metrokc.gov/parks

Railroad Trail (Scudder Pond Trail) • Bellingham Parks & Recreation Dept. • 3424 Meridian • Bellingham, WA 98225 • 360-676-6985

Rainer Multiple Use Trail (Issaquah Trail) • Issaquah Parks & Recreation Dept. • P.O. Box 1307 • Issaquah, WA 98027 • 425-837-3300

Republic Rail-Trail • City of Republic • County Courthouse • Republic, WA 99166 • 509-775-5231

Sammamish River Trail • King County Park System Headquarters, Luther Burbank Park • 2040 84th Ave. SE • Mercer Island, WA 98040 • 206-296-4232 • http://www.metrokc.gov/parks

Scott (Larry) Memorial Trail • Jefferson County Parks & Recreation • P.O. Box 2070 • Port Townsend, WA 98368 • 360-385-9160 • http://www.co.jefferson.wa.us/publicworks/park-srec/default.htm

Ship Canal Trail • Seattle Transportation, Bicycle & Pedestrian Program • 600 4th Ave., Room 708 • Seattle, WA 98104 • 206-684-7583 • http://www.ci.seattle.wa.us/td/bicycle.asp

South Ship Canal Trail • City of Seattle Engineering Dept. • 210 Municpal Building • 600 4th Ave. • Seattle, WA 98104 • 206-684-8022

Snohomish's Centennial Trail • Snohomish County Parks & Recreation Dept. • 3000 Rockefeller Ave., MS 303 • Everett, WA 98201 • 425-388-6621 or 425-388-6600 • http://www.co.snohomish.wa.us/parks

Snoqualmie Centennial Trail • Superintendent of Parks, City of Snoqualmie • P.O. Box 987 • Snoqualmie, WA 98065 • 206-888-5337 • http://www.ci.snoqualmie.wa.us

Snoqualmie Centennial Trail • King County Park System Headquarters, Luther Burbank Park • 2040 84th Ave. SE • Mercer Island, WA 98040 • 206-296-4232 • http://www.metrokc.gov/parks

Snoqualmie Ridge Trail • King County Park System Headquarters, Luther Burbank Park • 2040 84th Ave. SE • Mercer Island, WA 98040 • 206-296-4232 • http://www.metrokc.gov/parks

Soos Creek Trail • King County Park System Headquarters, Luther Burbank Park • 2040 84th Ave. SE • Mercer Island, WA 98040 • 206-296-4232 • http://www.metrokc.gov/parks

South Bay Trail • Bellingham Parks & Recreation Dept. • 3424 Meridian • Bellingham, WA 98225 • 360-676-6985

Spokane River Centennial Trail • Riverside State Park, North • 4427 A.L. White Parkway • Spokane, WA 99205 • 509-456-3964

Sylvia Creek Forestry Trail • Lake Sylvia State Park • P.O. Box 701 • Montesano, WA 98563 • 360-249-3621

Thompson (Tommy) Parkway Trail • City of Anacortes • P.O. Box 547 • Anacortes, WA 98221 • 360-293-1918

Waterfront Trail (Port Angeles Waterfront Trail or Olympic Discovery Trail) • City of Port Angeles, Parks & Recreation • 240 W. Front • Port Angeles, WA 98362 • 206-447-0411, ext. 215

Whatcom County & Bellingham Interurban Trail • Whatcom County Parks & Recreation Board • 3373 Mount Baker Highway • Bellingham, WA 98226 • 360-733-2900

Willapa Hills State Trail (Raymond to Southbend Riverfront Trail) • Willapa Bay Organization • 408 2nd St. • Raymond, WA 98577 • 360-942-9963 • http://www.willapabay.org

Woodard Bay Trail • Thurston County Parks & Recreation • 2617-A 12th Court SW • Olympia, WA 98502 • 360-786-5595 • http://www.thurston-parks.org

Woodard Bay Trail • City Engineer, City of Raymond • 230 2nd St. • Raymond, WA 98577 • 360-942-3451

Yelm-Tenino Trail • Thurston County Parks & Recreation • 2617-A 12th Court SW • Olympia, WA 98502 • 360-786-5595 • http://www.thurston-parks.org

West Virginia

General Information

Mid-Atlantic Rail-Trails • http://www.his.com/~jmenzies/urbanatb/rtrails/index.htm

West Virginia Bicycle & Pedestrian Coordinator, West Virginia Dept. of Highways • Building 5, Room A-816, 1900 Kanawha Blvd. East. • Charleston, WV 25305 • 304-558-3113 • http://www.state.wv.us

West Virginia Division of Tourism, Bicycle & Trails Coordinator • 2101 Washington St., East • Charleston, WV 25305 • 800-CALL-WVA, 800-225-5982 or 304-558-2279 • http://www.call-wva.com

West Virginia Rail-Trails Council • http://www.wvrtc.org

Trail Information

Caperton Trail • Marion County Parks & Recreation Commission • P.O. Box 1258, 316 Monroe St. • Fairmont, WV 26554 • 304-363-7037

Caperton Trail • Mon River Trails Conservancy • 304-293-2941 ext. 2414 • http://www.mon-trails.com

Cheat Haven Trail • Marion County Parks & Recreation Commission • P.O. Box 1258, 316 Monroe St. • Fairmont, WV 26554 • 304-363-7037

Cheat Haven Trail • Mon River Trails Conservancy • 304-293-2941 • ext. 2414 • http://www.montrails.com

Cranberry-Tri-Rivers Trail • Richwood Area Chamber of Commerce • 1 E Main St. • Richwood, WV 26261 • 304-846-6790

Cranberry-Tri-Rivers Trail • Monongahela National Forest • 304-636-1800

Cranberry-Tri-Rivers Trail • Drawer F • Richwood, WV 26261 • 304-846-2862 or 304-846-3041

Cranberry-Tri-Rivers Trail • Richwood Convention & Visitors Bureau • 304-846-6790 • http://www.richwoodwv.com

Deckers Creek Trail • Marion County Parks & Recreation Commission • P.O. Box 1258, 316 Monroe St. • Fairmont, WV 26554 • 304-363-7037

Deckers Creek Trail • Mon River Trails Conservancy • 304-293-2941 ext. 2414 • http://www.montrails.com

Greater Wheeling Trail: East-West • Department of Development, City-County Building • 1500 Chapline St. • Wheeling, WV 26003 • 304-234-3701 • http://www.cityofwheeling.com

Greater Wheeling Trail: North-South • Department of Development, City-County Building • 1500 Chapline St. • Wheeling, WV 26003 • 304-234-3701 • http://www.cityofwheeling.com

Greenbrier River State Park Trail • Pocahontas County Convention & Visitors Center • P.O. Box 275 • Marlinton, WV 24954 • 800-336-7009 • http://www.greenbrierrivertrail.com or http://www.pocahontascountywv.com

McPark Trail (Marion County Trail) • Marion County Parks & Recreation Commission • P.O. Box 1258, 316 Monroe St. • Fairmont, WV 26554 • 304-363-7037

McPark Trail (Marion County Trail) • Mon River Trails Conservancy • 304-293-2941 ext. 2414

• http://www.montrails.com

Mon River Trail (South) • Marion County Parks & Recreation Commission • P.O. Box 1258, 316 Monroe St. • Fairmont, WV 26554 • 304-363-7037

Mon River Trail (South) • Mon River Trails Conservancy • 304-293-2941 ext. 2414 • http://www.montrails.com

North Bend State Park Rail-Trail • North Bend Rails-to-Trails Foundation Inc. • P.O. Box 206 • Cairo, WV 26337 • 800-899-NBRT or 800-899-6278 • http://www.wvweb.com/www/travel_recreation/state_parks/north_bend_rail/north_bend_rail.html

North Bend State Park Rail-Trail • North Bend State Park • Route 1 Box 221 • Cairo, WV 26337 • 800-CALL-WVA, 800-225-5982 or 304-643-2931 • http://www.wvweb.com/www/travel_recreation/state_parks/north_bend_rail/north_bend_rail.html

Prickett's Fork Trail • Marion County Parks & Recreation Commission • P.O. Box 1258, 316 Monroe St. • Fairmont, WV 26554 • 304-363-7037

West Fork River Trail • Marion County Parks & Recreation Commission • P.O. Box 1258, 316 Monroe St. • Fairmont, WV 26554 • 304-363-7037

West Fork Trail • Monongahela National Forest, Greenbrier Ranger District • P.O. Box 67 • Bartow, WV 24920 • 304-456-3335

West Fork Trail • Mon River Trails Conservancy • 304-293-2941 ext. 2414 • http://www.montrails.com

Wisconsin
General Information
Bicycle Federation of Wisconsin • 106 E Doty St., Suite 110 • Madison WI 53703 • 800-362-4537 or 608-251-4456 • http://www.bfw.org

Biking Wisconsin's Rail-Trails (Rail-Trail & Bike Trail Maps), Adventure Publications Inc. • 820 Cleveland St. S • Cambridge, MN 55008 • 800-678-7006 • http://www.BikingUSARailTrails.com

Lake Michigan Car Ferry • 701 Maritime Dr. • Ludington, MI 49431 • AND • 900 S Lakeview Dr. • Manitowoc, WI 54220 • 800-841-4243 • http://www.ssbadger.com

Wisconsin Bicycle-Pedestrian Coordinator, Wisconsin DOT • P.O. Box 7913 • Madison, WI 53707 • 608-267-7757

Wisconsin Bureau of Parks & Recreation, Wisconsin DNR • P.O. Box 7921 • Madison, WI 53707 • 608-266-2181 • http://www.wiparks.net

Wisconsin Department of Tourism • 800-432-TRIP or 800-432-8747 • http://www.tourism.state.wi.us

Trail Information
Aaron (Henry) State Trail • Wisconsin DNR • 2300 N Dr. Martin Luther King Jr. Dr., Box 12436 • Milwaukee, WI 53212 • 414-263-8711 • http://www.dnr.state.wi.us/org/land/parks/specific/index.html#86

Ahnapee State Trail • Friends of the Ahnapee • P.O. Box 93 • Algoma, WI 54201 • 920-487-2041

Ahnapee State Trail • Door County Parks Dept. • 3418 Park Dr. • Sturgeon Bay, WI 54235 • 920-743-3636

Baraboo-Devils Lake State Park Trail • Devils Lake State Park • 55975 Park Rd. • Baraboo, WI 53913 • 608-356-8301

Baraboo-Devils Lake State Park Trail • Baraboo Area Chamber of Commerce • P.O. Box 442 • Baraboo, WI 53913 • 800-227-2266

Bearskin State Trail • Wisconsin DNR • 518 W Somo Ave. • Tomahawk, WI 54487 • 715-453-1263

Bugline Recreation Trail • Waukesha County Parks & Planning Commission • 1320 Pewaukee Rd., Room 230 • Waukesha, WI 53188 • 414-548-7790

Capital City State Trail • Dane County Parks • 4318 Robertson Rd. • Madison, WI 53714 • 608-246-3896 • http://www.co.dane.wi.us

Cheese Country Recreation Trail • Green County Clerk • 1016 16th Ave. • Monroe, WI 53566 • 608-328-9430 • http://www.state.wi.us/agencies/tourism.html

Chippewa River State Trail • Chippewa River State Trail • 921 Brickyard Rd. • Menomonie, WI 54751 • 715-232-1242 • http://www.wiparks.net

Elroy-Sparta State Trail • Wisconsin DNR c/o Wildcat Mountain State Park • P.O. Box 99 • Ontario, WI 54651 • 608-337-4775

400 State Trail • Wisconsin DNR c/o Wildcat Mountain State Park • P.O. Box 99 • Ontario, WI 54651 • 608-337-4775

Gandy Dancer State Trail • Burnett County: Burnett County Forest & Parks Dept. • 7410 County Highway K, #106 • Siren, WI 54872 • 800-788-3164 or 715-349-2157 • http://www.mwd.com/burnett/

Gandy Dancer State Trail • Polk County: Polk County Information Center • 710 Highway-35 South • St. Croix Falls, WI 54024 • 800-222-7655 or 800-222-POLK • http://www.polkcountytourism.com

Glacial Drumlin State Trail • Glacial Drumlin State Trail, Wisconsin DNR • 1213 S Main St. • Lake Mills, WI 53551 • 414-648-8774

Glacial River Trail • Jefferson County Parks Department Courthouse • 320 S Main St. • Jefferson, WI 53549 • 414-674-7260

Great River State Trail • Perrot State Park • P.O. Box 407 • Trempealeau, WI 54661 • 608-534-6409

Green Circle Trail • Portage County Parks • 1462 Strongs Ave. • Stevens Point, WI 54452 • 715-346-1433

Hiawatha State Trail • Lincoln County Forestry Land & Parks • 1106 E 8th St. • Merrill, WI 54452 • 715-536-0327

Hillsboro State Trail • Juneau County Forest & Parks Dept. • 250 Oak St. • Mauston, WI 53948 • 608-847-9390

Kenosha County Bicycle Trail • Kenosha County Parks • P.O. Box 549 • Bristol, WI 53104 • 262-857-1869

La Crosse River State Trail • Wisconsin DNR c/o Wildcat Mountain State Park • P.O. Box 99 •

Ontario, WI 54651 • 608-337-4775

Lake County Recreation Trail • Waukesha County Parks & Planning Commission • 1320 Pewaukee Rd., Room 230 • Waukesha, WI 53188 • 414-548-7790

Mascoutin Valley State Trail • Winnebago County Parks • 500 E County Road-Y • Oshkosh, WI 54901 • 920-424-0042

Military Ridge State Trail • Military Ridge State Trail • 4350 Mounds Park Rd., P.O. Box 98. • Blue Mounds, WI 53517 • 608-437-7393 • http://www.military.ridge@mail01.dnr.state.wi.us or http://www.wiparks.net

Mountain-Bay State Trail (Delly Trail) • Brown County: Brown County Park Dept. • 305 E Walnut, P.O. Box 23600 • Green Bay, WI 54305 • 414-448-4466

Mountain-Bay State Trail (Delly Trail) • Marathon County: Marathon County Park Dept. • 500 Forest • Wausau, WI 54403 • 715-847-5235

Mountain-Bay State Trail (Delly Trail) • Shawano County: Shawano County Planning Dept. • 311 N Main St. • Shawano, WI 54166 • 715-526-6766

New Berlin Recreation Trail, Waukesha County Parks & Planning Commission • 1320 Pewaukee Rd., Room 230 • Waukesha, WI 53188 • 414-548-7790

Oak Leaf Trail (Old-76 Bike Trail), Milwaukee County Parks • 9480 Watertown Plank Rd. • Wauwatosa, WI 53226 • 414-527-6100 • http://www.countyparks.com

Old Abe State Trail • Chippewa County Forest & Parks Dept. • 711 N Bridge St. • Chippewa Falls, WI 54729 • 715-726-7880 • http://www.chippewachamber.org

Old Plank Road Trail • Sheboygan Chamber of Commerce • 712 Riverfront Dr., Suite 101 • Sheboygan, WI 53081 • 800-457-9497

Old Plank Road Trail • Sheboygan County Planning & Resources Dept. • 615 N 6th St. • Sheboygan, WI 53081 • 414-459-3060

Omaha Trail • Juneau County Forestry & Parks • 650 Prairie St. • Mauston, WI 53948 • 608-847-9389 or 608-847-9390

Osaugie Trail • Superior Parks & Recreation • 1407 Hammond Ave. • Superior, WI 54880 • 715-394-0270

Ozaukee Interurban Trail • Cedarburg Chamber of Commerce & Visitor Center • W61N480 Washington Ave. • Cedarburg, WI 53012 • 800-237-2874 or 262-377-5846 • www.cedar-burg.org

Pecatonica State Trail • Green County Clerk • 1016 16th Ave. • Monroe, WI 53566 • 608-328-9430

Pine Line Trail • Price County Tourism Office • 126 Cherry St. • Phillips, WI 54555 • 800-269-4505

Pine Line Trail • Taylor County Tourism • P.O. Box 231 • Medford, WI 54451 • 715-748-4729 • 888-6-TAYLOR or 888-682-9567

Pine River Recreation Trail • Wisconsin DNR, PR/1 • P.O. Box 7921 • Madison, WI 53707 • 608-267-7459

Pine River Recreation Trail • U.W. Extension • 1100 Highway 14 West • Richland Center, WI 53581 • 608-647-6148

Racine County Bicycle Trail (Burlington to Waukesha County Line Trail) • Racine County Public Works Dept. • 14200 Washington Ave. • Sturtevant, WI 53177 • 262-886-8440

Racine County Bicycle Trail (M.R.K. Trail) • Racine County Public Works Dept. • 14200 Washington Ave. • Sturtevant, WI 53177 • 262-886-8440

Racine County Bicycle Trail (North Shore Trail) • Racine County Public Works Dept. • 14200 Washington Ave. • Sturtevant, WI 53177 • 262-886-8440

Racine County Bicycle Trail (Racine-Sturtevant Trail) • Racine County Public Works Dept. • 14200 Washington Ave. • Sturtevant, WI 53177 • 262-886-8440

Red Cedar State Trail • Chippewa River State Trail • 921 Brickyard Rd. • Menomonie, WI 54751 • 715-232-1242 • http://www.wiparks.net

Rock/Springbrook/Kiwanis Trails • Janesville Park Dept. • 17 N Franklin St. • Janesville, WI 53545 • 608-755-3030 • http://www.ci.janesville.wi.us

Sugar River State Trail • Sugar River State Trail • 418 Railroad St. • New Glarus, WI 53574 • 608-527-2334 or 608-527-2335

Sunset/Hidden Bluff Trails • Peninsula State Park • P.O. Box 218 • Fish Creek, WI 54212 • 920-868-3258

Tomorrow River State Trail • Portage County Parks Dept. • County Rd. I • Stevens Point, WI 54481 • 715-346-1433

U.S. Route 2 Duluth-Superior Bike Trail • Superior Parks & Recreation • 1407 Hammond Ave. • Superior, WI 54880 • 715-394-0270

U.S. Route 2 Duluth-Superior Bike Trail • City Trail Coordinator, Forestry Division • 2nd Floor, City Hall • Duluth, MN 55802 • 218-723-3586 • www.ci.duluth.mn.us

Tri-County Recreation Corridor Trail • Tri-County Recreation Corridor Commission • P.O. Box 503 • Ashland, WI 54806 • 715-372-5959 or 800-472-6338

Waukesha Bike Trail • Waukesha County Parks & Planning Commission • 1320 Pewaukee Rd., Room 230 • Waukesha, WI 53188 • 414-548-7790

Waukesha Bike Trail • Waukesha City Planning, City Hall • Room 200, 201 Delafield St. • Waukesha, WI 53188 • 414-524-3752

Wild Goose State Trail • Fond du Lac County Planning & Parks Dept. • 160 S Macy St. • Fond du Lac, WI 54935 • 920-929-3135 • http://www.dodgecountywi.com/planning/recreation/trails-wildgoose.html

Wildwood Trail • St. Croix County Parks Dept. • 1049 Rustic Rd. 3 • Glenwood City, WI 54013 • 715-265-4613 • http://www.co.saint-croix.wi.us

Wiouwash State Trail (Oshkosh to Hortonville) • Regional Trails Coordinator, Wisconsin DNR • 1125 N Military Ave. • Green Bay, WI 54303 • 920-492-5823

Wiouwash State Trail (Oshkosh to Hortonville) • Outagamie County Parks • 1375 E Broadway Dr. • Appleton, WI 54915 • 414-832-4790

Wiouwash State Trail (Split Rock to Aniwa) • Regional Trails Coordinator, Wisconsin DNR • 1125 N Military Ave. • Green Bay, WI 54303 • 920-492-5823

Wyoming

General Information

Wyoming Bicycle Coordinator, Wyoming DOT, Planning • 5300 Bishop Blvd. • Cheyenne, WY 82009 • 307-777-4719 • http://www.wydotweb.state.wy.us/Docs/Modes/Bicycle/Bicycle.html

Wyoming Travel & Tourism Division, Wyoming Business Council • I-25 at College Dr. • Cheyenne, WY 82002 • 800-225-5996 or 307-777-7777 • http://www.wyomingtourism.org

Trail Information

Wyoming Heritage Trail • Fremont County Recreation Board • 213 E Lincoln Dr. • Riverton, WY 82501 • 307-856-3820

Bicycle Safety & Equipment

This article used with permission from Harvard Pilgrim Health Care, copyright 1996.

Bicycling offers many rewards, among them a physically fit body and a pleasant means of transportation. But the sport has its hazards, which can lead to serious accidents and injuries. We have provided rules, facts and tips that can help minimize the dangers of bicycling while you're having fun.

Choose the Right Bicycle
Adults and children should ride bicycles with frames small enough to be straddled easily with both feet flat on the ground, and with handlebars that can be easily reached with elbows bent. Oversize bikes make it difficult to ride comfortably and maintain control. Likewise, don't buy a large bike for a child to grow into—smaller is safer.

Learn to Ride the Safe Way
When learning to ride a bike, let a little air out of the tires, and practice steering and balancing by "scootering" around with both feet on the ground and the seat as low as possible. The "fly-or-fall" method—where someone runs alongside the bicycle and then lets go—can result in injuries.

Training wheels don't work, since the rider can't learn to balance until the wheels come of. They can be used with a timid rider, but the child still will have to learn to ride without them. Once the rider can balance and pedal (without training wheels), raise the seat so that the rider's leg is almost straight at the bottom of the pedal stroke.

Children seldom appreciate the dangers and hazards of city cycling. Make sure they understand the traffic laws before letting them onto the road.

Use this Important Equipment:
Headlight: A working headlight and rear reflector are required for night riding in some states. Side reflectors do not make the rider visible to drivers on cross streets.

Safety seat for children under 40 lbs.: Make sure the seat is mounted firmly over the rear wheel of the bike, and does not wobble when going downhill at high speed. Make sure the child will not slide down while riding. The carrier should also have a device to keep the child's feet from getting into the spokes.

Package rack: Racks are inexpensive, and they let the rider steer with both hands and keep packages out of the spokes.

Obey Traffic Laws
Car drivers are used to certain rules of the road, and bicyclists must obey them too. The following rules should be taught to a child as soon as he or she can ride a bicycle:

Make eye contact with a driver before entering or crossing lanes.

Signal and glance over your shoulder before changing lanes.

Watch for openings in the traffic stream and make turns from the appropriate lane.

When riding off-road, be sure you are on a trail that permits bicycles.

Before riding in the road, these rules should be practiced until they become habit and can be performed smoothly. Adults must set good examples-children imitate them regardless of verbal instructions.

Beware of Dangerous Practices

Never ride against traffic. Failure to observe this rule causes the majority of car-bicycle collisions. Motorists can't always avoid the maneuvers of a wrong-way rider since the car and bike move toward each other very quickly.

Never make a left turn from the right lane.

Never pass through an intersection at full speed.

Never ignore stop light or stop signs.

Never enter traffic suddenly from a driveway or sidewalk. This rule is particularly important when the rider is a child, who is more difficult for a motorist to see.

Don't wear headphones that make it hard to hear and quickly respond to traffic.

Don't carry passengers on a bike. The only exception is a child under 40 lbs. who is buckled into an approved bike safety seat and wears a helmet as required by law.

Passenger trailers can be safe and fun. Be aware, though, that a trailer makes the bike much longer and requires careful control. Passengers must wear helmets.

Find Safe Places to Ride

Most cities have some bicycle-friendly routes, as well as some high-traffic areas that require skill and experience. It's safest to ride on secondary roads with light traffic. When choosing a route, remember that the wider the lane, the safer the cycling.

Get a Bike That Works with You

Skilled riders who use their bikes often for exercise or transport should consider buying multi-geared bikes, which increase efficiency while minimizing stress on the body. (These bikes may not be appropriate for young or unskilled riders, who may concentrate more on the gears than on the road.) The goal is to keep the pedals turning at a rate of 60-90 RPM. Using the higher gears while pedaling slowly is hard on the knees, and is slower and more tiring than the efficient pedaling on the experienced cyclist.

Have a safe trip!

Bicycle Helmets

Reprinted from July 1989 "Mayo Clinic Health Letter" with permission of Mayo Foundation, for Medical Education and Research, Rochester, Minnesota.

"It's as easy as falling off a bicycle." The adage has been around for decades. Unfortunately, it makes light of the potential for tragedy if you should take a serious fall while riding a bicycle.

With an increasing number of people riding bicycles on our streets and highways, the risk of injury—in particular, head injury—continues to rise. Each year, nearly 50,000 bicyclists suffer serious head injuries. According to the most recent statistics, head injuries are the leading cause of death in the approximately 1,300 bicycle-related fatalities that occur annually. To a large extent, these head injuries are preventable.

Wearing a helmet can make a difference. Until recently, advocates of the use of protective headgear for cyclists found their stance lacked scientific support. But wearing protective headgear clearly makes a difference. Recent evidence confirms that a helmet can reduce your risk of serious head and brain injury by almost 90 percent should you be involved in a bicycle accident.

Bicycle riding is an excellent form of aerobic exercise that can benefit your musculoskeletal and cardiovascular systems. Make the investment in a helmet and take the time to put in on each time you ride.

What to Look for in a Bicycle Helmet:

We endorse these guidelines for bicycle helmets recommended by the American Academy of Pediatrics:

The helmet should meet the voluntary testing standards of one of these two groups: American National Standards Institute (ANSI) OR Snell Memorial Foundation. Look for a sticker on the inside of the helmet.

1) Select the right size. Find one that fits comfortably and doesn't pinch.

2) Buy a helmet with a durable outer shell and a polystyrene liner. Be sure it allows adequate ventilation.

3) Use the adjustable foam pads to ensure a proper fit at the front, back and sides.

4) Adjust the strap for a snug fit. The helmet should cover the top of your forehead and not rock side to side or back and forth with the chain strap in place.

5) Replace your helmet if it is involved in an accident.

A Few More Bike Safety Tips

By Shawn E. Richardson

Rail-Trail Courtesy & Common Sense

1) Stay on designated trails.

2) Bicyclists use the right side of the trail (Walkers use the left side of the trail).

3) Bicyclists should only pass slower users on the left side of the trail; use your voice to warn others when you need to pass.

4) Get off to the side of the trail if you need to stop.

5) Bicyclists should yield to all other users.

6) Do not use alcohol or drugs while on the trail.

7) Do not litter.

8) Do not trespass onto adjacent land.

9) Do not wear headphones while using the trail.

Emergency Toolkit

When venturing out on bicycle tours, it is always smart to take along equipment to help make roadside adjustments and repairs. It is not necessary for every member of your group to carry a complete set of equipment, but make sure someone in your group brings along the equipment listed below:

1) Standard or slotted screwdriver

2) Phillips screwdriver

3) 6" or 8" adjustable wrench

4) Small pliers

5) Spoke adjuster

6) Tire pressure gauge

7) Portable tire pump

8) Spare innertube

9) Tire-changing lugs

A Few Other Things

When embarking on a extended bike ride, it is important to give your bike a pre-ride check. To ensure that your bike is in premium condition, go over the bike's mechanisms, checking for any mechanical problems. It's best to catch these at home, and not when they occur "on the road." If you run into a problem that you can't fix yourself, you should check your local yellow pages for a professional bike mechanic.

When you are planning a longer trip, be sure to consider your own abilities and limitations, as well as those of any companions who may be riding with you. In general, you can ride about three times the length (time-wise) as your average training ride. If you have a regular cycling routine, this is a good basis by which to figure the maximum distance you can handle.

Finally, be aware of the weather. Bring plenty of sunblock for clear days, and rain gear for the rainy ones. Rain can make some rides miserable, in addition to making it difficult to hear other traffic. Winds can blow up sand, and greatly increase the difficulty of a trail.

Trains from the past along the Mickelson (George S.) Trail (SD).

About the Author

Shawn E. Richardson has worked as a cartographer for the Ohio Department of Transportation since 1988. He specializes in photogrammetry, the process of creating maps using aerial photography. He received his Bachelor of Science degree in environmental geography with emphasis on cartography from Kentucky's University of Louisville in 1985. Born in California and growing up in Kentucky, Shawn has lived in Ohio since 1988.

Shawn enjoys bicycle touring, and his excursions can last anywhere from a few hours to several days. Although he has biked back roads through many states, the majority of his touring has been on trails. He is an active member of the Rails-to-Trails Conservancy and has belonged to the Columbus Outdoor Pursuits, the American Youth Hostels, and to the Louisville Wheelmen. Biking U.S.A.'s Rail-Trails is Shawn's fourth book. If you have questions or comments for Shawn, you can contact him by writing to him in care of Biking U.S.A.'s Rail-Trails, P.O. Box 612, Worthington, OH 43085.

Shawn E. Richardson bikes his first rail-trail as a teenager across Wisconsin.

Author Shawn E. Richardson and his wife Joyce are biking rail-trails through every state!